Jean Mabillon

Life and works of Saint Bernard, Abbot of Clairvaux

Jean Mabillon

Life and works of Saint Bernard, Abbot of Clairvaux

ISBN/EAN: 9783742866776

Manufactured in Europe, USA, Canada, Australia, Japa

Cover: Foto ©Lupo / pixelio.de

Manufactured and distributed by brebook publishing software (www.brebook.com)

Jean Mabillon

Life and works of Saint Bernard, Abbot of Clairvaux

CATHOLIC STANDARD LIBRARY.

WORKS OF SAINT BERNARD.

LIFE AND WORKS
OF SAINT BERNARD,

ABBOT OF CLAIRVAUX.

EDITED BY

DOM. JOHN MABILLON,

Presbyter and Monk of the Benedictine Congregation of S. Maur.

Translated and Edited with Additional Notes,

BY

SAMUEL J. EALES, M.A., D.C.L.,

Sometime Principal of S. Boniface College, Warminster.

VOL. II.

Second Edition.

JOHN HODGES,
HENRIETTA STREET, COVENT GARDEN, LONDON.
1889.

Lewes:
SOUTH COUNTIES PRESS LIMITED.

CONTENTS.

		PAGE
I.	NOTE ON THE SEAL OF S. BERNARD	457
II.	DESCRIPTION OF THE POSITION AND SITE OF THE ABBEY OF CLAIRVAUX	460
III.	LETTERS No. CXLVI. TO No. CLXXXIX.	468
IV.	NOTE TO THE FOLLOWING TREATISE	549
V.	LETTERS No. CXC. TO No. CCCLXXX.	565

NOTE.

The following list of editions carries on the bibliography given by Dom. J. Mabillon in his second edition, and adds some particulars not therein contained.

1. Editions by J. M. Horst were published in 1642 (*Parisiis*, 5 Tom.); in 9 vols. (1667—1668); and *Coloniæ Agrippinæ* (Cologne) 1641, 1672. (The first and last volumes of this edition are differently dated from the others.) The Editor was J. C. Schluter; and this was the last edition founded on Horst.

2. The second edition of Dom. J. Mabillon, which has ever since been the standard, was issued in 2 vols. folio (*Parisiis*, 1690).

A third, *tertiis curis* J. Mabillon, also in 2 vols. folio (*Parisiis*, 1719): and again in 3 vols. with additions by Dom. J. Martene (*Venetiis*, 1726).

Lastly, in 1839, was issued in Paris in 6 vols. 4to, by Gaume Frères, a fourth edition, *emendata et aucta,* of which precise details are given in Vol. i., pp. 74, 75; and the text of which has been used in this translation.

It is printed with remarkable correctness, a verification of the references having thus far shown but very few errors.

Volume ii. contains the great bulk of S. Bernard's Letters. The remainder, which are short and comparatively unimportant, will follow at the beginning of Vol. iii.

S. J. E.

NOTE

ON

THE SEAL OF S. BERNARD.

WE owe it to the kindness of M. Deville, Director of the Museum of Antiquities at Rouen, that we are able to reproduce the following note, with the exact design of S. Bernard's seal spoken of in this note.

NOTE ON THE SEAL OF S. BERNARD.

Copy of a letter addressed to the Permanent Secretary of the Academy of Inscriptions.

Rouen, Aug. 16, 1837.

SIR,—

A happy circumstance has just put into my hands the original seal of S. Bernard. The Academy will doubtless be interested at hearing that the seal of this celebrated man, who played so important a part in the religious and political events of his day, still exists; and I may, perhaps, be allowed to send it some account of this little memorial of the twelfth century—one of the most precious that it has left us. It is of yellow copper, and of oval form, about 40 millimètres long (about 1½ inch), 30 millimètres broad in its widest part (nearly 1¼ inch); its thickness is about ⅛ inch, and its weight about an ounce. The figure of S. Bernard is hollowed out, in monastic costume; his head is tonsured and bare,[1] his chin shaven, and he is sitting on a folding chair, the arms of which terminate in a serpent's head. The Saint holds in his right hand, which becomes

---

[1] S. Bernard would never use the mitre, which in his time the abbots were beginning to assume. He strongly withstood the innovation.

the left in the impression, a very simple staff, with a crook after the style of the ancient lituus; and in his left hand, which is stretched out like the right, an object which the roughness and minuteness of the work make it difficult to recognize. I think it to be a church-door divided into two parts by a column, surmounted by a capital. [Mabillon has taken this for a book; the owner of the seal took it for a sand-glass.] The following inscription is traced on the margin of the seal round the figure (a cross patée is placed just above the head of the Saint): ✠ Sigillum : Bernardi : Abbatis Clarævall.

With the exception of the *g* of the word *Sigillum*, of the *d* of *Bernardi*, and of the *e* of *Claravall*, which are of the Gothic character, the letters resemble the Roman uncials, and do not depart otherwise from the characters in use in the twelfth century.

The absence of the word *Saint* before Bernard is enough to prove, if necessary, that this seal is contemporary with him whose name it bears, and that it really belonged to him, because we know that S. Bernard, who died in 1153, was canonized not many years after his death, viz., in 1174, by Pope Alexander III. If this seal—the use of which in that case would be inexplicable—was posterior to the canonization, they would not have failed to add the significant word *Sanctus;* it could scarcely have been without it.

The only objection, perhaps, to a skilled eye that could be raised against the authenticity of the seal is that the style of the design, the costumes and the details, as well as the shape of the seal, seem to assign it to the latter half, or almost to the middle of the twelfth century. But S. Bernard having taken the pastoral staff A.D. 1115, the question arose why his official seal, which must have been executed at that time, had not the marks of that time; for the difference, after the long study that I had devoted to these monuments, was most apparent to my eyes. Such was the question that I had to consider.

On reading again the Letters of S. Bernard I found its solution. S. Bernard, writing to Pope Eugenius III., A.D.

1151, tells him that he has been forced to change his seal because of an abuse of confidence, and that he had had a second engraved, on which were traced his figure and name (ep. 284). It is this second seal which is in my possession. The effigy and name of S. Bernard are engraved on it: its shape and execution correspond exactly with the style of the time when S. Bernard informs us that he had had it made; it has in every way all the marks of genuineness that can be wished for.

It only remains for me now to inform the Academy of the way in which I became possessed of this inestimable piece of antiquity. I owe it to the generosity of a retired officer, M. Pays, of Issoudun, who wrote to me a few days ago, on sending it: "This seal was bought of a second-hand salesman, who became possessed in 1790 of the old copper articles of the Collegiate Church of S. Cyr, of Issoudun, which was affiliated to Clairvaux. How it came there I do not know." Subjoined is an impression of the seal, which I beg you to bring under the notice of the Academy. I forgot to say that the reverse is flat and of one piece, and with no mark of handle or hook. It is evident that the seal was pressed on the wax by the finger only.

Receive, etc.,
DEVILLE.

COPY OF AN IMPRESSION OF S. BERNARD'S SEAL.

DESCRIPTION OF THE POSITION AND SITE OF THE ABBEY OF CLAIRVAUX.

If you wish to know the site of Clairvaux, these lines will describe it for you as if in a mirror. The abbey is built at the foot of two mountains, which are separated from each other by a narrow valley, and leave between them a distance which widens as they descend from the side of the abbey. One of these mountains has its side occupied by one half of the abbey, and the other half is on the corresponding side of the other. The one mountain is fertile with vineyards, the other with corn; and each of them offers to the eye a beautiful sight, and supplies a needful support for the inmates. So that whilst on one of the ridges rises the corn upon which the brethren live, on the other is grown the wine which they drink. The top of the mountain is the scene of numerous labours of the monks; works as pleasant as they are peaceable—to collect dry branches, and gather them in bundles to burn them; to grub up the brushwood which disfigures the ground, and to prepare it for the fire, for which alone it is fit; to uproot the brambles and destroy them; to dig the soil; to scatter (as I may say after Solomon) the "bastard slips"[2] which choke the roots or entangle the boughs of the rising trees, so that there may be no impediment to the sturdy oak which salutes the heavens with its lofty top, to the graceful lime-tree which spreads its arms, to the ash-tree whose wood is so elastic and easily split, or to the leafy beech, as the one shoots upwards and the other spreads its lateral shade.

Behind the house extends a broad plain, of which a wall shuts in no small part, and encloses the abbey with an extended boundary. Within this enclosure the trees are

---

[2] *Spuria vitulamina*, the VULGATE version of Wisd. v. 3. The Greek word μόσχευμα is rare; and as μόσχος has the double meaning of "a shoot" and "a calf," the fact no doubt led to the rendering, which is clearly incorrect, and is noticed by S. Augustine (*De Doctr. Christ.* ii. 12).—[E.]

numerous and varied, fertile in fruit of various kinds, and form an orchard like a forest. Beside it rise the cells of the sick, and the neighbourhood of the trees is no slight alleviation of the infirmities of the brethren, to whom the orchard offers a vast space for walking, and gives a pleasant shade against the heat of the sun. The sick are wont to sit upon the green turf, and when the excessive heats of the dog-days burn the earth and dry up the rivers they sit sheltered under the trees, and defended from the heat of their shadow. Under their leafy screen the sun's rays are softened, and their sufferings are soothed as they breathe the air fragrant with the scent of hay. The pleasant green of the trees and of the turf rests their eyes, and the fruit which hangs before them promises them delight when ripened. They might say with reason: *I have sat under the shade of the tree which I desired, and its fruit was sweet to my taste* (Cant. ii. 3). Their ears are agreeably occupied by the sweet and harmonious concerts of birds of varied plumage. See how, in order to cure one sickness, the goodness of God multiplies remedies, causes the clear air to shine in serenity, the earth to breathe forth fruitfulness, and the sick man himself to inhale through eyes, and ears, and nostrils the delights of colours, of songs, and of odours. Where the orchard ceases begins the garden, through which run little channels of water, or rather little streams separate and divide it into squares. For although the water appears to be still, yet it has a steady current, though slow. Here, too, is a pleasing sight afforded to the eyes of the sick brethren when they go to sit on the verdant bank of a pool filled with pure and running water, where they can watch the sports of the little fish in water clear as crystal, which swim to and fro in shoals like marching armies. The water of these pools serves at the same time for nourishing the fish and for watering the vegetables in the garden; it is introduced by a constant current derived from the Aube, a river well known. This stream passes and repasses the many workshops of the abbey, and everywhere leaves a blessing behind it for its faithful service.

The river climbs to this height by works laboriously constructed, and passes nowhere without rendering some service, or leaving some of its water behind. It divides the valley into two by a sinuous bed, which the labour of the brethren, and not Nature, has made, and goes on to throw half of its waters into the abbey, as if to salute the brethren, and seems to excuse itself for not coming in its whole force, the canal which receives it being too small for it. If sometimes the stream, swollen by an inundation, rushes on with violent current, it is stopped by a wall, under which it is obliged to pass, and so turned back upon itself, meets and checks the descending stream. As much, however, as the wall, like a faithful porter, allows to enter passes on at once to drive the wheels of a mill; there, lashed into foam by their motion, it grinds the meal under the weight of the mill-stones, and separates the fine from the coarse by a sieve of fine tissue.

A little farther on, in the next building, it fills a boiler, and is heated for brewing, that drink may be prepared for the brethren, if it should happen that the vintage should not respond kindly to the labour of the vine-dresser; so that, in default of the juice of the vine, the want may be supplied by the extract of grain. But not even yet is its usefulness completed, for the fullers call it to their aid who labour beside the mill; sound reason requiring that, as in the mill, care is taken for the food of the brethren, so by these their clothing should be prepared. But the river does not hesitate nor refuse any who require its aid; and you may see it causing to rise and fall alternately the heavy pestles, that is to say, hammers, or wooden foot-shaped blocks (for that name seems to agree better with the treading-work, as it were, of the fullers), and so relieves them of the heaviest part of their labour. And if it is permitted to them to mix jokes with serious work, it relieves the sadness of their sins. O God, how many consolations Thou givest to Thy poor, so that they may not be entirely weighed down by the extreme stress of their labour! What alleviations of punishment to the penitent, that they may not be altogether absorbed by excessive sorrow! How many horses would this labour tire! of how many men would it weary the arms! And the kindly stream relieves us from it altogether, although without it we should have neither food to eat, nor raiment prepared to put on. It shares with us our fatigues, and for all the labour which it undertakes the whole day long it expects no other recompense than that when it has completed diligently all its tasks it may be permitted to go free upon its way. Thus, after having made to revolve in its quick movement so many wheels, rapid as itself, it emerges foaming, you would say that it is, so to speak, mealy, and that it has been made softer.

From thence it passes into the workshop of the curriers, where it contributes its laborious assistance to the preparation of the sandals which are needful for the use of the Brothers. Coming from there, it is divided into numerous threads of water, and thus distributed; it penetrates all the workshops, and lends itself to everyone's need, everywhere looking for assistance that it may be able to render. Thus it helps to cook the food, to sift the grain, to drive wheels and pestles, to damp, wash, and soak, and so to soften, objects; everywhere it stands ready to offer its help. Lastly, in order that I may not omit any thanks due to it, nor leave the catalogue of its services in any way imperfect, it carries away all dirt and uncleanness, and leaves all things clean behind it. Then, after having accomplished industriously the purpose for which it came, it returns with rapid current to the stream, and renders to it in the name of Clairvaux, thanks for all the services which it has performed, and replies to its salutation with worthy response. Immediately it receives into its bosom the waters that it had lent to us, and the two streams become only one; they are so perfectly mixed that you can find no trace of their union; only on re-entering into its bed, it hastens the course of the stream, which had been delayed, diminished, and rendered less active in its course, by the withdrawal of part of its waters.

But since we have restored it to its place, let us return

to the little streams which we have left behind us. They are drawn from the river, and wander in careless curves through the meadows, to penetrate into the earth and refresh it, so that it may bring forth seed for fear that at the return of spring, when the fruitful earth opens to let the new growth appear, the infant plants should be dried up for want of water; nor have they any need of the drops from the clouds because sufficiently fed by the bounty of the neighbouring river. These little streams, or rather watercourses, after they have fulfilled their office, are absorbed in the stream which had given them out, and the Aube having regained all its waters, resumes its rapid course down the valley. But as we have accompanied it so far, and it, following the word of Solomon, *returns to its place*, (Eccles. i. 7), let us too return to the point from whence we started, and traverse with rapid description the vast plain of meadows.

That spot has much charm, it greatly soothes weary minds, relieves anxieties and cares, helps souls who seek the Lord greatly to devotion, and recalls to them the thought of the heavenly sweetness towards which they aspire. The smiling countenance of the earth is painted with varying colours, the blooming verdure of spring satisfies the eyes, and its sweet odour salutes the nostrils. But while I view the flowers, while I breathe their sweet scent, the meadows recall to me the histories of ancient times; for while I drink in the sweetness of the flowers, the thought occurs to my mind of the fragrance of the clothing of the Patriarch Jacob, which the Scripture compares to the odour which mounts from a fruitful field. When I delight my eyes with the bright colours of the flowers, I am reminded that this beauty is far above that of the purple robe of Solomon, who in all his glory, could not equal the beauty of the lilies of the field, although to him there was wanting neither richness of material, nor wisdom and taste in arrangement. In this way, while I am charmed without by the sweet influence of the beauty of the country, I have not less delight within in reflecting on the mysteries which are hidden beneath it. This, meadow, then is irrigated by the little stream which flows through it, and sends its moisture to the roots of its vegetation, so that they will not fear the heats of summer when it shall come. It is extended so far that at the time when the covering of the greensward falls under the scythe, and is dried to make hay, the gathering-in of it is a heavy task for the whole force of the Abbey during twice ten days. Yet that labour is not left wholly to the monks, but with them an unnumbered multitude of lay brothers, brothers lent from other Houses, and a crowd of hired labourers, collect the hay when dried, and clear the shorn soil with rakes.

This meadow is shared between two farms, which the Aube divides equally and fairly, in order to avoid dispute, assigning to each its domain, of which it forms the boundary on either side, so that the one may not cross to encroach upon the land of the other. You would not suppose that these farm-houses only serve for the dwelling-place of lay-brothers; you would take them for cloisters of monks, if the yokes of oxen, ploughs, and other instruments fitted for the labours of countrymen did not make manifest the kind of inhabitants whom the houses shelter, and if you did not remark that no books are lying open among them. For as relates to the buildings, you would say that it was suitable for a great convent of monks, both by sight, size, and beauty.

In the part of the meadow which is near to the wall, a pool of water has been made out of the solid plain; there, where previously the labourer, pouring with sweat, was cutting the hay with his sharp scythe, there the brother fisherman, borne in a light skiff, as it were upon a wooden horse, scours the watery plain; for spurs he has a light oar with which he urges his boat to speed and turns its course where he will. He unfolds his net under the waves, in which the fishy tribe are entangled, to prepare for him a prey which he loves to see placed upon the table; or he uses the secret hook, with which the imprudent fish is taken. By the example of which we may be taught to despise pleasures, because pleasure is bought with pain, and is injurious, nor can anyone be ignorant of the sad fate of those who yield to it, except those who either have not sinned, or, having sinned, have not the benefit of repentance. May God keep far from us the pleasure, at the entrance to which Death is placed; according to the description of a wise man, "like bees in their flight, who seek a drop of honey, and are pierced through with a dart" (Boethius). The banks of the lake are strengthened by a high palisade woven of flexible osiers, so that the earth may not crumble away by the percolation of the water. This lake is fed by the river which flows by, at a distance of scarcely thirty-six feet, from which the water is let through narrow passages into the lake which it feeds. Overflow pipes lead back from it, and keep the water always at the same level.

But while I am carried on in this description of the meadows, while I breathlessly mount the steep slopes, or traverse the brightly-coloured surface of the meadow, painted by the hand of Wisdom, or describe the ridges of the mountains clothed with trees, I am accused of ingratitude by that sweet fountain of whose waters I have so often drunk, which has merited so well of me, and which I have repaid so ill. It reminds me in a tone of reproach that it has often quenched my thirst, that it has given me water to wash my hands and even my feet, that it has rendered to me many such offices of kindness and benevolence. It says to me that all these good offices I have repaid with ingratitude; that it has been the last mentioned of all the places I have described, and indeed that it scarcely found a place at all; whereas for the respect I owe to it, it should have been placed first. And, indeed, I am unable to deny that I remembered it too late; and that I should have thought of it earlier. But does it not roll its waters silently through subterranean channels, so that not even the lightest murmur marks its passage, like the waters of Siloah which roll in silence, as if fearing to be betrayed, and hide themselves from all eyes? Why should I not have supposed that it wished for secrecy, when I see that it does not wish to be beheld except under a roof? This fountain, then (which is said to be an indication of a good fountain), has its source opposite to the rising sun, so that at the time of the spring solstice it salutes the ruddy face of the scintillating aurora. A hut of turf, or, to speak more respectfully of it, a pavilion small and pretty, covers and protects it, that nothing unclean may fall into it on any side. But the place where the mountain permits it to issue forth is also the place where the valley engulfs it; where it is born, it also as it were dies, and is buried. But do not expect a sign like that of Jonas the prophet, that it should lie hidden three days and three nights in the soil; it seems to be raised up almost immediately from the heart of the earth, and reappears at a thousand feet distance, within the enclosure of the monastery. It might be said that it returns to life where it appears, offering itself to charm the sight and supply the wants of the brethren, as if it were not willing to have communication with any others than saints.

LETTER CXLVI.

TO BURCHARD, ABBOT OF BALERNE.[1]

Bernard rejoices that his efforts to train Burchard to the Religious life have not been in vain; the happy issue is to be attributed to God alone.

1. Your style has been filled with fire and power, and with that fire, too, which the Lord has sent on the earth. I read your letter, and my heart burned within me; I blessed that furnace from whence such sparks had flown forth. Did not your heart burn within you as you dictated such words? A good man out of the good treasure of his heart bringeth forth good things. If I laboured for you, as you humbly say, I rejoice at it. I ploughed, in hope, no doubt, of receiving fruit, and my hope has not deceived me. Lo, with the fruit of my works my heart is satisfied in a strange land; and I see by experience that my seed has not fallen by the wayside, nor on stony ground, nor amongst thorns, but into a good and fertile soil. And if I had sorrow when I brought them forth, yet now I remember no more the travail, for joy that a child has been born into the world. A child, I mean, in malice, not in understanding; one whom the Saviour could set forward for an example to the old, saying, *Except ye be converted and become as little children, ye shall not enter into the kingdom of heaven* (S. Matt. xviii. 3); such a child as can say, *I am wiser than the aged, because I have sought Thy commandments* (Ps. cxix. 100); and, *I am small and despised, yet do I not forget Thy precepts* (Ps. cxix. 141).

2. I thank Thee, O Father, Lord of Heaven and earth, because Thou hast hid these things from the wise and prudent, and hast revealed them unto babes; even so, Father, for so it seemed good in Thy sight. By Thy will, not by their merits are they what they are. For Thou dost

---

Balerne was of the Cistercian order, in the Diocese of Besançon, and was founded A.D. 1136. Its first Abbot was Burchard; the judgment passed on him may be seen in the *Life of S. Bernard*, at the end of lib. i.

not come to find, but goest before to give merit. We all
have sinned, and need to be prevented by grace. Do thou,
then, my brother, acknowledge that thou hast been prevented, and prevented with the blessings of goodness, not
by me, who am nothing, but by Him who, by His holy
inspiration, prevented me, and so caused me to warn thee
to save thyself. For. to attribute a great deal to myself, I
planted, I watered; but without Him who giveth the increase, what am I? To Him in all humility submit thyself,
to Him with utmost devotion cling. Use me as His servant, thy fellow servant, thy companion in the way, thy
future co-heir in our country, that is to say, if I shall have
faithfully fulfilled the ministry to which I was sent on your
behalf, and if I shall have done what I could to enable you
to lay hold of the inheritance of salvation. This is my
answer to your complaint. I will occupy myself with your
necessities as my own when I come.

LETTER CXLVII. (A.D. 1138.)
To Peter, Abbot of Cluny.[1]

*Peter had consoled Bernard, who was engaged abroad in
several difficult labours for the Church, by sending him
Gebuin, Archdeacon of Troyes. He gratefully acknow-*

[1] This reply of Bernard's is wanting in not a few copies, and in the first
editions was placed after ep. 307. But this ep. 147 is an answer to two of
Peter's, one of which is ep. 29 in lib. ii.; the other, ep. 37, is here subjoined,
that it may be seen how closely these two holy souls clung to each other; *cf.*
also notes to ep. 228. The epistle is as follows:—

"To my venerable and dearly beloved lord, BERNARD, Abbot of Clairvaux, his
brother PETER, humble Abbot of the Cluniacs, sends greeting, desiring that he
may be always strong in the Lord.

"How great are the reverence and the love that my inmost soul feels for you,
He knows whom in you I venerate and love. I still felt all this even when He
hid from me your bodily presence; because rumour, that travels faster than the
body can, brought before my mind's eye the form of your blessed soul. But
when I at length attained what had been so long time denied me, and when
the images of dreams disappeared before the light of truth, my soul clung to
yours and refused to be again separated from your love. So did your love
claim me wholly thenceforth, so did your virtues and the beauty of your
character seize me, that nothing of my own was left me which was not yours,.

ledges this kindness, and predicts a happier state for the Church by the extinction of the then existing schism.

To dom PETER, the very Reverend Father, Abbot of Cluny, his friend BERNARD wishes health, and all that he could desire for his friend.

1. May the Dayspring from on high visit you, my excellent friend, for you have visited me in a strange land, and consoled me in the place of my pilgrimage. You have done well to think upon the poor and needy. I was absent, and absent too for a long time, and you, a great man, full of important matters, yet forgot not my name. Blessed be thy holy angel, who put loving thought for me into thy heart: blessed be our God who moved thee. Lo, I hold in my hand your letter, of which I may make my boast among strangers, and in which you have poured out your full heart to me. I rejoice that you hold me in favour as well as in memory. I rejoice in the privilege of your love, I am refreshed out of the abundant sweetness of your heart. nothing of yours was suffered to remain with you which was not also mine. From that time there abode in me (and may the cause of Christ to which you have set your hand so abide in you) that brotherly love, which alone, because it can never perish, has preserved its nature perfectly so far as I am concerned. And since I have stored this up in my bosom, and hold it dearer than all the gold in the world, more precious than all jewels, I wonder that for so long a time I have not received from you, such tokens as I could wish for, of the love that you keep for me. I am thankful, indeed, that by the chance salutations you occasionally send, you show that you have not wholly forgotten your friend. But I complain that you have not given me yet surer proofs by letter. I say 'surer,' because the paper cannot alter what has been written on it, while the tongue of the speaker can too often change by addition or subtraction, the truth that has been uttered. Hence, because as a chosen warrior, prepared for the day of battle, because of the dangers that threaten the Church of God, you fight with the arms of righteousness on the right hand and the left, I securely commend to your friendship the messengers whom I am sending to my lord the Pope; being assured that one who assists strangers in their cause will not be wanting to his friends in their need. That my complaint may be set at rest, send me word by letters and not by word of mouth only, how you are, how my lord, the Pope, is situated, and about his return. Would that you were set free from an exacting Curia and I from a perilous charge,[1] as I have always longed for, so that one place never to be changed might hold us both, one charity unite us, one Christ receive us!"

[1] *Cura.*

And not only so, but I glory in tribulations also, if I have been counted worthy to endure any for the sake of the Church. This, truly, is my glory and the lifting up of my head—the Church's triumph. For if we have been sharers of her trouble, we shall be also of her consolation. We must work and suffer with our mother, lest she complain of us, saying, *My kinsmen stand afar off: they also that seek after my life lay snares for me* (Ps. xxxviii. 11, 12).

2. But thanks be to God who hath given her the victory, has crowned her labours, and glorified her in them. Our sadness has been turned into rejoicing, our mourning into gladness. The winter is passed, the rain is over and gone; the flowers appear on the earth, the time of pruning is here, the useless branch, the rotten member has been cut off. The wicked man who made Israel to sin, he has been swallowed up by death,[1] and given over to the pit of hell. In the words of the Prophet, he had entered into a covenant with death, and made an agreement with hell (Is. xxviii. 18), and therefore, as Ezekiel says, *Destruction has come to him and he shall be no more for ever* (Ezek. xxviii. 19). Another enemy, too, the greatest of all and the worst of all, has none the less been cut off.[2] And he was one of the friends of the Church, of whom she is wont to complain, saying: *My lovers and my neighbours did stand looking upon my trouble, and my kinsmen stood afar off* (Ps. xxxviii. 11). If any remain I hope for speedy judgment against them. I shall soon be returning to my brethren, if God preserves my life, and I shall hope to pay you a visit in passing. Meanwhile I commend myself to your holy prayers. I salute brother Hugh, the Chamberlain, and all who are with you, with the rest of your sacred congregation.

---

[1] The Antipope Anacletus died A.D. 1138. The manner of his death is described by Ernald (*Life of S. Bernard*, lib. ii. c. 7). Ordericus (p. 915) says that his death was sudden. Victor was chosen in his place by the rivals of Innocent.

[2] This seems to be Gerard, Bishop of Angoulême, who died A.D. 1136 (ep. 126 notes). Ordericus, speaking of his death (p. 908), calls him a most learned man, "and of great reputation and authority in the Roman Senate in the times of Popes Paschal, Gelasius, Calixtus, and Honorius."

LETTER CXLVIII. (A.D. 1138.)

TO THE SAME.

He replies to Peter only in a few words, proposing to write at greater length later.

To dom PETER, Abbot of Cluny, BERNARD sends humble and respectful salutations.

When I had read your letter I was made joyful that one so great as you should trouble to prevent one so insignificant as I with the blessings of goodness. But when shall we have an opportunity of seeing each other, and of conversing with each other? When will there be convenient place, or fitting occasion? Meanwhile I send a few words in reply to your short letter, and will gladly send more, when I know that they will not be burdensome to you. Else how could my littleness dare to write at all, were it not that you in your humility stoop to give me access to your exalted dignity?

LETTER CXLIX. (A.D. 1138.)

TO THE SAME.

Bernard advises him not to press on so eagerly the affair of the Abbey of Saint Bertin.

I think that you are well aware how unwilling I am ever to do anything which may be hostile to your Reverence. And having this confidence I do not hesitate to make suggestions to you when necessary. With respect to the monastery of S. Bertin[1] I could wish you to act less eagerly

---

[1] The monastery of S. Bertin at S. Omer, otherwise Sittich, after having come to great want, was handed over by Abbot Lambert to Hugh, Abbot of Cluny, A.D. 1101, and then it became so prosperous in point of wealth, piety, and the number of its monks, that where twelve monks could before hardly live the number increased to 150, and from them many monasteries of Belgium and France received the regular discipline, as Hermann, the monk, says (*Spicil.* Vol. xii. p. 443), with whom Iperius agrees. On the death of Hugh, Abbot of Cluny, the monks of Sittich shook off the yoke and entered into a suit with

than you have done. For even if you could bring it to submit to you in peace and without any contention, I do not see how you would gain even then. For I should not suppose that you would find any pleasure in honour accompanied by such responsibilities. But now that you cannot obtain the submission of this monastery without great labour, nor hold it, they say, peacefully, you have a good excuse afforded you for retiring gracefully from the attempt, in the fear of causing trouble and strife.

LETTER CL. (A.D. 1133.)

To Pope Innocent.

He praises the Pope for various acts of authority; and then urges him to oppose strongly the ambition of Philip, who was endeavouring to obtain the Archbishopric of Tours by illegitimate means.

1. May the members share in the health of the head! May the anointing oil which descended to the beard from the head also run down to the utmost skirts of the clothing! If when the shepherd is smitten the sheep are scattered, may they return to their pasture without fear when he is strong and well! What I mean is this: Many a report of your frequent glorious successes is making glad the city of God. It is, therefore, but fitting that your prosperity should be the strengthening of the Church; and that, when God exalts him that He has chosen out of His people, she also may see herself exalted, and feel the stronger by an increase of vigour. For if she have suffered with him, she ought also to reign with him. That is at once worthy of you and necessary for us. What is it then? If in times of fear and

their abbot without the knowledge of the Cluniacs. The quarrel was so kept up that at the instance of Peter the Venerable Innocent II. deposed two abbots, John and Simon; but at length Peter was persuaded by Bernard to yield his rights and give the monks of S. Bertin their independence. *Cf. Apolog.* (notes Vol. ii.).

distress the arm of justice was not shortened, nor the zeal for equity cooled, are we to give way now that we are nearing the goal? Shall the virtue which shone brightly in weakness succumb in power?

2. To come to the point, with how strong a hand has the famous monastery of Vezelay[1] been set in order? The Apostolic majesty thought that it ought not to give way, no, not for a moment, either to the insane outbreaks of an armed populace, or to the unbridled madness of mutinous and wrathful monks, or to what was more powerful than all —the forces of mammon. What shall I say of S. Benedict?[2] Was the indignation of a king able to repress the spirit of liberty kindled and girded to battle against flesh and blood?

---

[1] Vezelay, in the Diocese of Autun, was founded by Gerard, Count of Nevers, and Bertha, his wife, about the year 821, for nuns, who were afterwards replaced by monks, and they by regular canons, A.D. 1537. A reformation of this monastery was first instituted at the instance of Henry, Duke of Burgundy, by William, a follower of S. Mayeul, Abbot of Cluny. Then, again, Hugh, another Abbot of Cluny, restored its waning discipline. From this it came to pass that Paschal II. had it placed entirely, A.D. 1103, under the Abbot of Cluny. *Cf.* Duchesne (notes, *ad Bibliothth. Cluni*). But the monks of Vezelay, attempting to throw off the yoke gradually, were again compelled by Innocent II. to submit. The historian of Vezelay thus speaks of this: "Although the monks of Vezelay had for nearly three hundred years from the first foundation of their house quietly and without opposition enjoyed the liberty of choosing for their head one of their own number, or a brother from some other monastery, yet the Cluniacs, a much later foundation, endeavoured to surreptitiously gain a supremacy over them by first claiming an assenting voice, then the right of election, falsely asserting that the charge of the Order of the Abbey of Vezelay had been given them by Paschal II. From the same cause a grievous scandal arose under Innocent II. on their reclaiming their natural liberty; but a certain Alberic was thrust upon them by the Cluniacs, who were supported by force by Innocent and the Count of Nevers, and all the brethren nearly of the monastery were thrown into fetters."

[2] This was S. Benedict's on the Po, which had been dealt with by Popes Gregory VII. and Calixtus II. as Vezelay had been, that is to say, it was forbidden to choose its Abbot without the counsel, provision, and precept of the Abbot of Cluny, and the man of their choice was prohibited from seeking episcopal benediction without the Abbot's commendatory Letters. But, when the monks began to act differently, Innocent, at the instance of Peter the Venerable, gave order by Letter (*Bull. Clement.* iii., A.D. 1187, *Biblioth. Cluni*, col. 2452), that Abbot William, having been elected and admitted without the consent of the Cluniacs, should appear before them and pay them due obedience and reverence.

So in a wonderful way were the churches of S. Memmius[1] and S. Satyrus[2] transformed, from being synagogues of Satan to become again sanctuaries of God, whether the workers of wickedness would or no. Nor at Liege was the threatening and savage sword of a passionate and angry king able to enforce acquiescence in his urgent and wicked demands.[3] Who can sufficiently praise the bolt that was hurled, even though it was from a distance, against the dis-

[1] S. Memmius was sprung from the once famous family of Memmii at Rome, was sent by S. Peter into Gaul, and became first Bishop of Chalons. A famous Church of Canons was founded in his honour in the same city, which afterwards, by the command of Innocent II., took the rule of the Regular Canons of S. Augustine.

[2] Matilda, wife of Godfrey de Bouillon (or Boulogne, on the English Channel, according to William of Tyre, lib. ix. c. 5), and first King of Jerusalem, sought and obtained from Pope Paschal the body of S. Satyrus, whose memory is kept on March 7th, and erected for it at Bourges a collegiate house of secular Canons. But so easily do we deteriorate, that within a few years they had degenerated into worldliness and licence, and were expelled by the order of Innocent and replaced by Augustinian Canons, as the *Memoriale Historiarum* says:—"In the year 1138 there flourished the Order of Canons of S. Victor of Paris, whose name was famous throughout the world for the high character and great learning of its members, whom it sent forth into various Churches throughout the world, as a fruitful vine gives forth its branches to be transplanted. For at this time there were two professed Canons made prelates of the Roman Church; the Cardinals, Hugh, Bishop of Tusculum, and Master Ivo, as well as nine Abbots. In the Church of S. Satyrus, at Bourges, Abbot Ralph," etc. The Necrology of S. Victor, of Paris, adds to this, on the 5th of February, the name of "Dom Andrew, Abbot of S. Satyrus, and Canon of our Order." Stephen, Abbot of S. Geneviève, at Paris, and afterwards Bishop of Tournay, commends in a Letter to Pope Lucius III. the grave and regular discipline of this monastery. Add to this that in a terrier of the episcopal estates and the benefices of France this Abbey is said to be under the rule of S. Augustine.

[3] We must, it seems, understand this of the right of investiture claimed by Lothaire, and resisted by Innocent. Abbot Conrad of Ursperg says that "at this very time the Pope went to Lothaire to seek his help against Peter and his supporters." Doubtless the Emperor thought this too good an opportunity to be lost, and proceeded to demand from the Pope a restoration of the right of investiture, which had been held for so long by his predecessors. The Pope accordingly was not a little perplexed, and sorry that he had ever come, and anxious, too, that he might depart. For he was unable to grant the request of the Emperor in a matter in which the Church had before suffered so many troubles. However, by the intervention of S. Bernard, he was able to leave the Emperor in safety. Otto of Frisingen gives a more favourable account of the transaction (lib. vii. c. 18).

turbers of the church of Orleans,[1] by the same powerful hand in the last few days? Truly the bow of Jonathan turned not back, nor his sword returned empty. Nevertheless, by this word the king indeed was disturbed, but not all Jerusalem with him. He himself at last allowed his anger to cool. He was, indeed, fearful and scrupulous of taking up arms against the Lord, and against His Anointed. Your majesty has been exalted above the heavens, but only in order that so good a beginning may be adorned with a fitting ending. This, indeed, is what all who love you are eagerly looking for, and they are demanding its speedy arrival.

3. With equal zeal, and with as powerful an arm, it is necessary for help to be immediately lent to the Church of Tours. Otherwise she is even now on the point to perish, unless you speedily help her. The spirit of Gislebert[2] lives

---

[1] Who these were we learn from Letters used by D'Achery (*Spicil.* Vol. iii., p. 153). First, from a Letter of Archembald, Subdean of the Church of Orleans, to Henry, Archbishop of Sens, we gather that the instigator of this trouble was a certain John of Orleans, who afterwards ordered Archembald to be put to death (ep. 161), and who had been intruded into the office of Archdeacon. When Archembald and other clerks opposed him, they suffered grievous injuries, and the loss of nearly all their goods at the hands of him and his supporters, Bartholomew Capicer, Zacharias Paganus, the Archdeacon, James, Subdeacon of S. Anianus, and others. Hence, at the end of the Letter he asks that "full justice may be done him against the malefactors." Archbishop Henry, to whom they had fled for help, owing to the See of Orleans being vacant, was asked "to give order that the Church which had been defiled with bloodshed and sacrilege, should put an end to such things, or suffer interdict, and not to delay to avenge these men's misdeeds, which affected even his Lordship the Pope." There is extant also another Letter of the same tenor sent by Geoffrey, Bishop of Chartres, to the same Henry. It may be that this intruder John was maintaining his position by the support of the King. At length, however, Pope Innocent entrusted the charge of this matter to the above-named Geoffrey of Chartres, acting as his legate, and thus compelled the guilty to make satisfaction.

[2] Gislebert or Gilbert, the predecessor of Hildebert, who was translated, A.D. 1125, from the See of Le Mans to that of Tours, which he held for six years and six months (*cf.* note to ep. 122). On his death, Philip, nephew of Gislebert, by his evil attempts on the See, in which he was supported by Anacletus, gave occasion for the writing of this Letter and of the next, which, however, was the first written. Philip being compelled to retire, Hugh was canonically elected (*cf. Analect*), Vol. iii. p. 338).

again, they say, in Philip, who is at once his nephew according to the flesh, and the heir of his ambition. With what a lust for power this youth burns is shown by the protracted and cruel tortures inflicted on his mother church, by which the unhappy man has almost disembowelled her, in order that he may be brought forth to honour. However, by the will of God an end has at last been put to his misdoings, that is to say, if only what has been done against him, as justice dictated, and his wickedness compelled, and peace called for, be ratified by Apostolic authority. But God forbid that the benign majesty of the Holy See should confound its faithful servants, to whom the settling of this matter was graciously entrusted. God forbid it that cruel ambition should find a supporter in the defender of innocence. This is what his audacity is bidding him try for, this is what he madly hopes to find. Once and again has the despiser of the Apostolic decree eluded the stroke of justice; and does he now again, with still more impudent rashness, venture none the less to present himself before the face of your equity? Is there any one who cannot see the impiety of the attempt of this man, who places no confidence whatever in righteousness, to attack the tower of strength with the forces of mammon? But we are safe; it is Innocent who is to be tempted, and the son of iniquity shall not come nigh to hurt him.

4. As to the rest, most sweet Father, while we sigh for your presence, we talk to each other of the memory of your abundant kindness; the one consoles us for the want of the other. This is never absent from our hearts; it is often in our mouths, it is salt to every speech, it soothes the ear, sweetens the mouth, refreshes and enkindles our hearts. It is foremost at the meetings of the saints, it is their chief topic of conversation; it lends wings to their petitions, and nerves them to prayer. And now I pray earnestly for you and yours that the Eternal One, for Whom and on behalf of Whom you labour in time, may count you worthy of eternal memory. Amen.

LETTER CLI. (A.D. 1133.)

To Philip, the Intruded Archbishop of Tours.[1]

He expresses the great grief he felt that Philip should attempt to gain the Archbishopric of Tours by illegitimate means.

I am grieved for you, my dear Philip, but I beseech you mock not at my grief. For if by any chance you think that there is no cause for grief, then you are the more to be grieved for. Whatever you may think about yourself, for my part I think that a fount of tears is insufficient to lament for you. My grief is not one that calls for ridicule, but for compassion; for it is not a grief for flesh and blood, not for the loss of things that perish, but for you yourself, Philip. I cannot better describe the greatness of my grief than by saying that Philip is the cause of it. And when I say this, I declare the great lamentation of the Church, who once cherished you in her bosom, as a lily springing up, adorned with every celestial gift. Who, then, was there that did

[1] "On the death of Hildebert, Bishop of Tours, A.D. 1137, the Canons of that Church were expelled by violence by Count Geoffrey. Then when they were to elect another Bishop they were divided into two parts. For some of them, contrary to the decrees of the sacred canons, elected a certain Philip, nephew of the ambitious predecessor of Hildebert in the same See, who was called Gilbert. This was opposed by others. Philip immediately hurried away to the pseudo-pope Anacletus for confirmation and consecration, and then returned to Tours. Meanwhile Hugh, a wise and noble man, was canonically elected by the wiser part of the same clergy, and was consecrated in Le Mans by Guy and his comprovincials. When Philip heard of this he fled secretly, carrying off with him the ornaments of the Church." The above is taken from the Acts of the Bishops of Le Mans given in the third volume of the *Analecta*. While all this was going on, Bernard, who was then staying at Viterbo, wrote this Letter to Philip. Then he, having become more reckless, harassed the Church of Tours by his ambition, on the death of Anacletus, and the Saint wrote in the following year, 1138, the preceding Letter to Pope Innocent against him. But under Archbishop Hugh, who at length silenced Philip, that happened which Innocent III. speaks of (lib. iii. ep. 79) : "The party of Dôl has added that Eugenius III., our predecessor of good memory, entrusted to Abbot Bernard, of Clairvaux, of happy memory, the task of allaying the controversy between the Churches, whose decision the Church of Tours refused to abide by." This Letter was written long afterwards by Innocent III. in the cause of the Church of Tours against the metropolis of Dôl.

not loudly proclaim you to be a youth of good hope, a young man of good disposition? But, alas! the fair promise has disappeared. From what hope has France, who bore and nourished you, fallen! O, did you but know! But if you would apply your heart unto wisdom, you would also learn to grieve, and your grief would prevent mine from being sterile. I should go on if I were to give way to my feelings, but I do not wish to say much while in uncertainty, or to fight as one that beats the air. But I have written this that you may know my affection for you, and may learn that I am near you, if perchance God should inspire you with a desire for a conference, and if you should be willing to grant me what I greatly long for, an interview. I am at Viterbo,[1] and I hear that you are staying at Rome. Vouchsafe to write back to me to say how you receive this letter of mine, that I may know what I ought to do, whether I am to grieve more or less. But if you despise everything, and will in no way listen to me, I for my part shall not lose the fruit of my letter, for it proceeds from charity; but you will have to give an answer for your contempt before the dread tribunal.

LETTER CLII. (*Circa* A.D. 1135.)

To Pope Innocent, on behalf of the Bishop of Troyes.

The indiscipline of the clergy increases with the slothful indulgence of the Bishops. The Bishop of Troyes is hated by a part of his clergy because he has corrected them.

The evil living of the clergy, the mother of which is Episcopal negligence, is everywhere disturbing and weakening the Church. The Bishops give what is holy to dogs, and cast pearls before swine, who turn again and rend

---

[1] Bernard was staying, therefore, at Viterbo, in Etruria, and in the year 1133, when he was sent by Innocent into Germany to Lothaire; and from this place the preceding Letter to Innocent seems to have been written. For more about his stay at Viterbo see Sermon 2 *in Cantica*, n. 14.

them. But it is only right that they should have to suffer from those that they foster. They do not correct those whom they enrich with the goods of the Church, and therefore they are grieved and wearied with their misconduct. The clergy are made wealthy from other men's labours; they eat the fruit of the earth and give no money for it, and their iniquity cometh from their own fat (Ps. lxxiii. 7, VULG.). The old saying of the Scripture exactly applies to them of the present day, *The people sat down to eat and to drink, and rose up to play* (1 Cor. x. 7). A mind that has accustomed itself to delights, and that has not trained itself with the disciplinary rod, contracts many a stain. And what is more, if you attempt to rub off its long-standing rust, they will not suffer you to touch it with even the tips of your fingers; but as it is written, *Jeshurun waxed fat, and kicked* (Deut. xxxii. 15). False witnesses have risen up, men whose delight is ever to carp at the lives of others and neglect their own. Your son supplicates for the Bishop, whose sole fault in this quarrel, unless I am mistaken, has been that he has rebuked the clergy for their evil lives. Thus much for the Bishop; now let me offer excuses for myself. My father knows that I did not receive before the Nativity of the Blessed Virgin his gracious letter, in which he preferred to courteously entreat me to come to him, when he might have ordered me. And so I do not say, I have bought five yoke of oxen, or I have bought a piece of ground, or I have married a wife; but I confess simply, what, indeed, you are not ignorant of, that I am feeding my children with milk, and therefore I do not see how I can leave them without running the risk of causing scandal, or leaving them exposed to danger.

LETTER CLIII. (A.D. 1135.)

TO BERNARD DESPORTES,[1] OF THE CARTHUSIAN ORDER.

His correspondent had asked for an Exposition of the

[1] In the *Codex Cisterciencis* we read: "It should be recollected that there were two Bernard Desportes, one the prior, the other the sub-prior, who

Canticles. *He replies by pleading his inability to perform so great a task, and to satisfy the expectation of others.*

1. You ask importunately, but I refuse as constantly, not as despising you, but as sparing myself. I wish that I could produce something that was worthy of your eager wish, and of your intelligence. I would, if I could, give for you the light of my eyes; yea, my soul itself, my dearest friend, my brother, to be embraced in the bowels of Christ by me most of all with the fulness of spiritual love. But where is the ability, or when shall I have leisure enough to undertake what you ask for? Nor do you seem to ask for anything trifling or worthless, such as lies in my power. You would not be thus pressing for what was of little moment. For your numerous letters, and the eagerness that animates them, sufficiently show your wish. Therefore, the more ardent I see your feelings to be, the more do I shrink from gratifying them. Why is this? I am afraid of bringing forth a ridiculously insignificant mouse, while you expect great things. I am afraid of this, and this is the cause of my hesitation. And what wonder is it that I am afraid of giving what I should be ashamed to publish? I am unwilling, I confess, to give you anything, because I think I should be rather issuing some contemptible work than publishing something that would be useful. Who can wish to give what would only cause shame to the giver, without benefiting the receiver? Willingly do I give what I have, but unwillingly do I throw

afterwards was made a Cardinal." The prior had been an Ambrosian monk, and founded the Carthusian Portæ, A.D. 1115. We read of him in the *Necrology*: —"On the 12th of February died Bernard, first Prior of Portæ, A.D. 1125." Long before that time he had resigned his office, and was succeeded by another Bernard as Prior of Portæ, after having resigned the see of Bellay, as Peter Francis Chifflet says in his *Manuale Solitariorum*, who also thinks that this and the next Letter were directed to this second Bernard. He adds, moreover, a third Bernard during the same period, after the blessed Nathelmus, prior of the same place, which Bernard was afterwards Bishop of Die. It is evident from n. 2 of this Letter that the Bernard to whom this Letter was written, as well as the following, was not prior in the year 1135, when the Letter was penned, for Bernard salutes "my lord the prior," *i.e.*, Bernard, the first inhabitant and Prior of Portæ. Portæ is in Beaujé, in the Diocese of Lyons, near the Rhone, three leagues from Bellay, the Episcopal city.—*Cf. ep.* 250.

it away. I know that when great things are expected lesser things are generally displeasing. But what is not gratefully received is thrown away, not given.

2. It is your aim, since you have leisure and freedom, to seek from all quarters for fuel for the fire with which you burn, that you may burn the more, and fulfil the will of the Lord, who says, *And what do I wish, except that it burn brightly?* (S. Luke xii. 49, VULG.). I praise your aim, but not if you seek to obtain it in a quarter where you are likely to complain afterwards of having been disappointed. You err if you seek it with me. I ought rather to beg for such fuel from you. I know, indeed, how much *more blessed it is to give than to receive;* but that is true only when what is given is honourable to the giver, expedient for the receiver, and such a gift you will in vain seek from me. But such as I have, I am afraid that if I brought it forward, you would be ashamed of having wished for it, and would repent of having asked for it. But still, will it not after all be better for you to make my excuses to yourself? Let your own eyes judge for themselves. I yield to your importunity, to take away suspicion. I am dealing with a friend. I no longer spare my modesty, and henceforth while your desire is gratified, I will not make mention of my folly. I am having transcribed for you some sermons lately delivered on the beginning of the *Canticles*, and I send them to you before they are made public. When I have time, according as Christ assigns me my tasks, I will endeavour to proceed with this work. Ask this for me in your prayers. I warmly salute through you my lord and father your Prior, with the rest of your brethren, and I humbly entreat them to remember me before God.

LETTER CLIV. (*Circa* A.D. 1136.)

TO THE SAME.

He excuses himself for having been unable, on account of business, to visit the Chartreuse, as he had promised. He sends some of his Sermons on the Canticles.

I can no longer conceal the sorrow of my heart, nor hide my distress, from you, my very dear Bernard. I recollect my long-standing promise; it has been my purpose and strong desire to pass by your way, to visit again those whom my soul loveth, to ask for rest on my journey, some strength to bear my labours, some remedy for my sins; and in punishment of my sinfulness it has come to pass that though I have the will, yet I have not the power to visit you. Be assured, O man of God, that this is by no means due to the disinclination, or idleness, or negligence of your friend, but that a cause has intervened which might not be neglected, and that was the cause of God. None the less I am devoured by vexation as by a gnawing worm, and my heaviness is ever in my sight. And, indeed, I have more than enough of other troubles, but none so great as this. It is more than the toils of travelling, the unpleasantness of the heat, the anxieties of my affairs. Lo! I have opened my wound to a friend; it is yours now to sympathize with me, to bear with me what I suffer, that I may be relieved. I earnestly ask for your prayers, and for those of the saints who are with you. I am sending on to you the promised sermons on the beginning of the Canticles, which you asked for. And when you have read them, I beg you to give me your advice as soon as possible whether I ought to give them up or proceed with them.

LETTER CLV. (*Circa* A.D. 1135.)

To Pope Innocent, on behalf of the same Bernard when elected Bishop.[1]

Bernard Desportes, who is destined for a Bishopric in Lombardy, though well worthy of that honour, is not

[1] This was perhaps to the See of Pavia, which at that time was vacant through the death of Peter. This election did not hold, but S. Bernard's advice was followed, and Bernard Desportes was elected to the See of Bellay, which dignity he resigned A.D. 1147, as has been said above, for the office of Prior of Portæ.

altogether fit for such a place, and would be better reserved for a fitter place.

I have heard, reverend Father, that Bernard Desportes, a man beloved of God and men, is by your irresistible call to undertake the office and work of a Bishop. It is probably true, for it well becomes your Apostleship to bring into the light a light that was hidden; lest he who is capable of drawing others to the Life should live for himself alone. For how long is one that can give light to others to lie concealed and only burn? Let it be placed, if you see good, on a candlestick, that it may be a burning and a shining light; but at the same time let it not be in a place where the force of the storms is great, lest it be perchance extinguished. Who is there that does not know of the evil-living and turbulence of the Lombards? Who knows them better than yourself? You know better than I how weakened is the episcopal power there, how rebellious a house it is. What am I to think is likely to be done by a man whose health is shattered, and who has been accustomed to a hermit's quiet, in the midst of a barbarous, riotous, and passionate populace? When are such holiness and such iniquity likely to agree? or when will such simplicity and such hypocrisy live in concord? Let him be reserved, if you see good, for a more congenial sphere, and for another flock, that he may profit that over which he presides; and let not hasty action destroy the fruit which in due time he will be able to bring forth.

LETTER CLVI. *(Circa* A.D. 1135 OR 1136.)

To the Same, on behalf of the Clergy of Orleans.

For how long is the unhappy Church of Orleans to knock at the heart of the Father of the fatherless and the Judge of widows? How long now has the noble virgin of Israel been lying in the dust, bereft not only of her husband,[1] but also of the dear pledges of his affection! Alas! there is none to lift her up. How long will it be before you send away the children crying after you with their unhappy mother? I mean those who having lost their houses and their goods have only saved their lives by flight. Why hangs back the powerful hand, which never yet has shrunk from avenging the oppressed, or from smiting the haughty? Why delays it, I ask, to rescue the afflicted from the hand of the strong, and to mete out punishment to the proud? Even if it delays, let it not rest idle for ever. Help that has been withheld should, when it is given, come in greater force, and render more thorough service. Let this be the reward, if you see good, for painful waiting, that both those who in their arrogance have abused the patience of the Apostolic See, should in the end gain nothing by it; and also that those who have patiently endured, trusting in your word, should never have any cause to repent them of their patience.

LETTER CLVII. (A.D. 1135.)

To Haimeric, on behalf of the Same.

To his special friend HAIMERIC, by the grace of God Cardinal-deacon, and Chancellor of the Apostolic See, his Brother BERNARD, of Clairvaux, sends greeting, and his wish that he may shine ever more and more with the light of wisdom and virtue.

If I did not know your sympathy with the afflicted, and your indignation against wrong-doers, I would at every opportunity importunately beseech you on behalf of Master

---

[1] After the death of Bishop John, which took place A.D. 1133, the See was for four years vacant, according to the *Annals of Orleans* by Charles Soussay. When Hugh, the Dean, who had been elected, was returning from the King's Court, he was set upon and killed by ruffians on the road, as Ordericus Vitalis says (A.D. 1134). This Letter and the next were written by Bernard before his third journey to Rome in A.D. 1137.

William, of Meun,[1] and his companions; I would stir you up against their oppressors and calumniators. But as it is, it is enough to have mentioned them to you; it is yours swiftly to act as necessity requires.

LETTER CLVIII. (A.D. 1135.)

To Pope Innocent, on the Murder of Master Thomas, Prior of S. Victor, of Paris.[2]

To his most loving Father and Lord, INNOCENT, Supreme Pontiff, BERNARD, unworthy Abbot of Clairvaux, sends greeting, with the assurance of his prayers and his feeble services.

[1] Maudunum, or Magdunum (Meun), is a town near Orleans, on the Loire, where there was a Collegiate Church of S. Lifardus, and a palace belonging to the Bishop of Orleans.

[2] S. Bernard in this Letter earnestly exhorts the Pope to exercise his power and punish the sacrilegious persons who had murdered Thomas, Prior of S. Victor, of Paris. He hints at the occasion of the murder, viz., that Thomas, fired with zeal for ecclesiastical discipline, withstood the covetousness and unjust exactions with which the Archdeacon of Paris was oppressing the clergy. Inflamed with hatred at this, the Archdeacon meditated revenge, until his nephews, either sharing his vindictive hatred, and so identifying themselves with the cause of their kinsman, or hired and urged by him to the wickedness, attacked Thomas on the road, and, indeed, in the very company of the Bishop. Stephen, Bishop of Paris, at once excommunicated the author of the murder with his aiders and abettors; and, deeply stirred by the enormity of the crime, he for a time retired to Clairvaux as though to seek to alleviate his sorrow, and from thence sent the following Letter to Geoffrey, Legate of the holy Roman Church, and Bishop of Chartres:—

"To GEOFFREY, by the grace of God Bishop of Chartres, and Legate of the Apostolic See, STEPHEN, by the same grace, unworthy minister of the Church of Paris, and now an ill-starred herald of misery and affliction, sends greeting in the Lord.

"1. I know not how to find fitting words to bring to your ears and heart the weight of this new calamity. My news is of things hard and difficult to speak of, painful to all to whom the reproach of Jesus Christ and our holy Mother Church is a hard and grievous thing, and especially to us placed under the habit and seal of religion, to whom these things are likely to be more serious, as the injury more specially affects us; I speak of the fall of one man, whose death portends oppression and ruin to us all. Master Thomas, Prior of the monastery of S. Victor, a man well tried and proved, beloved as a friend by all good men, my most devoted and zealous coadjutor and champion in the defence of the Holy Church, has been, you must know, cut off by the hands of wicked men, put to death in the flesh, but, as we have sure and certain hope, alive in Christ. For Christ, in whose cause he died, will not be absent from him in glory; for as he breathed out his last in my arms, he protested with a loud voice that he died for the sake of righteousness, most confident of his own righteousness past and present, in which he had fought against the ungodly within the Church of Christ, leaving a proof to us that in that righteousness he would be perfected. This was the first and this was the last cause of his sufferings; for he was then with me on behalf of righteousness itself. For I, mainly by his urgency, which he was wont to show in these things, and with the command and assent of the King, who had also been similarly moved by him, had been to correct and set in order the house of nuns at Chelles, having taken with me several Religious, viz., the Abbot of S. Victor, and of S. Magloire, and the sub-prior of S. Martin's, and many other monks, canons, and clerks; and when the business had been finished to the best of our ability, and I was on my way home, as we were near the Castle of the lord Stephen, which is called Gournay, we were suddenly attacked by the nephews of Archdeacon Theobald, who were lying in wait for us. And as we were going on our way, in peace and unarmed (it being the Lord's Day), they suddenly rushed on us with drawn swords, and paying no respect to God, nor His holy day, nor to me, nor to the Religious with me, they slew the innocent in the midst of us, and threatened me too with death if I did not speedily take me out of their sight. But we, having more trust in God, threw ourselves into the midst among their swords, and rescued him, half-dead and dreadfully hacked. Then standing round him we bade him make his confession, and forgive the wickedness of his enemies. Then he joyfully forgave all who had sinned against him, and sought forgiveness for his own sins, and received the communion of the Body and Blood of Christ, and then testified with a loud voice before all that he died for righteousness' sake, and so gave up the ghost.

"2. Hence, therefore, although we have sure and certain hope of his salvation and glory, wherein we rejoice and although we know that right dear in the sight of the Lord is the death of his saints, yet the grief and deep mourning, which are consuming us for the loss of our friend, and the great dishonour done to us all, are tempered by no consolation that we can feel. For I behold myself slain in him, and even much more slain than he, for by his death I see myself exposed to dangers from which he has been set free. It remains, therefore, that since you see me now desolate and in misery, you delay not to come at once to console and counsel me. For as I cannot bear to see the place of so detestable a crime, I have fled to Clairvaux, and shall await you there, that we may take counsel together what we ought to do to wipe out this intolerable dishonour done to our holy Church. This onslaught threatens us all with death, and it will come unless the Lord prevent it. I, therefore, bid you, and with all my power beseech you, to hasten without any delay to Clairvaux, for dangers, which brook no laggard counsel, are threatening me on every side."

Having received this Letter, Geoffrey hurried to Clairvaux, and by Apostolic command bade the Bishops of Rheims, Rouen, Tours, and Sens to assemble in force at a Synod to be held at Jouarre. Then when they assembled, Hugh, Bishop of Grenoble, and the community of Chartreuse, wrote, "asking and beseeching them to unsheathe the sword of ecclesiastical rigour against the sacrilegious murderers." Innocent, too, informed of the facts by S. Bernard, replied to the decree of the Fathers, confirming it and making it still more severe. John Picard, in his notes to the Letter of Innocent, and others who follow him, assign this murder to the year 1130, but it is placed by Baronius in the year 1135. But this (former) opinion cannot be admitted. For from ep. 159 it is evident that Thomas was killed on a Sunday, and on the 20th August, as we read in the Necrology of S. Victor: "The anniversary of the death of Magister Thomas, Prior of this Church, who was cruelly slain by the enemies of righteousness for his defence of righteousness, and so both by his life and death he left behind him a noble example of an honourable and patient life for his successors to strive to imitate." On Picard's authority, too, the Kalendar of S. Guinail, of Corbeil, agrees with this. The day, therefore, that was consecrated by the blood of Thomas ought to bear the same dominical letter as the year 1130; but it does not, for the dominical letter of that year is E, but the corresponding letter of 20th August is A. Picard adds two other arguments in support of his contention. One that the death of Prior Thomas preceded that of Hugh, of Grenoble, since he wrote with the Carthusians to the Fathers assembled in council at Jouarre to urge them to avenge Thomas. But he says that the *Life of S. Hugh*, by Guy, Abbot of the Grand Chartreuse, places his death in the year 1132; and therefore the death of Thomas is to be referred, not, indeed, to the year 1131, when Innocent was in Gaul, accompanied the whole time by Bernard, and would not need to be petitioned by so many letters, but to the year 1130, in which Innocent was made Pontiff. The second argument is that Innocent, about the beginning of the year 1131, visited Paris, and went to the Church of S. Victor, and ordered the body of the blessed Thomas to be carried from the cloister into the Church on March 9th. It had been buried, therefore, in the August of the preceding year. But neither argument is conclusive; certainly not the first. For what is there to hinder our saying that this Letter was written by the successor of S. Hugh, who bore the same name? Nor can the second be pressed closely. For, granted that Innocent ordered the body to be moved into a more honourable place, yet it cannot be affirmed that he did so in person; nay, the mandate was sent from Italy, as is manifest from D'Achery (*Spicil.*, Vol. v. ep. on p. 567), where we find that he rebukes the Archbishops of Rheims and Sens for their delay in carrying out the excommunication of the murderers of Thomas. He concludes: "Therefore we command that the body of the above-named good man, who now bears testimony to his righteousness and innocence before the Supreme Judge, and whose life was a life of obedience, and who was slain in the service of his Bishop, be honourably buried in his Church. Given at Pisa Dec. 21." Therefore we must say that this murder took place, not in the year 1130, but in the year 1133, in which the dominical letter E corresponds with the letter of the 20th August, and in which year, too, a second Hugh was occupying the See of Grenoble in succession to S. Hugh; in which Innocent was at Pisa for the Council held there; in which, lastly, Bernard was sent from Italy into Germany to arrange terms of peace between

1. The wild beast which has laid waste Joseph, unable to meet the eager attack of our dogs, is said to have fled to you for shelter. What madness has seized the wretched creature, a wanderer, and stranger, and fugitive on earth, to cause it to fly thither of all places where it should have most to fear! Most accursed one! thinkest thou that the seat of strictest justice is a cave of robbers or a lurking-place of lions? Do you dare, with jaws still foaming, and mouth yet marked with the blood of the son you have but just now slain, to flee to the breast of the mother and appear before the eyes of the father? Yet if it is penance that he seeks, let it not be denied him. If it is a hearing, let him, if you please, obtain such an one as Moses gave the people worshipping their molten image, or such as Phinehas gave the fornicating Israelite, or such as Mattathias gave to him who offered sacrifice to devils, or, to take an example from your own house, such as Ananias and Sapphira gained from blessed Peter, such an audience, lastly, as the Saviour gave those who bought and sold in the temple. Do we not know that the sins of certain men go before them to judgment? Does not the voice of your brother's blood cry out against you from the ground? I believe that the spirit of our martyr, whom but a few days since you cruelly delivered to death, joins with the souls of the others who have been slain, in crying with a loud voice from under the altar, and in demanding vengeance, and that the more urgently as his blood has been more newly poured forth on the earth.

2. But he will reply, Was it I who actually slew him?

Lothaire and Conrad, and having returned into Gaul stayed there long enough to be present at a Cistercian Chapter, duly held in this year on the 13th September, as appears from the address of a Letter sent in this year by Peter of Cluny to the said Chapter (Pet. Ven. lib. i. ep. 36), at which he is spoken of as being present. Ordericus, too, favours this opinion of mine (lib. xiii., A.D. 1134), who, in giving a summary of several events which had taken place in the preceding year, after naming the death of John, Bishop of Orleans, and Hugh, the Dean, his successor-designate, which took place, according to the Annals of Orleans, in A.D. 1133, goes on to say: "Then, too, was killed Thomas, of S. Victor, a man of great authority."

No, not directly, but it was your friends who did, and for your sake. Whether at your instigation, may God see and judge. If you are to be excused, whose teeth are spears and arrows, whose tongue is a sharp sword, then the Jews ought not to be held guilty of the death of Christ, inasmuch as they were wary enough to withhold their hands from it. This man had been wont to abuse his office of Archdeacon, to grind the presbyters with unlawful exactions, and when this was put an end to by the zeal and diligence of the blessed Thomas, a lover and upholder of righteousness, this man held him in hatred, and was often in the habit of threatening him with death. Many, whose testimony is not to be rejected, declare that they have heard him so threaten. Lastly, let him say, if he can, what other complaint his nephews had against Thomas, that they should lay their impious hands on the saint of the Lord. If, then, the man who, as nearly all suspect, is the occasion, the instigator, and the plotter of this wickedness is to go, as he impudently presumes, unpunished by the Apostolic authority, what provocation will be given to sin in the Church without fear of punishment? One of two things must inevitably follow : either that none of the noble or powerful of this world will hereafter be admitted to ecclesiastical honours, or that the clergy will everywhere have free permission to abuse their sacred office for every unworthy end; lest, perchance, anyone kindled with zeal for God should attempt to prevent them, and for so acting be slain as a champion of righteousness by the soldier's sword. And then what is left for the spiritual sword, for ecclesiastical censure, for the law and discipline of Christ, for the reverence due to the priesthood, and for the fear of God, if no one dares to whisper a protest against the evil lives of the clergy from dread of the secular power? For what can be more monstrous or more disgraceful to the Church than that each one should maintain his own ecclesiastical dignity by armed violence instead of by moral integrity? Wherefore, my lord and father, I pray you to give such a decision, according to your wisdom, concerning this man as shall be to the Church's profit, so that the salvation given now may flow down to our children, and that another generation may hear not only how audacious was the crime, but also how terrible was the vengeance. Otherwise, if the poison be allowed to have full play, if no antidote is given, it will destroy many— which God forbid.

LETTER CLIX. (A.D. 1133.)

To the Same, in the Name of Stephen, Bishop of Paris, and on the Same Subject.

To his most godly father, INNOCENT, Supreme Pontiff, STEPHEN, unhappy Bishop of the Church that is at Paris, sends greeting, praying for mercy and judgment.

1. A religious man, Master Thomas, Prior of S. Victor, while engaged in an office of charity, on a journey that piety had bidden him to undertake, in a holy work, in the midst of a company of saints, on the Lord's Day, has been cruelly murdered on my bosom, so to speak, and almost in my arms, for his righteousness, by the ungodly, and has been made obedient even unto death. There is no need for a lengthy petition, when tears flowing silently are better able to stir sympathy, and when love finds expression in sobs which interrupt my prayer. These surely, if they do not demand, at all events deserve compassion, inasmuch as they indicate and show a grief that is unfeigned, and banish all suspicion of simulation. I think, therefore, that, to touch the heart of my father with grief for the disaster that has befallen us, it will be enough for me to simply mention the circumstances. A sad and pitiful story speaks for itself, especially before you, and needs no glossing appeals for sympathy. O, my eyes! run ye down with floods of tears, for my strength and the light of my eyes has failed me, and he is no more with me. For I do not mourn for him, but for myself. How should I weep for him, who, by a quick and glorious death, has passed into life?

2. Who would not pursue with praises rather than with lamentations him to whom to live was Christ, and to die is gain? I used to bear the name of Bishop; he performed the labours. Casting aside all thought of honour, he bore the burden with all his strength. And therefore he truly, though dead, is enjoying life, while I, though living, am in the midst of death. He did not fall into the snares of death, but escaped them; and lo! the sorrows of death compass me about, and the overflowings of ungodliness make me afraid. It is I, therefore, it is I that am to be pitied, now that you are dead, my sweetest brother Thomas. I am like a weaned child, without the sweet refreshment that you gave me, bereft of your wise counsel, and left desolate by the loss of your sure protection. Better would it have been for me to die than to live without you. Therefore, my life is wasted away in grief, and my years in mourning. The Church grieves with me, but she grieves also for herself. Common is the loss, common the lamentation; the whole of the religious world deplores with me his loss, and all alike implore that they may receive consolation from their father. If Theobald Notier[1] come before you let him feel to his cost that the Lord hath heard the voice of my weeping. His nephews were the perpetrators of the crime; he was its cause; whether he instigated it is a matter to be ascertained. Do not listen to anything that he may say, till our messenger arrive, who will put you more fully in possession of the truth, and preserve you from lying lips and a deceitful tongue.

LETTER CLX. (A.D. 1133.)

To Haimeric, the Chancellor, in the name of the same Bishop.

To his dearest lord, HAIMERIC, venerable Cardinaldeacon and Chancellor of the holy Roman Church, his

[1] Archdeacon of Paris, as Stephen the Bishop of Paris testifies in the Letter given in the last note, which was perhaps written by S. Bernard himself in Stephen's name to Geoffrey of Chartres, the then legate.

servant STEPHEN, of Paris, sends loving and friendly greeting.

A friend is proved in time of necessity. I say this, not that I have any doubt of your holy friendship for me, but to prevent any doubt from arising. But arise it undoubtedly will if I shall now find no sign of friendly zeal in you. Further, know that it will be to me an inexcusable proof of your want of zeal if Theobald Notier does not meet with what he deserves whenever a fitting opportunity arises; for through his heartless ambition he has cut away by the hands of his nephews the half of my soul, leaving the remaining half for nothing but cruel suffering.

LETTER CLXI. (A.D. 1133.)

TO THE LORD POPE INNOCENT.

Against the murderers of Archembald, Subdean of Orleans.

The voice of the blood of Archembald,[1] subdean of Orleans, cries with a loud voice for vengeance. For, alas! that I should have to say it, according to the Prophet, *blood toucheth blood* (Hos. iv. 2), and when once they are joined they call to you still more loudly from France. The blood of both calls and shouts with so loud a shout that it might even strike the palace of heaven itself, so piteously that it might soften hearts of stone. What are you doing, O friend of the bridegroom, O guardian of the Bride of Christ, O shepherd of the sheep of Christ? Do you think

---

[1] For his murderers, see note to ep. 150. Peter the Venerable also complains of his murder (lib. i. ep. 17), and implies that he was taken off before Thomas of S. Victor in the following words:—"The impunity enjoyed by these men lends arms to their phrensy; and so the sword of the persecutors, after slaying the Subdean of Orleans, has been unsheathed against Thomas of Paris, just because the first was unavenged." Still, the contrary may be without difficulty inferred from this Letter of S. Bernard's. But John, the author of the death of Archembald, was possibly John, the Dean of Orleans, who met a like end. His death is recorded in the Lamentation of that Church given by Stephen of Tournay.

that it will be sufficient to ponder upon a remedy to meet this infamous and unheard of evil? Certainly one must be [not only thought of, but] found which may bring relief for the present to the wound lately inflicted on the Church, and may act as a caution for the future. Therefore gird thee with thy sword upon thy thigh, O thou most mighty. If Phinehas does not stand forth even now and make atonement the terror will not cease. If the Church's vigour spare those men, John, and Theobald Notier, by whose assent, and perhaps at whose instigation, if not by whose hand, innocent blood has been poured forth on the earth, then who is there that sees not what is to follow? How many in the ranks of the clergy will the impunity of these men cause to be promoted from fear of their friends rather than from what their holy living deserves! New diseases must be met with new remedies. It seems to many that the Apostolic sword would act with most expedience and justice in cutting off these men from every ecclesiastical dignity, so that they may be both deprived of what they have, and be prevented from ever rising to any others.

LETTER CLXII. (A.D. 1133.)

TO HAIMERIC,[1] THE CHANCELLOR, ON THE SAME SUBJECT.

I have often testified to my Lord the Bishop of Paris of your frequent and kindly mention of him. Lo! now the demand is made upon you to show not in word or in tongue, but in deed and in truth, both that I was not speaking, and that you have not written, anything but the truth. So this concerns you, not only for the Bishop's sake, but also for the sake of your other friends, who would certainly be greatly concerned about you, if by any chance this cause should happen to go contrary to their expectation.

---

[1] In the *Colbertine MS.*, No. 1038, and in a very old edition this epistle is given as to John of Crema, the next to Haimeric. But what is said in the latter of the two about the conversion of the person to whom it is addressed is more applicable to John.

LETTER CLXIII. (A.D. 1133.)

To John of Crema, Cardinal-Priest, on the Same Subject.

I shall never forget the love and consideration which you have condescended to show me, a man of no influence and no rank; and I wish continually and frequently pray that worthy fruits may follow from your repentance and conversion, which have been a source of joy and delight to me as well as to the Angels. Especially now does this Gallican Church of ours join me in looking for them, and I think not unseasonably. It concerns your reputation as well as mine that I do not count on you to my own confusion. Let it be then so clear to all that your zeal for truth and righteousness burns against the murderers of clerks, and against their instigators, that I may not be sorry for having made my boast of you.

LETTER CLXIV. (A.D. 1138.)

To Pope Innocent in the matter of the Church of Langres.[1]

1. When I was at Rome there happened to come there the Lord Archbishop of Lyons. With him came also Robert, Dean of the Church of Langres, and Odalric, Canon of the same church, seeking for themselves and the Chapter of Langres permission to elect a fresh Bishop. They had

---

[1] The events referred to here did not take place after the death of Guilencus, or Wilencus, Bishop of Langres, to whom Letters 59 and 60 were sent, but after the death of his successor, William de Sabran. The death of Guilencus took place August 1st, A.D. 1135, that of William in the year 1138. Then there was a disputed succession. Peter, Archbishop of Lyons, and Hugh of Burgundy, afterwards Duke, gave their support to a certain monk of Cluny; he was opposed by Robert, Dean of Langres, Pontius the Archdeacon, Odalric, and other Canons. Bernard was called in as arbiter, and finally the Cluniac monk was excluded, and Godfrey, Prior of Clairvaux, a relation of Bernard's, was elected. There are three Letters of Peter of Cluny about this controverted election of the Bishop of Langres; one which is ep. 29 of the first book, written to Bernard, in which he endeavours to clear the name of one of his monks, who had been chosen as Bishop of Langres, from unjust aspersions; the second, which is ep. 28 of the second book, to Pope Innocent, in which he asks that Innocent will refuse to confirm the election of the

received, indeed, a command from my lord the Pope to abstain by all means from acting till they had the advice of religious men. And when they wished and asked to obtain this permission through me, I altogether refused until I knew for a certainty that they intended to elect a good and fitting person. They replied that they would subordinate their purpose and intention to my opinion, and that they would do nothing but what I advised them. And this they promised me. But as their promise did not give me sufficient confidence, the Archbishop joined his entreaties to theirs, and promised faithfully the same thing. He added, moreover, that if the clergy should attempt to act otherwise he would not confirm or give his sanction to anything that they might do. My lord the Chancellor also gave a similar pledge. Not content with this, I went also before my lord the Pope to have what we had agreed upon confirmed by his sanction and authority. Nevertheless, a conference was held daily between us on the election to be held, and, out of the many names of which mention was

Abbot of Vezelay to the same See; the last, which is ep. 36 of the same book, to Innocent again, in which he asks that the Church of Langres in future episcopal elections may be allowed its full rights according to the canons. By comparing the first and third it is evident that they refer to the election of which Bernard here speaks. But it is more difficult to say whether the second also refers to it. My own opinion is that it must be understood of another person. For in the first, Peter the Venerable simply speaks of the elected man as "a monk of Cluny and my son," in the second "the Abbot of Vezelay." In the first he says that "he was met by Canons of Langres as he was on his return from Poitou, who told him of the election of his monk; in the latter he says that he had heard a rumour that "certain men were clamorously seeking from Innocent that the Abbot of Vezelay might be Bishop of Langres. In the first he does all he can to help forward the confirmation of his monk; in the second he strives to prevent the confirmation of the Abbot of Vezelay. Therefore I think that the opinion is not to be despised of those who say that Wilencus, Bishop of Langres, was succeeded by William de Sabran, who perhaps was taken from presiding over the Abbey of Vezelay to rule the See of Langres; and that Geoffrey, as will be shown presently, succeeded him. At length, the Cluniac having been excluded, Geoffrey was elected and confirmed A.D. 1138, that is when Bernard had returned into Gaul after the extinction of the schism. But we should observe in this history, as Baronius does (A.D. 1138), that although Peter of Cluny so warmly took the side of his monk, and although he was worsted by Bernard, yet he refused to change his kindly feelings towards Bernard and his monks (*Cf.* ep. 229, n. 5).

made, two at last were chosen, and it was agreed that we would none of us dissent from the election of either of the two. And so my lord the Pope decreed that our decision should be binding without any change, and both Archbishop and clerks promised faithfully to abide by it. When they had left I made a stay of several days longer in Rome, and when I was able to obtain permission from my lord to return I took my journey to my brethren.

2. And as I was crossing the Alps I found that the day was at hand on which the consecration to the See of Langres was to take place, of a person concerning whom I would that I had heard better reports and more honourable to him. But I am unwilling to repeat what it gave me pain to hear. I was persuaded by not a few religious who had come to salute me to turn aside to Lyons in order, if possible, to prevent the execution of the infamous act that was contemplated. For I, out of regard for my health and the weariness of my body, had determined to go home by a shorter way, especially because I had not given much credence to the rumours that had reached me. For who would have thought that so great a man would have been so fickle as to set aside his own promise so lately given, to say nothing of the command of his lord, and lay his hands without any fear on the head of one whose ill reputation was known? And so I listened to the advice of these religious, and turned my steps towards Lyons, and when I arrived I found that things were just as I had heard. The joyful (or rather unfortunate) festival had been prepared for. The Dean, however, and, unless I am mistaken, the greater part of the Canons of Lyons were in constant and open opposition. The shameful and grievous report had filled the city, too, and was hourly spreading and gaining strength.

3. What was I to do? I called on the Archbishop. With due reverence I reminded him of the agreement that he had entered into, and of the instructions that he had received. He admitted all that I said. But he said that the cause of his going from his promise was the refusal of the Duke's son to accept what we had determined, and he said that to pacify him he had been guilty of this change of purpose,

and had done as he did for the sake of peace. He went on to say that whatever he might have done before, he would do as I bade for the future. Then I said, in thanking him, "God forbid that it should be my will; nay, rather God's will be done. And what this will is, will doubtless be known, if the matter is brought before the Council of Bishops and other religious persons who have assembled at your summons, or will soon be here. But if, after invoking the Holy Spirit, the consent of all bids you proceed in the work that you have begun, then proceed in it; but if not, then listen to the Apostle who bids you *Lay hands suddenly on no man*" (1 Tim. v. 22). My advice seemed to please him. Meanwhile, that man is said to have arrived; but he went to an hostel, not to the palace. He came on Friday night; he left on Saturday morning. It is not for me to say why he was loath to put in an appearance at the Court, when that was the very object of his long journey. It might have been thought to be a monk's modesty, and a contempt for honour, were it not that what followed showed that it was otherwise. For what were we to conclude when the Archbishop returned from him, and declared before all that he could in no way induce him to acquiesce, but that he rejected wholly what had been done in the matter?

4. In short, the Archbishop soon after bade the election to take place. This is testified by some of the Canons of Langres, who were then present, as well as by a letter which can be produced. When it was brought forward and read before the Chapter of Langres, immediately another was read contrary to the first in every point, asserting that the consecration was postponed, not set aside, appointing a day and place to decide a cause which the first letter declared to have been decided already. You would think that in these letters it was not merely diverse, but adverse persons that were speaking and contradicting each other, if it were not that one and the same image was impressed on the wax, one and the same name signed at the bottom; and so it was manifestly declared, to the amazement of all that were present, that from one fountain there flowed both sweet and bitter. These contradictory letters are in our hands;

whichever you determine to obey, you must be held disobedient. If you obey the first that you open, you will be condemned by the last, or if you elect to follow the latter, the former one will complain. And would that the second letter could as well protect itself against a third as it overturned the first. But lo! we have letter upon letter, so that it is not with us as with the Prophet, *Line upon line* (Is. xxviii. 10), but rather line against line.

5. In the meantime the man who had shrunk from consecration, and rejected the election, hastened to the King. He obtained formal possession of the Regalia,[1] but by what title, he must say for himself. Presently letters were sent out, changing the place which had been appointed, and anticipating the day, in order that through the inconvenience of time and place opposers might be deprived of all chance of acting, and a march might be stolen on all who might wish to appeal. But no counsel can stand against that of God, by whose providence it came to pass that neither opposers nor appellants were wanting. An appeal was lodged by Falco, Dean of Lyons; by Ponce, Archdeacon of Langres; by Bonami, priest and Canon of Langres, and also by my brethren, Bruno and Geoffrey, who knew nothing of what these men had intended in their hearts, but who happened to arrive by chance, and no doubt by the will of God, who foresees all things. So little time, indeed, was left, that when I learnt the day scarcely four days were left for our messenger to go with letters to prevent what was more a sacrilege than a sacrament from being performed. He, too, nevertheless, opposed it, and summoned the consecrators and the man they proposed to consecrate to the Apostolic See. He whom I had sent was a Canon of Langres. I say the truth; I lie not. The Truth Himself is my witness that I have said nothing out of personal hatred, but that I have truthfully set down everything out of love of the truth alone.

---

[1] The investiture of the Regalia is the formal delivering by the king to the new bishop of the temporal jurisdiction and lands of the Church after the oath of fidelity has been taken. For the Regalia see also ep. 170, Suger (epp. 19 and 20), and Du Cange's *Glossary*.

LETTER CLXV. (A.D. 1138.)

To Falco, Dean, and Guy, Treasurer, of the Church of Lyons.

Great as you see, dearly beloved, is the plague that is threatening our Church, and great is the care needed; and not only is the plague great, but close at hand, so that we must with tears press on the heavenly Physician and say: "Lord, come down ere it die." There is one thing which makes our grief the more acute, and almost causes us to despair of a cure, and that is that the source of our tribulation is where we ought to have looked for its relief. For who is it, O, unhappy Church, that has brought this evil, of which you complain, upon you? It is no enemy, not one who hates you, but your bosom friend, your leader and metropolitan himself. Why comes this evil from the south and not from the north?[1] Surely there is no grief like unto my grief, since it is from those, and none others, on whom I most relied, that I have suffered these things. O, Lyons! my holy Mother Church, what a monster have you now chosen for a bridegroom for your daughter! No mother do we find you in this, but a step-mother. How far has this son-in-law of yours now degenerated from the honour, weight, and integrity for which you were once so renowned? Am I to say that that is an honourable marriage and an undefiled bed which has been brought about in such a way and with such a man? In defiance of all law, and order, and reason all things have been so confounded, nay, as all

---

[1] A reference may be conjectured to Ps. lxxv. 7: *Neither from the east, nor from the west, nor yet from the south.* But the resemblance in the Vulgate is much less strong: *Neither from the east, nor from the west, nor from the desert hills.* Compare, however, Ps. xlviii. 2, *upon the north side lieth the city of the great King;* Jer. vi. 1, *Evil appeareth out of the north;* Ps. cxxvi. 4, Turn again our captivity, O Lord, *as the streams in the south;* and the comment of Gerhohus on the latter passage.

There is not space to go into the subject here, but the north was taken in Mediæval times to be mystically the quarter whence evil came. In exorcisms, and the Renunciation during the Baptismal Office, if I mistake not, the officiant was directed to turn *towards the north;* and the *north side* of churchyards was usually chosen for the burials of criminals and persons under ecclesiastical censures.—[E.]

know, all things have been so fraudulently and rashly ordered and ventured on, that it would be most unseemly for a bailiff even, or receiver of tolls, to say nothing of a Bishop, to be appointed in this way. How can I sufficiently sing your praises, dearly beloved, who have alone mourned with your afflicted Church, and have once and again stood up in her defence when oppressed, rising on the other side, and opposing yourselves as a wall for the house of Israel? In that whole congregation not one has been found like you, to keep the law of the Most High, to obey the sacred canons, to put on the zeal of Phinehas and smite the fornicators with the sword of the tongue. And since these things redound more and more on all sides to the glory of God and your fame, it only remains for you to give a worthy ending to so good and praiseworthy a beginning, and do all you can to join the tail to the head of the victim.

LETTER CLXVI. (*Circa* A.D. 1138.)

TO POPE INNOCENT, ON THE SAME SUBJECT.

1. Again I call, again I knock, if not with clamorous cry, yet with tears and groanings. I am compelled to reiterate my crying by the reiterated injury inflicted on us by the wicked, and by those who prolong their iniquity. They have made themselves strong and added treachery to their evil-doing. They add sin to sin, and their pride is ever going up higher. Their phrensy has strengthened itself, while shame and the fear of God are no more. The man whom they did not hesitate to elect, my father, contrary to your wise and just arrangement, they have even dared to consecrate, or rather execrate, after an appeal had been made to you. This has been done presumptuously by the Archbishop of Lyons and the Bishops of Autun and Macon; all friends of Cluny. What a vast multitude of saints will be confounded by these men's fraud and audacity, if they are forced to bear such a yoke imposed on them in such a way. Wicked and shameful thing! If they are to accept it, it will be as if they were being forced to bow the knees to Baal, or, as the Prophet says, *to make a covenant with*

death and to be at agreement with hell (Is. xxviii. 15). I ask, Where are equity, law, the authority of the sacred canons, and reverence for your majesty? That appeal which is denied to none that is oppressed was of no profit to me alone. When gold sways the throne, and silver sits at the seat of judgment, laws and canons are silent, and right and equity have no place. With the same weapons, which is still more intolerable, they threaten to storm the heights of the Apostolic citadel itself. That, however, is but vain, for it is founded upon a Rock.

2. But what am I doing? I have gone too far, I confess; it is not for me to accuse or blame any one; it is enough for me to bewail my grief. After long delay, and many toils, which I undertook in the service of the Roman Church, when at last it seemed good to your Serenity to let me return to my brethren, I rejoiced, though I was but an unprofitable servant with shattered health, because of the sheaves of peace which I was taking back with me, and I arrived safely at my monastery. I thought that I had escaped from labour to rest, that it was allowed me to repair the losses of my spiritual studies, and the ruffling of the spirit's tranquillity which had met me outside my walls, and behold! tribulation and anguish have come upon me. As I lie upon my bed I am tortured more by the pangs of grief than by the body's pains. I do not complain of any temporal inconvenience. It is my soul that is in my hands, and its salvation that is at stake. Would you advise me to commit the keeping of my soul to a man who has lost his own? I know that you would not. Wherefore I have said to my soul that it is better for her to take flight from hence than to consume the remainder of my days with grief, and none the less to risk my salvation. But may God guide you to the course which is best; may He bring back to your recollection, if you think me worthy, in what manner I have dealt with you, and make you cast an eye of love upon your son, and free him from the anguish with which he is afflicted. Moreover, forget not what great things God hath done for you, and as some little return for

it all, annul and undo what has here been done so much amiss.

LETTER CLXVII. (A.D. 1138.)
To the Same, on the Same Subject.

Most gracious Father, did you not strictly enjoin that in the Church of Langres some suitable and religious person should be elected, with the advice of your son? Did not my lord of Lyons receive in person this same command from your Apostolic mouth, which he was to carry out as faithfully as it had been irrevocably given and frequently impressed on him? Did he not, moreover, promise to obey? What, then, has made him endeavour to set aside what had been most wisely and prudently determined, and to presumptuously take another course which was not convenient, to make your majesty contemptible, and my littleness a laughing-stock? How is it that this good man was not ashamed to have "yea and nay" found in his mouth, and to attempt to put so base a yoke on the necks of such a large number of religious men who are your servants, contrary to your command and his own promise? Ask, my Father, ask diligently, what kind of repute this man, on whom he is eager to lay his hands, bears, both with those that are near and those that are far off. Very shame prevents me from saying what common rumour says of him, nay, what his well-known evil reputation has made known to the world. What can I say? My soul is sorrowful even unto death. Perhaps even now I should have fled away had I not been kept back by the hope of the consolation that I look for from your kindness. I had it in my mind to write to you in order the distressing story of my misery; but my hand fails for very sadness, my mind clouds over, my tongue shrinks from speaking of the iniquitous treachery, the underhand dealing, the dishonesty, the audacity, the perfidy. What is it, then? Your son, Ponce the Archdeacon, who has shown himself in this matter constant and faithful, will tell you everything, my Father, both what we grieve for as already done, and what we implore may not be done. Trust him as myself. But this one thing I must say from the midst of my pangs, that unless these men are made to desist from their wicked and audacious undertaking, I feel that, as I am now, my life will fail in grief and my years in mourning.

LETTER CLXVIII. (A.D. 1138.)

To the Bishops and Cardinals of the Roman Court on the Same Subject.

1. You know, if you will deign to call it to your recollection, what manner of life mine was with you in the time of adversity, going out and coming in, and going forth at the King's bidding, perseveringly remaining with you in your temptations, so much so that my bodily strength was almost exhausted, and it was with difficulty that I was able to return home after God had given peace to the Church. I recall all this not boastfully or reproachfully, but to urge and implore you, to remind you, and to demand from you the debt of pity that you owe me. My necessity now forces me to appeal to all my debtors. But for myself, even if I have done all that I ought, yet, according to the word of the Lord, I reckon myself to be nothing else on that account, than an unprofitable servant. Nevertheless, if I did what was necessary or fit to be done, did I deserve to be beaten for it? And lo! when I went from you, I found trouble and anguish, and I called on the name of the Lord, but it was to no purpose; I called, too, on your name, but it availed me nothing; in truth, they that are as mighty gods on the earth have highly exalted themselves; I mean the Archbishop of Lyons and the Abbot of Cluny. They, trusting in their strength, and boasting themselves in the multitude of their riches, have come near me, and stood against me; and not merely against me, but against a great host of the servants of God, against you also, against themselves, against all equity and honesty, against God.

2. In one word, they have placed a man over our heads, whom, shameful to say, both the good abhor and the bad laugh at. By what order, or, I should better say, how *extraordinarily*, they have acted, let God see and judge; let the Roman Court see; let it see and grieve, let it have compassion, and gird itself to punish the evil and show honour to the good. Is it thy pleasure, O mistress of the world, thou that hast been placed over all to execute vengeance on the proud and to judge the oppressed, is it thy pleasure that the poor should be consumed when the wicked is lifted up, and the poor man too, who, when he had no wealth to expend in thy service, spared not his blood? Do you think it right that you should enjoy your peace, and care nothing for mine, or that you should not receive the partners of your toil to some share in the reward? If I have found grace in your sight, deliver the helpless from the hand of them that are stronger than he, the poor and needy from those that are robbing him. Otherwise I for my part will labour as I can amidst my grief, and my tears shall be my meat day and night; while to you I will say that verse, *He that ceases to have pity on his friend forsakes the fear of the Lord* (Job vi. 14), and again, *All my kinsmen stood afar off:* and another also, *My lovers and my neighbours did stand looking upon my trouble, and they also that sought after my life laid snares for me* (Ps. xxxviii. 11, 12).

LETTER CLXIX. (A.D. 1138.)

To Pope Innocent, on the Same Subject.

Bernard explains why he has detained the clergy of Langres who had been summoned to Rome; and indicates the persons to whom the election should be confided.

Your condescension has admitted me to intimacy, and that intimacy has made me to presume. Let your wonted kindness rule in your heart, lest haply my presumption breed indignation. Yet hear patiently not only what I have done, but why I did it; perhaps the cause may in some way excuse the deed. I ventured to keep back the clergy of Langres who had been summoned to appear before you, since peace had been made between them, and they had been persuaded to act for the future in holding the election according to your will and the counsel of good men, even as it is written in their letters. Moreover there was great necessity for their not leaving just now, because of the lands and possessions of the Church, which are given over to be plundered and stolen, while there is none to guard or defend them. And so, if it please you, let an order be given to these men, since they are no longer under suspicion, and since they seek not the things that are their own, but those of Christ Jesus, that they elect one who may be pleasing to God, that so this long-standing and unhappy trouble of the Church may find at length its ending. What else remains to be said I have committed to Herbert, Abbot of S. Stephen's of Dijon, and to the Archdeacon of Langres, and their companions. I add, moreover, a prayer that you would receive under your protection the Archdeacon of Langres and Bonami, presbyter of the same Church, since they have shown themselves faithful in God's cause. *For the workman is worthy of his hire* (S. Luke x. 7).

LETTER CLXX. (A.D. 1138.)

To Louis the Younger,[1] King of the French.

He endeavours to defend the election of Geoffrey, Prior of Clairvaux, to the See of Langres; to which the King had appeared adverse.

[1] Ordericus calls him Florus absolutely (lib. xi. p. 813.), Louis Florus more than once (lib. xiii. pp. 910, 911). In the first passage Louis the Fat is said to have made peace between Tedbald of Blois, and Ralph of Peronne, who were at discord, and also to have entrusted the Kingdom of Gaul to his son Louis Florus, whom three years before he had had crowned King at Rheims; and this in the year 1135. In the last passage, on the year 1137, Louis being at the point of death is said "to have entrusted Louis Florus his son to Tedbald, Count Palatine, and Ralph, of Peronne, his kinsman."

1. If the whole world were to conjure me to join it in some enterprise against your royal Majesty, I should still through fear of God not dare lightly to offend a King ordained by Him. Nor am I ignorant who it is that has said, *Whosoever resisteth the power resisteth the ordinance of God* (Rom. xiii. 2). Nor yet do I forget how contrary is lying to the Christian calling and still more so to my profession. I say the truth, I lie not; what was done at Langres in the matter of our Prior[1] was contrary to my expectation and my intention and that of the Bishops. But there is One who knows how to gain the assent of the unwilling, and who compels, as He wills, the adverse wills of man to subserve His counsel. Why should I not fear for him whom I love as my own soul, that danger which I have ever feared for myself? Why should I not shrink from the companionship of those who bind heavy burdens and grievous to be borne, and lay them on men's shoulders, but they themselves will not move them with one of their fingers? Still, what has been done, has been done; nothing against you, very much against me. The staff of my weakness has been taken from me, the light of mine eyes removed from me, my right arm cut off. All these waves and storms have gone over me. Wrath has swallowed me up, and on no side do I see any way to escape. When I fly from burdens, then I have them placed upon me to my great discomfort. I feel that it is hard for me to kick against the pricks. It would perhaps have been more tolerable for a willing horse than for one that is restive and

---

[1] This refers to Geoffrey, Bernard's kinsman, who after many disagreements had been at length unanimously taken from being third Prior of Clairvaux to be Bishop of Langres, A.D. 1138; that is to say, when the schism was at an end. For while Geoffrey was still Prior, Bernard wrote ep. 317, from Italy, within the Octave of Pentecost of that year, in which after his return from Italy the affair of this election at Langres took place, viz., when peace had been restored to the Church, as ep. 166 expressly says. How highly Bernard valued Geoffrey is evident from this epistle. *Cf.* also *Life of S. Bernard* (lib. ii. c. 5), and also the Preface to the third book of the *Life*. The election of Geoffrey was at length ratified A.D. 1132, as we gather from a deed given by Perard (p. 134), where the Church of S. Stephen of Dijon is said to have been consecrated by him A.D. 1141, " in the second year of his episcopate."

obstinate. For if there were any strength in me, would it not be easier for me to bear these burdens on my own shoulders than on those of others?

2. But I yield to Him that disposeth otherwise, to contend with whom in wisdom or strength is neither prudent nor possible for either me or the King. He is, indeed, terrible among the kings of the earth. It is a terrible thing to fall into the hands of the living God, even for you, O King. How grieved have I been to hear things of you so contrary to the fair promise of your early days! How much more bitter will be the grief of the Church, after having tasted first of such great joys, if, which God forbid, she shall chance to be deprived of her pleasant hope of protection under the shield of your good disposition, which up to the present has been held over her. Alas! the Virgin, the Church of Rheims, has fallen,[1] and there is none to lift her up. Langres, too, has fallen, and there is none to stretch out the hand to help. May the goodness of God divert your heart and mind from adding yet more to our grief, and from heaping sorrow upon sorrow. Would that I may die before seeing a king of whom good things were thought, and still better hoped for, endeavouring to go against the counsel of God, stirring up against himself the anger of the supreme Judge, bedewing the feet of the Father of the fatherless with the tears of the afflicted, knocking at heaven's door with the cries of the poor, the prayers of the saints, and with the just complaints of Christ's beloved Bride, the Church of the living God. May all this never happen. I hope for better things, and expect things more joyful. God will not forget to be gracious, nor shut up his

---

[1] This was after the death of Archbishop Reginald, which happened A.D. 1139, on January 13th. The Church of Rheims remained for nearly two years without its shepherd, not through any dissension among the clergy in the election, but through the violent opposition of the citizens for the institution of the "communia," as they called it, and the inborn hatred of Louis VII. against Theobald, Count of Champagne, which showed itself also against the counts and churches of the district. *Cf.* Bernard's complaint in ep. 318. Finally, on Bernard refusing the dignity, Samson was elected, A.D. 1140, whose election was for a time opposed, according to ep. 222. *Cf.* epp. 210 and 224.

loving kindness in displeasure. He will not make His Church sad through him, and because of him, by whom He has already made her so much to rejoice. By His long-suffering He will preserve him whom He freely gave us, and if you think anything otherwise, this also He will reveal to you, and will teach your heart in wisdom. This is my wish, this is my prayer night and day. Think this of me, think it of my brethren. The truth shall not be sinned against by us, nor the King's honour and the good of his kingdom diminished.

3. We give thanks to your clemency for the kindly answer which you deigned to send us. But still we are terrified to delay, as we see the land given over to plunder and robbery. The land is yours; and we plainly see and mourn the disgrace brought on your kingdom by your orders that we should abstain from our rights, inasmuch as there is no one to defend them. For in what else that has been done can the king's majesty be truly said to have been diminished? The election was duly held; the person elected is faithful, which he would not be if he wished to hold your lands otherwise than through you. He has not yet stretched out his hand to your lands, he has not yet entered your city, he has not yet put himself forward in any affair, though most earnestly pressed to do so by the united voice of clergy and people, by the oppression of the afflicted, and by the prayers of all good men. And since this is the state of affairs there is, you see, need for counsel to be quickly taken, not less for the sake of your honour than our necessity. And unless your Serenity give answer according to their petition, by the messengers who bring this, to your faithful people who look to you, the hearts of many religious men who are now devoted to you will be turned against you (which would not be expedient), and I fear that no little loss will accrue to the regalia belonging to the Church, which yet are yours.

LETTER CLXXI. (A.D. 1139.)

TO POPE INNOCENT.

On behalf of Falco, Archbishop elect of Lyons.

I think that I, who have so many times been listened to in the affairs of others, shall not be confounded in my own. I, my lord, hold the cause of my Archbishop to be my own, being a member of him, and knowing that there is nothing that affects the head but what touches me, which, nevertheless, I would not say if the man had taken this honour to himself, and had not been called by God, as was Moses. Nor can I think that it was the work of any but Him that the votes of so many men were so readily given him, that there was not even any hesitation, still less opposition. And deservedly so. He is distinguished not only for his high birth, but also for the nobility of his mind, for his knowledge, and his irreproachable life. In short, the integrity of his name fears not the tooth even of a foe. What, therefore, has been so done for so good a man is surely worthy to obtain the favour of the Apostolic See, the fulness of honour,[1] which is the only thing now lacking, to increase the joy of its people that has grown accustomed to its kindness, or, I may say, to the liberality which he has fully deserved. This is what the whole Church, with most earnest supplication, implores; this is what your son, with his usual presumption, entreats of you.

LETTER CLXXII. (A.D. 1139.)

TO THE SAME, IN THE NAME OF GODFREY, BISHOP OF LANGRES.

He expresses the same thought as in the preceding Letter.

Amidst the numerous evils which nowadays are seen in the churches on the occasion of elections the Lord hath looked down from heaven upon our Mother Church of

[1] *I.e.*, the pallium.—[E.]

Lyons, and has without strife given it a worthy successor to Peter of pious memory, its Archbishop, in the person of Falco, its Dean. I ask, my lord, that he who has been unanimously elected by his fellows, promoted for the good of all, and duly consecrated, may receive at your hands the fulness of honour that belongs to his office. And what makes me seek this is not so much consciousness of his merits, but of my duty—duty laid upon me not only by the metropolitan dignity of that Church, but because I am placed in this position in order that I may bear my testimony to the truth.

LETTER CLXXIII. (A.D. 1139.)

To the above-named Falco.

Bernard recommends to him the interests of certain Religious.

The Lord Bishop and I have written, as we thought we ought to do, to my lord the Pope on your behalf, and you have a copy of your letters. It is our determination to stand by you with all our might, because of the good which we hope for from you for the Church. It concerns you so to act that we may not be disappointed of our hope. For the rest, if I have found favour in your sight I pray you think of those poor and needy ones at the house of Benissons Dieu.[1] Whatsoever you do to one of them you will do to me, nay, to Christ. For they are both poor, and they live amongst the poor. I especially implore you to prevent the monks of Savigny from molesting them, for they are calumniating them unjustly, as I consider. Or if they think that they have justice on their side, judge between them. I ask also that my son, Abbot Alberic, though well deserving of your favour through his own merits, may

---

[1] Benissons Dieu was a Cistercian Abbey, an offshoot of Clairvaux, in the Diocese of Lyons, and was founded A.D. 1138. Alberic was its first Abbot. Not far from it was the monastery of Savigny, of the order of S. Benedict, in the same diocese. Its Abbot was Iterius, of whom Bernard here complains.

still be in even greater regard through my recommendation. For I love him tenderly, as a mother loves her only child, and he that loveth me will love him. In fact, I shall find out whether you care for me by the way you treat him. For the farther he is away from me the more necessary is it that he should have consolation from your fatherly care.

LETTER CLXXIV. (*Circa* A.D. 1140.)
TO THE CANONS OF LYONS, ON THE CONCEPTION OF S. MARY.

Bernard states that the Festival of the Conception was new; that it rested on no legitimate foundation; and that it should not have been instituted without consulting the Apostolic See, to whose opinion he submits.

1. It is well known that among all the Churches of France that of Lyons is first in importance, whether we regard the dignity of its See, its praiseworthy regulations, or its honourable zeal for learning. Where was there ever the vigour of discipline more flourishing, a more grave and religious life, more consummate wisdom, a greater weight of authority, a more imposing antiquity? Especially in the Offices of the Church, that of Lyons has always shown itself opposed to attempts at sudden innovation, and it is a proof of her fulness of judgment that she has never suffered herself to be stained with the mark of rash and hasty levity. Wherefore I cannot but wonder that there should have been among you at this time some who wished to sully this splendid fame of your Church by introducing a new Festival, a rite which the Church knows nothing of, and which reason does not prove, nor ancient tradition hand down to us. Have we the pretension to be more learned or more devoted than the Fathers? It is a dangerous presumption to establish in such a matter what their prudence left unestablished. And the matter in question is of such a nature that it could not possibly have escaped the diligence of the

Fathers if they had not thought that they ought not to occupy themselves with it.

2. The Mother of the Lord, you say, ought greatly to be honoured. You say well, but the honour of a queen loves justice. The royal Virgin does not need false honour, since she is amply supplied with true titles to honour and badges of her dignity. Honour indeed the purity of her flesh, the sanctity of her life, wonder at her motherhood as a virgin, adore her Divine offspring. Extol the prodigy by which she brought into the world without pain the Son, whom she had conceived without concupiscence. Proclaim her to be reverenced by the angels, to have been desired by the nations, to have been known beforehand by Patriarchs and Prophets, chosen by God out of all women and raised above them all. Magnify her as the medium by whom grace was displayed, the instrument of salvation, the restorer of the ages; and finally extol her as having been exalted above the choirs of angels to the celestial realms. These things the Church sings concerning her, and has taught me to repeat the same things in her praise, and what I have learnt from the Church I both hold securely myself and teach to others; what I have not received from the Church I confess I should with great difficulty admit. I have received then from the Church that day to be reverenced with the highest veneration, when being taken up from this sinful earth, she made entry into the heavens; a festival of most honoured joy. With no less clearness have I learned in the Church to celebrate the birth of the Virgin, and from the Church undoubtedly to hold it to have been holy and joyful; holding most firmly with the Church, that she received in the womb that she should come into the world holy. And indeed I read concerning Jeremiah, that before he came forth from the womb [*ventre:* otherwise *de vulva*] he was sanctified, and I think no otherwise of John the Baptist, who, himself in the womb of his mother, felt the presence of his Lord in the womb (S. Luke i. 41). It is matter for consideration whether the same opinion may not be held of holy David, on account of what

he said in addressing God: *In Thee I have been strengthened from the womb: Thou art He who took me out of my mother's bowels* (Ps. lxxi. 6); and again: *I was cast upon Thee from the womb: Thou art my God from my mother's belly* (Ps. xxii. 10). And Jeremiah is thus addressed: *Before I formed thee in the belly I knew thee; and before thou camest out of the womb I sanctified thee* (Jer. i. 5). How beautifully the Divine oracle has distinguished between conception in the womb and birth from the womb! and showed that if the one was foreseen only, the other was blessed beforehand with the gift of holiness: that no one might think that the glory of Jeremiah consisted only in being the object of the foreknowledge of God, but also of His predestination.

3. Let us, however, grant this in the case of Jeremiah. What shall be said of John the Baptist, of whom an angel announced beforehand that he should be filled with the Holy Ghost, even from his mother's womb? I cannot suppose that this is to be referred to predestination or to foreknowledge. For the words of the angel were without doubt fulfilled in their time, as he foretold; and the man (as cannot be doubted) filled with the Holy Ghost at the time and place appointed, as he predicted. But most certainly the Holy Ghost sanctified the man whom He filled. But how far this sanctification availed against original sin, whether for him, or for that prophet, or for any other who was thus prevented by grace, I would not rashly determine. But of these holy persons whom God has sanctified, and brought forth from the womb with the same sanctification which they have received in the womb, I do not hesitate to say that the taint of original sin which they contracted in conception, could not in any manner take away or fetter by the mere act of birth, the benediction already bestowed. Would any one dare to say that a child filled with the Holy Ghost, would remain notwithstanding a child of wrath; and if he had died in his mother's womb, where he had received this fulness of the Spirit, would endure the pains of damnation? That opinion is very

severe; I, however, do not dare to decide anything respecting the question by my own judgment. However that may be, the Church, which regards and declares, not the nativity, but only the death of other saints as precious, makes a singular exception for him of whom an angel singularly said, *and many shall rejoice in his birth* (S. Luke i. 14, 15), and with rejoicing honours his nativity. For why should not the birth be holy, and even glad and joyful, of one who leaped with joy even in the womb of his mother?

4. The gift, therefore, which has certainly been conferred upon some, though few, mortals, cannot for a moment be supposed to have been denied to that so highly favoured Virgin, through whom the whole human race came forth into life. Beyond doubt the mother of the Lord also was holy before birth; nor is holy Church at all in error in accounting the day of her nativity holy, and celebrating it each year with solemn and thankful joy. I consider that the blessing of a fuller sanctification descended upon her, so as not only to sanctify her birth, but also to keep her life pure from all sin; which gift is believed to have been bestowed upon none other borne of women. This singular privilege of sanctity, to lead her life without any sin, entirely befitted the queen of virgins, who should bear the Destroyer of sin and death, who should obtain the gift of life and righteousness for all. Therefore, her birth was holy, since the abundant sanctity bestowed upon it made it holy even from the womb.

5. What addition can possibly be made to these honours? That her conception, also, they say, which preceded her honourable birth, should be honoured, since if the one had not first taken place, neither would the other, which is honoured. But what if some one else, following a similar train of reasoning, should assert that the honours of a festival ought to be given to each of her parents, then to her grandparents, and then to their parents, and so on *ad infinitum?* Thus we should have festivals without number. Such a frequency of joys befits Heaven, not this state of exile.

It is the happy lot of those who dwell there, not of strangers and pilgrims. But a writing is brought forward, given, as they say, by revelation from on high,[1] as if anyone would not be able to bring forward another writing in which the Virgin should seem to demand the same honours to her parents also, saying, according to the commandment of the Lord, *Honour thy father and thy mother* (Exod. xx. 12). I easily persuade myself not to be influenced by such writings, which are supported neither by reason nor by any certain authority. For how does the consequence follow that since the conception has preceded the birth, and the birth is holy, the conception should be considered holy also? Did it make the birth holy because it preceded it? Although the one came first that the other might be, yet not that it might be holy. From whence came that holiness to the conception which was to be transmitted to the birth which followed? Was it not rather because the conception preceded without holiness that it was needful for the being conceived to be sanctified, that a holy birth might then follow? Or shall we say that the birth which was later than the conception shared with it its holiness? It might be, indeed, that the sanctification which was worked in her when conceived passed over to the birth which followed; but it could not be possible that it should have a retrospective effect upon the conception which had preceded it.

6. Whence, then, was the holiness of that conception? Shall it be said that Mary was so prevented by grace that, being holy before being conceived, she was therefore conceived without sin; or that, being holy before being born, she has therefore communicated holiness to her birth? But in order to be holy it is necessary to exist, and a person does not exist before being conceived. Or perhaps, when her parents were united, holiness was mingled with the conception itself, so that she was at once conceived and sanctified. But this is not tenable in reason. For how

---

[1] A writing of this kind is attributed to an English abbot named Elsin in the works of Anselm, pp. 505, 507 of the new edition.

can there be sanctity without the sanctifying Spirit, or the co-operation of the Holy Spirit with sin? Or how could there not be sin where concupiscence was not wanting? Unless, perhaps, some one will say that she was conceived by the Holy Spirit, and not by man, which would be a thing hitherto unheard of. I say, then, that the Holy Spirit came upon her, not within her, as the Angel declared: *The Holy Spirit shall come upon thee* (S. Luke i. 35). And if it is permitted to say what the Church thinks, and the Church thinks that which is true, I say that she conceived by the Holy Spirit, but not that she was conceived by Him; that she was at once Mother and Virgin, but not that she was born of a virgin. Otherwise, where will be the prerogative of the Mother of the Lord, to have united in her person the glory of maternity and that of virginity, if you give the same glory to her mother also? This is not to honour the Virgin, but to detract from her honour. If, therefore, before her conception she could not possibly be sanctified, since she did not exist, nor in the conception itself, because of the sin which inhered in it, it remains to be believed that she received sanctification when existing in the womb after conception, which, by excluding sin, made her birth holy, but not her conception.

7. Wherefore, although it has been given to some, though few, of the sons of men to be born with the gift of sanctity, yet to none has it been given to be conceived with it. So that to One alone should be reserved this privilege, to Him who should make all holy, and coming into the world, He alone, without sin should make an atonement for sinners. The Lord Jesus, then, alone was conceived by the Holy Ghost, because He alone was holy before He was conceived. He being excepted, all the children of Adam are in the same case as he who confessed of himself with great humility and truth, *I was shapen in iniquity, and in sin hath my mother conceived me* (Ps. li. 6).

8. And as this is so, what ground can there be for a Festival of the Conception of the Virgin? On what principle, I say, is either a conception asserted to be holy

which is not by the Holy Ghost, not to say that it is by sin, or a festival be established which is in no wise holy? Willingly the glorious Virgin will be without this honour, by which either a sin seems to be honoured or a sanctity supposed which is not a fact. And, besides, she will by no means be pleased by a presumptuous novelty against the custom of the Church, a novelty which is the mother of rashness, the sister of superstition, the daughter of levity. For if such a festival seemed advisable, the authority of the Apostolic See ought first to have been consulted, and the simplicity of inexperienced persons ought not to have been followed so thoughtlessly and precipitately. And, indeed, I had before noted that error in some persons; but I appeared not to take notice of it, dealing gently with a devotion which sprang from simplicity of heart and love of the Virgin. But now that the superstition has taken hold upon wise men, and upon a famous and noble Church, of which I am specially the son,[1] I know not whether I could longer pass it over without gravely offending you all. But what I have said is in submission to the judgment of whosoever is wiser than myself; and especially I refer the whole of it, as of all matters of a similar kind, to the authority and decision of the See of Rome, and I am prepared to modify my opinion if in anything I think otherwise than that See.

LETTER CLXXV. (A.D. 1135.)

To the Patriarch of Jerusalem.[2]

Having received many letters from him, Bernard replies in a friendly manner, and praises the soldiers of the Temple.

[1] The Church of Lyons was the Mother Church of Bernard because of its "metropolitan rights," as he himself says in Letter 172, since he was born at Fontaines, near Dijon, and lived at the monastery of Clairvaux, both of which places were in the Diocese of Langres and Province of Lyons.

[2] William a Gallo-Belgian, and a monk of Tours, was Patriarch of Jerusalem from A.D. 1130 to A.D. 1145. See, for more information about him, the history of the Blessed Mary of Fountains (*Spicilegium*, Vol. x. p. 369), where there is a

I shall seem ungrateful if I do not reply to the many patriarchal letters which you have vouchsafed me. But what more can I do than salute him who has saluted me? For you have prevented me with the blessings of goodness, you have graciously set me the example of sending letters across the sea, you have deprived me of the first share of humility and charity. What fitting return can I now make? In truth, you have left me nothing which in my turn I can give back; for even of your worldly treasures you have been careful to make me a sharer in giving me part of the Cross of the Lord. What then? Ought I to omit what I can do because I cannot do what I ought? I show you my affection at least and my goodwill by merely replying and returning your salutation, which is all that I can do at present, separated as we are by so great a tract of sea and land. I will show, if ever I have the opportunity, that I love not in word or in tongue, but in deed and in truth. Give a thought, I pray you, to the soldiers of the Temple, and of your great piety take care of these zealous defenders of the Church. If you cherish those who have devoted their lives for their brethren's sake you will do a thing acceptable to God and well-pleasing to man. Concerning the place to which you invite me, my brother Andrew[1] will tell you my mind.

description of the relics sent by him to Fountains through Lambert, a monk of the place. Ordericus says at the end of his thirteenth book: " In the year 1128 died Germundus, Patriarch of Jerusalem. After him succeeded Stephen of Chartres, who reigned in holy Sion for two years; after him came William of Flanders." The same author mentions a Ralph as Patriarch. But certainly, on the authority of William of Tyre, William buried King Baldwin A.D. 1142, and was succeeded by Fulcher in 1145. Either William had two appellations or Ordericus has made a mistake. Letter 393 was written also to the same Patriarch.

[1] Was this Andrew the uncle of S. Bernard, one of the Knights Templars, to whom Letter 288 was written? or was it his brother, a monk of Clairvaux, mentioned in the 184th Letter? or Andrew of Baudiment, mentioned in Letter 226, n. 2? The place mentioned here may be the one conceded to the Præmonstratensians by Bernard. See Letter 252.

LETTER CLXXVI. (*Circa* A.D. 1135.)

TO POPE INNOCENT, IN THE PERSON OF ALBERO, ARCHBISHOP OF TRÈVES.[1]

Bernard declares in the name of the Archbishop his own respect and obedience and that of the citramontane Churches towards Innocent.

It has long been the wish of my heart, and my eager desire, to pay you a visit, and see the welcome face of your Blessedness, and to know, moreover, more certainly how things are with you, and in turn to acquaint you more closely with my own affairs; and this motive has been long pressing and ceaselessly urging me to make a journey to you. But having been hindered by the wickedness of the world and of the times, and also, besides my daily troubles, by some matter important to you, I have not yet been able, nor am I even yet able to carry out my wish. But must a purpose that is sound and righteous be altogether given up because it cannot be wholly carried out? I have determined, therefore, to satisfy in some degree in the meantime the desire I have so long felt, and to make known to you my anxiety, by means of this venerable man, Hugh, Archdeacon of the Church of Toul. Nor could anyone be more faithful, more devoted, or more cautious than he in matters of importance, whether in bringing to you what I charge him with, or in bringing back to me whatever matters you may have been pleased to entrust to him. I desire, then, and implore you to inform me more fully in your goodness, of the state of the Court, of the safety of your person, and if by the Divine goodness any more favourable breeze has perchance blown upon the Church in her struggles against the wanton but ineffectual madness of the schismatics. For the rest you know that the Church on this side of the Alps, both here and in the realm of France, is strong in the faith, peaceful in unity, devoted in its obedience to you,

[1] Letter 30 was addressed to him when at Metz, when he was made Archbishop of Trèves. In the same Letter he is called "archangel of Trèves."

ready for your service. The loss of Beneventum, of Capua, nay, if God so will it, of Rome herself cannot terrify me; knowing that the position of the Church is not to be estimated by arms but by merits. Of her and of no other we recognize those words in the Psalm: *Though an host should encamp against me my heart shall not fear, and though there rose up war against me yet will I put my trust in Him* (Ps. xxvii. 3). Therefore we, because we are of the Church, will not fear while the earth is troubled and the mountains removed into the midst of the sea. The Sicilian tyrant may boast himself as much as he pleases, he may boast in wickedness because he is powerful in iniquity, but our strength is made perfect in weakness. Paul has learned that the weaker the Church is the more powerful she is (2 Cor. xii. 10). He has learnt directly and from Solomon that the prosperity of fools slays them (Prov. i. 32). He has learned when he sees a fool flourishing, to curse his beauty immediately (Job v. 3). Therefore with holy David he consoles himself in both ways, viz., in the fall of his enemies and in his own liberation. He says, indeed, *They put their trust in chariots and in horses, but we will call on the Name of the Lord our God. They are brought down and fallen, but we are risen and stand upright* (Ps. xx. 7, 8). These few words on matters about which I am quite sure, I thought ought to be addressed to you by faithful testimony in the way of comfort; to relieve in some degree that anxiety which the care of all the churches incessantly brings upon you. I add this also, that the king,[1] God strengthening him, is zealous, and is making ready for the liberation of the Church, and is collecting an exceedingly great army; and that I also am labouring for this end with all my strength, and am exhorting and stirring up every one that I can. When the time comes I will spare neither expense nor my own person.

[1] The Emeror Lothaire.

LETTER CLXXVII. (*Circa* A.D. 1139.)

TO THE SAME, IN THE PERSON OF THE SAME.

He complains of the pastoral charge laid upon him. He is hindered in its discharge by the envy of certain persons, not without fault in the Pope himself.

Did I ever seek the episcopate from you, my lord? And if ever I aspired to a bishopric it was certainly not that of Trèves. For I knew it to be an exasperating house, a stiff-necked people. I hated them because they had always wallowed in discord, and always resisted the Church. For her if I have ever undergone any labours I grieve not, but I never hoped or wished for any such fruit as this. I have laboured arduously, but willingly, and not with any hope of reward. I have been assigned for my sins a difficult province. Amongst my other troubles there is this, that my suffragans are young and nobly born.[1] They ought to be assistants, and would that they were not opponents. But I pass this by. I prefer that their characters and pursuits be made known to you by another, if you are ignorant of them. Still, I say that law, right, integrity, and religion have perished out of our episcopates. The evil, which the duty I owe to my office will not allow me to conceal, I have briefly pointed out, that what it does not please your providence should be corrected by me may, at all events, be made known to you who can correct it, lest I seem altogether to bear in vain the name of archbishop. And, indeed, it would have been better for me not to have ascended my throne than thus shamefully to descend. But what does it matter about myself? Let me suffer what I deserve, inasmuch as I do amiss. Let me be, as I am, a scorn to my friends, who have been frustrated of the hope which they had conceived about me in wishing me to preside over them, whilst they see that the dignity of the Church is by

---

[1] Viz., Stephen of Metz, from A.D. 1120, sister's son to Calixtus II.; Albero of Verdun, from A.D. 1126, son of Arnulf, Count of Chisney; Henry of Toul, from A.D. 1124, son of Theodoric, Duke of Lorraine. Many praiseworthy actions are recorded of them all.

me rather diminished, instead of its old losses being repaired, as they had expected they would be. All these things I bear patiently, if not willingly, that I may not seem to kick against the obedience I owe you, for which I confess I am willing, if need be, to lay down my life. But I wish that you would carefully consider this, that injury done to the thing created reflects on the creator. The strength which you withdraw from me you rob yourself of, and my scorn and helplessness casts disgrace on you. I have many things to complain of to you about yourself, but I leave them to be explained by the messenger, whom I know to be diligent and faithful for this purpose. I tell you also that we are in danger amongst false brethren. The ambassadors of the schismatics come and go to some of our supporters more freely than they used to, and the messages of the Sicilian tyrant are admitted frequently.

LETTER CLXXVIII. (A.D. 1139.)

To the Same, on behalf of the Same.

He complains that some evil-disposed persons abuse their powers to the injury of the Church, while zealous prelates are powerless.

To his most loving Father and Lord, INNOCENT, Supreme Pontiff, his BERNARD writes in entire devotedness.

1. I write confidently because I love faithfully. For that is no sincere love which cherishes doubt, and retains the dregs of suspicion. The complaint of my Lord of Trèves is not his alone, but of many, and of those especially who love you with a more sincere affection. The one cry of all who faithfully preside over the flock among us is that justice in the Church is perishing, that the keys of the Church are mere ornaments, that the Episcopal authority is altogether become vile, since no one of the Bishops is able to avenge the wrongs done to God, nor is allowed to punish for misdeeds, however glaring, no, not even in his

own diocese. They refer the cause to you and to the Roman Curia. You annul, they say, what they have rightly established, and establish what they have justly annulled. All the evil and quarrelsome men, whether from the clergy or the monasteries, hasten to you when they are expelled, and then return and boast, and rejoice that they have obtained as protectors those whom they ought to have felt as their chastisers. Was not the sword of Phinees most promptly and righteously unsheathed to punish the incestuous alliance of Drogo and Milis? But it returned to its sheath dulled and blunted, being met by the shield of an Apostolic defence. Alas! what ridicule has this caused, and is still causing, among the enemies of the Church, and especially among those very men who have made us wander out of the right way through fear or favour. Our friends are confounded, the faithful are insulted, the Bishops everywhere come into shame and contempt. And when their just judgments are contemned your authority is also diminished.

2. It is these very men who are zealous for your honour, who labour faithfully, if fruitlessly, for your peace and exaltation. Why do you lessen their influence?—why do you weaken their power? For how long will you blunt the weapons of those who are faithfully fighting for you, and lower the standards raised in defence of your power and safety? The Church of S. Gengulph at Toul grievously bewails her desolation, and there is none to comfort her. For who can oppose himself to the stroke of a powerful arm, to the force of a torrent, to the decision of the Supreme Power? The Church of S. Paul at Verdun[1] complains that it suffers the same violence, as the Arch-

[1] The monastery of S. Paul of Verdun, of the Order of Benedictines, having relaxed the bonds of discipline, had fallen into great license; and therefore Albero II., Bishop of Verdun, who had succeeded Ursio in the year 1131, had it transferred to the Præmonstratensians, with the approval of Pope Innocent. The monks of the place for a long time withstood the change; and even Peter the Venerable, generally a most retiring man, warmly expostulated with Matthew, Bishop of Albano. Innocent, somewhat shaken by their complaints, was preparing to rehear the cause, but was persuaded by S. Bernard to let the matter stand; and he, therefore, confirmed by letter what Albero had done.

bishop has now no power to defend it against the violence of the monks; and as though they were not outrageous enough, they are further supported by the Apostolic See. What fresh reason, I ask, has been found why that should again come into court and be brought under discussion which has been once granted, wisely and without question, to canons of good fame and life, then confirmed and, as they say, again renewed? Indeed, the establishment of both those places above mentioned is said to have been first sanctioned by you, and yet is now revoked. With such sacrifices God is not well-pleased. Alas! His anger is not turned away, His grace is not won, His mercy is not called forth. For these and such things the wrath of the Lord is not yet averted; but His arm is stretched out still, and the rod mentioned by Jeremiah is ever ready for our sins.

3. In truth, God is wroth with the schismatics; but He is by no means well-pleased with the Catholics. The Church of Metz is, as you have found, in danger, through a grievous quarrel between the Bishop and the clergy. You know what it may be your pleasure to decide about it; but there is there no peace yet, nor is it hoped for in the near future. I (not to conceal what seems best to my unworthiness) think that this and the troubles of the Churches of Toul and Verdun can be most safely and conveniently settled by the Metropolitan, who knows all the facts, has had great experience, and by the testimony of the Church has been found faithful. Moreover, think what evil you are inflicting on those two dioceses of Toul and Metz;[1] for, to speak truth,

[1] The charges brought here by S. Bernard against the Bishops of Metz and Toul are to be understood of Stephen of Metz and Henry of Toul, since this Letter was written during the schism of Anacletus, about the year 1135. The first Appendix of the *History of the Bishops of Metz* speaks of Stephen as follows: "Stephen, illustrious for his birth, still more illustrious for his virtue and uprightness, succeeded Poppo as Bishop of the Burgundians and Lorrainers in A.D. 1120, the second year of Calixtus II. Henry V. was at that time Emperor, and owing to the contest between the Church and State, refused to put him in possession of his See; and accordingly Stephen was consecrated at Rome by the Supreme Pontiff, and honoured with the pall and title of Cardinal." It is not easy to conjecture why S. Bernard complains of him so bitterly. For besides the quotation above, we also find it said of him in the same History: "If I were to try to reckon up and record the good deeds done by him and

they seem to be without Bishops, and I would that they were without tyrants. When such men are protected, supported, honoured, cherished, many are greatly amazed and scandalized; since they most surely know of that in their characters and lives, which in any of the laity, to say nothing of a Bishop, should be severely censured and execrated. What it is I should be ashamed to write, and it would not befit you to read. Be it so, that without an accuser they cannot be deposed, yet why should those whom common rumour accuses be honoured, and yet further exalted, with the special favour of the Apostolic See?

4. For by what merit of his own, whether of his sanctity as priest, or honour as bishop, has the Bishop of Metz obtained leave to quash, together with the liberty of the Church, at his mere bidding, an election duly made by the Canons, and to have the Primicerius[1] elected on his recommendation against the privileges of the Church?[2] Would it not be more just and honest, if

worthy to be handed down I should have more matter than paper." Nay, S. Bernard himself, in his 29th Letter, congratulates him on the restoration of peace to the Church at Metz, and in Letter 367 commends him to Guido, the Chancellor. It is possible that Stephen may have displeased S. Bernard through having stirred up several contests, caused cities to be besieged, and castles to be destroyed in trying to recover the goods of the Church which had been stolen by the nobles. It was things of this sort, as described in the same History, which made S. Bernard call him, in Letter 230, "a lion rather than a shepherd of the sheep." When Albero was chosen for the Bishopric of Liége, in the year 1135, and the Canons had duly chosen a successor to him, Stephen attempted to intrude a nominee of his own. Thence ensued a bitter strife which Innocent endeavoured to put an end to directly, passing over the jurisdiction of the Metropolitan, the Archbishop of Trèves. It is this that S. Bernard here complains of. As far as Henry of Toul is concerned, perhaps S. Bernard was in the same way badly informed about the protracted negotiations with respect to war carried on with Frederick, Count of Toul, and at length brought to an end in the year 1136.

[1] With respect to this title, see Note on Letter 30.—[E.]
[2] The Archbishop of Trèves claimed for himself the monastery of S. Maximin, near Trèves, against the Abbot and monks. On the other hand, Henry, Count of Luxembourg, endeavoured to claim obedience to himself in temporal matters as the advocate of the monastery. This claim caused strife, led to war and great slaughter on both sides. This explains S. Bernard's allusion when he says that the Archbishop had recovered the Church's goods, and had freed the captive Church from a lay-hand.

it should seem good to your discretion, that a man worthy of greater honour should not be deprived of that which is deservedly his own? I mean the Archbishop of Trèves, whom, to the great indignation of many who fear God, you have excluded from ending these and other matters in his diocese, as though he were under suspicion, or were inexperienced. Believe your faithful servant that, as far as I have found, this is wholly injurious to that province.

5. In writing these things I should fear the charge of presumption if I knew not to whom I am writing, and who I am that write. But I know your natural gentleness, and I feel assured that you know both me and the disposition with which I venture on these matters with you, my most sweet and loving father. One word more with regard to the Archbishop; in order that you may know how his messenger ought to be regarded, I may mention to you that he holds a high position in that realm, that he is a man faithful and constant to you and the Church of God, and gives no countenance to our ill-wishers, and to those who would overturn you, by whom he is frequently and sorely tempted; and that we shall be derided if by any chance he should not be listened to by you. I wished lastly to commend the messenger to you, but the merit of his honesty sufficiently commends him, and especially his exceeding love and faithful devotion to you. Indeed, if I thought he had not this, I would by no means send by his hand such private letters.

LETTER CLXXIX. (A.D. 1139.)

To the Same, on behalf of the Same.

He maintains the cause of Albero, Archbishop of Trèves, against the Abbot of S. Maximin and his rebellious monks.

Is it possible that wickedness can thus overcome wisdom? You know, holy Father, you know the Archbishop of Trèves. I am sure that you know him. But do you know also that unholy Abbot of the holy Maximin? I suspect that you do not. Who is worthier of honour than the first? Who more deserving of shame than the second? Yet the latter has been honoured, the former given to reproach. How has the Archbishop sinned? He has recovered the goods plundered from his Church, he has freed his captive Church from lay-hands. Why is evil returned him for his good, and hatred for his goodwill? Let your loving eye, I pray you, rest on this; lay aside for a moment your other occupations, and consider what he has been robbed of; that such a man as the one—I am ashamed to say what he is— should hold up to scorn to his neighbours and enemies such a man as yourself know the Archbishop to be. Holy Father, it is filial affection which speaks. So far I have sympathized with the unhappy and much-to-be-pitied Archbishop. But if after this, this injustice is not rectified, the grief of my heart, and my deep compassion will wholly pass over to him by whom it could have been rectified. There are other wrongs done to the same man, and in alleviating them you will undoubtedly be labouring for yourself. Whatever stains the name of my most sweet Lord pierces my heart.

LETTER CLXXX. (*Circa* A.D. 1136.)

TO THE SAME ON BEHALF OF THE SAME.

He commends to the Pontiff the cause of the Archbishop of Trèves.

Again supplication and prayers, though ten times repeated, shall not cease. I desist not because I distrust not. I have a good cause and a just judge, who will not hesitate to annul whatever has been stealthily gained, when the truth is evident, so that he who wished to scoff will not be able to find cause for his malicious humour, but as it is written, *His iniquity deceived himself* (Ps. xxvi. 12, VULG.). The Apostolic See is wont to have this virtue especially, that it is not ashamed to recall a grant when it has discovered it to have been extracted by fraud, and not to be truly deserved. It is most just and praiseworthy that no one should benefit by a lie, especially at the hand of the supreme and holy See. Knowing this, your son supplicates without fear on behalf of the Archbishop of Trèves, and is thus urgent, not as uncertainly. I certainly know his merits, his cause, his mind. For which of these do his monks wish to stone him? Because he has deserved ill of them? But he faithfully helped them, and served them greatly. For the injustice of his cause? But no one but an unjust man will speak of him as unjust. Because he freed them from a lay-hand? Nay, he recovered their monastery for the episcopal See, as though wringing his club out of the hand of Hercules with a stronger hand. Is it because of the wickedness of his intention? But it is a pious deed to do as he intended, viz., to reform religion in a monastery. The Lord help the heart of my lord, that it may not again be stolen away by monks, who are not so much, as they pretend, seeking liberty, but really flying from discipline.

LETTER CLXXXI. (*Circa* A.D. 1136.)

To the Chancellor Haimeric.

He protests his gratitude for the benefits he has received.

If I wished to repay you in words for the good deeds with which you overwhelm me it would be as if one, attacked with arrows, should defend himself with straws; except that this last would seem a mere game, the other deceit. Deeds ought to be repaid by deeds. But such return is difficult for me who am poor and in low station. Poor I am in goods and strength, but not in good wishes. Your kindnesses, then, which I cannot repay with good deeds I will with prayers. I am rich in good wishes, I abound in affection. And surely a true benefactor asks no more. For in what way is a man beneficent if he is not also benevolent? Besides, the benevolent man thinks nothing dearer to himself than the very benevolence from which he is called benevolent and is beneficent. Again, the fruit of beneficence is benevolence, unless perchance any one think that to be a benefit bestowed which he has sown in hope or lost through fear. But who does not see that this last is abandoned, the other sold, neither given? A benefit, therefore, to be real must be gratuitous. And so, to be repaid anything by the receiver, cannot be so pleasing to the giver as to have gratitude felt for what he has gratuitously given. And this benevolence in the mind of the receiver springs from the benevolence in that of the giver, a beneficent act intervening. In this benevolence I confess myself rich; this I offer to my benefactor from a full heart as a worthy return; this I devoutly send up to the Creator of all as a sacrifice of praise for the salvation of my benefactor.

LETTER CLXXXII. (*Circa* A.D. 1136.)
To Henry, Archbishop of Sens.[1]

He blames him for harshness in deposing his Archdeacon against rule.

Often, I confess, I have been going to write to you on behalf of many, and I had determined not to do so because of your hateful harshness, but charity shall prevail. I wish to retain for you your friends, and you disdain it; I wish to reconcile your enemies, and you suffer it not. You wish not for peace, but for shame and deposition;[2] you are hastening on your confusion with hands and feet. You are multiplying your accusers, alienating your supporters. You

---

[1] This is a severe Letter, and is written to the same Bishop to whom in Letter 42 he gave such wholesome advice about the office and character of Bishops. This Letter was written close upon A.D. 1140, certainly before A.D. 1144, in which year Henry died, and was succeeded by Hugh. About his death see Letter 102.

[2] That he was suspended A.D. 1136 is evident from the fact that Hugh, Abbot of Pontigny, was consecrated Bishop of Auxerre, at Ferrara, by Geoffrey, Bishop of Chartres, "because of the suspension of the Metropolitan Henry."—*Labbe's History of the Bishops of Auxerre*, c. 55.

are stirring up against yourself quarrels long laid to rest, provoking your adversaries, offending your protectors. You do all from caprice and not from reason, all for power, nothing from the fear of God. Who is there of your enemies that does not laugh at you, who of your friends that does not complain? Why do you degrade a man who is not only not convicted after trial, but not even heard? What scandal will this cause! how many mouths will it stir to derision, how many hearts to indignation! And do you suppose that justice has perished out of the earth as it has out of your heart, that a man should lose his archdeaconry taken from him in this way? But you perhaps are better pleased to give it back after seizing it, rather than to deserve his gratitude by suffering him to retain it: but this you have lost by your way of acting. Do not, I beseech you, do not do this thing; all who hear of it will be amazed, no one will praise you. These words that I have written are more biting and more bold than you may like, but if you are willing to correct your ways, you will see that they are not unwise, nor to your disadvantage.

LETTER CLXXXIII. (A.D. 1139.)

To Conrad, King of the Romans.

He urges upon him reverence for the Apostolic See.

Your letters and salutations I receive as gladly as I am unworthy of them; unworthy I mean in dignity, not in devotion. The complaints of the King are also mine, and especially those which you rightly make about the invasion of the Empire. I have never wished for the disgrace of the King, or the diminution of his kingdom; the violent my soul abhorreth. I have read indeed: *Let every soul be subject unto the higher powers; he who resisteth the power resisteth the ordinance of God* (Rom. xiii. 1, 2). Which sentence I ask and warn you to observe in every way, by showing reverence to the supreme Apostolic See, and to the Vicar of Blessed Peter, just as you wish it shown to you by the whole empire. There are some matters which I have thought it best not to write of, but which I could more suitably perhaps speak of in person.

LETTER CLXXXIV. (A.D. 1140.)

To the Lord Pope Innocent.

He excuses himself for not being well able to send the monks asked of him.

We have received again my brother Andrew [1] safe and in good spirits, and bringing good news of your safety and glory, of the peace and prosperity of the Church, of the flourishing and powerful state of the Roman Curia, and lastly of the favour and good-will which you still have for me. God in His mercy has dealt well with me: He has made me joyful. But your wish that we should send brothers to you will be with difficulty complied with, chiefly because we have not the number of members we once had. Indeed, besides those who have been destined in twos or threes to different cells, three new monasteries have been wholly founded out of them since I left you, and others are about to be founded. Still I will take care to summon from all our houses some whom I may send you, as I desire in all things to obey your commands.[2]

LETTER CLXXXV. (A.D. 1138.)

To Eustace, Intrusive Occupier of the See of Valence.

Bernard exhorts him to think of his age and his approaching death, and not to give ear to the perfidious counsels of flatterers.

[1] Either Andrew, Bernard's brother, a Cistercian, or the one mentioned in Letter 176, or Andrew of Baudiment, mentioned in Letter 226.

[2] The Pontiff wished to have a colony of Cistercians placed at Rome in the Church of S. Anastasius at Aquæ Salviæ. Another colony which was under the rule of another Abbot Bernard, who was afterwards Eugenius III., had been sent to Farfa, and this he placed at Aquæ Salviæ A.D. 1140. See the third book of his *Life*, n. 23, and also S. Bernard's Letters 343 and 345.

LETTER CLXXXV.

To the illustrious EUSTACE, Brother BERNARD sends greeting.

1. I often wish your salvation, my illustrious brother, though I do not often write. Who shall forbid the wish? Neither laws govern, nor princes hold sway over the affections. They are free, especially if led by the Spirit, for *where the Spirit of the Lord is, there is liberty* (2 Cor. iii. 17). Thence it is that I am now venturing to write to your greatness as though I were some great one, though, I confess, I have neither been bidden, nor asked, nor invited by you to do so. But what if charity bid me? Another may, perhaps, take it differently; I have determined by this letter, so far as in me lies, and with true charity, to remind an illustrious man of his salvation, to arouse him from sleep, to recall him to himself, to summon him to grace. Who knows whether God will turn, and pardon, and leave a blessing behind Him? Nay, who knows not what and how great are the riches of His goodness, and long suffering, which a merciful and compassionate God has treasured up for him? In short, He is merciful, He spares, waits, and hides Himself even till now, having made Himself as a man who heareth not, and in whose mouth are no reproofs, delaying to strike, ready to pardon. But thou, my Lord, how long? Thou, I say, O good man, how long wilt thou hide thyself from Him? how long wilt thou despise Him? *It is hard for thee to kick against the pricks* (Acts ix. 5). Knowest thou not *that the goodness of God is leading thee to repentance? How long wilt thou, after thy hardness and impenitent heart, heap up for thyself wrath against the day of wrath?* (Rom. ii. 4, 5).

2. Or is it not according to thy hardness indeed, but according to thy shame? What matters it according to what you are perishing? O, shame, void of reason, enemy of salvation, ignorant of all honour and honesty! This truly is that of which the Wise Man says, that *there is a shame which bringeth sin* (Ecclus. iv. 21). Is it, then, a shame for a man to be overcome by God, and is it to be held a disgrace to humble one's self under the mighty hand of the Most High?

That glorious King David says thus: *Against Thee only have I sinned and done this evil in Thy sight, that Thou mightest be justified in Thy sayings and mightest overcome when Thou art judged* (Ps. li. 4). The highest kind of victory is to yield to the Divine Majesty; and not to strive against our mother, the Church, is the highest honour and glory. O, perversity! You are not ashamed to be polluted, and yet you are ashamed to be cleansed. There is a shame, according to the Wise Man, which brings glory (Ecclus. iv. 21), viz., that which keeps from sin. But even if you are not ashamed to sin, there remains a glory, though it comes late, viz., when shame brings back that which guilt had banished. They, *whose iniquities are forgiven and whose sin is covered* (Ps. xxxii. 1), hold the second place of blessedness. An honourable covering is that of which it is said, *Confession and beauty are in his sight* (Ps. xcvi. 6, VULG.). Who will grant me to see you in golden apparel, so that I can say to you also: *Thou hast put on confession and honour, thou hast clad thyself with light, as with a garment* (Ps. civ. 1, 2); *Return, O Shunamite, that we may see thee* (Cant. vi. 13); *Awake, awake, put on thy strength, put on the garment of salvation* (Isa. lii. 1); *Awake thou that sleepest, and arise from the dead, and Christ shall give thee light* (Eph. v. 14); *Confession perisheth from the dead as from one who is not* (Ecclus. xvii. 28).

3. How long will you forget yourself, for ever? How long will you sleep in death, O ornament of the noble, but grief of the faithful? How long will you be stubbornly opposed to your spiritual good, an exile from your honour, a rebel against your salvation? Why do you proceed to consummate your previous excellent character and actions with so different an ending? How can such an old age, which ought to be spent quietly in fruitful deeds of mercy, wipe out the punishment due to all your past days, or blot out their guilt? Why, alas! should your hoary head alone, which should be reverenced, be robbed of its accustomed veneration; why should it alone sink unhonoured into the grave, when it should have been especially respected?

Have pity on thy soul by pleasing God (*Ibid.* xxx. 23); *For they who please men have been put to confusion, for God hath despised them* (Ps. liii. 5). The time of man is short; to the old man death is at the door. You have a short, a very short time with those who say to you, Well! well! Let it be also a light thing to you to be judged by them, or by man's little day, since you are even now ready to be brought before the scrutiny of angels; and, unhappy man that you are, are being hastened by the very failure of nature before the dread tribunal of Christ. You ought to be preparing yourself for that judgment, to be conforming yourself to that world, to be seeking the favour of that Court, and dreading rejection from it. Why are you disturbed by the opinion of those whose praise at that day will be found not to render you approved, nor their abuse to condemn you? In short, *the children of men are vanity, the children of men are a lie in the scales, that they may alike deceive in their vanity* (Ps. lxii. 9).

4. Besides, those who call you blessed lead you into error; they give you words and take back gifts. Vain both, but especially the words. And you deceive from vanity like them; but you are more deceived, they less. For you give what at all events is worth something, and you give it to the ungrateful and undeserving. Indeed, they love your goods, not you; nay, rather they love neither you nor yours, but they seek their own. Your goods, as far as they can, they will hunt after with their empty and lying flatteries. Their *words are smoother than oil, and yet they are very darts* (Ps. liii. 21). And therefore David said: *The oil of the sinner shall not anoint my head* (Ps. cxli. 5). By them *the sinner is praised in the desires of his soul and the wicked is blessed* (Ps. x. 3). It is not I, then, but the Wise Man who bids you beware of them. *My son, if sinners entice thee, consent thou not* (Prov. i. 10). Attend rather to Him who judges in equity for the meek of the earth; the meek whom your pastoral care does not feed, but whom your secular power oppresses, over whom you would have no power at all except it were

given you from above. But this is your hour and the power of darkness. But listen to this: *Judgment is severe for those who govern, and mighty men shall be mightily tormented* (Wisd. vi. 6, 7). If you fear this you will take care; if you disregard it you will fall into it, and it is *a fearful thing to fall into the hands of the living God* (Heb. x. 31). May the one true God avert this, who *wishes not the death of a sinner, but rather that he should be converted and live* (Ezek. xviii. 23, 32). My mind bids me say more, but you perchance would not listen. Rough words please not, although true and wholesome, because they are bitter and disagreeable to the taste. Therefore I will put my finger on my lip till I know how this is received; but you may believe that I will be agreeable to you if I can, yet not with pen or with tongue, but in deed and in truth.

LETTER CLXXXVI. (*Circa* A.D. 1140.)

To Simon, Son of the Castellan of Cambray.[1]

Bernard recommends to his protection the monks of Vaucelles, and begs him to ratify the donation of his father.

I have heard, dearly beloved, from Ralph, Abbot of Vaucelles, that you greatly long to see and speak to me, and I was greatly pleased with your so great devotion to me, nor am I ungrateful for your goodwill. You know it is my wish to satisfy your desire; but I am hindered from carrying out my wish not only by bodily illness, but also by very many, and very important, matters of business. But though absent in the body I am present in spirit, until such a time as I may be, if God will, present with you in body and in spirit. If, however, we love not in mouth and tongue only, but in deed and in truth, the truth of our love

[1] Cambray is wanting in all copies; some have D'Oisy. Both are right; for in this Letter mention is made of the monks of Vaucelles, of the Cistercian Order, founded near Cambray A.D. 1132. The author of the *Life of S. Goswin*, Abbot of Anchin, praises Simon of Oisy (lib. ii. c. 19).

will best appear in action. And so this is what I ask, that you will love, cherish, and whenever necessary protect the brothers of Vaucelles and their Church, so that in this you may afford a signal mark of your liberality, and that there may be a clear proof of that affection which you promise me. That affection I wish now first to make trial of in this one point: Will you ratify to me the lands of Ligecourt, which your father conferred on me in person for the support of that monastery, so as not to make void the grant of your father? I, for my part, giving thanks for past kindnesses, and hoping for the like in the future, offer up my prayers for you and yours to Him who performs the wish *of those who fear him, and hears their prayer* (Ps. cxlv. 19). We pray for the welfare of you and your wife, and all who belong to you.

LETTER CLXXXVII. (A.D. 1140.)

To Call Together the Bishops of the Archdiocese of Sens against Peter Abaelard.[1]

He urges the Bishops to energetic action in the cause of religion against Abaelard.

---

[1] Peter was born in the neighbourhood of Nantes; his father's name was Berengarius, his mother's Lucia. He first studied philosophy at Paris under William of Champeaux, then mathematics under Roscelin, and then theology under Anselm at Laon, not without envy and admiration. He afterwards entered on the interpretation of the Scriptures at Paris, and attracted many disciples, amongst them Heloise, a niece of Fulbert, a Canon of Paris, whose mind he trained, but violated her body. Fulbert being enraged at this injury revenged himself on Abaelard, who wished to repair by marriage the wrong that he had done, by breaking into his room at night and cruelly mutilating him. Both lovers then sought hiding places for their shame, one became a nun at Argenteuil, near Paris, the other a monk of S. Denys. But everywhere he was unlucky, or he made himself obnoxious, and he soon retired to a cell near the monastery at Deuil, and there he publicly lectured on theology. But he gave the reins too much to his own genius and to human reason, and, using expressions inconsistent with the faith, he was summoned to a Council held at Soissons, A.D. 1121, by the Legate Conon, and there was compelled to burn his book *On the Trinity; or, Introduction to Theology*, which contained suspected statements. He was then handed over to the monastery of S. Medard at Soissons. At length, tired of society, he was allowed to depart to a cell situate

in a lonely part of the Diocese of Troyes, where he built an oratory, which he dedicated first to the Holy Trinity, and afterwards to the Paraclete. But not even here was quiet allowed him. The monks of S. Gildas, in Brittany, in the Diocese of Vannes, summoned him to be their Abbot, and he found them, as he says in his *History of His Calamities*, "though Christians and monks, harsher and worse than heathen." He then returned to his oratory of the Paraclete, and handed it over to Héloise, with her sisters, who had been driven from the monastery of Argenteuil by Suger, Abbot of S. Denys, who claimed it for the Abbey under an old charter, A.D. 1127. He continued his perverse writings and teaching, and more now began to discuss his writings, especially William, Abbot of S. Thierry, who wrote a refutation of some heads of his errors, and sent his refutation to Geoffrey, Bishop of Chartres, and Bernard, Abbot of Clairvaux, to stir them up to avenge the wrong done to their faith. (See Letters 326 and 327.) But Abaelard, indignant at being branded as a heretic, challenged S. Bernard, as the author of the charge, to a public encounter at a Council held at Sens, A.D. 1140. S. Bernard went to the Council, though against his will. Impious doctrines of Abaelard were quoted from his writings, which he was bidden to deny if they were not his opinions, to abjure if they were. But he became confused, and unable to speak, as Geoffrey of Auxerre relates in his *Commentary on the Apocalypse*, or he was afraid of popular violence, as Otto of Frisingen says, or he thought it was safer for him to plead his cause at Rome, as S. Bernard says, because he had some Cardinals and clergy amongst his disciples, and so he appealed to the Roman Curia. The Fathers of the Council, none the less, proceeded to condemn his errors, and sent a list of them to Innocent, and S. Bernard wrote various Letters, both in his own name and in that of the Fathers, to Innocent and the Cardinals. Amongst Abaelard's works there are extant the heads of 17 errors which the Synod transmitted to the Pope; in the Letter of S. Bernard (No. 190) and in that of William of S. Thierry we have nearly 390. Innocent, on the receipt of the Synodal Letter, immediately wrote back the one numbered 194 to the Fathers of the Council, condemning the errors; and he added another, giving sentence against Abaelard in these words:—

"INNOCENT, Bishop, servant of the servants of God, to his venerable Brothers SAMSON, Archbishop of Rheims, HENRY, Archbishop of Sens, and to his beloved son in Christ, BERNARD, Abbot of Clairvaux, health and Apostolic benediction:—

"By these presents we command you, brethren, to cause Peter Abaelard and Arnold of Brescia, perverse manufacturers of dogma, and impugners of the Catholic faith, to be imprisoned separately in houses of religion wherever it may seem best to you, and to cause their books to be burnt wherever they may be found.

"Given at the Lateran, xviii. Kal. Aug."

On this Letter was written: "Show this transcript to no one till this Letter shall have been presented to the Archbishops in the assembly at Paris." So Abaelard, finding that he had been condemned at Rome, desisted from his appeal on the advice of Peter, Abbot of Cluny, by whom he was kindly received into the monastery. Afterwards, by Peter's intervention, he was reconciled with S. Bernard, and then, with Innocent and the Church; and having spent two years at Cluny with great submission, he died, A.D. 1142, in the 63rd year of his age, in the monastery of S. Marcellus, of Chalons-sur-Saône, whither he had been sent by Peter to be cured of a disease that he was suffering from. Peter the Venerable, in a Letter to Héloise (No. 21, Book iv.), recounts the eminent virtues that he displayed in this last part of his life. Abaelard has his too partial supporters, who go so far as to say that he was innocent of all error. Firstly, they state that Bernard fought against shadows; secondly, they overturn the authority of the Council of Soissons; and, thirdly, they reverse the verdict of the Roman Court given against Abaelard. A brief answer must be made to these three counts.

1. Against Bernard there is first of all set the authority of Otto of Frisingen, who, although he held Bernard in great veneration as his own Abbot, that is to say, as the head of his order, yet writes that he, "because of his zeal for the Christian religion was somewhat of a fanatic, and from his habitual meekness was credulous; so that from the first he detested those teachers who might put too much reliance on human reason and worldly wisdom, and from the second he was ready to lend a favourable ear to any account, however much against those teachers." Otto, indeed, says this in *De Gestis Frederici* (lib. i. c. 47), but it is in connection with Gilbert de la Porrée; it is an argument, however, in favour of Abaelard. But Radevicus testifies, in the same work (lib. ii. c. 11), that Otto, being too partial to Gilbert, declared, on his death-bed, that if he had said anything with regard to his sentence which could offend anyone, he would wish it corrected. This must be taken, therefore, as a retractation. Further, Otto himself, in what follows, says clearly enough what he thought of Abaelard. He says: "From his early years he was devoted to the study of letters, and to other elegant pursuits; but he was so arrogant, and had such confidence in his own abilities, that he would scarcely deign to descend from his intellectual height to listen to teachers." And again: "Holding the meaning of words and names in their natural sense, he applied them incautiously in theology. Wherefore, in writing and teaching about the Holy Trinity, he over-refined about the Three Persons, and used inapt illustrations." Add to this that Abaelard, on Otto's own confession, was adjudged a Sabellian heretic at the Council of Soissons. So much for the authority of Otto against Bernard. Then, in the second place, the testimony of Peter the Venerable is brought forward in Abaelard's favour, who, in the Letter to Héloise already referred to, says of him: "Germanus was not more humble, nor Martin himself more poor." Peter of Cluny is here speaking of those last days which Abaelard spent at Cluny, and truly enough. But was Bernard attacking his future merits? And can he, therefore, be said to have been fighting against shadows? The *Chronicle of Cluny*, speaking of Peter the Venerable, says well: "Abaelard, whose name was Peter, was recalled from his errors by Peter the Venerable, our Abbot, and by Bernard, Abbot of Clairvaux, and abjured what he had held from want of faith against the faith, and became a Cluniac monk. And then his thoughts, words, and deeds were always divine; ... and, as is said of Gregory the Great, no moment passed that he was not praying, or reading, or writing, or dictating. Wherefore Peter the Venerable carefully commending him," &c. Many other remarks of this kind are quoted, extolling either the disposition, or

the doctrine, or the excellent death of Abaelard, as though anyone of these affected Bernard.

II. A want of power or jurisdiction is then alleged against the Synod of Soissons, because neither the Archbishop of Sens nor of Rheims, who were present, had any jurisdiction over Abaelard, as Abbot of S. Gildas, in the Diocese of Vannes, but only the Metropolitan of Tours, who was absent. But having returned twelve years before to the oratory of the Paraclete, which was in the Diocese of Troyes, he was under the Archbishop of Sens. In the next place, he had as judges men whom he himself had chosen, as Bernard says, in Letter 191, written in the name of the Council to Innocent. "He appealed," he says, "from the place and the judges that he himself had chosen to the Apostolic See." Neither did Bernard, as some mistakenly say, call this Synod against Abaelard, but rather Abaelard forced Bernard to it against his will, as is plainly stated in Letters 187 and 189; moreover, Geoffrey of Auxerre, a former disciple of Abaelard, says in his *Commentary on the Apocalypse*: "Abaelard demanded of the Metropolitan of Sens that a great Council should as early as possible be summoned in his province, because the Abbot of Clairvaux was secretly bringing charges against his books. He said that he was ready to defend his writings in public, and asked that the aforesaid Abbot should be summoned to the Council that people might hear what he had to say." He was then rightly condemned, because, as jurisconsults say, anyone has jurisdiction over those who willingly submit themselves to it. The second engine brought up to shake the authority of the Synod is the testimony of Peter Berengarius, of Poictiers, who, in his *Apology for Abaelard*, his teacher, written against the Fathers of the Council, and Bernard in particular, utters such shameless falsehoods and such disgraceful libels that it is a wonder that any man of ordinary good feeling should put up with them, or bring forward such an audacious and unscrupulous man, who scoffs at venerable Bishops as "drunkards, dogs, pigs," thus exposing himself not only to the ridicule, but also to the just indignation of his readers. But let us see what in his more lucid moments he wrote to the Bishop of Mende about S. Bernard: "Why, they say, now that you have finished the first volume, do you not proceed with the second as you had promised? Because, in course of time, I had a clearer apprehension, and I came to be of the same mind as Bernard. I was unwilling to be the patron of the articles charged against Abaelard, because though their meaning was good, their form was bad. Well, then, they say, when you decided to leave the second book alone why did you not destroy the first? I would have done so, I reply, if it were not that my work might be of use in furnishing examples," &c.

III. In the third place there is alleged against the sentence of the Roman Pontiff an indecent haste in pronouncing it, because he condemned Abaelard without hearing his defence. But were not the acts of the Council of Soissons, at which Abaelard was present, sufficient evidence? Was there any one of the Cardinals or clergy of the Roman Curia who was not well acquainted with his opinions, or who would not, if it had been possible, have tried to save him from condemnation whom very many of them had had as teacher? Therefore, let the sentence of Innocent stand, let the authority of the Council and of S. Bernard stand unshaken, and let Abaelard have no other excuse for his error than his own,

The news has gone abroad amongst many, and I suppose has reached you, why we are convoked at Sens, within the Octave of Pentecost, and provoked to a contest in defence of the Faith, although the servant of the Lord must not strive, but rather be patient to all. If it were my own cause, the son of your Holiness might not undeservedly, perhaps, boast himself in your protection. But now since it is also yours, nay, more yours than mine, I bid you the more confidently, and ask you the more importunately, to show yourselves friends in need. I mean, friends not to me, but to Christ, whose Bride calls to you that she is well-nigh choked in the midst of a forest of heresies, and a crop of errors which are springing up under your care and protection. The friend of the Bridegroom will not desert Her in Her time of trouble. Nor wonder that I invite you so suddenly and within so short a time; it is because the opposite side in its wiliness and craft is preparing to attack the unprepared, and to force the unarmed to join battle.

LETTER CLXXXVIII. (A.D. 1140.)

To the Bishops and Cardinals of the Curia on the Same Subject.

He warns them to vigilance against the errors of Peter Abaelard.

To the Lords and reverend Fathers, the Bishops and Cardinals who are of the Curia, the son of their holiness sends greeting.

No one doubts that to you it specially belongs to remove scandals from the kingdom of God, to cut down thorns as they arise, and to allay quarrels. For so Moses enjoined

viz., the correction of his life and false opinions. Héloise herself, after the death of her Abaelard, acted far more wisely than these his defenders, when she asked leave from Peter the Venerable to be buried in Abaelard's tomb (as is recorded in the Cluniac Library and in Abaelard's works), which some rely on in framing their Apologies, as an excuse for the errors which he at the last did not cease to wash away with penitence and tears. But enough of this.

when he ascended the Mount, saying, *You have Aaron and Hur with you, if any question arise you shall refer it to them* (Ex. xxiv. 14). I speak of that Moses who went through water, and not through water only, but through water and blood. And He is therefore more than Moses, because He went through blood. And since in place of Aaron and Hur the zeal and authority of the Roman Church presides over the people of God, to it we rightly refer not only doubtful questions, but attacks on the faith, injuries done to Christ, scorn and contempt cast on the Fathers, the scandals of the living, the dangers to posterity. The faith of simple folk is scoffed at, the hidden things of God are exposed, questions about the most exalted truths are rashly ventilated, the Fathers are derided because they held that such things are rather to be tasted than solved. Thence it comes to pass that the Paschal Lamb, contrary to the command of God (Ex. xii. 9), is either cooked with water, or is eaten of raw in a rude and bestial fashion. What is left is not burnt with fire but is trodden under foot; so human reason usurps for itself everything, and leaves nothing for faith. It tries things above it, tests things too strong for it, rushes into Divine things; holy subjects it rather forces open than unlocks, what is closed and sealed it rather plunders than opens; and whatever it finds out of its reach it holds to be of no account and disdains to believe. Read if you please the book of Peter Abaelard, which he calls a book of Theology, for it is in your hands (since, as he boasts, it is read by many at the Curia), and see what things are said about the Holy Trinity, about the generation of the Son, about the procession of the Holy Spirit, and many other things he says repugnant to Catholic ears and minds. Read too that other book which they call a book of his *Sentences*,[1] and that one

[1] Abaelard denies in his Apology that he had ever written any book of this name, and therefore brings forward the accusation that it had been put forth against him through malice or ignorance; and Duchesne asserts the same in his notes. "S. Bernard," he says, "attributes to Abaelard this book of *Sentences* in ignorance in his 188th Letter," as though he had attributed to him the books of *Sentences* written by Peter Lombard. But Peter was not so un-

which is entitled *Know Thyself,* and notice what a crop of blasphemies and errors is there flourishing. See what he thinks about the Soul of Christ, about the Person of Christ, about the descent of Christ into Hades, about the sacrament of the altar, about the power of binding and loosing, about original sin, about concupiscence, about the sin of delight, about the sin of infirmity, about the sin of ignorance, about the work of sin, about the will to commit sin. And if you think that I have rightly stirred, bestir also yourselves; and bestir not yourselves in vain; act for the place you hold, the dignity of your office, the authority you have received, in such a way that he who has exalted himself to heaven may be cast down to hell, so that the works of darkness which have had the audacity to come forward into the light may be reproved by the light; so that while he who sins publicly is publicly reproved, others may learn to restrain themselves, putting, as they do, darkness for light, disputing at the cross roads about Divine things, speaking evil in their writings, and writing it in their books; and that so the mouth of them who speak wickedness may be stopped.

LETTER CLXXXIX. (A.D. 1140.)

To Pope Innocent, on the Same Subject.

He expresses his grief at the errors of Abaelard, which he warns the Pope to oppose.

To his most loving Father and Lord INNOCENT, by the grace of God, Supreme Pontiff, BERNARD, called Abbot of Clairvaux, writes as his humble servant.

known to S. Bernard that he should fall into this mistake. He sings his praises in Letter 410. Moreover, when this Letter was written Peter had not published his *Sentences.* We have certainly a book which is undoubtedly Abaelard's, commonly called *Sic et non,* the heading of which runs: "Here begin sentences taken from the Holy Scriptures which seem opposed to each other: because of which opposition this compilation is called *Sic et non.*" S. Bernard may have alluded to this when he wrote. Besides the other works of Abaelard named by Duchesne we have a book of his on the six days of creation dedicated to Héloise.

1. It is necessary that offences come. It is necessary but not pleasant. And therefore the Prophet says, *O that I had wings like a dove, for then would I flee away and be at rest* (Ps. lv. 6). And the Apostle wishes to be dissolved and to be with Christ. And so another of the Saints: *It is enough, O Lord, take away my life, for I am not better than my fathers* (1 Kings xix. 4). I have now something in common with the Saints, at least in wish if not in desert. For I could wish myself now taken from the midst of this world, overcome, I confess, by the fearfulness of my spirit and by the troubles of the time. I fear lest I be found better disposed than prepared. I am weary of life, and whether it is expedient to die I know not; and so perhaps even in my prayers I differ from the Saints, because they are provoked by the desire of better things, while I am compelled to depart by scandals and anxieties. He says in fact, *To be dissolved and to be with Christ is far better* (Phil. i. 23). Therefore in the Saint desire prevails, and in me sense; and in this unhappy life neither is he able to have the good he desires, nor I not to have the trouble which I suffer. And for this reason we both desire indeed to depart, with the same wish, but not from the same cause.

2. I was but just now foolishly promising myself some rest, when the schism of Leo was healed and peace restored to the Church. But lo! that is at rest, but I am not. I knew not that I was in a vale of tears, or I had forgotten that I dwell in a land of forgetfulness. I paid no attention to the fact that the earth in which I dwell brings forth for me thorns and thistles, that when they are cut down others succeed, and when these are destroyed others grow ceaselessly, and spring up without intermission. I had heard these things indeed, but, as I now find out, vexation itself gives better understanding to the hearing. My grief has been renewed, not destroyed, my tears have overwhelmed me, because evil has strengthened, and when they had endured the frost, the snow fell upon them. Who hath power to resist this frost? By it charity freezes, that

iniquity may abound. We have escaped the lion, Leo, to fall on the dragon (*i.e.*, Peter Abaelard), who perhaps may do us not less injury by lurking in ambush than the former by raging on high. Although I would that his poisonous pages were still lying hid in bookcases, and not read at the cross-roads. His books fly abroad; and they who hate the light because they are evil have dashed themselves against the light, thinking light darkness. Over cities and castles is darkness cast instead of light; instead of honey, or rather in honey, his poison is on all sides eagerly drunk in. His books have passed from nation to nation, and from one kingdom to another people. A new gospel is being fashioned for peoples and nations, a new faith propounded, another foundation laid than that which is laid. Virtues and vices are discussed immorally, the Sacraments of the Church unfaithfully, the mystery of the Holy Trinity craftily and extravagantly; but everything is given in a perverse spirit, in an unprecedented manner, and beyond what we have received.

3. Goliath advances, tall in stature, clad in his armour of war, preceded by his armour-bearer, Arnold of Brescia. Scale overlaps scale, and there is no point left unguarded. Indeed, the bee which was in France[1] has sent his murmuring to the Italian bee, and they have come together against the Lord and against His anointed. They have bent their bow, they have made ready their arrows within the quiver, that they may privily shoot at them which are true of heart. In their life and habits they have the form of godliness, but they deny its power, and they thereby deceive many, for they transform themselves into angels of light, when they are Satan's. Goliath standing with his armour-bearer between the two lines, shouts against the armies of Israel, and curses the ranks of the Saints, and that the more boldly because he knows that no David is present. In short, he puts forward philosophers with great

---

[1] An allusion to Isaiah vii. 18. The French bee is Abaelard, the Italian, Arnold of Brescia, a city of Italy. For more about him see notes on Letter 195.

praise and so affronts the teachers of the Church, and prefers their imaginations and novelties to the doctrine and faith of the Catholic Fathers; and when all fly from his face he challenges me, the weakest of all, to single combat.

4. The Archbishop of Sens, at his solicitation, writes to me fixing a day for the encounter, on which he in person, and with his brother bishops, should determine, if possible, on his false opinions, against which I had ventured to lift my voice. I refused, not only because I am but a youth and he a man of war from his youth, but also because I thought it unfitting that the grounds of the faith should be handed over to human reasonings for discussion, when, as is agreed, it rests on such a sure and firm foundation. I said that his writings were enough for his condemnation, and that it was not my business, but that of the Bishops, whose office it is to decide on matters of faith. He none the less, nay, rather the more on this account, lifted his voice, called upon many, assembled his accomplices. What he wrote about me to his disciples I do not care to say. He spread everywhere the report that on a fixed day he would answer me at Sens. The report reached everyone, and I could not but hear of it. At first I held back, nor was I much moved by the popular rumour. At length I yielded to the advice of my friends (although much against my will, and with tears), who saw how all were getting ready as if for a show, and they feared lest from my absence cause of offence should be given to the people, and the horn of the adversary be exalted; and, since the error was likely to be strengthened if there were no one to answer or contradict it, I betook myself to the place appointed and at the time, unprepared, indeed, and unarmed, except that I revolved in my mind those words, *Take no thought how ye shall answer, for it shall be given you in that hour what ye shall say* (S. Matt. x. 19); and, again, *The Lord is my helper, I will not fear what man may do unto me* (Ps. cxviii. 6). There had assembled, besides bishops and abbots, very many religious men,

masters of the schools from different states, and many learned clergy; and the King, too, was present. And so in the presence of all, my adversary standing opposite, I produced certain articles taken from his books. And when I began to read them he departed, unwilling to listen, and appealed from the judges that he had himself chosen, a course I do not think allowable. Further, the articles having been examined, were found, in the judgment of all, opposed to the faith, contrary to the truth. I have written this on my own behalf, lest I should be thought to have shown levity, or at all events rashness, in so important a matter.

5. But thou, O successor of Peter, wilt determine whether he, who assails the faith of Peter, ought to have shelter at the See of Peter. Thou, I say, the friend of the bridegroom, wilt provide measures to free His Bride from lying lips and from a deceitful tongue. But that I may speak a little more boldly with my Lord, do thou, most loving Father, take heed to thyself, and to the grace of God which is in thee. Did He not, when thou wast small in thine own eyes, place thee over nations and kingdoms? For what, but that thou shouldst pull down, and destroy, and build, and plant? See what great things He, who took thee from thy father's house, and anointed thee with the oil of His mercy, has since done for thy soul: what great things for His Church, by your means, in His vineyard, Heaven and Earth being witnesses, have been, as powerfully as wholesomely, uprooted and destroyed; what great things, again, have been well built, planted, and sown. God raised up the madness of schismatics in your time, that by your efforts they might be crushed. I have seen the fool in great prosperity, and immediately his beauty was cursed; I saw, I say, I saw the impious highly exalted and lifted up above the cedars of Lebanon, and I passed by, and lo he was gone. It is necessary, S. Paul says, *that there be heresies and schisms, that they that are approved may be made manifest* (1 Cor. xi. 19). And, indeed, in schism, as I have just said, the Lord has proved and known you. But that nothing be wanting to your crown, lo!

heresies have sprung up. And so, for the perfection of your virtues, and that you may be found to have done nothing less than the great Bishops, your predecessors, take away from us, most loving Father, the foxes which are laying waste the vineyard of the Lord while they are little ones; lest if they increase and multiply, our children despair of destroying what was not exterminated by you. Although they are not even now small or few, but imposing and numerous, and will not be exterminated save by you, and by a strong hand. Iacinctus[1] has threatened me with many evils; but he has not done, nor could he do, what he wished. But I thought that I ought to bear patiently concerning myself what he has spared neither to your person nor to the Curia; but this my friend Nicholas, as he is also yours, will better tell in person.

[1] It is uncertain who this Iacinctus, or Hyacinctus, is. It may be he who was afterwards created Cardinal by Lucius II., under the name of Bobo, and title of S. Mary in Cosmedin. Mention seems to be made of him in Letter 508. Nicholas was a monk of Clairvaux, and afterwards S. Bernard's notary; *v.* Letter 298.

NOTE
TO
THE FOLLOWING TREATISE.

1. The following Letter, which is the 190th of S. Bernard, was ranked by Horst among the Treatises, on account of its length and importance. It was written on the occasion of the condemnation of the errors of Abaelard by the Council of Sens, in 1140, in the presence of a great number of French Bishops, and of King Louis the Younger, as has been described in the notes to Letter 187. In the Synodical Epistle, which is No. 191 of S. Bernard, and in another, which is No. 337, the Fathers of the Council announced to Pope Innocent that they had condemned the errors of Abaelard, but had pronounced no sentence against him personally out of respect for the appeal which he had made to the Holy See; and they add that "the chief heads of his errors are more fully detailed in the Letter of the Bishop of Sens." I think that the Letter of which mention is thus made can be no other than that given here, and in which we find, in fact, the chief heads of Abaelard's errors, with a summary refutation of each. They are also the same as those which William, who had become a simple monk at Igny, after having been Abbot of Saint Thierry, had addressed to Geoffrey, Bishop of Chartres, and to Bernard, in a Letter which is inserted among those of Bernard.

2. As regards the different errors imputed to Abaelard, there are some which he complained were wrongly attributed to him. Others, on the contrary, he recognized as his, and corrected them in his Apology, in which he represents Bernard as being his only opponent, his malignant

and hasty denouncer. Two former partizans of Abaelard himself, but who had long recoiled from his errors, Geoffrey, who afterwards was the Secretary of Bernard, and "a certain Abbot of the Black Monks," whose name is unknown, attempted to justify Bernard against these calumnies. Duchesne had spoken of these two writers in his notes to Abaelard, but the Treatises of both of them were lately printed in Vol. iv. of the "Bibliotheca Cisterciensis," whose learned Editor, Bertrand Tissier, remarks that this unknown Abbot is some other person than William of Saint Thierry.

3. Of the heads of errors attributed to Abaelard, some are wanting in his printed works, which has given occasion to some writers for accusing Bernard, as if he had attributed errors to Abaelard without foundation, and so had himself been fighting against shadows and phantoms. But it is certain that most of these errors are to be found even in his printed writings, as we shall show each in its place. As for those which are no longer discoverable, William of Saint Thierry, Geoffrey, and this unknown Abbot, who had been once a disciple of Abaelard, and was perfectly acquainted with his doctrine, quote word for word statements both from his *Apology* and from his *Theology*, which do not appear in the printed editions; and certainly Abaelard himself, in Book ii. of his "Commentary on the Epistle to the Romans," p. 554, reserves certain points to be treated in his *Theology* of which there is no mention in the printed copies, which close thus: "The rest is wanting," so that it appears that the printed copies of the Theology have been mutilated.

4. Those writers have, therefore, done a very ill service to Religion, to say nothing of the injury to Bernard, who, in order to justify Abaelard, accuse Bernard of having been hurried on by the impulse of a blind zeal. They ought at least to acknowledge, as Abaelard himself did, and also Berengarius, his defender, that he had erred in various matters. And, indeed, Abaelard himself, in his *Apology*, acknowledges, though perhaps not quite sincerely, that in

some respects he was wrong. "It is possible," he says, "that I have fallen into some errors which I ought to have avoided, but I call God as a witness and judge upon my soul that in these points upon which I have been accused, I have presumed to say nothing through malice or through pride." It may well be that he might be able to clear himself of the reproach of malice, and even of that of heresy; but, at least, he could not deny that he had fallen into various errors—a liking for new words and phrases, levity, and perhaps even pride and an excessive desire for disputation. However this may be, Pope Innocent bade the Bishops by a rescript that the man was to be imprisoned and his books burned, and Godfrey declares that the Pope himself had them thrown into the flames at Rome. But Peter Abaelard at length returned to better views. He desisted from his Appeal by the advice and request of Peter the Venerable, Abbot of Cluny, who has described his last days in pleasing terms in a Letter which he wrote to Heloïse.

5. Bernard did not attack Abaelard in his discourses and writings with impunity. Not only was Abaelard impatient of his censure, but also Berengarius, his disciple and defender, dared to accuse Bernard of having spread certain errors in his books. "You have certainly erred," says Berengarius, addressing Bernard, "in asserting the origin of souls from Heaven" (p. 310). And on p. 315: "The origin of souls from Heaven is a fabulous thing, and this I remember that you taught in these words (Serm. in Cantica, No. 17): 'The Apostle has rightly said, *our conversation is in heaven.*' These words which you have expounded with great subtilty, savour much to the palate of a Christian mind of heresy." But enough of this foolish and impudent slanderer. The unknown Abbot reports another calumny of Abaelard against Bernard at the end of his second book: "It is very astonishing to me that for such a long time no reply should have been made by so many great men whose teaching enlightens the Church, as the light of the sun is reflected upon the moon, to our Abae-

lard, who accused the Abbot of saying that God, and Man assumed by God, are one Person in the Trinity. Whereas Man is a material body composed of various limbs and dissoluble, while God is neither a material body, nor has any limbs, nor can be dissolved. Wherefore, neither ought God to be called Man, nor Man to be called God," etc. Thus Abaelard shows himself a Nestorian, while petulantly accusing Bernard of error. Rightly does William of Saint Thierry reply in his 8th chapter to Abaelard with regard to this passage: " Thus we say similarly that Christ is the Son of Man in the nature of His Humanity, but not from that according to which He has union with God, and is One of the Three Persons in the Trinity; because, as God Incarnate was made the Son of Man on account of the human nature which He assumed, so the man united to the Son of God has become the Son of God on account of the Divine Nature which has united him to itself."

6. Besides the heads of errors which Bernard refutes in these books, he groups together some others in No. 10, contenting himself with exposing them; these have been refuted by other authors, viz., by William, and by the unknown Abbot. As to the Eucharistic species or the accidents, which, according to Abaelard, remain in the air after consecration, this was the view of William: "It appears to me, if you agree with me," he says, writing to Geoffrey, Bishop of Chartres, and to Bernard, " that those accidents, *i.e.*, the form of the earlier substance, which, I believe, is nothing else than a harmonious combination of accidents into one, if they still exist, do so in the Body of the Lord, not forming it, but by the power and wisdom of God working upon them, shaping and modifying it, that it may become capable, according to the purpose of the mystery and the manner of a Sacrament, of being touched and tasted in a form different from that proper to it, which it could not do in its own." He says again in his book to Rupertus, *De Corpore et Sanguine Domini,* c. 3: " In opposition to every conception and mode of reasoning in secular philosophy, the substance of bread is changed into another substance,

and has carried with it certain accidents into the Eucharistic mystery, but without altering them from what they were, and in such a manner that the Body of the Lord is not either white or round, though whiteness and roundness are associated with it. And it so retains these accidents that although they are truly present with His Human Body, yet they are not in It, do not touch it, or affect it," etc.

7. It was not only with respect to the Incarnation of Our Lord that Abaelard thought, or at least expressed himself, in an erroneous manner. He was equally in error on the subject of the grace of Christ, which he reduced simply to the reason granted to man by God, to the admonitions of the Holy Scriptures, and to good examples, and thus made it common to all men. "We may say, then," he taught, " that man, by the reason which he has received from God, is able to embrace the grace which is offered him; nor does God do any more for a person who is saved before he has embraced the offered grace, than for one who is not saved. But just as a man who exposes precious jewels for sale, in order to excite in those who see them the wish to purchase; thus God makes His grace known before all, exhorts us by the Scriptures, and reminds us by examples, so that men, in the power of that liberty of will which they have, may decide to embrace the offer of grace." And a little farther on he continues: " That vivification is attributed to grace: because Reason, by which man discerns between good and evil, and understands that he ought to abstain from the one and to do the other, comes from God. And therefore it is said that he does this under the inspiration of God: because God enables him by the gift of Reason which He has bestowed to recognize what is sinful." Such were the errors William has extracted, among many others, from the writings of Abaelard, and without doubt from his *Theology*, which, perhaps because of these and other similar passages, was mutilated by his scholars. Nor can we refuse to credit the good faith of William, who was a learned and pious man: especially as Abaelard in his Book iv., on the Epistle to the Romans, teaches the same hurtful doctrine (p. 653

and following). We learn from all these expressions of Abaelard that he thought, or at least certainly wrote, with the same impiety concerning the grace of Christ as he did on the Incarnation, and that Bernard was perfectly correct in saying (Letter 192): "He speaks of the Trinity like Arius, of grace like Pelagius, and of the Person of Christ like Nestorius." Proof of the truth of these words of Bernard as concerns the two last charges will be found in reading the letter given here; and as to the third, it will be sufficient to show that Bernard has in nowise exaggerated, to read the end of Book iii. of the *Theology* of Abaelard; there it will be found in his own words, "that those who abhor our words respecting the faith may be easily convinced when they hear that God the Father and God the Son are joined with us according to the sense of the words." In what manner? "Let us ask, then," he continues, "if they believe in the wisdom of God of which it is written: *Thou hast made all things with wisdom, O Lord,* and they will reply without hesitation that they do so believe. But this is to believe in the Son; as for believing in the Holy Ghost, it is nothing else than believing in the goodness of God." These words seem clearly to be not only Arian, but even Sabellian, although, as I must frankly confess, Abaelard formally rejects that error in its logical consequences in another passage on p. 1069. But especially in matters of faith, it is a matter of importance, not only to think rightly, but also to speak and write with exactness. Thus it is with reason that William of Saint Thierry says in citing the very words of Abaelard with respect to the brass and the seal, and with respect to power in general and a certain power: "As for the Divine Persons, he destroys them like Sabellius, and when he speaks of their unlikeness and their inequality, he goes straight to the feet of Arius in his opinion." I only cite these passages to make those persons ashamed who, although they detest these errors, yet take up the defence of Abaelard against Bernard, and do not hesitate to accuse the latter of precipitation and of excess of zeal against him. William de

Conches expresses himself in almost the same manner as Abaelard with respect to the mystery of the Holy Trinity, and Abbot William of S. Thierry confutes his errors also in his letter to Bernard. Nor is there anything worse that can happen to religion than that philosophers should attempt to explain the mysteries of our faith by the power of Reason alone.

8. Geoffrey, secretary of S. Bernard, gives an account of the whole business of Abaelard in a letter to Henry, Cardinal and Bishop of Albano: "I have heard also that your Diligence desires to know the entire truth respecting the condemnation of Peter Abaelard, whose books Pope Innocent II., of pious memory, condemned to be burned solemnly at Rome in the Church of S. Peter, and declared him by Apostolical authority to be a heretic. Some years before a certain venerable Cardinal, Legate of the Roman Church, by name Conon, once a Canon of the Church of S. Nicholas of Artois, had already condemned his *Theology* in the same way to be burned, during a council at Soissons in which he presided, the said Abaelard having been present and having been condemned of heretical pravity. If you desire it he will satisfy you by the book of *The Life of S. Bernard,* and by his letters sent to Rome on that subject. I have found also at Clairvaux a little book of a certain Abbot of Black Monks, in which the errors of the same Peter Abaelard are noted, and I remember to have seen it on a previous occasion; but for many years, as the keepers of the books assert, the first four sheets of this little book, although diligently sought for, could not be found. Because of this I have had the intention to send some one into France to the Abbey of the writer of that little book, so as, if I should be able to recover it, to have it copied, and send it to you. I believe that your curiosity will be completely satisfied in learning in what respects, how, and wherefore he was condemned."

It is thus that Geoffrey expresses himself. (Notes of Duchesne to Abaelard.) I pass over the vision related by Henry, Canon of Tours, to the Fathers of the Synod of Sens and to Bernard (*Spicileg.*, Vol. xii. p. 478 *et seqq.*).

9. After I had written what precedes, our brother, John Durand, who was then occupied at Rome, sent me the *Capitula Hæresum Petri Abaelardi,* which were placed at the head of the following letter, taken from the very faulty MS. in the Vatican, No. 663. These were, without doubt, those which Bernard, at the end of this letter, states that he had collected, and transmitted to the Pontiff. It seems well to place them here for the illustration of the letter.

HEADS OF HERESIES OF PETER ABAELARD.

I.—*The shocking analogy made between a brazen seal, and between genus and species, and the Holy Trinity.*

"The Wisdom of God being a certain power, as a seal of brass is a certain [portion of] brass; it follows clearly that the Wisdom of God has its being from His Power, similarly as the brazen is said to be what it is from its material: or the species derives what it is from its genus, which is, as it were, the material of the species, as the animal is of man. For just as, in order that there may be a brazen seal, there must be brass, and in order that there may be man, there must be the genus *Animal,* but not reciprocally: so, in order that there may be the Divine Wisdom, which is the power of discernment, there must be the Divine Power; but the reciprocal does not follow." And a little further on we read: "The Beneficence, the name under which the Holy Spirit is designated, is not in God Wisdom or Power."

II.—*That the Holy Spirit is not of the Substance of the Father.*

"The Son and the Holy Spirit are of the Father, the One by the way of generation, the Other by that of procession. Generation differs from procession in that He who is generated is of the very Substance of the Father, whilst the essence of Wisdom itself is, as was said, to be a certain Power." And a little further on we read: "As for the Holy Spirit, although He be of the same Substance with the Father and the Son, whence even the Trinity itself is called consubstantial (*homoousion*), yet He is not at all of the Substance of the Father or of the Son, as He would be if generated of the Father or the Son; but rather He has of them the Procession, which is that God, through love, extends Himself to another than Himself. For like as anyone *proceeds* through love from his own self to another, since, as we have said above, no one can be properly said to have love towards himself, or to be beneficent towards himself, but towards another. But this is especially true of God, who having need of nothing, cannot be moved by the feeling of beneficence towards His own self, to bestow something on Himself out of beneficence, but only towards creatures."

III.—*That God is able to do what He does, or to refrain from doing it, only in the manner or at the time in which He does so act or refrain, and in no other.*

"By the reasoning by which it is shown that God the Father has generated the Son of as great goodness as He was able, since otherwise He would have yielded to envy; it is also clear that all which He does or makes, He does or makes as excellent as He is able to do; nor does He will to withhold a single good that He is capable of bestowing." And a little farther on we read: "In everything that God does, He so proposes to Himself that which is good, that it may be said of Him that He is made willing to do that which He does rather by the price (as it were) of good, than by the free determination of His own Will." Also: "From this it therefore appears, and that both by reason and by the Scriptures, that God is able to do that only which He does." And a little farther: "Who, if He were able to interfere with the evil things which are done, would yet only do so at the proper time, since He can do nothing out of the proper time; consequently I do not see, in what way He would not be consenting to sinful actions. For who can be said to consent to evil, except he by whom it may be interfered with at the proper time?" Also: "The reason which I have given above and the answers to objections seem to me to make clear that God is able to do what He does, or to refrain from doing it, only in the manner or at the time, in which He does so act or refrain, and in no other."

IV.—*That Christ did not assume our flesh in order to free us from the yoke of the devil.*

"It should be known that all our Doctors who were after the Apostles agree in this, that the devil had dominion and power over man, and held him in bondage of right." And a little farther on: "It seems to me that the devil has never had any right over man, but rightly held him in bondage as a jailer, God permitting; nor did the Son of God assume our flesh in order to free us from the yoke of the devil." And again: "How does the Apostle say that we are justified or reconciled to God by the death of His Son, when on the contrary, He ought to have been more angry still against man, who had committed in putting His Son to death, a fault much more great than in transgressing His first precept by eating one apple; and would it not have been more just? For if that first sin of Adam was so great, that it could not be expiated except by the death of Christ; what is there which can be capable of expiating the Death of Christ itself, and |all the great cruelties committed upon Him and His Saints? (See Letter V. 21.) Did the death of His innocent Son please God so much, that for the sake of it He has become reconciled to us, who have caused it by our sins, on account of which the innocent Lord was slain? And could He forgive us a fault much less great, only on condition that we committed a sin so enormous? Were multiplied sins needful in order to the doing of so great a good, as to deliver us from our sins and to render us, by the death of the Son of God, more righteous than we were before?" Again: "To whom will it not seem cruel and unjust that one should have required the innocent blood, or any price whatever, or that the slaughter of the innocent, under any name or title, should be pleasing to him? Still less that God held the death of His Son so acceptable that He would, for its sake, be reconciled to the world. These and similar considerations raise questions of great importance, not only concerning redemption, but also concerning our justification by the death of our Lord Jesus Christ. But it seems to me that we were nevertheless justified by the Blood of Christ, and reconciled with God by the special grace shown to us when His Son took upon Him our nature, and in it gave us an example both by word and deed, until His Death. He has united us so closely with Him by His love for us, that we are fired by so great benefit of Divine grace, and will hesitate at no suffering, provided it be for Him. Which benefit indeed we do not doubt aroused the ancient Fathers, who looked forward to this by faith, to an ardent love of God, as well as those of more recent time." And below: "I think then that the cause and design of the Incarnation was to enlighten the world with the wisdom of God, and arouse it to love of Him."

V.—*Neither God-and-Man, nor the Man who is Christ, is one of the three Persons in the Trinity.*

"When I say that Christ is one of the Three Persons in the Trinity I mean this: that the Word, who was from eternity one of the Three Persons in the Trinity, is so; and I think that this expression is figurative. For if we should regard it as literal, since the name of Christ means He who is God-and-Man, then the sense would be, that God-and-Man is one of the Three Persons of the Trinity. Which is entirely false." And a little farther on: "It should be stated that although we allow that Christ is one of the Three Persons in the Trinity, yet we do not allow that the Person who is Christ is one of the Three Persons in the Trinity."

VI.—*That God does no more for a person who is saved, before he has accepted grace offered, than for one who is not saved.*

"It is frequently asked whether it is true, as is said by

some persons, that all men need to be saved by the mercy of God, and that their need is such that no one is able to have the will to do good unless by the preventing grace of God, which influences his heart and inspires in him the will to do good, and multiplies it when produced, and preserves it after having been multiplied. If it is true that man is not able to do anything good by himself, and that he is incapable of raising himself up in any way whatever by his free will for the reception of Divine grace, without the help of that grace, as is asserted, it does not appear on what ground, if he sins, he can be punished. For if he is not able to do anything good of himself, and if he is so constituted that he is more inclined to evil than to good, is he not free from blame if he sins, and is God who has given to him a nature so weak and subvertible deserving of praise for having created such a being? Or, on the contrary, does it not rather seem that He merits to be reproached?" And a little farther on: "If it were true that man is unable to raise himself up without the grace of another, in order to receive the Divine grace, there does not seem to be any reason wherefore man should be held culpable; and it would seem that if he has not the grace of God the blame should be rather reflected upon his Creator. But this is not so, but very far otherwise, according to the truth of the case, for we must lay down that man is able to embrace that grace which is offered to him by the reason which has, indeed, been bestowed upon him by God; nor does God do anything more for a person, who is saved before he has accepted the grace offered to him, than for another who is not saved. In fact, God behaves with regard to men in like manner as a merchant who has precious stones to sell, who exhibits them in the market, and offers them equally to all, so that he may excite in those who view them a desire to purchase. He who is prudent, and who knows that he has need of them, labours to obtain the means, gains money and purchases them; on the contrary, he who is slow and indolent, although he desires to have the jewels, and although he may be also more robust in body than the other, because he is indolent does not labour, and, therefore, does not purchase them, so that the blame for being without them belongs to himself. Similarly, God puts His grace before the eyes of all, and advises them in the Scriptures and by eminent doctors to avail themselves of their freedom of will to embrace this offered grace; certainly he who is prudent and provident for his future, acts according to his free will, in which he can embrace this grace. But the slothful, on the contrary, is entangled with carnal desires, and although he desires to attain blessedness, yet he is never willing to endure labour in restraining himself from evil, but neglects to do what he ought, although he would be able by his free will to embrace the grace offered him, and so he finds himself passed over by the Almighty."

VII.—*That God ought not to hinder evil actions.*

"In the first place, we must determine what it is to consent to evil, and what not to do so. He, then, is said to consent to evil who, when he can and ought to prevent it, does not do so; but if he ought to prevent it, but has not the power, or if, on the contrary, though he has the power, he ought not to do so, he is blameless. Much less if he neither has the power, nor ought, if he had, to prevent it, is he to be blamed. And, therefore, God is far from giving consent to evil actions, since He neither ought, nor has the power, to interfere with them. He ought not, since if an action develops by His goodness in a particular manner, than which none can be better, in no wise ought He to wish to interfere with it. He is, furthermore, not able, because His goodness, though it has chosen a minor good, cannot put an obstacle to that which is greater."

VIII.—*That we have not contracted from Adam guilt, but penalty.*

"It should be known that when it is said, Original sin is in infants, this is spoken of the penalty, temporal and eternal, which is incurred by them through the fault of their first parent." And a little farther on: "Similarly it is said, *In whom all have sinned* (Rom. v. 12), in the sense that when he (our first parent) sinned we were all in him in germ. But it does not, therefore, follow that all have sinned, since they did not then exist; for whoever does not exist does not sin."

IX.—*That the Body of the Lord did not fall to the ground.*

"On the subject of this species of Bread and Wine which is turned into the Body of Christ it is asked whether they continue to exist in the Body of Christ, in the substance of bread and wine as they were before, or whether they are in the air. It is probable that they exist in the air, since the Body of Christ had its form and features, as other human bodies. As for the Eucharistic species of bread and wine, they serve only to cover and conceal the Body of Christ in the mouth." And a little farther on: "It is asked again concerning this, that it seems to be *multiple* . . . wherefore it is ordered to be preserved from one Saturday to the next, as we read was done with the shew bread. It seems also to be gnawed by mice, and to fall to the ground from the hands of a priest or deacon. And, therefore, it is asked, wherefore God permits such things to happen to His Body; or whether, perhaps, these things do not really happen to the Body, but are only so done in appearance, and to the species? To which I reply, that these things do not really affect the Body, but that God allows them to happen to the species in order to reprove the negligence of the ministers. As for His Body, He replaces and preserves it as it pleases Him to do."

X.—*That man is made neither better nor worse by works.*

"It is frequently asked what it is that is recompensed by the Lord: the work or the intention, or both. For authority seems to decide that what God rewards eternally are works, for the Apostle says *God will render to every man according to his works* (Romans ii. 6). And Athanasius says:

'They will have to give account of their own works.' And a little farther on he says: *And those who have done good shall go into life eternal, but those who have done evil into eternal fire* (S. Matt. xxv. 46, and S. John v. 29). But I say that they were eternally recompensed by God either for good or for evil; nor is man made either better or worse because of works, at least only so far as that while he is doing them his will towards either good or evil gathers force. Nor is this contrary to the Apostle, or to other authors, because when the Apostle says *God will render to each*, etc., he puts the effect for the cause, that is to say, the action for the will or intention.

XI.—*That those who crucified Christ ignorantly committed no sin ; and that whatsoever is done through ignorance ought not to be counted as a fault.*

"There is objected to us the action of the Jews who have crucified Christ; that of the men who in persecuting the Martyrs thought that they were doing God service; and finally that of Eve, who did not act against her conscience since she was tempted, and yet it is certain that she committed sin. To which I say that in truth those Jews in their simplicity were not acting at all against their conscience, but rather persecuted Christ from zeal for their law ; nor did they think that they were acting wickedly, and, therefore, they did not sin ; nor were any of them eternally condemned on account of this, but because of their previous sins, because of which they rightly fell into that state of darkness. And among them were even some of the elect, for whom Christ prayed, saying: *Father, forgive them, for they know not what they do* (S. Luke xxxiii. 34). He did not ask in this prayer that this particular sin might be forgiven to them, since it was not really a sin, but rather their previous sins."

XII.—*Of the power of binding and loosing.*

"That which is said in S. Matthew, *whatsoever thou shalt bind on earth*, etc. (xvi. 19) is thus to be understood: *Whatsoever thou shalt bind on earth, i.e.,* in the present life,

shall be bound also in heaven, i.e., in the present Church."
And a little farther on: "The Gospel seems to contradict
us when we say that God alone is able to forgive sins, for
Christ says to His disciples *receive ye the Holy Ghost;
whosoever's sins ye remit, they are remitted unto them*
(S. John xx. 22, 23). But I say that this was spoken to the
Apostles alone, not to their successors." And immediately
he adds: "If, however, anyone shall say that this applies
also to their successors, it will be needful in that case to
explain this passage also in the same manner in which I
have explained the preceding."

XIII.—*Concerning suggestion, delectation, and consent.*

"It should be known also that suggestion is not a sin for
him to whom the suggestion is made, nor the delectation
which follows the suggestion, which delectation is produced
in the soul because of our weakness, and by the remembrance of the pleasure which is bound in the accomplishment of the thing which the tempter suggests to our mind.
It is only consent, which is also called a contempt of
God, in which sin consists." And a little farther on:
"I do not say that the will of doing this or that, nor even
the action itself is sin, but rather, as has been said above,
that the contempt itself of God in some act of the will that
constitutes sin."

XIV.—*That Omnipotence belongs properly and specially to the Father.*

"If we refer power as well to the idea of Being as to
efficacy of working, we find Omnipotence to attach properly
and specially to the *proprium* of the Person of the Father:
since not only is He Almighty with the Two other Persons,
but also He alone possesses His Being from Himself and
not from another. And as He exists from Himself, so He
is equally Almighty by Himself."

LETTER CXC. (A.D. 1140.)

TO THE SAME, AGAINST CERTAIN HEADS OF ABAELARD'S HERESIES.

To his most loving Father and Lord, INNOCENT, Supreme Pontiff, Brother BERNARD, called Abbot of Clairvaux, sends humble greeting.

The dangers and scandals which are coming to the surface in the Kingdom of God, especially those which touch the faith, ought to be referred to your Apostolic authority. For I judge it fitting that there most of all, the losses suffered by the faith should be repaired, where faith cannot suffer defect. This, truly, is the prerogative of your see. For to what other person [than Peter] has it ever been said, *I have prayed for thee, Peter, that thy faith fail not?* (S. Luke xxii. 32). Therefore that which follows is required from the successor of Peter: *And when thou art converted strengthen thy brethren.* That, indeed, is necessary now. The time is come, most loving Father, for you to recognize your primacy, to prove your zeal, to do honour to your ministry. In this plainly you fulfil the office of Peter, whose seat you occupy, if by your admonition you strengthen the hearts that are wavering in the faith, if by your authority you crush the corrupters of the faith.

CHAPTER I.

He explains and refutes the dogmas of Abaelard respecting the Trinity.

1. We have in France an old teacher turned into a new theologian, who in his early days amused himself with dialectics, and now gives utterance to wild imaginations upon the Holy Scriptures. He is endeavouring again to quicken false opinions, long ago condemned and put to rest, not only his own, but those of others; and is adding fresh ones as well. I know not what there is in heaven

above and in the earth beneath which he deigns to confess ignorance of: he raises his eyes to Heaven, and searches the deep things of God, and then returning to us, he brings back unspeakable words which it is not lawful for a man to utter, while he is presumptuously prepared to give a reason for everything, even of those things which are above reason; he presumes against reason and against faith. For what is more against reason than by reason to attempt to transcend reason? And what is more against faith than to be unwilling to believe what reason cannot attain? For instance, wishing to explain that saying of the wise man: *He who is hasty to believe is light in mind* (Ecclus. xix. 4). He says that a hasty faith is one that believes before reason; when Solomon says this not of faith towards God, but of mutual belief amongst ourselves. For the blessed Pope Gregory denies plainly that faith towards God has any merit whatever if human reason furnishes it with proof. But he praises the Apostles, because they followed their Saviour when called but once (Hom. in Evang. 26). He knows doubtless that this word was spoken as praise: *At the hearing of the ear he obeyed me* (Ps. xviii. 44), that the Apostles were directly rebuked because they had been slow in believing (S. Mark xvi. 14). Again, Mary is praised because she anticipated reason by faith, and Zacharias punished because he tempted faith by reason (S. Luke i. 20, 45), and Abraham is commended in that *against hope he believed in hope* (Rom. iv. 18).

2. But on the other hand our theologian says: "What is the use of speaking of doctrine unless what we wish to teach can be explained so as to be intelligible?" And so he promises understanding to his hearers, even on those most sublime and sacred truths which are hidden in the very bosom of our holy faith; and he places degrees in the Trinity, modes in the Majesty, numbers in the Eternity. He has laid down, for example, that God the Father is full power, the Son a certain kind of power, the Holy Spirit no power. And that the Son is related to

the Father as force in particular to force in general, as species to genus, as a thing formed of material, to matter,[1] as man to animal, as a brazen seal to brass. Did Arius ever go further? Who can endure this? Who would not shut his ears to such sacrilegious words? Who does not shudder at such novel profanities of words and ideas? He says also that "the Holy Spirit proceeds indeed from the Father and the Son, but not from the substance of the Father or of the Son." Whence then? Perhaps from nothing, like everything created. But the Apostle does not deny that they are of God, nor is he afraid to say: *Of whom are all things* (Rom. xi. 36). Shall we say then that the Holy Spirit proceeds from the Father and the Son in no other way than all things do, that is, that He exists not essentially but by way of creation, and is therefore a creature like all other things. Or will this man, who is always seeking after new things, who invents what he does not find, affirms those things which are not, as though they are, will he find for himself some third way, in which he may produce Him from the Father and the Son? But, he says, "if He were of the substance of the Father, He would surely have been begotten, and so the Father would have two Sons." As though everything which is from any substance has always as its father that from which it is. For lice and phlegm and such things, are they sons of the flesh, and not rather of the substance of the flesh? Or worms produced by rotten wood, whence derive they their substance but from the wood? yet are they not sons of the wood. Again, moths have their substance from the substance of garments, but not their generation. And there are many instances of this kind.

3. Since he admits that the Holy Spirit is consubstantial with the Father and the Son, I wonder how an acute and learned man (as at least he thinks himself) can yet deny that He proceeds in substance from the Father and the Son, unless perchance he thinks that the two first persons proceed from the substance of the third. But this is an

[1] *Materialum; materiu.*

impious and unheard of opinion. But if neither He proceeds from their substance, nor They from His, where, I pray, is the consubstantiality? Let him then either confess with the Church that the Holy Spirit is of their substance, from whom He does not deny that He proceeds, or let him with Arius deny His consubstantiality, and openly preach His creation. Again he says, if the Son is of the substance of the Father, the Holy Spirit is not; they must differ from each other, not only because the Holy Spirit is not begotten, as the Son is, but also because the Son is of the substance of the Father, which the Holy Spirit is not. Of this last distinction the Catholic Church has hitherto known nothing. If we admit it, where is the Trinity? where is the Unity? If the Holy Spirit and the Son are really separated by this new enumeration of differences, and if the Unity is split up, then especially let it be made plain that that distinction which he is endeavouring to make is a difference of substance. Moreover, if the Holy Spirit does not proceed from the substance of the Father and the Son, no Trinity remains, but a duality. For no Person is worthy to be admitted into the Trinity whose substance is not the same as that of the others. Let him, therefore, cease to separate the procession of the Holy Spirit from the substance of the Father and the Son, lest by a double impiety he both take away number from the Trinity and attribute it to the Unity, each of which the Christian faith abhors. And, lest I seem in so great a matter to depend on human reasonings only, let him read the letter of Jerome to Avitus, and he will plainly see, that amongst the other blasphemies of Origen which he confutes, he also rejects this one, that, as he said, the Holy Spirit is not of the substance of the Father. The blessed Athanasius thus speaks in his book on the Undivided Trinity: "When I spoke of God alone I meant not the Person only of the Father, because I denied not that the Son and the Holy Spirit are of this same Substance of the Father."

CHAPTER II.

In the Trinity it is not possible to admit any disparity: but equality is every way to be predicated.

4. Your holiness sees how in this man's scheme, which is not reasoning but raving,[1] the Trinity does not hold together and the Unity is rendered doubtful, and that this cannot be without injury to the Majesty. For whatever That is which is God, it is without doubt That than which nothing greater can be conceived.[2] If, then, in this One and Supreme Majesty we have found anything that is insufficient or imperfect in our consideration of the Persons, or if we have found that what is assigned to one is taken from another, the whole is surely less than That, than which nothing greater can be conceived. For indubitably the greatest which is a whole is greater than that which consists of parts. That man thinks worthily, as far as man can, of the Divine Majesty who thinks of no inequality in It where the whole is supremely great; of no separation where the whole is one; of no chasm where the whole is undivided; in short, of no imperfection or deficiency where the whole is a whole. For the Father is a whole, as are the Father, the Son and the Holy Spirit; the Son is a whole, as are He Himself and the Father and the Holy Spirit; the Holy Spirit is a whole, as are He Himself and the Father and the Son. And the whole Unity is a whole neither superabounding in the Three, nor diminished in Each Person. For they do not individually divide between Them that real and highest Good which they are, since they do not possess It in the way of participation, but are essentially the very Good. For those phrases which we most rightly use, as One from Another, or One to Another, are designations of the Persons, not division of the Unity. For although in this ineffable and incomprehensible essence of the Deity we can, by the requirements of the properties of the Persons, say One and Another in a sober and Catholic sense, yet

---

[1] *Non disputante, sed dementante.*

[2] Anselm greatly approves this idea respecting God in his *Monologium* and his *Apologeticus* at the commencement.

there is not in the essence One and Another, but simple Unity; nor in the confession of the Trinity any derogation to the Unity, nor is the true assertion of the Unity any exclusion of the *propria* of the Persons. May that execrable similitude of genus and species be accordingly as far from our minds as it is from the rule of truth. It is not a similitude, but a dissimilitude, as is also that of brass and the brazen seal; for since genus and species are to each other as higher and lower, while God is One, there can never be any resemblance between equality so perfect and disparity so great. And again, with regard to his illustration of brass, and the brass which is made into a seal, since it is used for the same kind of similitude, it is to be similarly condemned. For since, as I have said, species is less than and inferior to genus, far be it from us to think of such diversity between the Father and the Son. Far be it from us to agree with him who says that the Son is related to the Father as species to genus, as man to animal, as a brazen seal to brass, as force to force absolutely. For all these several things by the bond of their common nature are to each other as superiors and inferiors, and therefore no comparison is to be drawn from these things with That in which there is no inequality, no dissimilarity. You see from what unskilfulness or impiety the use of these similitudes descends.

CHAPTER III.

The absurd doctrine of Abaelard, who attributes properly and specifically the absolute and essential names to one Person, is opposed.

5. Now notice more clearly what he thinks, teaches, and writes. He says that Power properly and specially belongs to the Father, Wisdom to the Son, which, indeed, is false. For the Father both is, and is most truly called, Wisdom, and the Son Power, and what is common to Both is not the *proprium* of Each singly. There are certainly some other names which do not belong to Both, but to One or the Other alone, and therefore His own Name is peculiar to

Each, and not common to the Other. For the Father is not the Son, nor the Son the Father, for He is designated by the name of Father, not because He is the Father with regard to Himself, but with regard to His Son, and in like manner by the name of Son is expressed not that He is Son with regard to Himself, but to the Father. It is not so with power and many other attributes which are assigned to the Father and the Son in common, and not singly to Each taken by Himself. But he says, "No; we find that omnipotence belongs especially to the *proprium* of the Person of the Father, because He not only can do all things in union with the other two Persons, but also because He alone has His existence from Himself, and not from Another, and as He has His existence from Himself, so has He His power." O, second Aristotle! By parity of reasoning, if such were reasoning, would not Wisdom and Kindness belong properly to the Father, since equally the Father has His Wisdom and Kindness from Himself, and not from another, just as He has His Being and His Power? And if he does not deny this, as he cannot reasonably do, what, I ask, will he do with that famous partition of his in which, as he has assigned Power to the Father and Wisdom to the Son, so he has assigned Loving Kindness to the Holy Spirit properly and specially? For one and the same thing cannot well be the *proprium* of two, that is, to be the exclusive property of each. Let him choose which alternative he will: either let him give Wisdom to the Son and take It from the Father, or assign It to the Father and deny It to the Son; and again, let him assign Loving Kindness to the Spirit without the Father, or to the Father without the Spirit; or let him cease to call attributes which are common, *propria;* and though the Father has his Power from Himself, yet let him not dare to concede It to Him as being a *proprium*, lest on his own reasoning he be obliged to assign Him Wisdom and Loving Kindness which He has in precisely the same way, as His *propria* also.

6. But let us now wait and see in how theoretic a manner our theologian regards the invisible things of God. He says, as I have pointed out, that omnipotence properly

belongs to the Father, and He makes it to consist in the fulness and perfection of Rule and discernment. Again, to the Son he assigns Wisdom, and that he defines to be not Power simply, but a certain kind of Power in God, namely, the Power of discernment only. Perhaps he is afraid of doing an injury to the Father if he gives as much to the Son as to Him, and since he dares not give Him complete power, he grants Him half. And this that he lays down he illustrates by common examples, asserting that the Power of discernment which the Son is, is a particular kind of Power, just as a man is a kind of animal, and a brazen seal a particular form of brass, which means that the power of discernment is to the power of Rule and discernment, *i.e.*, the Son is to the Father, as a man to an animal, or as a brazen seal to brass. For, as he says, "a brazen seal must first be brass, and a man to be a man must first be an animal, but not conversely. So Divine Wisdom, which is the power of discernment, must be first Divine Power, but not conversely " (Abael. *Theol.* B. ii. p. 1083). Do you, then, mean that, like the preceding similitudes, your similitude demands that the Son to be the Son must first be the Father, *i.e.*, that He who is the Son is the Father, though not conversely? If you say this you are a heretic. If you do not your comparison is meaningless.

7. For why do you fashion for yourself the comparison, and with such beating about the bush, apply it to questions long ago settled and ill-fitted for debate? Why do you bring it forward with such waste of energy, impress it on us with such a useless multiplicity of words, produce it with such a flourish, if it does not effect the purpose for which it was adduced, viz., that the members be harmonized with each other in fitting proportions? Is not this a labour and a toil, to teach us by means of it, the relation which exists between the Father and the Son? We hold according to you, that a man being given an animal is given, but not conversely, at least by the rule of your logic; for by it it is not that when the genus is given we know the species, but the species being given we know the genus. Since, then, you com-

pare the Father to the genus, the Son to the species, does not the condition of your comparison postulate, that in like manner, when the Son is known you declare the Father to be known and not conversely; that, as he who is a man is necessarily an animal, but not conversely, so also, He who is the Son is necessarily the Father, but not conversely? But the Catholic faith contradicts you on this point, for it plainly denies both, viz., that the Father is the Son, and that the Son is the Father. For indubitably the Father is one Person, the Son another; although the Father is not of a different substance from the Son. For by this distinction the godliness of the Faith knows how to distinguish cautiously between the *propria* of the Persons, and the undivided unity of the Essence; and holding a middle course, to go along the royal road, turning neither to the right by confounding the Persons, nor looking to the left by dividing the Substance. But if you say that it rightly follows as a necessary truth that He who is the Son is also the Father, this helps you nothing; for an identical proposition is necessarily capable of being converted in such a way that what was true of the original proposition is true of the converse; and your comparison of genus and species, or of brass and the brazen seal does not admit of this. For as it does not follow as a necessary consequence that the Son is the Father, and the Father the Son, so neither can we rightly produce a convertible consequence between man and animal, and between a brazen seal and brass. For though it be true to say, "If he is a man he is an animal," still the converse is not true, "If he is an animal he is a man." And again, if we have a brazen seal it necessarily follows that it is brass; but if we have brass it does not necessarily follow that it is a brazen seal. But now let us proceed to his other points.

8. Lo! according to him we have omnipotence in the Father, a certain power in the Son. Let him tell us also what he thinks of the Holy Spirit. That loving-kindness, he says, which is denoted by the name of the Holy Spirit is not in God power or wisdom (Theol. ii. 1085). *I*

saw Satan as lightning fall from heaven (S. Luke x. 18). So ought he to fall who exercises himself in great matters, and in things that are too high for him. You see, Holy Father, what ladders, nay what dizzy heights, he has set up for his own downfall. All power, half power, no power. I shudder at the very words, and I think that very horror enough for his confutation. Still, I will bring forward a testimony which occurs to my troubled mind, so as to remove the injury done to the Holy Spirit. We read in Isaiah: *The Spirit of wisdom, the Spirit of ghostly strength* (Is. xi. 2). By this his audacity is plainly and sufficiently answered, even if it is not crushed. Be it that blasphemy against the Father or the Son may be forgiven, will blasphemy against the Spirit? The Angel of the Lord is waiting to cut you asunder; for you have said "The Holy Spirit in God is not power or wisdom." So the foot of pride stumbles when it intrudes [where it ought not].

CHAPTER IV.

Abaelard had defined faith as an opinion or estimate: Bernard refutes this.

9. It is no wonder if a man who is careless of what he says should, when rushing into the mysteries of the Faith, so irreverently assail and tear asunder the hidden treasures of godliness, since he has neither piety nor faith in his notions about the piety of faith. For instance, on the very threshold of his theology (I should rather say his stultology) he defines faith as private judgment; as though in these mysteries it is to be allowed to each person to think and speak as he pleases, or as though the mysteries of our faith are to hang in uncertainty amongst shifting and varying opinions, when on the contrary they rest on the solid and unshakable foundation of truth. Is not our hope baseless if our faith is subject to change? Fools then were our martyrs for bearing so cruel tortures for an uncertainty, and for entering, without hesitation, on an everlasting exile, through a bitter death, when there was a doubt as to the recompense of their reward. But far be it from us to think

that in our faith or hope anything, as he supposes, depends on the fluctuating judgment of the individual, and that the whole of it does not rest on sure and solid truth, having been commended by miracles and revelations from above, founded and consecrated by the Son of the Virgin, by the Blood of the Redeemer, by the glory of the risen Christ. These infallible proofs have been given us in superabundance. But if not, the Spirit itself, lastly, bears witness with our spirit that we are the sons of God. How, then, can any one dare to call faith opinion, unless it be that he has not yet received that Spirit, or unless he either knows not the Gospel or thinks it to be a fable? *I know in whom I have believed, and I am confident* (2 Tim. i. 12), cries the Apostle, and you mutter in my ears that faith is only an opinion. Do you prate to me that that is ambiguous than which there is nothing more certain? But Augustine says otherwise: "Faith is not held by any one in whose heart it is, by conjectures or opinions, but it is sure knowledge and has the assent of the conscience." Far be it from us, then, to suppose that the Christian faith has as its boundaries those opinions of the Academicians, whose boast it is that they doubt of everything, and know nothing. But I for my part walk securely, according to the saying of the teacher of the Gentiles, and I know that I shall not be confounded. I am satisfied, I confess, with his definition of faith, even though this man stealthily accuses it. *Faith,* he says, *is the substance of things hoped for, the evidence of things not seen* (Heb. xi. 1). The substance, he says, of things hoped for, not a phantasy of empty conjectures. You hear, that it is a substance; and therefore it is not allowed you in our faith, to suppose or oppose at your pleasure, nor to wander hither and thither amongst empty opinions, through devious errors. Under the name of substance something certain and fixed is put before you. You are enclosed in known bounds, shut in within fixed limits. For faith is not an opinion, but a certitude.

10. But now notice other points. I pass over his saying that the spirit of the fear of the Lord was not in the Lord; that there will be no holy fear of the Lord in the world to

come ; that after the consecration of the bread and of the cup, the former accidents which remain are suspended in the air ; that the suggestions of devils come to us, as their sagacious wickedness knows how, by the contact of stones and herbs ; and that they are able to discern in such natural objects strength suited to excite various passions; that the Holy Spirit is the *anima mundi;* that the world, as Plato says, is so much a more excellent animal, as it has a better soul in the Holy Spirit. Here while he exhausts his strength to make Plato a Christian, he proves himself a heathen. All these things and his other numerous silly stories of the same kind I pass by, I come to graver matters. To answer them all would require volumes. I speak only of those on which I cannot keep silence.

CHAPTER V.

He accuses Abaelard for preferring his own opinions and even fancies to the unanimous consent of the Fathers, especially where he declares that Christ did not become incarnate in order to save man from the power of the devil.

11. I find in a book of his sentences, and also in an exposition of his of the Epistle to the Romans, that this rash inquirer into the Divine Majesty attacks the mystery of our Redemption. He admits in the very beginning of his disputation that there has never been but one conclusion in our ecclesiastical doctors on this point, and this he states only to spurn it, and boasts that he has a better ; not fearing, against the precept of the Wise Man, *To cross the ancient boundaries which our fathers have marked out* (Prov. xxii. 28). It is needful to know, he says, that all our doctors since the Apostles agree in this, that the devil had power and dominion over man, and that he rightly possessed it, because man, by an act of the free will which he had, voluntarily consented to the devil. For they say that if any one conquers another, the conquered rightly becomes the slave of his conqueror. Therefore, he says, as the doctors teach, the Son of God became incarnate under this necessity, that since man could not otherwise

be freed, he might, by the death of an innocent man, be set free from the yoke of the devil. But as it seems to us, he says, neither had the devil ever any power over man, except by the permission of God, as a jailer might, nor was it to free man that the Son of God assumed flesh. Which am I to think the more intolerable in these words, the blasphemy or the arrogance? Which is the more to be condemned, his rashness or his impiety? Would not the mouth of him who speaks such things be more justly beaten with rods than confuted with reasons? Does not he whose hand is against every man, rightly provoke every man's hand to be raised against him? All, he says, say so, but so do not I. What, then, do you say? What better statement have you? What more subtle reason have you discovered? What more secret revelation do you boast of which has passed by the Saints and escaped from the wise? He, I suppose, will give us secret waters and hidden bread.

12. Tell us, nevertheless, that truth which has shown itself to you and to none else. Is it that it was not to free man that the Son of God became man? No one, you excepted, thinks this; you stand alone. For not from a wise man, nor prophet, nor apostle, nor even from the Lord Himself have you received this. The teacher of the Gentiles *received from the Lord what he has handed down to us* (1 Cor. xi. 23). The Teacher of all confesses that His doctrine is not His own, for *I do not*, He says, *speak of Myself* (S. John vii. 16 and xiv. 10), while you give us of your own, and what you have received from no one. *He who speaketh a lie speaketh of his own* (*Ibid.* viii. 44). Keep for yourself what is your own. I listen to Prophets and Apostles, I obey the Gospel, but not the Gospel according to Peter. Do you found for us a new Gospel? The Church does not receive a fifth Evangelist. What other Gospel do the Law, the Prophets, apostles, and apostolic men preach to us than that which you alone deny, viz., that God became man to free man? And if an angel from heaven should preach to us any other Gospel, let him be anathema.

13. But you do not accept the Doctors since the Apostles,

because you perceive yourself to be a man above all teachers. For example, you do not blush to say that all are against you, when they all agree together. To no purpose, therefore, should I place before you the faith and doctrine of those teachers whom you have just proscribed. I will take you to the Prophets. Under the type of Jerusalem the prophet speaks, or rather the Lord in the prophet speaks to His chosen people: *I will save you and deliver you, fear not* (Wisd. iii. 16). You ask, from what power? For you do not admit that the devil has or ever has had power over man. Neither, I confess, do I. It is not, however, that he has it not because you and I wish it not. If you do not confess it, you know it not; they whom *the Lord has redeemed out of the hand of the enemy,* they know it and confess it. And you would by no means deny it, if you were not under the hand of the enemy. You cannot give thanks with the redeemed, because you have not been redeemed. For if you had been redeemed you would recognize your Redeemer, and would not deny your redemption. Nor does the man, who knows not himself to be a captive, seek to be redeemed. Those who knew it called unto the Lord, and the Lord heard them, and redeemed them from the hand of the enemy. And that you may understand who this enemy is, He says: *Those whom He redeemed from the hand of the enemy He gathered out of all lands* (Ps. cvii. 2, 3). But first, indeed, recognize Him Who gathered them, of Whom Caiaphas in the Gospel prophesied, saying that Jesus should die for the people, and the Evangelist proceeds thus: *And not for that nation only, but that He might gather together into one all the children of God which were scattered abroad* (S. John xi. 51, 52). Whither had they been scattered? Into all lands. Therefore those whom He redeemed he gathered together from all lands. He first redeemed, then gathered them. For they were not only scattered, but also taken captive. He redeemed and gathered them; but redeemed them from the hand of the enemy. He does not say of the enemies, but of the enemy. The enemy was one, the lands many. Indeed, he gathered them not from one land, but from the lands, from the east and from the west, from the north and from the south. What Lord was there so powerful, who governed not one land but all lands? No other, I suppose, than He who by another prophet is said to drink up a river, that is, the human race, and not to wonder; and to trust that he can also draw up into his mouth Jordan, *i.e.*, the elect (Job xl. 18). Blessed are they who so flow in that they can flow out, who so enter that they can go out.

14. But now perhaps you do not believe the Prophets, thus speaking with one accord of the power of the devil over man. Come with me then to the Apostles. You said, did you not? that you do not agree with those who have come since the Apostles; may you agree then with the Apostles; and perhaps that may happen to you which one of them describes, speaking of certain persons: *If God, peradventure, will give them repentance to the acknowledging of the truth, and that they may recover themselves out of the snare of the devil, who are taken captive by him at his will* (2 Tim. ii. 25, 26). It is Paul who thus asserts that men are taken captive by the devil at his will. Do you hear? "at his will;" and do you deny his power? But if you do not believe Paul, come now to the Lord Himself, if perchance you may listen to Him and be put to silence. By Him the devil is called *the prince of this world* (S. John xiv. 30), and the *strong man armed* (S. Luke xi. 21), and the *possessor of goods* (S. Matt. xii. 29), and yet you say that he has no power over men. Perhaps you think the house in this place is not to be understood of the world, nor the goods of men. But if the world is the house of the devil and men his goods, how can it be said he has no power over men? Moreover, the Lord said to those who took Him: *This is your hour and the power of darkness* (S. Luke xxii. 53). That power did not escape him who said: *Who hath delivered us from the power of darkness, and hath translated us into the kingdom of His dear Son* (Col. i. 13). The Lord then neither denied the power of the devil even over Him, nor that of Pilate, who was a member of the devil. He said: *Thou couldst have no power against me at all except it were given thee*

from above (S. John xix. 11). But if that power given from above so violently raged against the green tree, how is it that it did not dare to touch the dry? Nor I suppose will he say, that it was an unjust power which was given from above. Let him, therefore, learn that not only had the devil power over man, but also a just power, and in consequence let him see this, that the Son of God came in the flesh to set man free. But though we say that the power of the devil was a just one we do not say that his will was. Whence it is not the devil who usurped the power, who is just, nor man who deservedly was subjected to it; but the Lord is just, who permitted the subjection. For anyone is called just and unjust, not from his power but from his will. This power of the devil over man though not rightly acquired, but wickedly usurped, was yet justly permitted. And in this way man was justly taken captive, viz., that the justice was neither in the devil, nor in man, but in God.

CHAPTER VI.

In the work of the Redemption of man, not only the mercy, but also the justice, of God is displayed.

15. Man therefore was lawfully delivered up, but mercifully set free. Yet mercy was shown in such a way that a kind of justice was not lacking even in his liberation, since, as was most fitting for man's recovery, it was part of the mercy of the liberator to employ justice rather than power against man's enemy. For what could man, the slave of sin, fast bound by the devil, do of himself to recover that righteousness which he had formerly lost? Therefore he who lacked righteousness had another's imputed to him, and in this way: The prince of this world came and found nothing in the Saviour, and because he notwithstanding laid hands on the Innocent he lost most justly those whom he held captive; since He who owed nothing to death, lawfully freed him who was subject

to it, both from the debt of death, and the dominion of the devil, by accepting the injustice of death; for with what justice could that be exacted from man a second time? It was man who owed the debt, it was man who paid it. *For if one,* says S. Paul, *died for all, then were all dead* (2 Cor. v. 14), so that, as One bore the sins of all, the satisfaction of One is imputed to all. It is not that one forfeited,[1] another satisfied; the Head and body is one, viz., Christ. The Head, therefore, satisfied for the members, Christ for His children, since, according to the Gospel of Paul, by which Peter's[2] falsehood is refuted, He who died for us, *quickened us together with Himself, forgiving us all our trespasses, blotting out the handwriting of ordinances that was against us, and took it out of the way, nailing it to His cross, having spoiled principalities and powers* (Col. ii. 13, 14).

16. May I be found amongst those spoils of which the opposing powers were deprived, and be handed over into the possession of my Lord. If Laban pursue me and reproach me for having left him by stealth, he shall be told that I came to him by stealth, and therefore so left him. The secret power of sin subjected me, the hidden plan of righteousness freed me from him; or I will reply, that if I was sold for nothing shall I not be freely redeemed? If Asshur has reproached me without cause, he has no right to demand the cause of my escape. But if he says, "Your father sold you into captivity," I will reply, "But my Brother redeemed me." Why should not righteousness come to me from another when guilt came upon me from

---

[1] *Forefecit, i.e.,* offended or transgressed. *Forisfactura* or *forefactum* denoted the crime or offence: and the former word is also used to signify the *penalty* of a crime. *Forisfactus* is the criminal himself. *Servus forisfactus* is a free man who has been reduced to slavery as a punishment for crime (*Legibus Athelstan. Reg.* c. 3). From this word is the French *forfaire, forfait;* and the English forfeit, forfeiture.

It will be seen that the word is a legal term adopted into the language of theology. The earliest instance of its use is apparently in the *Glossa* of Isidore.

See Du Cange's *Glossary s.v. Forisfacere.* Forcellini's ed. of Facciolati does not give the word.—[E.]

[2] *i.e.,* Abaelard.

another? One made me a sinner, the other justifies me from sin; the one by generation, the other by His blood. Shall there be sin in the seed of the sinner and not righteousness in the blood of Christ? But he will say, "Let righteousness be whose it may, it is none of yours." Be it so. But let guilt also be whose it may, it is none of mine. *Shall the righteousness of the righteous be upon him, and the wickedness of the wicked not be upon him?* It is not fitting for the son to bear the iniquity of the father, and yet to have no share in the righteousness of his brother. But now by man came death, by Man also came life. *For as in Adam all die, even so in Christ shall all be made alive* (1 Cor. xv. 21, 22). I attain to one and to the other in the same way: to the one by the flesh, to the other by faith. And if from the one I was infected with concupiscence from my birth, by Christ spiritual grace was infused into me. What more does this hired advocate bring against me? If he urges generation, I oppose regeneration; and add that the former is but carnal, while the latter is spiritual. Nor does equity suffer that they fight as equals, but the higher nature is the more efficacious cause, and therefore the spirit must necessarily overcome the flesh. In other words, the second birth is so much the more beneficial as the first was baneful. The offence, indeed, came to me, but so did grace; and *not as the offence so also is the free gift; for the judgment was by one to condemnation, but the free gift is of many offences unto justification* (Rom. v. 16). From the first man flowed down the offence, from the highest heaven came down the free gift: both from our father, one from our first father, the other from the Supreme Father. My earthly birth destroys me, and does not my heavenly much more save me? And I am not afraid of being rejected by the Father of lights when I have been rescued in this way from the power of darkness, and justified through His grace by the blood of His Son: *It is God that justifieth, who is he that condemneth?* He who had mercy on the sinner will not condemn the righteous; I mean that I am righteous, but it is in His righteousness, for

Christ is the end of the law for righteousness to every one that believeth (Rom. x. 4). In short, *He was made our righteousness by God the Father* (1 Cor. i. 30). Is not that righteousness mine which was made for me? If my guilt was inherited, why should not my righteousness be accorded to me? And, truly, what is given me is safer than what was born in me. For this, indeed, has whereof to glory, but not before God; but that, since it is effectual to my salvation, has nothing whereof to glory save in the Lord. *For if I be righteous,* says Job, *yet will I not lift up my head* (Job x. 15), lest I receive the answer: *What hast thou that thou didst not receive? now if thou didst receive it, why dost thou glory as if thou hadst not received it?* (1 Cor. iv. 7).

CHAPTER VII.

He severely reproves Abaelard for scrutinizing rashly and impiously, and extenuating the power of, the secret things of God.

17. This is the righteousness of man in the blood of the Redeemer: which this son of perdition, by his scoffs and insinuations, is attempting to render vain; so much so, that he thinks and argues that the whole fact that the Lord of Glory emptied Himself, that He was made lower than the angels, that He was born of a woman, that He lived in the world, that He made trial of our infirmities, that He suffered indignities, that at last He returned to His own place by the way of the Cross, that all this is to be reduced to one reason alone, viz., that it was done merely that He might give man by His life and teaching a rule of life, and by His suffering and death might set before him a goal of charity. Did He, then, teach righteousness and not bestow it? Did He show charity and not infuse it, and did He so return to His heaven? Is this, then, the whole of the great *mystery of godliness, which was manifested in the flesh, justified in the Spirit, seen of angels, preached unto the Gentiles, believed on in the world, received up into*

glory (1 Tim. iii. 16). O, incomparable doctor! he lays bare to himself the deep things of God, he makes them clear and easy to every one, and by his false teaching he so renders plain and evident the most lofty sacrament of grace, the mystery hidden from the ages, that any uncircumcised and unclean person can lightly penetrate to the heart of it: as though the wisdom of God knew not how to guard or neglected to guard against what Itself forbade, but had Itself given what is holy to the dogs and cast its pearls before swine. But it is not so. For though it was manifested in the flesh, yet it was justified in the Spirit: so that spiritual things are bestowed upon spiritual men, and the natural man does not perceive the things which are of the Spirit of God. Nor does our faith consist in wisdom of words but in the power of God. And, therefore, the Saviour says: *I thank Thee, O Father, Lord of heaven and earth, because Thou hast hid these things from the wise and prudent, and hast revealed them unto babes* (S. Matt. xi. 25). And the Apostle says: *If our Gospel be hid, it is hid to them that are lost* (2 Cor. iv. 3).

18. But see this man scoffing at the things which are of the Spirit of God, because they seem to him folly, and insulting the Apostle who speaks the hidden wisdom of God in a mystery, inveighing against the Gospel and even blaspheming the Lord. How much more prudent would he be if he would deign to believe what he has no power to comprehend, and would not dare to despise or tread under foot this sacred and holy mystery! It is a long task to reply to all the follies and calumnies which he charges against the Divine counsel. Yet I take a few, from which the rest may be estimated. "Since," he says, "Christ set free the elect only, how were they more than now, whether in this world or the next, under the power of the devil?" I answer: It was just because they were under the power of the devil, by whom, says the Apostle, *they were taken captive at his will* (2 Tim. ii. 26), that there was need of a liberator in order that the purpose of God concerning them might be fulfilled. But it behoved Him to set them

free in this world, that He might have them as freeborn sons in the next. Then he rejoins: "Well, did the devil also torture the poor man who was in the bosom of Abraham as he did the rich man who was condemned, or had he power over Abraham himself and the rest of the elect?" No, but he would have had if they had not been set free by their faith in a future Deliverer, as of Abraham it is written: *Abraham believed God, and it was counted unto him for righteousness* (Gen. xv. 6). Again: *Abraham rejoiced to see My day, and he saw it and was glad* (S. John viii. 56). Therefore even then the Blood of Christ was bedewing Lazarus, that he might not feel the flames, because he had believed on Him who should suffer. So are we to think of all the saints of that time, that they were born just as ourselves under the power of darkness, because of original sin, but rescued before they died, and that by nothing else but the blood of Christ. For it is written: *The multitudes that went before and that followed, cried saying, Hosanna to the Son of David, Blessed is He that cometh in the Name of the Lord* (S. Matt. xxi. 9). Therefore blessing was given to Christ coming in the flesh, both before he came and afterwards, by multitudes of those who had been blessed by Him, although those who went before did not obtain a full blessing, this, of course, having been kept as the prerogative of the time of grace.

CHAPTER VIII.

Wherefore Christ undertook a method of setting us free so painful and laborious, when a word from Him, or an act of His will, would alone have sufficed.

19. Then he labours to teach and persuade us that the devil could not and ought not to have claimed for himself any right over man, except by the permission of God, and that, without doing any injustice to the devil, God could have called back his deserter, if He wished to show him mercy, and have rescued him by a word only, as though

anyone denies this; then after much more he proceeds: "And so what necessity, or what reason, or what need was there, when the Divine compassion by a simple command could have freed man from sin, for the Son of God to take flesh for our redemption, to suffer so many and such great privations, scorn, scourgings, and spittings on, in short, the pain and ignominy of the cross itself, and that with evil doers?" I reply: The necessity was ours, the hard necessity of those sitting in darkness and the shadow of death. The need, equally ours, and God's, and the Holy Angels! Ours, that He might remove the yoke of our captivity; His own, that He might fulfil the purpose of His will; the Angels', that their number might be filled up. Further, the reason of this deed was the good pleasure of the Doer. Who denies that there were ready for the Almighty other and yet other ways to redeem us, to justify us, to set us free? But this takes nothing from the efficacy of the one which He chose out of many. And, perhaps, the greatest excellence of the way chosen is that in a land of forgetfulness, of slowness of spirit, and of constant offending, we are more forcibly and more vividly warned by so many and such great sufferings of our Restorer. Beyond that no man knows, nor can know to the full, what treasures of grace, what harmony with wisdom, what increase of glory, what advantages for salvation the inscrutable depth of this holy mystery contains within itself, that mystery which the Prophet when considering *trembled at, but did not penetrate* (Habak. iii. 2 in LXX.), and which the forerunner of the Lord thought himself *unworthy to unloose* (S. John i. 27).

20. But though it is not allowed us to scrutinize the mystery of the Divine Will, yet we may feel the effect of its work and perceive the fruit of its usefulness. And what we may know we may not keep to ourselves, for to conceal their word is to give glory to kings, but God is glorified by our investigating His sayings. [Prov. xxv. 2. But the sense of the text is the reverse of this.] Faithful is the saying and worthy of all acceptation, that *while we were yet sinners we were reconciled to God by the death of His*

Son (Rom. v. 10). "Where there is reconciliation there is also remission of sins. For if, as the Scripture says, *our sins separate between us and God*" (Is. lix. 2), there is no reconciliation while sin remains. In what, then, is remission of sins? *This cup,* He says, *is the new testament in My Blood which shall be shed for you for the remission of sins* (S. Matt. xxvi. 28). Therefore where there is reconciliation there is remission of sins. And what is that but justification? Whether, therefore, we call it reconciliation, or remission of sins, or justification, or, again, redemption, or liberation from the chains of the devil, by whom we were taken captive at his will, at all events by the death of the Only Begotten, we obtain that we have been justified freely by His blood, *in whom,* as S. Paul says again, *we have redemption through His blood, the forgiveness of sins, according to the riches of His grace* (Eph. i. 7). You say, Why by His blood when He could have wrought it by His Word? Ask Himself. It is only allowed me to know that it is so, not why it is so. *Shall the thing formed say to Him that formed it, "Why hast Thou made me thus?"*

21. But these things seem to him foolishness, he cannot restrain his laughter; listen to his jeering. "Why does the Apostle say," he asks, "that we are justified, or reconciled to God by the death of His Son, when He ought to have been the more angry with man, as he sinned more deeply in crucifying His Son, than in transgressing His first command by tasting of the apple?" As if the iniquity of the malignant were not able to displease, and the godliness of the sufferer to please God, and that in one and the same act. "But," he replies, "if that sin of Adam was so heinous that it could not be expiated but by the death of Christ, what expiation shall suffice for that homicide which was perpetrated upon Christ?" I answer in two words, That very Blood which they shed, and the prayer of Him whom they slew. He asks again: "Did the death of His innocent Son so please God the Father that by it He was reconciled to us, who had committed such a sin in Adam, that because of it our innocent Lord was slain?

Would He not have been able to forgive us much more easily if so heinous a sin had not been committed?" It was not His death alone that pleased the Father, but His voluntary surrender to death; and by that death destroying death, working salvation, restoring innocence, triumphing over principalities and powers, spoiling hell, enriching heaven, making peace between things in heaven and things on earth, and renewing all things. And since this so precious death to be voluntarily submitted to against sin could not take place except through sin, He did not indeed delight in, but He made good use of, the malice of the wrongdoers, and found the means to condemn death and sin by the death of His Son, and the sin [of those who condemned Him]. And the greater their iniquity, the more holy His will, and the more powerful to salvation; because, by the interposition of so great a power, that ancient sin, however great, would necessarily give way to that committed against Christ, as the less to the greater. Nor is this victory to be ascribed to the sin or to the sinners, but to Him who extracted good from their sin, and who bore bravely with the sinners, and turned to a godly purpose whatever the cruelty of the impious ventured on against Himself.

22. Thus the Blood which was shed was so powerful for pardoning that it blotted out that greatest sin of all, by which it came to pass that it was shed; and, therefore, left no doubt whatever about the blotting out of that ancient and lighter sin. Thus he rejoins: "Is there anyone to whom it does not seem cruel and unjust, that anyone should require the blood of an innocent man as the price of something, or that the death of an innocent man should in any way give him pleasure, not to say that God should hold so acceptable the death of His Son as by it tô be reconciled to the whole world?" God the Father did not require the Blood of His Son, but, nevertheless, He accepted it when offered; it was not blood He thirsted for, but salvation, for salvation was in the blood. He died, in short, for our salvation, and not for the mere exhibition of charity, as this man thinks and writes. For he so concludes the numerous calumnies and reproaches, which he as impiously as

ignorantly belches out against God, as to say that "the whole reason why God appeared in the flesh was for our education by His word and example, or, as he afterwards says, for our instruction; that the whole reason why He suffered and died was to exhibit or commend to us charity.

CHAPTER IX.

That Christ came into the world, not only to instruct us, but also to free us from sin.

23. But what profits it that He should instruct us if He did not first restore us by His grace? Or are we not in vain instructed if the body of sin is not first destroyed in us, that we should no more serve sin? If all the benefit that we derive from Christ consists in the exhibition of His virtues, it follows that Adam must be said to harm us only by the exhibition of sin. But in truth the medicine given was proportioned to the disease. *For as in Adam all die, even so in Christ shall all be made alive* (1 Cor. xv. 22). As is the one, so is the other. If the life which Christ gives is nothing else but His instruction, the death which Adam gave is in like manner only his instruction; so that the one by his example leads men to sin, the other by His example and His Word leads them to a holy life and to love Him. But if we rest in the Christian faith, and not in the heresy of Pelagius, and confess that by generation and not by example was the sin of Adam imparted to us, and by sin death, let us also confess that it is necessary for righteousness to be restored to us by Christ, not by instruction, but by regeneration, and by righteousness life (Rom. v. 18). And if this be so, how can Peter say that the only purpose and cause of the Incarnation was that He might enlighten the world by the light of His wisdom and inflame it with love of Him? Where, then, is redemption? There come from Christ, as he deigns to confess, merely illumination and enkindling to love. Whence come redemption and liberation?

24. Grant that the coming of Christ profits only those who are able to conform their lives to His, and to repay to Him

the debt of love, what about babes? What light of wisdom will he give to those who have barely seen the light of life? Whence will they gain power to ascend to God who have not even learned to love their mothers? Will the coming of Christ profit them nothing? Is it of no avail to them that they have been planted together with Him by baptism in the likeness of His death, since through the weakness of their age they are not able to know of, or to love, Christ? Our redemption, he says, consists in that supreme love which is inspired in us by the passion of Christ. Therefore, infants have no redemption because they have not that supreme love. Perhaps he holds that as they have no power to love, so neither have they necessity to perish, that they have no need to be regenerated in Christ because they have received no damage from their generation from Adam. If he thinks this, he thinks foolishness with Pelagius. Whichever of these two opinions he holds, his ill-will to the sacrament of our salvation is evident; and in attributing the whole of our salvation to devotion, and nothing of it to regeneration, it is evident too that, as far as he can, he would empty of meaning the dispensation of this deep mystery; for he places the glory of our redemption and the great work of salvation, not in the virtue of the Cross, not in the blood paid as its price, but in our advances in a holy life. But *God forbid that I should glory save in the Cross of our Lord Jesus Christ* (Gal. vi. 14), in which are our salvation, life, and resurrection.

25. And, indeed, I see three chief virtues in this work of our salvation: the form of humility in which God emptied Himself; the measure of charity which He stretched out even to death, and that the death of the Cross; the mystery of redemption, by which He bore that death which He underwent. The former two of these without the last are as if you were to paint on the air. A very great and most necessary example of humility, a great example of charity, and one worthy of all acceptation, has He set us; but they have no foundation, and, therefore, no stability, if redemption be wanting. I wish to follow with all my strength the lowly Jesus; I wish Him, who loved me and gave Himself

for me, to embrace me with the arms of His love, which suffered in my stead; but I must also feed on the Paschal Lamb, for unless I eat His Flesh and drink His Blood I have no life in me. It is one thing to follow Jesus, another to hold Him, another to feed on Him. To follow Him is a life-giving purpose; to hold and embrace Him a solemn joy; to feed on Him a blissful life. *For His flesh is meat indeed, and His blood is drink indeed. The bread of God is He who cometh down from Heaven and giveth life to the world* (S. John vi. 56, 33). What stability is there for joy, what constancy of purpose, without life? Surely no more than for a picture without a solid basis. Similarly neither the examples of humility nor the proofs of charity are anything without the sacrament of our redemption.

26. These results of the labour of the hands of your son, my lord and father, you now hold, such as they are, against a few heads of this new heresy; in which if you see nothing besides my zeal, yet I have meanwhile satisfied my own conscience. For since there was nothing that I could do against the injury to the faith, which I deplored, I thought it worth while to warn him, whose arms are the power of God, for the destruction of contrary imaginations, to destroy every high thing that exalteth itself against the knowledge of God, and to bring every thought into captivity to the obedience of Christ. There are other points in his other writings, not few nor less evil; but the limits of my time and of a letter do not allow me to reply to them. Moreover, I do not think it necessary, since they are so manifest, that they may be easily refuted even by ordinary faith. Still, I have collected some and sent them to you.

LETTER CXCI. (A.D. 1140.)

To the Same, in the Person of the Archbishop of Rheims.

That the Pope should use his authority to repress the arrogance of Abaelard.

To their most revered Lord and dear Father, INNOCENT,

by the grace of God Supreme Pontiff, SAMSON, Archbishop of Rheims, JOSCELIN, Bishop of Soissons, GEOFFREY. Bishop of Chalons, and ALVISUS, Bishop of Arras, send their willing testimony of the obedience they owe.

1. As your time is occupied with many things we send a short account of a lengthy matter, and the more especially as a longer and fuller account is contained in the letters of the Bishop of Sens. Peter Abaelard is endeavouring to destroy the virtue of the Christian faith, inasmuch as he thinks that he is able to comprehend the whole that God is by his unaided human reason, he is ascending to the skies, he is descending to the depths. There is nothing which can escape him, either in the heights above or in the depths beneath. He is a man great in his own eyes, a disputer of the faith against the faith, a man who busies himself about great and wonderful matters which are out of his reach, a prier into the Majesty of God, a manufacturer of heresies. He had not long since put forth a treatise on the Trinity, which was tried by the fire under the command of the Legate of the Roman Church,[1] because iniquity was found in it. Cursed was he who rebuilt the ruins of Jericho. That book has risen from the dead, and with it the heresies of many which had slept have arisen, and appeared unto many. Now, his heresy is spreading out its boughs unto the sea, and its branches even to Rome. It is his boast that his book has where to lay its head even in the Roman Curia. Hence his phrensy is strengthened and confirmed. Therefore, when the Abbot of Clairvaux, armed with zeal for the faith and for righteousness, was arguing about his heresies in the presence of the Bishops, he neither confessed nor denied, but in order to prolong his wickedness, though he had received neither injury nor wrong, he appealed from the place and judge which he had himself chosen to the Apostolic See. Then the Bishops who had assembled for the purpose of deciding did nothing against his person, in deference to your authority, but only censured, as a medicinal necessity, to prevent the disease spreading, the

[1] Viz., Conon, who presided at Soissons in A.D. 1121. See notes to Letter 187.

articles from his books which had already been condemned by the holy Fathers. Because, then, the man is drawing a multitude after him, and has a whole people as believers in him, it is necessary for you to meet this contagion with a swiftly-working remedy, for

> When ills through long delays grow strong.
> Too late is medicine prepared.[1]

We have advanced in this matter as far as we dared. For the rest it is your part, Blessed Father, to take care that in your days no spot of heretical depravity stains the fair beauty of the Church. To thee, O friend of the bridegroom, has the bride of Christ been entrusted; it is thine to present her, a chaste virgin, to one husband, even to Christ.

LETTER CXCII. (A.D. 1140.)

TO MAGISTER GUIDO DU CHATEL,[2] WHO HAD BEEN A DISCIPLE OF PETER, ON WHICH PETER PRESUMED TOO MUCH, AND WHO WAS AFTERWARDS POPE CELESTINE.

He warns him not to cherish the errors of Abaelard in his love for the man himself.

To his venerable Lord and dear Father, GUIDO, by the grace of God Cardinal-priest of the holy Roman Church, BERNARD, called Abbot of Clairvaux, desires that he decline neither to the right hand nor to the left.

I should do you an injury if I were to suppose that when you love anyone you are in love also with his errors. Whoever so loves another knows not yet how to love as he ought. For such love is earthly, sensual, devilish, injuring alike the lover and the loved. Others may think of others as they please; I cannot yet think of you anything that is contrary to reason, or to the strict rule of equity. Some

---
[1] Ovid, *De Remedio Amoris*, vv. 91, 92.
[2] He was created A.D. 1130 Cardinal of S. Laurence, in Damasus, when a Canon of S. Victor, at Paris. See Letter 144. Being sent as legate into Gaul, he excommunicated Ralph, Count of Vermandois. See Letters 216 and 218.

decide first and try afterwards; I will not decide whether a drink is sweet or bitter before I have tasted it. Master Peter puts forth in his books many blasphemous novelties, both of terms and senses; he disputes about the faith against the faith, and attacks the law with the words of the law. He sees nothing through a glass darkly, but beholds all things face to face, and busies himself in great and wonderful matters above him. Better would it be if (according to the title of his book[1]) he did know himself, and did not go beyond his measure, but thought soberly. I do not accuse him before the Father; there is one who accuses him, even his book, in which he has such ill-founded pleasure. When he discourses of the Trinity he savours of Arius; when of grace, of Pelagius; when of the Person of Christ, of Nestorius. I do not question your goodness, in asking you earnestly to prefer no one to Christ in Christ's own cause. But know this, that it is expedient for you, to whom power has been given by the Lord, it is expedient for the Church of Christ, it is expedient also for the man himself, that he be silenced, for his mouth is full of cursing, and bitterness, and guile.

LETTER CXCIII. (A.D. 1140.)

To Cardinal Ivo, on the Same Subject.

That it is an unworthy thing that Abaelard should find partisans even in the Court of Rome.

To his beloved Ivo, by the grace of God Cardinal-priest of the holy Roman Church, BERNARD, Abbot of Clairvaux, desires that he love righteousness and hate iniquity.

Master Peter Abaelard, a monk without a rule, a prelate without a cure, neither keeps his order, nor is kept in order by it. He is a man inconsistent with himself, within a Herod, without a John; a thorough hypocrite, having nothing of a monk but the name and habit. But this is nothing to me.

---

[1] Viz., "*Scito te ipsum.*"

Each one will bear his own burden. There is something else, which I cannot keep silence about, which belongs to all who love the name of Christ. He loudly utters iniquity, he is corrupting the integrity of the faith, and the chastity of the Church. He crosses over the boundaries which our fathers have marked out in his discussions and writings about the faith, about the Sacraments, about the Holy Trinity; at his pleasure he alters, adds to or diminishes them. In his books and works he shows himself a manufacturer of falsehood, and a worshipper of false dogmas; proving his heresy, not so much by his error as by his obstinate adherence to his error. He is a man who goes beyond his measure, and who, by his skill in words, lessens or destroys the power of the Cross of Christ. He is ignorant of nothing in heaven or in earth, except himself. He was condemned at Soissons, with his work, in the presence of the Legate of the Roman Church. But as though that condemnation were not enough for him, he is again acting so as to be again condemned, and his last error now is worse than the first. Still he feels secure, since, as he boasts, he has the Cardinals and clergy of the Curia as his disciples; and he assumes that those, whose judgment and condemnation he ought to fear, are defenders of his past and present error. If anyone has the Spirit of God, let him call to mind that verse, *Do not I hate them, O Lord, that hate Thee, and am not I grieved with those that rise up against Thee* (Ps. cxxxix. 21)? May God, by you and His other sons, free His Church from lying lips and from a deceitful tongue!

LETTER CXCIV. (A.D. 1140.)

Rescript of Pope Innocent against the Heresies of Peter Abaelard.

INNOCENT, Bishop, servant of the servants of God, to his venerable brothers, HENRY, Archbishop of Sens, SAMSON, Archbishop of Rheims, and their suffragans, and to his beloved brother in Christ, BERNARD, Abbot of Clairvaux, health and Apostolic benediction.

1. On the testimony of the Apostle, as one Lord, so *one faith is to be known* (Eph. iv. 5), on which the inviolate firmness of the Catholic Church is built, as on an immovable foundation, beside which no man can lay another. Thence it was that Blessed Peter, the chief of the Apostles, merited, through his noble confession of faith, to hear from our Lord and Saviour the words, *Thou art Peter, and on this rock I will build my Church* (S. Matt. xvi. 18), manifestly meaning by the rock the firmness of his faith and the solidity of Catholic unity. This is the seamless robe of our Redeemer for which the soldiers cast lots, but which they could not divide. Against it in the beginning the heathen raged, and the nations imagined vain things. *The kings of the earth stood up and their rulers were gathered together* (Ps. ii. 1, 2). But the Apostles, as leaders of the Lord's flock, and the Apostolic men, their successors, inflamed with the ardour of charity and zeal for righteousness, did not hesitate to defend the faith, and to implant it in the hearts of others by shedding their own blood. At length the Lord gave commands to the winds; the violence of the persecutors ceased, and there was a great calm in the Church.

2. But since the enemy of the human race is ever going about seeking whom he may devour, he now stealthily uses the deceitful fallacies of heretics in order to undermine the sincerity of the faith. Against these heretics the pastors of the churches have boldly risen and condemned their evil teachings, with their authors. For in the great Council of Nicaea Arius was condemned as a heretic; the Synod at Constantinople condemned Manes as a heretic by a fitting sentence; at the Ephesine Synod Nestorius received the condemnation of his error, which he deserved. The Council of Chalcedon also justly condemned the Nestorian heresy, and the Eutychian, with Dioscorus and his accomplices. Moreover, Marcian, though a layman, yet a Christian emperor, being inflamed with love of the Catholic faith, says, among other things, when writing to our predecessor,

Pope John, against those who were endeavouring to profane the sacred mysteries: " Let none of the clerical order, or of the military, or of any other rank, endeavour for the future to discourse publicly about the Christian faith. For, for anyone to take on himself to explain and again dispute of matters once determined on and rightly settled, is an injury to the decision of the most holy Council; " and he adds, as a penalty to any who should break this law, that if any clerk should dare to treat of religion in public, he should be removed from the fellowship of clerks as if guilty of sacrilege.[1]

3. We lament, therefore, that, as we gather from your letters, and from the heads of the errors sent us by your Fraternity, in these last days when perilous times are approaching, the heresies of the aforenamed, and other perverse doctrines contrary to the Catholic faith, have begun to show their heads in the pernicious teaching of Peter Abaelard. But by one thing we are specially consoled, and we give thanks to Almighty God for it, viz., that He has raised up in your parts such worthy successors of the Fathers, and in the time of our Apostolate has granted to us such noble pastors, who study to meet the calumnies of the new heretic, and to present His spotless Bride as a chaste virgin to one Husband, even Christ. And, therefore, we who sit in the seat of Blessed Peter (to whom it was said by the Lord: *And when thou art converted strengthen thy brethren*) (S. Luke xxii. 32), however unworthily we seem to occupy it, have, by the common advice of our brethren, the Bishops and Cardinals, condemned, with their author, all the articles sent us in the exercise of your discretion, and all the perverse doctrines of Peter himself, by the authority

[1] A double mistake seems to have crept in here, one of the inscription, the other of the name of the existing Pope. This letter or decree of Marcian's is extant among the acts of the Council of Chalcedon, held in the time of Leo the Great, A.D. 451, but addressed to the citizens of Constantinople, not to Leo, much less to John, who succeeded to the Roman See more than 80 years after the death of Marcian. Perhaps the passage should be restored by reading the name of the Pope as an Ablative Absolute, in this way, "the most holy Leo, our predecessor, being Pope," etc.

of the sacred canons, and we have imposed perpetual silence on him as a heretic. We decree, also, that all the followers and supporters of his error be cut off from the fellowship of the faithful, and be bound with the chain of excommunication.

Given at the Lateran xvii. a.d. Kal., August.

LETTER CXCV. (A.D. 1140.)
To the Bishop of Constance[1] about Arnold of Brescia.

Bernard advises him to expel Arnold of Brescia from his Diocese.

1. *If the good man of the house had known in what watch the thief would come he would have watched, and would not have suffered his house to be broken up* (S. Matt. xxiv. 43). Do you know that a thief has broken into your house by night, yet not your house, but the Lord's entrusted to your care? But there can be no doubt that you know what is taking place at your door, when news of it has penetrated even to us who are so far distant. It is no wonder that you could not foresee the hour, or perceive the night attack of the thief, but it will be a wonder if you do not recognize that he has been caught, if you do not hold him fast and prevent him from carrying off your goods, nay, rather the most precious spoils won by Christ, souls which He has stamped with His own image and redeemed with His own blood. Perhaps you are yet in the dark and wonder who it is I mean. I speak of Arnold of Brescia,[2] and I wish he

[1] It is uncertain whether this Constance is the one in France or the one on the Rhine. I am inclined to think the latter, because Arnold when expelled from France is said to have turned his steps to this place. Herman was then Bishop of this See, the same that met Bernard at Frankfort and took him to Constance (*Miracles of Bernard* lib. vi. c. i.).

[2] Otto of Frisingen (*de Gestis Friderici* lib. ii. c. 20) thus describes Arnold—He was born at Brescia, a city of Italy, and being ordained reader he became a clerk in the Church there. He had formerly had Abaelard as his teacher. He was a man of quick intelligence, more distinguished for a flow of words than for the weight of his matter, " a man who affected singularity and sought after novelty, one of those dispositions ever ready to manufacture heresies and to stir up divisions.

were of as sound doctrine as he is of strict life. And if you wish to know more, he is a man who comes neither eating nor drinking, but with the devil alone he is hungering and thirsting for the blood of souls. He is one of the number of those whom the watchfulness of the Apostle takes note of when he says, *Having the form of godliness, but denying the power thereof* (2 Tim. iii. 5). And the Lord Himself says: *They shall come to you in sheep's clothing, but inwardly they are ravening wolves* (S. Matt. vii. 15). Up to the present time, in whatever place he has lived, he has left such foul and destructive tracks that he dares not return to any place wherever he has imprinted his footmark. For example, he grievously stirred up and troubled the land in which he was born, and he was, therefore,

On returning from Gaul to Italy he assumed the religious habit in order to impose on people the more easily. He mangled and gnawed at everything as a dog might, he spared no one, he spoke contemptuously of Bishops and clergy, he persecuted the monks, and reserved his flatteries for the laity. For he was in the habit of saying that no clergy with private property, no Bishops with estates, no monks with possessions of their own, could in any way be saved; that all these things belonged to the King, and that they ought to give up possession of them and hand them over to the laity. Besides this he seems to have held erroneous ideas on the Sacrament of the Altar and on Baptism of children." The same author adds: "In the year 1138 he was condemned to silence by a Council held at Rome, was banished from Italy, retired to the town of Thurgau, and scattered his false doctrines broadcast. When at last he heard of the death of Innocent he returned to Rome in the early days of Eugenius, and urged on the people to further sedition, putting before them the examples of the Romans of old, who in the later days of the Senate had brought the world under their sway. And, therefore, he exhorted them to rebuild the Capitol, to restore the Senatorial dignity, and to recreate the equestrian Order. He said that no part of the government of the city belonged to the Pontiff, that he ought to be content with ecclesiastical jurisdiction. The evils springing from this pernicious teaching grew to such a head at last that not only were the houses and splendid palaces of the Roman nobles or Cardinals pulled down, but violent hands were laid by the furious populace on the sacred persons of the Cardinals, and some were disgracefully injured." The same author says (*Chronicles* lib. vii. c. 20) that Jordan, the son of Peter Leonis, was elected into the Patrician Order. "At last," he says, "falling into the hands of certain people in Tuscany, he was arrested, was brought before the Prince for examination, and at last was bound to a stake by the Prefect of the city, and, the pyre having been reduced to ashes to prevent the foolish populace from paying honour to his body, his remains were scattered upon the Tiber."

accused before the Pope of grievous schism, and was banished from his native soil, and also compelled to swear that he would not return except by the Pope's permission. For a like reason this notable schismatic has been driven out from the kingdom of France. When anathematized by Peter the Apostle he joined himself to Peter Abaelard, and with him, and for him, he endeavoured to defend vigorously and stubbornly all his errors, which had been already exposed and condemned by the Church.

2. And in all these incidents his phrensy was not abated, but his hand was stretched out still. For though he is a fugitive and wanderer on the earth, he does not cease to do amongst men of other countries what he is not allowed to do amongst his own countrymen, and goes about as a roaring lion, seeking whom he may devour. And I hear that he is now working mischief amongst you, and is eating up your people as it were bread. *His mouth is full of cursing and bitterness, his feet are swift to shed blood. Destruction and unhappiness are in his ways, and the way of peace has he not known.* He is an enemy of the cross of Christ, a sower of discord, a manufacturer of schisms, a disturber of peace, a divider of unity; *his teeth are spears and arrows, and his tongue a sharp sword, his words are smoother than oil, and yet they are very darts.* Thence it is that he is wont to entice to himself by flattering words and the pretences of virtues the rich and the powerful, according to the verse: *He sitteth lurking in thievish corners with the rich that he may slay the innocent* (Ps. x. 8). Depend upon it, when he feels that he has securely gained their goodwill and affection, you will see the man openly rise against the clergy; and, relying on military tyranny, he will rise against the Bishops themselves, and run a tilt against all ecclesiastical order. Knowing this, I do not know what better or more wholesome thing you can do at such a crisis than, according to the admonition of the Apostle, *to remove the evil man from among you* (1 Cor. v. 13), though the friend of the bridegroom will see that he is

bound rather than put to flight, lest he be able to travel about again, and so do more harm. Our Lord the Pope, when he was here, gave in writing the same directions, because of the evils which he heard were being done; but there was no one to do the good action. To end, if the Scripture soundly warns us *to take the little foxes which spoil the vine* (Cant. ii. 15), should not a powerful and fierce wolf much rather be bound fast, lest he break into the sheep-folds of Christ, and slay and destroy His sheep?

LETTER CXCVI. (A.D. 1140.)

To Guido, the Legate, on the Same Subject.

Bernard warns him against familiarity with Arnold of Brescia.

1. Arnold of Brescia is said to be with you, a man whose discourse is as sweet as honey, whose doctrine is poison; whose head is that of a dove, his tail a scorpion's; whom Brescia cast forth, Rome was horrified at, France rejected, Germany abominates, Italy is unwilling to take in. See, I beseech you, that your authority lend no protection to his further mischief; for he has both the art and the wish to do injury, and if he gain your favour he will be likely, like a threefold cord which is not easily broken, to be, I am afraid, above measure mischievous. And if it is true that you have the man with you, I suppose one of two things—either that you do not know him, or, which is more likely, that you are hoping for his repentance. Would it were not a vain hope! Who can from this stone raise up a child to Abraham? How welcome a gift would it be to our mother the Church to receive him as a vessel for honour, whom she had so long borne with as a vessel to dishonour! It is lawful to make the attempt, but a wise man will be careful not to go beyond the number laid down by the Apostle, when he says, *A man that is an heretic after the first and second admonition reject, knowing that he that is such is subverted and sinneth, being condemned of himself*

(Tit. iii. 10, 11). Otherwise, to be on intimate terms with him, and to admit him frequently to private conversation, not to say to your house, is suspiciously like showing him favour, and is a powerful weapon in the hands of the enemy. A member of the household, and a private friend of the Legate of the Apostolic See, will preach with impunity and persuade whom he will. For who can suspect any wrong to come from the side of our Lord the Pope? But although he manifestly speak perverse things, who will dare lightly to oppose himself against one who is at your side?

2. And do you know what kind of footprints he has left in every place he has dwelt in? It is not without cause that Apostolic energy has forced him to cross the Alps from Italy which gave him birth, and does not suffer him to return to his native country. What man is there amongst the foreigners to whom he was driven who does not heartily wish that they had sent him back to his home? And certainly the fact that his bearing towards all is such that he incurs the hatred of all is an approbation of the condemnation under which he labours, so that no one can say that it was obtained from our Lord the Pope by surprise. With what excuse, then, can he flout the sentence of the Supreme Pontiff when, though his tongue disclaims it, his life loudly proclaims its justice? And so to show him favour is to go against our Lord the Pope, to oppose our Lord God. For by whomsoever a righteous sentence may have been given, it is certain that it proceeds from Him who says by the mouth of the Prophet, *I who speak righteousness* (Is. lxiii. 1). But I have confidence in your wisdom and honesty, and that when you have read this letter, and know the truth, you will not be led away to give your consent in this matter to anything, save what is becoming to you and expedient to the Church of God, on behalf of which you are discharging the office of legate. You have my heart, and may reckon on my obedience.

LETTER CXCVII. (A.D. 1141.)

To Peter, Dean of Besançon.

Bernard blames his injurious conduct towards the Abbot of Charlieu.

I hear such an account of the pilgrimage of the Abbot of Charlieu[1] that I look upon him as already dead. Whatever danger threatens him, whatever suffering he has to undergo, is (to my great grief) imputed to you most of all. I neither expected this, nor deserved it at your hands. I thought you one thing, I find you another. Those who were present at the affair bear their testimony against you that you have not behaved in it straightforwardly or justly. And I partly believe it. For the Venerable Abbot of Beauvais[2] is by no means pleased with you. Do not, I implore you, do not persecute the servants of God, to whom you read that He said: *He that toucheth you toucheth the apple of my eye* (Zach. ii. 8). Do not pluck up by the roots whatever good feeling I formerly had towards you. And I write this, not because I love you not, but to take away whatever may cause me not to love you. For I tell you, as

---

[1] Charlieu, in the Diocese of Besançon, was a daughter house of Clairvaux, and founded A.D. 1131. Its first Abbot was Guy, mentioned in this and the following Letter. He being attacked and unjustly oppressed by a monk named Peter, went on appeal to Innocent with commendatory letters from Bernard. His enemy, however, was able to get the case sent back to judges in Gaul, and it was entrusted to John, Bishop of Valence, by the Abbot of Bonneval, a Cistercian monastery, who, with the Bishop of Grenoble, was to compose the differences. And then it first came to pass that questions which concerned their Order were submitted to the Cistercians for decision, because of their tried uprightness. And this becoming an established custom, was the cause of that famous and honourable exception to the law that no one may be a judge in his own cause, or in any cause in which he is interested, viz., if the judge is of such a nature that no suspicion is likely to attach to him, *e.g.*, if he is a Cistercian monk this law may be dispensed with, and such a judge is not to be refused. (*Tiraquellus de Pœnis*, temp. aut. remitt. 15, n. 60 and many others.) Sentence having been given in favour of the Abbot of Charlieu, the aforesaid Peter again appealed to Innocent, and Bernard wrote to him Letter 199 to request him to confirm the just sentence of the Bishops.

[2] Beauvais is situated in the Diocese of Besançon, close to the city. For Charlieu, see *Life of S. Bernard*, B. iv. n. 40; for Beauvais, n. 7.

your friend, that it is not expedient for you nor for your Church that the Pope should hear how you have acted.

LETTER CXCVIII. (A.D. 1141.)

To Pope Innocent.

Bernard requests that he will avenge the violence and unjust aggression which Abbot Guy has suffered.

1. In the cause which is brought before you by our dear brother Guy, Abbot of Charlieu, I have no doubt that you see plainly enough the injury of the assailant, the innocence of the sufferer, and the carelessness of the judge. The poor man, disregarding the toil of the journey, the expense and the dangers of the time, has been forced to appeal to you in person by the violence of the accuser, and by the denial of justice. He, a lover of quiet, has joined hands with death that he should not live in turmoil. I beseech you look favourably on his need and poverty, and listen to his complaint with a father's sympathy, so that his toil and sorrow may not be productive of but small results. Before this I have testified to you by my letter once and again that the man who is now attacking the Abbot is both untrue to his monastic vows and a squanderer of the means of the monastery.[1] But now I tell you, even weeping, that he is an enemy of the cross of Christ, a most violent oppressor of the saints who are in his neighbourhood, and a defrauder of the poor. Since he has hardly anything of his own to waste, he seizes violently, after the fashion of a tyrant, on his neighbours' goods on every side. A monk in habit, though a false one, a robber in fact, he shows himself altogether heedless of the Rules of his Order, he

[1] This monastery seems to be identical with the Abbey of S. Mary of Favernay, which Anseric, Archbishop of Besançon, gave, A.D. 1133, to Stephen of Mercœur, then Abbot of Chaise-Dieu. Bernard rightly calls this Stephen a man full of religion, since he is said to have been well-known for his miracles; he died the 29th March, A.D. 1146. See Letter 391.

despises the laws and canons. He has a brazen forehead, knows no scruples, is void of godliness, is easily provoked, ready to dare any crime, and to inflict any injustice. And I wonder how the Abbot of Chaise-Dieu, a man full of religion, can either be ignorant of or conceal such vices, and such glaring vices, in his own monk.

2. But what is this to me? Let him see to it. To his own master he standeth or falleth. It is enough for me to be set free from his hands. I most earnestly implore this from you, which has been in vain attempted in other ways. I looked round and there was none to help. We now have recourse to the refuge of all, we fly to him by whom we hope to be set free. You have the power, may you have the will. And, indeed, it is one of the privileges of the apostolic see that men should in the last resource look most for help to your supreme authority and plenary power. But among the other ornaments of your sole primacy, this one thing more specially and more gloriously ennobles and makes your Apostolate famous, viz., the rescue of the poor man from the hands of those who are stronger than he. In my judgment, there is no more precious jewel in your crown than the zealous care with which you are wont to strive for the oppressed, and to prevent the rod of the sinners from coming upon the lot of the righteous. Doubtless because of that which follows—*that the righteous stretch not out their hands to iniquity* (Ps. cxxv. 3); or else because of that which is said elsewhere: *When the ungodly is exalted the poor man is put to rebuke* (Ps. ix. 23, VULG.). And what tortures the body of the one destroys the soul of the other more grievously.

3. There is also a monastery of our Order near this place, which, in a similar way, is grievously harassed by the attacks of evil men, and there is no one to redeem it, or save it. And for this also your son does not shrink from stirring your fatherly compassion with his tears and prayers. Who the men are, and the occasion of their oppression, the Abbot who brings this letter will tell you by word of mouth, and truly. May Almighty God preserve

you to us for a long time, to protect us all, who are passing a life in poverty, and in the habit and purpose of repentance, in order *that we being delivered out of the hand of our enemies might serve Him without fear* (S. Luke i. 74.)

LETTER CXCIX. (A.D. 1141.)
To the Same.

Bernard begs that the decision already given in favour of certain Religious unjustly oppressed may be ratified.

How long is the ungodly to be exalted and the poor put to rebuke? How long is so great innocence to be vexed by such shamelessness, and this while Innocent lives? It is our sins doubtless which cause that my lord is so late in discovering the characters of those who lie to him, so slow in listening to those who call to him in this cause. For in other cases I know it is customary to my lord both to come to an understanding quickly and to show mercy readily. For the sake of Him who chose you and placed you as a refuge of the oppressed, put now at length an end to the malice of the oppressor, and to the sufferings of the afflicted, because both have been by this time brought into the light and manifested. In short, at the command and good pleasure of my lord the cause has been discussed and ended, and it only remains that the sentence pronounced by his authority be confirmed. If, then, the man come to you with his lies shall he be heard against the testimony of such men as the Bishops of Valence and Grenoble?[1] Again, I implore you, and I fall at the feet of my lord with the most anxious mind possible, do not suffer a religious house to be destroyed by this wicked and deceitful man. For he who has nearly destroyed his own will not spare ours. And, therefore, I add, with my wonted presumption, if you believe your son, then send back to his own cell this man who abuses your loving kindness, and give orders to the Abbot of Chaise-Dieu that he promote a man full of

[1] See Notes to Ep. 197.

religion to the place in the monastery which this man
occupies uselessly, and that he order the convent according
to the Rule. This is what is worthy of your Apostolate, this
will be well-pleasing to God, this will be an honour to the
Abbot of Chaise-Dieu, and to his monastery. And so, too,
you may set free the soul of the aforesaid man, and the
monastery itself, on which he is a burden.

LETTER CC. (A.D. 1140.)

To Magister Ulger, Bishop of Angers, concerning the Grievous Quarrel existing between him and the Abbess of Fontevrault.[1]

1. I am more inclined to shed tears than write a letter.
But since charity is not unable to do either the one or the
other, it is my duty to give the latter and not omit the
former. The one is due to you, the other to me, and to
the many weak ones like me who are made to stumble.
You say, perhaps, that the scandal is not caused by you.
Will you deny that it exists because of you? I would bear
the rest easily enough if only you were not in the cause.
For I do not dare to say you are in the wrong. It is not
my place to discuss this; there is One who seeketh and
judgeth. Woe to that man by whom the offence cometh.
Whosoever is the guilty, whether it be he or she, shall
surely bear the punishment. But my discourse is now
with you. Bear a little with my folly. What I have once

[1] Petronilla, first Abbess, who was succeeded by Matilda A.D. 1150. The death of Petronilla is placed in the Necrology on April 24th, and she is said to have been chosen for Abbess by Robert, founder of the Order of Fontevrault, a famous nunnery in the Diocese of Poictiers, not far from the borders of Tours and Angers. A bitter quarrel with the nuns was kept up by Ulger, Bishop of Angers, whose religion and learning Ordericus speaks of (lib. xii. p. 882), till the year 1124, when he was substituted for Reynold, who had been translated to the See of Rheims. He was a man excelling the other Bishops of his age in wisdom, character, and holiness (*Acts of the Bishops of Le Mans*, Vol. iii. p. 335). Because of this suit he did not at once betake himself to Rome, to Innocent and Lucius, who had undertaken the defence of the nuns, as appears from their bulls given in the *History of Fontevrault*. See Letter 340.

begun I will say to my Lord. I will satisfy in some degree, though imperfectly, the zeal and affection which prompt me to speak. I will not fear the age, I will not be terrified by the dignity, I will not pause at the great name of Magister Ulger. For the greater the name the greater the scandal. Therefore I will go beyond myself, and will be a fool. I will chide my senior, I will reprove a Bishop. I will endeavour to teach a teacher, to give counsel to the wise. The love and the emulation which I formerly conceived for your sanctity and the glory of your name may well excuse any kind of presumption. To me it is no light matter, nor is it to the Church of God, which used everywhere to rejoice with great joy in this noon-day sun, that the spiritual odour of this glory which was poured out everywhere should be interrupted even in a small degree by the envy of the devil.

2. But it is plain enough how utterly you despise your own glory. I praise you in this, but not if it is to the injury of God. I praise, too, the constancy with which you yield nothing of what you think your rights even to the highest powers, but I praise you not if you should seem to do this with more obstinacy than constancy. How much more to your glory, and certainly to your holiness, would it be if you were to bear bravely an injustice done to you, and so keep your good name for the glory of God. And yet I cannot think how you keep even your conscience in safety under this scandal. For it is no excuse even if you can rightly throw the blame on another. Be it that another has caused the scandal, surely it is in your power to end it. Will you be guiltless if you are unwilling to end it? or will the wish to end it be without glory? If the ill which you repress is your own it will redound to your righteousness; if another's, to your glory. Whoever may be the author of the scandal, on all grounds it is your duty to end it; and I can only say that on one condition only are you free from blame, viz., if it is out of your power to end it. And, finally, is it not the work of angels to remove scandals from the kingdom of God (S. Matt. xiii. 41)? If you say, What is that to the point? the verse will answer you, *The priest's*

lips keep knowledge, and they ask for the law at his mouth, for he is a messenger[1] *of the Lord* (Matt. ii. 7). If, then, you do not, when you can, end this scandal, you simply do not fulfil your ministry. And you shall judge for yourself whether that be no fault. But I do not mean to say this alone is enough; you must show it honour by acting on it.

3. There is another thing also I would add if I were not, I confess, more timid than I professed myself. But I bring forward with more safety as a teacher a Bishop who is not afraid to speak the plain truth to a Bishop. *There is utterly a fault among you,* he says, *because ye go to law one with another. Why do ye not rather suffer wrong* (1 Cor. vi. 7)? He has set up the mirror, the Sun of righteousness has shone forth, truth has shone, the spot has been made apparent. Of what importance is that little, trivial possession that it should have power any longer to cast a shade over such manifest truth, or hinder so longed-for an ending of strife? May God inspire you so as to yield to this counsel, which is not so much mine, as the counsel of all who are jealous for you with a godly jealousy, reverend father, who art worthy to attain all honour.

LETTER CCI.

To Baldwin,[2] Abbot of the Monastery of Riéti.

Bernard begs him to apply himself strenuously to the duties of his charge.

1. The letter which you have sent me is full of your affection; it stirs mine. And I am grieved that I cannot reply as I feel. Nor will I waste time in making excuses, knowing that I speak to one who knows me. You are aware

[1] *Angelus.*
[2] Not the same as Cardinal Baldwin, a disciple of Bernard, for whom turn to Letters 144 and 245. For he was a Cardinal when the other Baldwin was ruling the Cistercian Monastery of Riéti, which was in two divisions, one dedicated to S. Matthew, the other to the Holy Shepherd, and over this last Baldwin was placed.

under what a load I groan, and my groaning is not hid from you. But do not judge my affection by the shortness of my letter, for no speech would be able to express it by its length. And the trouble of my many occupations, indeed, is able to bring it about that I write in few words, but not to diminish my love. It may exclude action, or impede it, but never affection. As a mother loves her son, so did I love you when you were with me, and delighted my heart. Let me love you when absent, lest I seem to have loved you for the pleasure I received from you, and not for yourself. You were very necessary to me; and from this it may most clearly be seen how sincere is my love. I mean that I should not be this day feeling your loss if in you I had sought merely my own good. But now you see that, disregarding my own advantage, I envied not your gain when I placed you in a position from whence at some time you may be placed over all the goods of your Lord.

2. But do you see that you are found a faithful and prudent servant. See that you give their heavenly bread to your fellow servant without grudging, and that you pray without ceasing; and do not make any empty excuse about your being new to the office, and inexperienced, for this, perhaps, you feel or put on. For a barren modesty is unpleasing, and humility beyond the bounds of truth is not praiseworthy. Attend then to your office. Drive away false shame by considering the dignity of your office. Act as a teacher. You are a novice, but you are a debtor; and recognize that you became a debtor from the time you bound yourself. Will inexperience be any excuse to the creditor for the loss of his gains? Does the usurer suffer the first part of the time to go unreckoned? But I am not, you will say, sufficient for these things. As though your devotion were not accepted from what you have, and not from what you have not! Prepare to give an answer about the one talent entrusted to you, and be easy about the rest. If you have received much, give much, but if little, then give that little. For he that is not faithful in the least will

not be faithful in the greatest. Give all, because all will be asked for again from you, even to the last farthing, but only what you have, not what you have not.

3. Remember also to give to your voice the utterance of power. What is that, do you say? That your works harmonize with your words; nay, rather your words with your works; that is to say, that you take care to do first, and then to teach. It is a most beautiful and most wholesome order of things that you should first bear yourself what you impose as a burden on another, and so learn from yourself how you ought to rule others. Otherwise the Wise Man will address you as the sluggard, to whom *it is a labour to lift up his hand to his mouth* (Prov. xxvi. 15). The Apostle, too, will reprove you: *Thou that teachest others, dost thou not teach thyself?* (Rom. ii. 21). Moreover, you will be stamped with the fault of the Pharisees, who *bind heavy burdens, and grievous to be borne, and lay them on men's shoulders, but they themselves will not move them with one of their fingers* (S. Matt. xxiii. 4). The example set by actual work is indeed a speech that is living and efficacious, easily making that which is said persuasive, by showing that that which is ordered can be done. On these two kinds of commands, viz., of word and example, understand that there hang the whole of your duty, and the safety of your conscience. Yet if you are wise you will add a third, viz., devotion to prayer, as a kind of complement of that threefold repetition in the Gospel concerning feeding the sheep (S. John xxi. 15-17). In this way you will find that the Sacrament of this Trinity is in nothing made void by you if you feed by word, by example, and by the fruit of holy prayers. And now abideth these three—word, example, prayer; but the greatest of these is prayer. For although, as I said, work is the life of the word spoken, yet prayer gives both to work and word grace and efficacy. Alas! I am called away; I must go; I cannot write more. Let me, however, briefly implore you to take care to free me as soon as you can from one heavy care, and forget not to say more plainly what you mean when you complain,

among other things, that you have received a wound from one from whom you did not expect it. For that gives me much anxiety.

LETTER CCII. (A.D. 1144.)

TO THE CLERGY OF THE ARCHDIOCESE OF SENS.

He warns them that the election of a new Prelate should not be entered upon rashly or precipitately.

Now that you have been deprived of your blessed pastor[1] it is your duty, dearly beloved, to take great care in the selection of a successor to him. It must not be taken in hand hastily, confusedly, or inconsiderately, lest perchance what is done presumptuously against reason and due order be annulled, and so you begin to enter on the same weary round as some of your neighbours have done. Take an example, if you please, from the neighbouring churches,[2] and let their troubles be a warning to you in the present case. It is a great matter that you are engaged on, this of supplying a pastor to the renowned Church of Sens. It is truly a great matter, and not one to be lightly undertaken. Wait for the advice of the suffragan bishops, wait for the assenting voice of all the faithful in the diocese, and transact in common this matter which is of importance to all in common. Otherwise, dearly beloved, believe me, we shall to our grief behold your Church under tribulation. To our grief we shall have to look upon your confusion. Both of which will readily take place if such action take place as will have to be recalled. Therefore, let a fast be proclaimed, let the Bishops be assembled, let the Religious be invited to be present, so that the election of so exalted a priest may be duly celebrated, and may not be deprived of its proper solemnity, which God forbid. We believe that so the Holy Spirit will assist your prayers; that honour will be added to you if you honour your ministry, provided

---

[1] Henry, succeeded A.D. 1144 by Hugh, Abbot of Pontigny.
[2] Viz., Orleans (Ep. 156), Chalons (Ep. 224), Langres (Ep. 164, *et seq.*)

you diligently seek, with prayer and common counsel, alike what is most for the glory of God, and the good of the people.

LETTER CCIII. (*Circa* A.D. 1140.)

To the Bishop and Clergy of Troyes.

Bernard presses them to forbid marriage and a military career to a clerk named Anselle.

We read: *If any of you do err from the truth, and one convert him, let him know that he which converteth the sinner from the error of his ways shall save a soul from death and shall hide a multitude of sins* (S. James v. 19, 20). Our friend Anselle is erring, is erring. Who doubts it? If we dismiss him thus, he will not err alone. How many will the illustrious youth not draw after him by his example? And we judge to be involved in the same error not only those who follow him, but also all who may be able to call him back and do not. I am clean from his blood. I have both told him before by letter, and I now tell you that he is presumptuously undertaking what is forbidden. It is not the part of a clerk to fight in worldly warfare, nor of a subdeacon to marry. Tell the sinner his duty, lest he die in his sins, and He who redeemed him with His own precious blood require his blood at your hands. Lo He cries from Heaven: *The Virgin of Israel is fallen; there is none to raise her up* (Amos v. 2). How long is gold to lie in the mire? Remove this pearl, remove, take up this most splendid and precious jewel from the dunghill. Take it up before it be trodden under foot by swine, that is by unclean spirits, and be no more a vessel for honour but for dishonour.

LETTER CCIV. (*Circa* A.D. 1140).
To the Abbot of S. Aubin.[1]

Bernard declares his affection for him and his wish to see him.

Though you are unknown to me by face, yet you are not by renown; and it is very precious to me to know you thus. For such an image of you has stolen into my heart through this report, that though I am occupied with many things, yet, my dear brother, that pleasing thought of you often calls me from them all, so that I dwell on it willingly and with pleasure. But the more I cherish the thought of you, the more eagerly do I long to see you. But when will that be? or will it ever be? Certainly if not before, at all events we shall meet in the city of our God, if here we have no abiding city, but seek one above. There, there shall I see you, and my heart shall rejoice. In the meanwhile I shall be delighted and pleased none the less with what I hear from you, hoping and expecting to see you face to face in the day of the Lord, that my joy may be full. Add, I pray you, to those good things which are always coming to me from you and about you, my dear and longed-for brother, your own prayers and those of your brethren for me.

LETTER CCV. (*Circa* A.D. 1140.)
To the Bishop of Rochester.[2]

Bernard complains of the severity of his letter, which he has done nothing to deserve.

You write severely to one who does not deserve it.

---

[1] Others read S. *Albans*, a famous monastery in England, founded by King Offa. But our reading of S. Aubins is to be preferred; this was a monastery in Anjou, from which William went, and "was received by the Abbot Bernard, and displayed such grace in his virtues that his sanctity seemed marvellous even to the perfect."

[2] Ascelin or Anselm was then presiding over this English See. He succeeded John, A.D. 1137, and was Bishop of it for 10 years.—[Mabillon's Note.] But according to the Diocesan Registers, the Diocese was administered by John of Seez for five years from A.D. 1137, and Ascelin was consecrated in A.D. 1142. This Letter should therefore be dated not before 1142. See note on next page.—[E.]

What have I done wrong? If I advised Master Robert Pullen[1] to spend some time at Paris, because of the sound learning which is known to be gained there, it was because I thought it necessary for him, and I still think so. If I asked your Highness to permit it, I would again make the same request, if I were not aware that you had rejected my former petition. If I said that the man is supported by the kindness of his friends, whose influence at the Curia is by no means small, I said it because I had fears for you, and I still have. For in that after appeal was made, you, as I hear, stretched out your hand to the property of the appellant; I neither praised you in this, nor do I now. But certainly I never advised him, nor do I now, to go against your wish in any way. For the rest I am your servant,

[1] An Englishman by birth. He first studied letters at Paris, and then, returning to his native land, restored the school at Oxford, which had well nigh perished. He was then summoned to Rome, because of his intellectual gifts and great learning, by Innocent II., who created him a Cardinal under the title of S. Eusebius. He was the first Cardinal of his nation, unless a certain Ulrinus is earlier than he. But in what year? In 1134, if we believe Onuphrius and Ciaconius. One thing is very evident, and that is, that he had not obtained this dignity when this Letter was written, which from its place in the list of S. Bernard's Letters seems to have been penned about A.D. 1140. In the next place Godwin says that this Letter was sent to Anselm, or Ascelin, who, in the year 1137, was made Bishop of Rochester. Again, at the end of his Letter Bernard thanks the Bishop of Rochester for having shown care for "his children, the sons that he had sent into Ireland." But that no monks of the Cistercian Order lived in Ireland before the year 1139, when S. Malachy first went to Clairvaux, is evident from what S. Bernard says in his life of him (cxvi.), where he writes that some of his companions had been sent by the holy Bishop to Clairvaux to learn the Cistercian rule, who took it back with them to Ireland in the year 1141, when the monastery of Mellifont was founded, which was the first Cistercian foundation in that province, except that of S. Mary at Dublin, which some writers say submitted itself to the Cistercian rule about the year 1139. And, therefore, the opinion of the Anglo-Benedictine writer is preferable (it is referred to in the preface to the works of Pullen), who holds that Robert Pullen was invited to Rome by Innocent, was again proclaimed Cardinal by his successor, Lucius, afterwards obtained the dignity of Chancellor, and died under Eugenius III. They call him the oldest of Theologians; his remains, which were indexed by Pitsæus, prove his great learning. They would have altogether perished had they not been rescued by Hugh Mathoud, head of the Benedictine house of S. Columba, at Sens, who published eight books of his Sentences, illustrated by learned notes. If more about him is wanted it will be found in the notes to Letter 334.

ready always to hold and honour your crown[1] in due and worthy veneration. I venture again on the strength of this consciousness to pray and advise you that Master Robert with your full goodwill may be allowed to spend some time at Paris. May the Lord repay you in eternal life the good you have done to my offspring, I mean my sons whom I have sent into Ireland.

LETTER CCVI.
To the Queen of Jerusalem.[2]

Bernard recommends to her one of his relatives; and exhorts the Queen so to live that she may reign for ever.

Men tell me that I have some influence with you, and many who are about to set out for Jerusalem ask for a recommendation from me to your Excellency. Amongst whom is this young relation of mine, a youth, they say, bold in arms, and of polished manners. And I rejoice that at his age he has chosen to fight for God rather than for the world. And so do according to your custom, and let it be well with him for my sake, as it has always been with all my other relations who have been able by my means to make themselves known to you. As to the rest, see that the pleasure of the flesh and worldly glory do not block up your road to the heavenly kingdom. For what advantage is it to reign for a few days over the earth and to lose the eternal kingdom in the Heavens? But I trust in the Lord that you will do better; and if the testimony is true which my dear uncle Andrew bears concerning you, and I place great reliance on him, you will, by the mercy of God, reign both here and in eternity. Bestow care on pilgrims, the needy, and prisoners, for with such sacrifices God is well pleased. Write to me more often; for it will not hurt you, and will help me if I know more fully and more certainly of your state[3] and of your good dispositions.

---

[1] S. Bernard not unfrequently addresses Bishops, *more veterum*, as having a crown, i.e., royal honour. See Ep. 221.

[2] This was Melisendis, to whom Letters 289, 354, 355 were written.

[3] *Esse vestrum*: i.e., *statum*.

LETTER CCVII. (A.D. 1139.)

To Roger, King of Sicily.

Bernard begs him to be kind and liberal towards poor Religious.

Far and wide the renown of your magnificence has spread over the earth. For what lands are there to which the glory of your name has not reached?[1] But listen to the advice of me who loves you. Endeavour as much as in you lies to refer this same glory to Him from whom it comes, if you do not wish to destroy it, or to be destroyed by it. This certainly will happen if you open the eye of discretion upon those whom the well-known report of your magnificence calls to you from afar, and if you stretch out your hand not so much to the greedy as to the poor. Truly, *Blessed is he that considereth* not the greedy, but *the poor and needy* (Ps. xli. 1). The poor, I repeat, who asks unwillingly, receives modestly, and when he receives glorifies his Father which is in Heaven. Since, then, His own glory will be so faithfully given to God from the mouth of the needy because of your gift, that fount of glory must flow for you with more fruitful stream,

---

[1] Bernard now addresses Roger in very different terms from what he had used before; doubtless because, as he was not in the habit of sparing sinners, so he was gentle and kind to the repentant; and when the character had been changed he knew how to change his style, as he says at the end of Letter 224. It seems, then, that Roger had repented himself of having been a foe to the Church, a disturber of peace, a fomenter of schism, a persecutor of Pope Innocent, and a rival of the Emperor. His ferocity had been so great that he spared neither sacred things nor persons, nor his dead enemies (Otto of Frisingen lib. vii. c. 23; *Baronius* Vol. xii., year 1136). Thence Bernard had spoken of him as, "the Sicilian tyrant" in Letters 130 and 136; as "an intruder upon the royal crown, the Sicilian usurper," in Letter 139; as "the Duke of Apulia whom Pope Anacletus had drawn to his side by the ridiculous bribe of an usurper's crown," in Letter 127. Peter, Abbot of Cluny, speaks of him in high terms (lib. iv. ep. 37). At all events, when he had submitted to Pope Innocent, although he held him captive, he obtained a confirmation of his royal crown (*Baronius, Annals*, year 1139), and invited to his realms religious, both Cluniacs and Cistercians. He had, too, a great desire to see Bernard, as appears from the next Letter.

VOL. II.

for *He loves those who love Him, and glorifies those who glorify Him; just as he who sows blessings shall reap blessings* (2 Cor. ix. 6). For this reason I beseech you cast your eyes on the bearer of this letter, for most certainly it is not greed that has drawn him to your presence, but necessity that has forced him to come. Necessity, I say, not his own, but of his brethren, viz., the many faithful servants of God by whom he has been sent. Hear patiently what they have to be patient under; hear and suffer with them; for if you suffer with them you shall reign with them. To reign with such is not to be scorned, even by a king. For the kingdom of heaven is theirs who have despised the life of the world. *Make to yourself friends of the mammon of unrighteousness, that when you fail out of your earthly kingdom they may receive you into their heavenly kingdom* (S. Luke xvi. 9).

LETTER CCVIII. (A.D. 1139.)

To the Same.

The King had desired to see him; he sends some of his brethren in his place.

If you ask for me, here am I, and my children which God has given to me. For my humility is said to have found favour with the King's majesty, so that he seeks to see me. And who am I that I should go against the good pleasure of the King? I hasten and say to him who sought me: Lo! here I am, not in the weak bodily presence which Herod mocked in the Lord (S. Luke xxiii. 11), but in my children. For who shall separate me from them? I will follow them wherever they go; even if they dwell in the uttermost parts of the sea, they shall not be without me. You have, O King, the light of my eyes, you have my heart and my soul. What if my meanest part is absent? I mean my worthless body, that vile possession, which necessity retains, though the will would gladly give it up. It is not able to follow the will, since it is weak, and almost the only thing awaiting it is the tomb. But why need this be a care? My soul shall dwell among the good, when my seed shall inherit the earth. My seed, my good seed shall spring up, that is if it falls into good soil. My soul shall rejoice and delight herself in fatness, because, I trust, there shall be given to her of the fruit of her hands. This hope of mine is laid up in my heart, so that I can patiently bear to be separated from them in body. Do not wonder, O King. I would rather have been absent from the body, than to send them away, if the cause had not been God's alone. Receive them as strangers and pilgrims, as fellow citizens with the saints and of the household of God; nay, not citizens, they are kings. For theirs is the kingdom of heaven by the right and merit of poverty. It is not fitting that they should have been summoned from afar to no purpose, and wander as exiles from their home in a useless pilgrimage. Do you suppose they will be able to sing the Lord's song in a strange land? But perhaps I am wrong in calling it a strange land, for it has opened its heart of its own accord to receive the good seed, and has taken in the precious deposit to be piously fostered in its kindly bosom. It has fallen, I see, the good seed has fallen into a good, nay, an excellent, soil; I hope in the Lord that it will take root, spring up, multiply, and *bring forth fruit with patience* (S. Luke viii. 15). Then will I share this with the King, and *each one shall receive according to his labour* (1 Cor. iii. 8).

LETTER CCIX.

To the Same.

Bernard praises the King's munificence in receiving and maintaining the Religious sent to him.

You have what you asked for, you have done what you promised. Those whom, according to your word, we selected and sent abroad to you have been received with princely generosity. You have met them with bread, you have brought them into a pleasant place, you have placed them on a lofty spot, that they may eat the fruits of the fields, suck honey out of the rock, and oil from the hard stone; may have butter and milk from the herd, and from the sheep, and honey with the flour of wheat, and may drink the choicest blood of the grape. These, indeed, are earthly blessings, but they purchase heavenly. Such is the way to heaven; with such sacrifices God is well pleased. For the kingdom of heaven is theirs who in the land of the living will have power to render to the earthly king for these earthly benefits life and everlasting glory. I have sent you Master Bruno, formerly for a long time the companion of my solitude, but now the father of many souls who rejoice in Christ indeed, but are poor in this world's goods. Let him, too, experience the generous hand of the King that the number of those may be increased who may receive him into everlasting habitations. What you do for him, you do for me; for what he lacks has to be supplied by me. But, as my purse is not very full, I have directed Christ's poor monk to look to yours, which, as everyone knows, is somewhat more full than mine.

LETTER CCX. (*Circa* A.D. 1139.)

To Pope Innocent.

He recommends to the Pontiff the Archbishop of Rheims.

I recommend the Lord Bishop of Rheims[1] to your Holiness, not merely as one of many, but as one above the rest. And I do so the more confidently as I am confident of his faithful devotion to you, his sincere love, his submissive and obedient disposition. Let him be honoured, since he is a vessel made to honour. Let him be made to feel, as much as in you lies, that he does not honour his ministry in vain, that it is not in vain that he excels in those virtues by which God is honoured and the Church adorned, which, in short, become the priest of the Lord.

[1] Samson.

LETTER CCXI. (*Circa* A.D. 1139.)
To the Same.

He recommends the cause of the Archbishop of Canterbury and of the Bishop of London.

My Lord of Canterbury,[1] a good man, and one who has the testimony of good men, is unjustly dragged into a dispute, and violently held back from acting. He was preparing to start (for in your presence the dispute was to be settled), when he was stopped by a hurricane and tempest of wars. Please excuse him, for the necessity of excusing himself is a trouble to him, not only because he is sure of getting justice at your hands, but also because he greatly desired to see your face. Your son adds also this, that if the venerable priest[2] should make any other request of you, please grant it the more quickly, as he who makes it is the more worthy. As I have begun, I venture to say one thing more to my lord. Your old friend, faithful servant, and devoted son, Robert, Bishop of London, appeals to you, because he who preceded him in the See[3] to which God has called him has appropriated the goods and lands of his Church, and refuses to make restitution.[4] And how injurious this is, and how it is to be corrected it ill would become my humility to dictate to so great wisdom.

LETTER CCXII. (A.D. 1139.)
To the Same.

He pleads pathetically with the Pontiff the cause of the Bishop of Salamanca, praising his remarkable humility.

[1] Theobald, formerly Abbot of Bec.

[2] Bernard everywhere, as a loving student of antiquity, retains old names; as here, Sacerdos, by which name those even of the first Order were wont to be called in olden times (above, Letters 61 and 202).

[3] This was apparently Anselm, Abbot of Bury, "elected A.D. 1134, but afterwards set aside." Robert's accession to the See was not until A.D. 1141: and according to English accounts, it was in 1147 that Archbishop Theobald, being oppressed by Henry of Blois, the Papal Legate, was driven into exile. So that the date of this Letter must be somewhat later than stated in the text.—[E.]

[4] *I.e.*, as securities.

That illustrious man who was formerly Bishop of Salamanca, when returning from Rome, did not think it too much trouble to turn aside to your son, nor thought it beneath him to ask help from one so feeble as I am.[1] And when I had heard him I called to mind the words of the prophet: *Every mountain and hill shall be made low before God, and the crooked places shall be made straight, and the rough places plain* (Is. xl. 4). Even so you know how to make sport of and repress the lofty, to abase the proud, and to reduce to their measure those who go beyond their rule. But when the man had told me in detail the history of his troubles, I commended the judge, I approved the verdict, but, I confess to you, I also felt compassion for the man, though condemned. And so, as it was, indeed, through the whole of that tearful account, he finished as one who would say with the prophet: *Having been exalted, I was humbled and put to confusion* (Ps. lxxxvii. 16, VULG.); and, *Thou hast raised me up only to cast me down* (Ps. cii. 10). And when I thought of your justice, and the nobility of mind which I know you to have, I began to think at the same time of the riches of your mercy, which in many cases I have made trial of, and I said, *Who knows whether the Lord will turn and pardon, and leave a blessing behind Him?* Certainly, I repeat, he has been taught, in all things, and in all ways, both to be jealous, and to pardon, both to tame the haughty, and by no means to spare the conquered; except that, following his Master, he is also accustomed to let mercy triumph over justice. And I, who am dust and ashes, consented to write with that wonted presumption of mine to my lord. And I found ground for hope, confidence for my request,

---

[1] This was the Peter who, when the Church of Salamanca was long labouring under a threefold schism, was summoned to Rome by Innocent while boasting himself in his rights of possession, and was degraded with the other litigants. Then Peter betook himself to Cluny, and then to Bernard, and would, perhaps, have obtained re-instatement in his dignity had not the Bishops of Toledo, Zamora, and Segovia, sent to Rome by King Alphonso, intervened, and secured the election of Berengarius, King Alphonso's Chancellor. (Manriquez, on the year 1139.)

reason for my doing him this kindness, in the fact that the man is not, as is usual, departing in indignation, filled with anger, and going back to his native land to cause scandals, to excite seditions; but he has given place to wrath, and has put on the spirit of meekness; he has turned aside to your monks of Cluny, and prostrated himself before the knees of the humble, and has joined them in their prayers as arms that are powerful from God. He has resolved to contend with you with these weapons, and he will endeavour to undermine with these engines of devotion, as he boasts, the wall of your severity which now stands in his way. He trusts also that you will regard the prayer of the humble, and not despise their petition, and that piety will overcome him before whom the powers of the world tremble. I, too, with confidence stretch out my hands with them, bend my knees, supplicate for the suppliant, boldly declare that his humility ought to help the unhappy man, since his pride has so injured him, and say that it is unbecoming for virtue to be surpassed by vice in receiving recompense.

LETTER CCXIII. (A.D. 1139.)
To the Same.

He expostulates that the reconciliation of Peter of Pisa, made by him with the Pope's own authority, has been held invalid.

Who will do me justice against you? If I had a judge before whom I could take you I would quickly show you what you deserve—I speak as one in travail. There is, indeed, the tribunal of Christ; but far be it from me to summon you there, for if it were necessary for you and possible to me, I would far rather stand there and answer for you with all my strength. And so I appeal to him to whom, for the present, power has been given to judge all things, *i.e.*, to you yourself. I summon you before yourself, to judge between us. In what, I ask, has your son deserved so ill from his father, that it has seemed good to you to brand and stamp him with the mark and the name of traitor? Did you not think it good to constitute me your Vicar in the matter of reconciling Peter of Pisa, if perchance God should vouchsafe to recall him by my means from the mire of schism? If you deny it I will prove it by the many witnesses that were in your Curia at the time. Was he not after this, according to the instructions of my lord, restored to his rank and honour? Who is it, then, who by his advice, or rather his craft, has stealthily undone what your indulgence granted, and made void the words which proceeded out of your lips? And I say this, not to blame your apostolic severity, and your zeal kindled from the fire of God against schismatics, which with a mighty wind breaks the ships of Tarshish, and like Phinehas slays the fornicators, according to the verse, *Do not I hate them, O Lord, which hate Thee, and am not I grieved with them that rise up against Thee* (Ps. cxxxix. 21)? But where the guilt is not equal, the punishment clearly should not be equal; nor ought he who has forsaken his sin to be under the same sentence as he whose sin has forsaken him. For the sake of Him who to spare sinners spared not Himself, take away my reproach; and, by re-establishing what you first established, consult the credit of your first sound and perfect opinion. I wrote to you before on this matter; but as I have received no reply, I presume that the letter did not reach you.

LETTER CCXIV. (*Circa* A.D. 1140.)

To the Same.

He recommends Nicholas, Bishop of Cambray, and Abbot Gottschalk.

If any regard for me, any recollection, however slight, of me, still remains in the heart of my lord, and if his child finds any small portion of the grace he once found in his sight, let him now experience it on behalf of that illustrious

and humble man, Nicholas,[1] Bishop of Cambray. I confess
that I am under obligation to him, and that I am in debt
for all that I can do, not only because he honours me and
mine, whenever he can, but also for his uprightness, meekness, and justice, virtues which can recommend him also to
you. And, if I mistake not, those who trouble him are
false men, and truth is not in their mouth. In short, you
are sure to approve of him, and there is no need for me to
multiply words about him. He has, too, with him a religious
and holy man, Abbot Gottschalk,[2] on behalf of whom, in
like manner, I earnestly ask a hearing for his requests, if
my intervention can lend any power to his merits. For I
believe that he will make no petition which is unworthy of
being granted.

LETTER CCXV. (*Circa* A.D. 1140.)

To the Same.

He intercedes on behalf of the Bishop of Auxerre.

I write to you very often, I, a worthless little worm; and
I am impelled to this boldness by the entreaties of my
friends. I confess I am bold, but not false.[3] Let not my
lord suspect that falsehood will be found in the words of
his child in any letter he sends him. I wish to comply with
the wishes of my friends, but not to my death. For I do not
forget what I have read: *A mouth that belieth slayeth the
soul* (Wisd. i. 11). I deny, then, falsehood, I confess importunity; this will find pardon, the rest I fear not. The
Bishop of Auxerre[4] is a special friend of mine. Who does
not know him? He is able to communicate anxiety to his

---

[1] In most copies neither the name, nor even the initial, is found. One copy only has the name in the margin. Nicholas presided over the Church of Cambray from A.D. 1140 to A.D. 1167.

[2] These words "of S. Martin's Mount" are wanting in all the manuscripts, and so is Gottschalk in some, others have the initial G. He was Abbot of Mount S. Martin at Arras, of the Order of Præmonstratensians, and is praised in Letter 253, n. 4; he was afterwards Bishop of Arras (see Letter 284).

[3] *Audax non mendax.*

[4] Hugh.

friend, but not falsehood. We bring before you a trustworthy defence of his dean, and we ask for absolution for him. I speak with my wonted presumption when I say that we are sons of the same father, viz., of yourself. I hope that my father will not reject his sons, but will do the will of them that *fear him, and will hear their cry, and will make them joyful* (Ps. cxlv. 19).

LETTER CCXVI. (A.D. 1142.)

To the Same.

He complains that Count Ralph, who had repudiated his wife and taken another, finds supporters in the Curia.

It is written: *Whom God hath joined together let not man put asunder* (S. Matt. xix. 6). Audacious men have arisen, and have not shrunk from disjoining those whom God has joined together.[1] Nor is that all; they have gone farther, and joined together persons whom it is forbidden to unite, thus adding sin to sin. The sacred rites of the Church are violated, and alas! the robe of Christ is rent, and that, to crown the sorrow, by the hands of those who ought to have kept it whole. *Thy friends and thy neighbours, O God, have come near and stood against Thee* (Ps. xxxvii. 12, VULG.). For they who are transgressing Thy command are not foreigners, not strangers to Thy sanctuary, but they hold the place of those to whom was said: *If ye love me keep My commandments* (S. John xiv. 15). Count Ralph and his wife had been joined together by God through the ministers of the Church, and by the

[1] The Bishops named here, who approved of the divorce of Ralph, Count of Vermandois, were Simon of Tournay his brother, Bartholomew of Laon, and Peter of Senlis. Count Ralph had conceived a desire to be married to the sister of Eleanor, Queen of the French, named Petronilla, and he consequently, with the approbation of the three Bishops named above, repudiated his lawful wife, a niece of Theobald, Count of Champagne, under the plea of consanguinity. A complaint about the matter came to the ears of the Pope through Count Theobald, and he pronounced his anathema against the Count, and suspended the three Bishops for some time from their office.

Church through God who had given such power unto men. Why did the Court disjoin those whom God had joined? And in so doing provision was made as was fitting for one thing only, viz., that the works of darkness should be done in darkness. For he who does wrong hates the light, and does not come into the light, that his works may be reproved by the light. What has Count Theobald deserved, what wrong has he done? If to love righteousness and hate iniquity be a sin, he cannot be excused. If it be a sin to render to the King the things which are the King's, and to God the things which are God's, he cannot be excused. If at your command he received the Archbishop of Bourges, this is his first and greatest sin.[1] Lo! this is the crime which is laid at his door. They who render evil for good calumniate him because he follows the thing that good is. Many are calling to you from the depths of their hearts to visit with fitting punishment the wrong done to your son, and the oppression the Church is subjected to, and to restrain the workers of this wickedness with their leader, with whatever Apostolic force you wish and are able to put forth, that so their wickedness may descend upon their own head.

LETTER CCXVII. (A.D. 1142.)
To the Same.

He complains that Count Theobald is suffering for the cause of justice, and for his fidelity to the Apostolic See.

Tribulation and anguish have found us out. The earth trembles and quakes at the deaths of men, at the banish-

---

[1] This was the cause of the hostility [of the King of France] to Theobald, about which we find Hermann saying: "The Pope consecrated as Archbishop of Bourges a certain clerk named Peter, a relation of his Chancellor; and because the King refused to receive him he was excommunicated." This was in the year 1144, after the death of Archbishop Alberic. You will gather more from the notes to Letter 219, where you will find how badly Theobald was treated by the King for giving an asylum to Peter *Cf.* Letter 219 and *Life of S. Bernard* lib. iv. n. 12.

ment of the poor, at the arrest and imprisonment of the rich. Even religion itself has come into shame and contempt. Only to make mention of peace is counted a disgrace amongst us. Nowhere are faith and innocence safe. Count Theobald, a lover of innocence, and a seeker after holiness, has been almost delivered over to the will of his enemies. He was struck at that he might fall, but the Lord sustained him; and it is a consolation to him that justice and obedience to you are at stake, because of the Apostle's words: *If ye suffer for righteousness sake, happy are ye* (1 S. Peter iii. 14). And again it is written in the Gospel: *Blessed are they who endure persecution for righteousness* (S. Matt. v. 10). Woe to us! we have been able to foresee, but not to take precautions against these evils. What more can I say? In order that the land might not be wholly laid desolate, and the whole kingdom, divided against itself, fall, that most devoted son of yours, and defender of the Church's liberty, has been compelled to promise under an oath that he would do what he could to induce you to remove the sentence of excommunication pronounced against the land and person of the adulterous tyrant,[1] who has been the head and originator of all these evils and sorrows, by your legate Ivo of good memory, as also against the adulteress herself, which the aforesaid prince did at the entreaty and advice of some faithful and wise men. For they said that without any injury to the Church it would be easy to obtain from you a renewal of the decree, and an irrevocable confirmation of the same sentence which had been justly pronounced; so would artifice be eluded by artifice and peace obtained; and he who boasts himself in wickedness and is powerful in iniquity would gain no advantage. I have many things to say to you, but there is no need to write about everything, when there is one present who knows all, and can acquaint you with them more plainly and completely by word of mouth.

[1] Ralph.

LETTER CCXVIII. (A.D. 1143.)

HIS LAST LETTER TO INNOCENT II.; IN SELF DEFENCE.

Bernard having remarked that he had lost the favour of Pope Innocent, on account of the will of Cardinal Ivo, humbly justifies himself.

To his lord and most reverend Father INNOCENT, BERNARD, a thing of nought, wishes health.

1. I used to think at one time that I was of some account, though of small; but now I feel I have simply been reduced to nothing while I knew it not. For I would never have said that I was nothing at all while the eyes of my lord were over his child, and his ears open to my prayers, whilst all that I wrote he received with open hands, read with smiling face, and while he answered most graciously and fully all my demands. But now I do not say that I am of small account, I am of none; because since yesterday and the day before his face has been turned away from me. Why is this? what wrong have I done? Much, I admit, if the money of Cardinal Ivo, of good memory, was distributed according to my will, and not according to his directions, for I am told that this has been brought before the notice of my lord. But I trust that by this time you know the truth of this matter, and the truth shall make me free. I am not so dull as not to know that whatever he left no directions about becomes the property of the Church.

2. But now hear the simple truth. If falsehood is found in my mouth, my own mouth shall condemn me. When the man put off his mortal frame I was absent, nay, at a long distance. But I heard from those who were present that he made his will, and had what he wanted written down; and of his property he divided what he would to whom he would, and whatever was over he entrusted to the two Abbots who were assisting him, and to me who was absent, with a view to its distribution; because the poorer places of the saints were known to us. Then the Abbots returned home, and not finding me (for I was kept at that time in accordance with your orders by the negotia-

tions for peace), they nevertheless divided the money as seemed good to them, I not only not conniving, but not even knowing what they had done. Let now, if you please, your indignation give place to this manifest truth, and henceforward look upon me not frowningly or in displeasure; but let your wonted serenity return to your kind and gracious countenance, and let your face once more assume its brightness and joy.

3. As to your complaint that you have found much in my letters to displease you, I shall not have to fear it any longer, for it is a fault which I will soon cure. I know it, I know it, I have presumed more than I ought to have done; not thinking sufficiently who I was and to whom I was presuming to scribble; but you will not deny that your kindness had armed me with that boldness. And then the love of my friends urged me to it; for I wrote very little on my own account, if I recollect aright. But enough of this. I will for the future put a rein on my zeal, be more wise, and put my finger to my lips. For it will be more tolerable to offend some of my friends than to weary with many prayers the Lord's anointed. And at this time too I have not ventured to write to you about the dangers overhanging the Church, and about the grievous schism which I fear, and the many evils we are suffering from. But I have written to the holy Bishops around your person; you can, if you wish it, hear from them what I have written.

LETTER CCXIX. (A.D. 1143.)

To Three[1] Bishops of the Curia; Alberic[2] of Ostia, Stephen of Præneste, Igmarus of Tusculum,[3] and to the Chancellor Gerard.

[1] The common reading "three" is better than "four," which is found in some MSS.; for Gerard the Chancellor was not a Bishop. He was afterwards made Pontiff under the name of Lucius II.

[2] Alberic of Verdun in France was dead; Bernard is recorded to have offered the Sacrifice of praise at his tomb (*Life*, lib. iv. n. 21). He is mentioned in Letter 241; Stephen in Letter 224.

[3] Igmarus, or Ymarus, was a Cluniac monk of S. Martin des Champs, then

Respecting the interdict laid on the realm of France on account of the Archbishop of Bourges.

1. How great an evil is schism in the Church, and how it is to be detested and in every way avoided, is plainly shown by the well known dreadful death of those men whom the earth swallowed up and sent down alive into hell because of this very pest. It has been shown too by the persecution of Guibert,[1] and the rashness of Bourdin, whom our times have seen separating between the kingdom and the priesthood, and so inflicting on them both an almost incurable wound and a cruel chastisement. It has been shown too by the mad schism of Leo, which after grievous and manifold trouble and loss to the Church has lately by the mercy of God received its death blow. Well then does the Saviour say in the Gospel: *Woe to that man by whom the offence cometh* (S. Matt. xviii. 7). Woe to us who live bewailing what we have endured, grieving for what we feel, and fearing what we expect. And what is worse, human affairs are come to such an evil pass that the guilty are not willing to be humbled, nor the judges to show mercy. We say to the wicked: *Deal not so wickedly;* and to the sinners: *Lift not up your horn* (Ps. lxxv. 5), and they will not listen to us, *for it is a rebellious house* (Ezek. ii. 5). We beseech those whose office it is to rebuke the sin to save the sinner, not to break the bruised reed, and not quench the smoking flax, and they all the more break the ships of Tarshish with a violent wind.

Prior of La Charité sur Loire, then Abbot of the New Monastery in Poictiers (under which name he took part in drawing up an agreement made between Louis the younger and Argrimus, Archdeacon of Orleans: see *Duchesne*, Vol. iv. p. 764), and was finally created a Cardinal by Innocent. He was a man of great integrity, as appears from the *Cluniac Chronicle* under the Abbot Pontius. To these Cardinals Letter 230 and the two following were also written.

[1] So named from Guibert, Bishop of Ravenna, whom the Emperor Henry IV. set up as antipope in opposition to Gregory VII., and the three following legitimate Pontiffs. Maurice Burdin also, Archbishop of Braga, was intruded into the Roman See by Henry V., and was at last compelled by Calixtus II. to retire to the monastery of Cava. His life was written in a pleasing style by Stephen Baluze (*Misc.* Vol. iii).

2. When, with the Apostle, we bid sons obey their parents in all things, we may as well beat the air. When we tell parents not to provoke their children to anger, we only call down their anger on our own heads. Sinners no longer will consent to give satisfaction, nor those who bear the rule or the rod in any wise to condescend. All follow their own pride and passion; and, pulling a rope with all their might in different directions, they break it. Alas! the scar of the wound so recently given to the Church[1] has hardly healed over, when they are again doing all they can to tear it open, to nail the Body of Christ to the cross, to pierce again His unoffending side, to divide His garments, and, though in vain, as far as in them lies, to rend asunder His robe which is woven without seam. If you have any feelings of piety, set yourselves against such evils, lest a schism take place on that soil where, as you well know, other schisms are wont to be healed. For if the author of a scandal is stricken specially by a tremendous curse from the mouth of his Judge, of what blessings may we suppose that they are worthy who conquer and put to flight this wickedness?

3. Of two wrongs I cannot acquit the King. For he both took an unlawful oath and perseveres in it contrary to justice.[2]

[1] Viz., the schism of Anacletus.

[2] William of Nangis thus relates the affair in his Chronicle:—"In the year 1142 a dispute arose between Pope Innocent and Louis, King of the French, by which the Gallican Church was disturbed. For on the death of Alberic, Archbishop of Bourges, Peter was consecrated and sent by the Pope to succeed him. But Louis rejected him, and refused to receive him because he had been consecrated without his consent. Now, King Louis had given permission to the Church of Bourges to choose whom they would, except Peter alone, and had taken an oath publicly that while he lived Peter should not be Archbishop. Yet for all that he was elected and went to Rome, and was consecrated by the Pope, who said, 'We must teach and curb this boy-king, lest he get used to such actions,' and he added, 'That is no true freedom of choice when an exception of any person is made by the King, unless he is proved before an ecclesiastical judge to be incapable of election. For then he has a hearing like anyone else.' But the King, as I said before, refused to receive the Archbishop on his return. Then Count Theobald welcomed him into his country, and he ruled the churches from there. This enraged the King, and he called together his vassals and made war on Theobald." This is William's account, and from it we must correct that of Matthew of Paris, who places the affair in the year 1146. This dispute reached

But he does so not so much from his own will as from a sense of honour ill-directed. For it is reckoned disgraceful, as you know, among the French, to break an oath, however much the oath may be against the public good, although no wise man doubts that unlawful oaths ought not to be kept. But not even so can I admit that he is to be excused. For I have not undertaken to excuse him, but to ask pardon. See whether passion, his age, or his high rank can in any degree be his excuse. It will avail him, no doubt, if you decide that mercy is to be exalted above judgment, viz., in so far as such excuse is to be taken into consideration in the case of a king, who is but a lad; so that for this time perhaps he may be spared, but on this understanding, that he does not count on similar leniency for the future. I mean that he may be dealt lightly with, if it can be done without endangering the liberty of the Church in any way; and if at the same time the honour that is due to an Archbishop consecrated by Apostolic hands is preserved. The King himself humbly asks this, this the whole Church on this side of the Alps suppliantly implores after her too long affliction. Otherwise we join hands with death, we pine and wither away for fear, and for looking after those things which are coming on the whole world. Indeed this has been my prayer since last year; and since my sins called for it, I received not a favourable answer but anger, and desolation over nearly the whole earth followed on the anger. If my zeal has caused anything to escape me which ought not to have been said, or ought to have been said otherwise than it was, let it be, I beg you, as if unsaid. But let not that be in vain which I have said as I ought, and when I ought.

such a point that not only did King Louis lay waste the territories of Theobald, but burnt to the ground Vitry, together with a large number of its inhabitants of both sexes; moreover, he forbade all elections and ordinations of Bishops within his realm, and handed over their estates to his brother Robert. S. Bernard bitterly complained of this in the case of Rheims, Paris, and Chalons, in his 222nd Letter to Joscelyn of Soissons, and again in his 234th to Stephen of Præneste. At length he succeeded in quashing this unfortunate divorce on the accession of Eugenius III. to the Papal See.

LETTER CCXX.

To Louis, King of France.

He repulses the unjust demand of the King on behalf of Count Ralph, and warns him not to oppress the innocent, and arouse against himself the anger of the King Supreme.

1. I ever readily strive and will strive to the utmost of my little power for the things which make for your honour and the good of your kingdom; and this you deign to admit, and your own conscience bears me witness. But with regard to your complaint to your humble servant about the anathema to be shortly renewed against Count Ralph,[1] and your wish that I should in every possible way endeavour to prevent it, because of the many evils which you think will ensue, to be plain with you I do not see how I can do this, and go against the Apostolic decree. Even if I had the power I do not see how I could do so reasonably. I shall be sorry certainly if evils ensue, but still we ought not therefore to do evil that good may come. It is better and safer to leave all this to the will and providence of Almighty God, who is able to bring to pass and confirm the good that He wishes, and either to prevent the evils which evil men contrive, or else bring on themselves the evils which they desire and seek for.

2. But I am very distressed by one thing which is contained in your Majesty's letter, viz., that this anathema must militate against the peace made between you and Count Theobald. Do you not know that it was a grievous offence that Count Theobald was obliged by the violence of your inroad to take an oath against God and against righteousness, not only because it sought, but also because it brought about the absolution of the aforesaid Count Ralph and his land, an absolution as little deserved as lawful. Do you wish again to add sin to sin, and to heap up the wrath of God against you?—which may He forbid. How has Count Theobald done wrong, that he deserves to

[1] For two reasons the King was enraged at the anathema pronounced against Ralph, because he was a relation, as Hermann of Tournay records, and also because he had taken as his second wife a sister of the Queen.

incur your anger again, when with so much toil and trouble he obtained the absolution of Count Ralph, though an unjust one, as you know, and has neither striven, nor is now striving for the renewal of the excommunication, though it is returning most justly, inasmuch as from fear of you he has even protested against it. Do not, my lord King, do not, I pray you, dare to resist so plainly your King, nay, the Creator of all, in His kingdom and territory, and with frequent and rash audacity to lift your hand against that terrible Being who takes away the breath of princes, and is terrible among the kings of the earth. I speak sharply, because I fear sharp things for you; and I should not fear for you so much if my affection for you were not so great.

LETTER CCXXI. (A.D. 1142.)
To the Same.

He gravely reproves King Louis, because he listens to bad advice and rejects counsels of peace.

1. God knows how great has been my affection for you from the time I first knew you, and how ardently I have wished for your honour; you too know with what toil and anxiety I throughout the past year strove together with your other faithful servants to obtain peace for you. But I am afraid that our labour in your cause has been fruitless. For you evidently are kicking with too much haste and fickleness against the good and wholesome advice you had received; and I hear that you are hurrying, under I know now what counsel of the devil, to those former evils, which you were but now bewailing, and properly bewailing, that you had been guilty of committing, and this while those wounds are still fresh. For from whom except from the devil can I say that this counsel proceeds which makes us add fires to fires and slaughter to slaughter?[1] which causes the cry of the poor, the groanings of the captives, and the blood of the slain, to strike a second time the ears of the *Father of the fatherless, and the Judge of widows?*

[1] This refers to the burning of Vitry and the people in it; see notes on Letter 224.

(Ps. lxviii. 5.) Doubtless that old victimiser *(hostis,* enemy*)* of our race, is pleased with these victims *(hostiis)*, for he is *a murderer from the beginning* (S. John viii. 44). And do not take occasion from Count Theobald to pile up excuses for your sins; it is useless; for he says he is prepared, and in every way he begs, to come to the terms arranged between you when peace was made, and he is willing to make satisfaction in all points, according to the decision of all who love your name, *i.e.*, those who acted as mediators between you; so that if he can be convicted of any wrong, and he is confident he cannot, he will not hesitate to make immediate amends to your honour.

2. But you neither entertain proposals for peace, nor keep to your agreements, nor listen to good advice; but by some judgment of God you so turn everything round that you consider disgrace honour and honour disgrace. You fear for what is safe, and neglect what should be feared, and you incur the rebuke which Joab is recorded to have given to the holy and glorious King David, *Thou lovest thine enemies and hatest thy friends* (2 Sam. xix. 6). For it is not your honour but their own advantage which they seek, who are instigating you to renew your former evil-doing against an innocent person. Nay, it is not so much their own advantage as the will of the devil, in order that they may have (which God forbid) the power of the king as an effectual worker of their hot-headed purpose, which they know that they cannot accomplish by their own strength. They are enemies to your crown, and manifest disturbers of the kingdom.

3. But whatever it may please you to do in a matter which concerns your crown, your soul, and your kingdom, we sons of the Church cannot wholly keep silence about the injuries done to our mother, and the way in which she is despised and trodden under foot; for we perceive that these evils, besides those which we lament piteously have already fallen upon her, are again partly inflicted afresh and partly threatened. We will certainly make a stand, and fight even to death, if need be, for our mother with the

weapons allowed us, not with shield and sword, but with prayers and lamentations to God. And I for my part recollect that, besides the daily prayers, which I call my Lord to witness, I humbly poured forth for your peace and salvation and for your kindgom, I also pleaded your cause by messengers and letters to the Apostolic See (I confess it), even to the damage of my own conscience, and (which I ought not to deny) to the anger of the supreme Pontiff himself against me. Now, I tell you, that provoked by your constant outrages, which you do not cease to renew daily, I begin to repent of my former folly, which made me more indulgent to your youth than I ought to have been. For the future, to the best of my little power, I will not hold back the truth.

4. I will not conceal the fact that you are doing all you can to again enter into alliance and fellowship with the excommunicated, that you are keeping company (so I am told) with robbers and freebooters for the murder of men, the burning of houses, the destruction of churches, and the dispersion of the poor, according to the saying of the Psalmist, *When thou sawest a thief then thou consentedst unto him, and hast been partaker with adulterers* (Ps. l. 18), as though you had not enough power of your own to work mischief. I will not hold back the fact that that unlawful and accursed oath foolishly taken by you against the Church of Bourges (through which so many and so great misfortunes have already deservedly followed) is still, notwithstanding all this, uncorrected by you; that you do not allow a pastor to be set over the sheep of Christ at Chalons; and moreover that you have the audacity to throw open Episcopal houses for the use of your brother[1] and his archers and cross-bowmen, against law and justice, and so expose the property of the Church to be squandered in nefarious uses of this kind. I tell you plainly that if you proceed in this

---

[1] Viz., Robert; for whom see Letter 224, n. 2, and 304. In Letter 293 (of Duchesne), the fathers complain to King Louis that Count Robert, his brother, "had eaten flesh in their Granges," contrary to the interdict of the Order. See Letter 224, respecting the Church of Chalons.

way the wrong will not be unavenged, and, therefore, my lord king, I warn you as a friend and advise you as a faithful servant to desist quickly from this wickedness, so that if [God] is now preparing His hand to strike, you may, like the King of Nineveh, prevent Him with penitence and humility. I speak severely, because I fear severe things for you; but remember that the Wise Man says, *Better are the wounds of a friend than the fraudulent kisses of an enemy* (Prov. xxvii. 6.)

LETTER CCXXII. (A.D. 1142.)

To Joscelyn, Bishop of Soissons, and Suger, Abbot of S. Denys.

He complains to them, as the King's counsellors, of his unjust attacks upon Count Theobald.

1. I had written to the King, rebuking him for the wrongs done in his kingdom, which are said to be done by his consent, and I have thought it fit to bring his reply before you who are of his council. For I wonder if he believes what he says, and if he does not, I wonder how he expects to make me believe it, when, as you know, I am aware of everything which took place with a view to making peace. For he says, as you can see in his letters, when he was trying to prove that the agreement had not been well kept by the Count, "Our Bishops still remain suspended, our land is still under an interdict," as though it belonged to Count Theobald to put an end to any ecclesiastical interdict whatever, or as if he ever promised that he would. He says, "Count Ralph was mocked and his excommunication renewed." And what has this to do with Count Theobald? Did he not faithfully carry out and effectually perform whatever promise he made about this matter? Rather, was not the King caught in his own craftiness, and did he not fall into the pit which he made? Was this the sole reason why the King made void the agreement which

he had made and which your lips pronounced? Was it right for this that the anger of the King should be kindled against God and against His Church, against himself and his kingdom? Because of this ought he to have so forgotten his honour as to send his brother to overcome his vassal, whom he had not even declared war against, much less warned privately or reasoned with, and that, too, through Chalons, and you know the agreement come to between the King and Count about this state especially.

2. But the King makes it a further complaint that the Count, contrary to the allegiance due to him, is endeavouring to ally himself by marriage with the Count of Flanders and Soissons.[1] Well, a suspicion about his fidelity is not a certitude; moreover, you can see the morality of setting aside fixed agreements because of empty suspicions. Nor ought suspicion of such a man as the Count to be entertained at all. Are, then, those to whom the Count allies himself necessarily the King's enemies, and not his vassals or his friends? Is not the Count of Flanders a relation of the King by blood, and, as he says himself, the staff of his kingdom? In what way, then, does his vassal and faithful servant act against the allegiance that he owes the King, if he allies himself by the marriage of those of his own house, to the King's friends? If any one were to consider the matter with an unprejudiced eye, would he not rather see that it greatly adds to the peace, strength, and security of the kingdom?

3. But I do wonder how the King can dare to say that he had ascertained that I knew that Count Theobald had endeavoured to draw over Count Ralph to his side against the King. For he said more to my messenger than he wrote; that I had very often told Count Ralph that I would take on myself the greatest part of his sins if he would join himself

[1] Bernard calls them Barons of the King in ep. 224 n. 3. Hermann of Tournay explains this passage, p. 394, where he speaks of Theodoric, Count of Flanders, who "had betrothed his daughter to Henry, son of Theobald, though the King of the French did his best to break off the alliance by saying that they were related within the third degree of consanguinity." Theobald meditated also allying his daughter to the Count of Soissons. See ep. 224 n. 4.

to Count Theobald. If the man exists by whom I sent such messages, let him come forward and accuse me openly. If I wrote it in letters, let them be produced. Let the King see whom he has believed. I am certain that I have never known anything of what he alleges. I think the same, too, about Count Theobald, for he denies it in every way. May God look upon and judge the King for accusing Count Theobald on suspicion, when he himself, against his agreements, against the precepts of God, and the sentence of the Supreme Pontiff, is keeping Count Ralph close by him, and is communicating with one that is an adulterer and excommunicate.

4. The King also says: "I have almost had upon my hands two bitter assailants." And the prophet answers in scorn: *They feared where no fear was* (Ps. xiv. 5). Lo! he says, I am assailed, I, who did not assail any one; I, who persecuted not, suffer persecution. Who, I ask, who is assailing him? Or who is persecuting him? Is not the Count entreating him, and that humbly? Is he not ready to honour the King, to serve and obey him as his liege-lord? Is he not earnestly praying for peace, and doing all he can to win the King's good will? Suppose that it is not so, but that it is the Count rather who is doing all this wrong to the King; should he not have had recourse to that which you know was determined on? For they agreed between them that, if any controversy or difference should arise about any of the articles agreed upon they would neither do nor seek any injury to each other until the matter had been ventilated and discussed between us three and the Bishop of Auxerre, for we were then the mediators; and if any quarrel arose we ought to have been called on to settle it. And that the Count in every way asks for, but the King refuses.

5. In short, even if the Count has deserved punishment, why has the Church of God deserved it? I mean not only the Church of Bourges, but also that of Châlons, and even of Rheims, and of Paris.[1] Suppose that the King has right on his side against the Count, by what right, I ask, by what

---

[1] See notes to ep. 216 and ep. 224.

right does he presume to lay waste the possessions and lands of the Church, to prevent pastors being set over the sheep of Christ, to forbid those elected to be promoted to their head? By what right does he bring about the postponement of an election (a thing hitherto unheard of) until he has swallowed up all the revenues, carried off the goods of the poor, and until the land is wholly made desolate? Do you advise him to this? It is wonderful, indeed, if it is done against your advice; still more wonderful and mischievous if it is by your advice. For to advise to this is manifestly to create a schism, to resist God, to make a tool of the Church, and to reduce to slavery our ecclesiastical liberty. If any one is a faithful servant of God and His Church, he will certainly stand up and oppose himself as a wall as far as he can in defence of the house of God. For how can you yourselves, if you desire the peace of the Church, as behoves children of peace, I do not say give such evil counsel, but even have any part in it? For whatever evil is done is rightly imputed, not to the King, but to his aged advisers.

LETTER CCXXIII. (A.D. 1143.)

To the Bishop of Soissons.

Bernard excuses himself courteously to the Bishop, who had replied to his former letter in such a way that this was the salutation, "Health in the Lord and not the spirit of calumny."

1. I do not think that I have in me anything of the spirit of calumny, but I know certainly that I have never wished nor wish now to curse anyone, especially a prince of my people. But whatever that may be by which your dignity thinks itself wronged, for it I ask pardon, for I know who said, *Being defamed we entreat* (1 Cor. iv. 13). I say, then, with blessed Job, *Would that I had not said what I have, and I will say no more* (Job xl. 5). When I

lately wrote to my lord the Abbot of S. Denys about your common complaint I answered both of you, and I thought that I had done enough, and since I see that your anger is not yet appeased, which more justly, perhaps, would have been kindled against the oppressors of the Church, I also say to you that I never said, wrote, or believed that you were schismatics or promoters of scandal, and I say so with an easy mind, for I am not afraid that my letter will convict me of falsehood. Examine it, if you please, and if you find that I said so I will confess that I have been guilty of great profanity, and that what you say is true, that I wrote the letter impelled by a spirit of calumny.

2. But lest my humble explanation seem to exclude the spirit of liberty, let me say that I grieved, and I do still, to find that you do not yet avenge the wrongs of Christ or defend the liberty of the Church with the liberty that is fitting. That grief compelled me to write severe things, but they were not of the spirit that you complained of. I thought certainly, and I would still think if I were not afraid that this would offend you, that it is by no means enough for you not to be the authors of the schism. You should, with all your strength, freely restrain those who are the authors, whatever their rank may be, and condemn their counsel and society. I should think it an honour to you if you too could say, *I have hated the congregation of the wicked, and will not sit among the ungodly* (Ps. xxvi. 5). Was it that prophet alone that zeal befitted, and is it not as much required now from a priest of the Lord to say with him, *Do not I hate them, O Lord, that hate Thee, and am not I grieved with those that rise up against Thee?* (Ps. cxxxix. 21). I much wish (and with no wish to anger your Serenity[1] I will say it) that you had exercised this zeal against the young King, who, more like a cruel tyrant than a boy,[2]

---

[1] A title which (ep. 170) he had before given to the King of the French. He here gives it to the Bishop, but only as the King's counsellor. He also salutes Innocent by the same name (ep. 337, n. 1).

[2] He calls Louis a boy after the manner of Holy Scripture, though he was married and over 22 years old. The same word is similarly used in ep. 170 and elsewhere.

has gone against your advice and his own promises, who, without cause, is disturbing his kingdom, stirring up all round him wars in heaven and earth, laying waste the churches, laying an impious hand on sacred things, exalting the wicked, persecuting the good, and destroying the innocent. I repeat that I wish you were sorry for these things, that you would withstand and resist them to the best of your power. But it is not my place to teach such an one as Magister Joscelyn, much less to rebuke a Bishop, who should rather punish me and other sinners and correct those who err. You see how much I fear you. Since you thought ill of my last letter being open I send you this one sealed, for certainly I meant nothing else by it than to follow the usual practice of not sealing with wax a letter[1] sent to different people. I now ask your pardon for so doing also.

LETTER CCXXIV. (A.D. 1143.)

To Stephen, Bishop of Praeneste.[2]

Bernard details the ill-doings of King Louis, and his injuries to the Church.

1. Jeremiah when addressing God for his enemies speaks in this way: *Remember that I stood before Thee to speak good for them, and to turn away Thy wrath from them;* and he goes on to say, *therefore deliver up their children to the famine, and give them into the power of the sword* (Jer. xviii. 20, 21). And he calls down on them other imprecations of this sort, and quite as grievous. I thought that I might now remind your Reverence of this passage, because I find that I am in a condition like that of the Prophet. For you know how I too stood up for the King

---

[1] Hence he says (ep. 304), "My seal is not at hand." Also in ep. 402. The name and likeness of Bernard were engraved on the seal (ep. 284, where see note).

[2] Stephen of Praeneste, to whom ep. 219 also was addressed, was a Cistercian, was made Cardinal in 1140, and died in 1144. Ernald in his *Life of S. Bernard* (lib. ii. n. 49) speaks of him as a man of great modesty. John of Salisbury also praises him above others. He was most likely of Châlons.

in the sight of my Lord, being, indeed, absent in body, but present in spirit, that I might speak good for him. He, indeed, promised well. But now that he returns evil for good I am compelled to write differently. I am ashamed of my mistake, and of the groundless hope which I entertained of him; and I am thankful that the prayer which I put up in my simplicity was not answered. I thought that I was serving a peaceful king, and I find that I was helping a bitter enemy to the Church.[1] Our holy things are trodden under his feet, and the Church is shamefully enslaved. For

---

[1] The state of the Church, as well as of the civil power, under Louis the Younger is plainly enough shown in epp. 216-222 above; here he depicts the tearful and sorrow-stricken face of the Gallican Church. Otto of Frisingen does the same (Chron. lib. vii. c. 21); he says: "Western[2] France on the death of the King, under his son Louis who succeeded him, suffered so grievously through fire and sword in the war between him and Theobald, that unless it had been brought to an end by the merits, prayers, and counsel of the Religious in that province, the whole country seemed likely to be consumed." Otto here describes the preservation of Gaul to the prayers and good counsel of the Religious. Who, then, can doubt that, as it was said, the world stands firm through the merits of the Saints? And who can doubt that among them Bernard led the van, the common counsellor and leader, not only of Gaul, or of Europe, but of the whole world? But in passing let me say how difficult it is to see how Louis could have been so praised by Historians, as, *e.g.*, Gordon, writing on the year 1180. Certainly if you take Bernard as a good witness in these Letters, and especially this one, you cannot call Louis very praiseworthy. But so are the ways of men: they praise and blame according to their affection. We need not go far for an instance. For at the present time how many different opinions are held and judgments given on the plans, expeditions, treaties, and other doings of kings and princes? Some make things turn to their praise and glory which others censure and condemn most severely. Some think that of this kind are the wars carried on to the harm of religion and the Church, the fostering of heresies, the profanation of places dedicated to God, the scorning of holy things, the oppression of the poor, the loss inflicted on the State, the weakening of the vigour and dignity of the Church. Yet you will find others glossing over these evils, or knowing how to palliate them, and exalting to the skies with their praises those by whose labour and under whose auspices such things are carried out. Still we have no wish to detract from the merits of King Louis, if he improved when he grew older. Perhaps when of riper years he atoned for the crimes of his youth by the noble deeds of his manhood. For he survived Bernard many years, dying in the year 1180. I read too that he gave S. Bernard himself proofs of his repentance. For Emilius speaks of him thus: "The King, in a great rage, attacked him [Theobald] and took and plundered Vitry which was in his domains. He burnt secular and sacred buildings without making any distinc-

[2] *Sic*; but should he not have said "Eastern France"?—[E.]

not only is it forbidden to hold elections of Bishops, but if the clergy anywhere have ventured to do so, the prelate of their choice is not allowed to exercise his episcopal functions. In short, the Church of Paris is sitting in sadness, deprived of her own pastor, and no one dares so much as to whisper about finding another.

2. It is not enough for him that the episcopal residences are spoiled of the goods now in them; his sacrilegious hand is raging against men and lands everywhere, for he claims from each for himself the revenues of the whole year as well. The Church of Châlons has, indeed, held an election, but he who was elected[1] has been now for a long time deprived of his honour, and you know that this cannot take place without grievous loss to the Lord's flock. The King has charged his brother Robert to administer the Bishopric, and he, exercising his power over all the lands and goods of the Church, and being not slothful in the execution of his office, is offering daily sacrifices to heaven, not, indeed, sacrifices of peace, but the cries of the poor, the tears of widows, the wailing of orphans, the groans of captives, and the blood of the slain. But that episcopate is too narrow for his wickedness, so he is now attacking

---

tion, and in one large church 1,500, both young and old were burnt, who had fled to the altars for protection. Afterwards the King, coming to himself, was seized with great grief; he afflicted himself and refused consolation. Bernard was sent for because he was renowned for his evident holiness already under King Louis le Gros; and though a disciple only, it was said, of the woods and glades, who had become very learned, under no other teacher, he had brought his holiness and learning out of solitude before crowds, out of darkness into light. He was then introduced, and was kindly received by the King, and when he saw his tears and had been told the cause, he said, 'These tears, if they do not quickly dry up, can extinguish all recollection of the burning of Vitry. Only add to them constancy and determination, and let not your lamentation be like a woman's, but show a manly and truly royal courage.'" What else is here said about the King's hindering the election of the Bishops may be seen in the notes to ep. 219.

[1] Geoffrey of Chalons, mentioned in ep. 66, died in the year 1142; in his place Guy, here spoken of, was elected. Samson, Archbishop of Rheims, because he supported Count Theobald, had been expelled by the King's servants, who also plundered the City Churches of S. Mary, S. Remigius, and S. Nicasius, and the suburban monastery of S. Thierry. See the mention here, as in ep. 222 n. 5, of the See of Paris, to which Theobald had been chosen on the death of Stephen.

Rheims, and carrying on his ill-deeds in the land of the saints, sparing neither clerks, nor monks nor nuns. In short, he has laid waste with the edge of the sword the fruitful fields and populous villages of S. Mary, S. Remigius, S. Nicasius, S. Thierry in such a way that he has reduced them all to almost a wilderness. The cry is frequently heard by all, *Let us take to ourselves the houses of God in possession* (Ps. lxxxiii. 12). So does the King improve upon the wrong he has done to the Church of Bourges under an oath like Herod's.

3. Moreover, when, after we had expended no little labour on the matter, he had made peace with Count Theobald, and as we thought, had entered on a treaty of firm friendship: but now he seeks occasion to withdraw from his friend. This is brought as a heinous charge against the Count, that he is making matrimonial alliances for his children with the King's barons. A loosening of friendship is suspected by the King in this, and he does not think himself a king if his chieftains love each other. Your wisdom may conjecture what kind of disposition he bears towards his subjects when he thinks himself the stronger, if there is hatred and discord between them. You may see and determine whether this man is of God, who trusts more in the mutual rivalry of his barons than their mutual love, when *God is love* (1 S. John iv. 8). He would hold this if he had the wisdom of him who said, *Love is strong as death, jealousy is cruel as the grave* (Cant. viii. 6). Besides, he openly breaks his conventions and terms of peace agreed on, and does not hold himself to the promises which his own lips have uttered. Lastly, he has recalled to his palace and to his Council an adulterous and excommunicate man [Ralph] whom he had agreed to banish, and in order to work greater wickedness, the King, and official guardian[1] of the Church, is a second time leagued with many other like worthless characters, excommunicated and perjured men, incendiaries, murderers, and this against one of whose love for the Church and willingness to defend her there is no

[1] *Advocatus.*

doubt, according to the saying of the Prophet, *When thou sawest a thief thou consentedst unto him, and hast been partaker with the adulterers* (Ps. l. 18).

4. In addition to all this, he compels bishops, after his custom, to curse those who should be blessed, and to bless those who should be cursed. And since he sets no bounds to what it may please him to do, he compasses sea and land to find perjurers by whose means those whom God has joined together may be by man put asunder. With what face, I ask, can he endeavour so hard to lay down laws to others about consanguinity when, as is well known, he is living with his cousins within the third degree?[1] I do not know (for I have never to my knowledge praised, nor do I now, any forbidden marriages) whether there is any consanguinity between the son of Count Theobald and the daughter of the Count of Flanders, and also between the Count of Soissons and the daughter of Count Theobald: but you know, and my lord knows, that their nuptials are forbidden. If it is lawful for them to be united, then their being forbidden is the disarming of the Church, and the withdrawal of strength from her. Nor do I suppose that the object of those who oppose him is anything else but to prevent those who venture to withstand the schism which is threatened, from finding refuge in the territories of the aforenamed princes. So far my zeal carries me. For I have no power to redress the faults which I have been able to point out. I have, however, been able to warn him who can. The zeal of my lord will do this. I thought it necessary that he should be informed of the great suffering and danger of the Church, and no one can do it so well as you, who share his counsels and spirit. And I pray you have me excused with him for writing with altered pen now that the King has altered, for you know that the Prophet of God

---

[1] John Besley, in his Gallican History of the Counts of Poictiers, thus explains the consanguinity between Louis VII. and Eleanor his wife, daughter of William, Count of Aquitaine:—Aldeardis, great grandmother of Eleanor, was sister to the wife of Humbert II., Count of S. Jean de Maurienne, and so aunt to Adela, mother of King Louis.

said to God, *With the innocent thou shall be innocent, and with the perverse man Thou shalt show Thyself perverse* (Ps. xviii. 26).

LETTER CCXXV. (A.D. 1143.)

To the Bishop of Soissons.[1]

Bernard urges him to promote peace.

We have worked hard, but it is a question whether we have made much progress. We have sown much, but reaped little. We want, I must tell you, your help and presence. You will hear from our common friend, the Abbot of S. Denys, why we did not seek your help before in our great strait. But now I appeal to your holy watchfulness to dissemble no more, but to labour for the things which make for peace according to the wisdom given you by God. For you ought not to need entreaty to take such action, since it is evident that by it your ministry is not only greatly honoured, but also that if you neglect it, it is greatly disgraced. I hope to see you at the festival announced to be held at S. Denys.[2]

LETTER CCXXVI. (A.D. 1143.)

To Louis, King of the French.

Bernard and Hugo complain of the King's persistence in ill-doing.

To Louis, by the grace of God illustrious King of the French, and Duke of Aquitaine, Hugh, Bishop of Auxerre, his humble servant, and Bernard, Abbot of Clairvaux, wish health, and desire that he should love righteousness, and judge his land in wisdom.

1. It is a long time since we left our homes and set aside our private interests in order to labour, as God

[1] Joscelyn.
[2] Was this an assembly of the nobles of the kingdom, or the Dedication Festival which is kept by S. Denys in February on S. Matthias' Day?

is our witness, for your peace, and the peace of your realm. We lament that so far we have reaped no fruit, or very little, in return for all our labour. Still the poor are crying after us, still the land is daily going to ruin. Do you ask what land? Yours, none other. For it is within your realm, and against your realm that all these evils are being perpetrated. For whether it be your friends or your enemies who are being impoverished, taken prisoners, and crushed by that war, they are from nowhere else than your kingdom. In it the saying of the Saviour seems to be daily coming true, that *every kingdom divided against itself shall be brought to desolation* (S. Luke xi. 17). To this there is added the fact that these dividers and desolators themselves have made you the head and leader of this wickedness, when they ought to have feared you especially as their opponent, and felt you most of all as their punisher. Still, we hoped that you, touched and illuminated by God, had perceived their great wickedness, had recognized your error, and were desirous under wiser counsels to withdraw your foot from this snare.

2. But the conference lately held between us at Corbeil, has dispelled any such hope. For you know how, and how unreasonably (by your leave be it said) you then left us. Whence it happened that your displeasure with us did not allow us to give you any clear explanation of that passage in our discourse which displeased you. But if you had deigned to await it with undisturbed mind you might, perhaps, have learnt that nothing was said by us that was an insult to your majesty, or unendurable in the present position of your affairs. But, as it is, since you have been provoked without any cause, you have disturbed and confused us, and you also keep us, being men who desire and seek your good, in doubt and anxiety as to what we are to do. What has disturbed you is nothing but the fraud of the wicked, and the idle talk of men who know little, who call evil good and good evil. But though we have been troubled, yet we do not altogether despair of the help of the Spirit, who, we see, has wholesomely smitten your mind for

your past evil deeds, and we still stand and wait till your better nature return, and you effectually accomplish what you have wisely begun. For this reason we have sent to you our dear brother Andrew of Baudiment,[1] who will tell you of these things more fully, and will faithfully bring back word to us of whatever reply you may have been pleased to give. But if (which God forbid) you persist in withstanding good advice, we are clean from your blood; God will not any longer suffer His Church to be trodden down either by you or yours.

LETTER CCXXVII. (A.D. 1143.)

To the Bishop of Soissons.

Bernard earnestly implores the help of the Bishop.

I have always stood in need of my friends' good offices, for I am a man greatly to be pitied in mind and body; but now especially is the need and time for pity when my conscience is troubling me, when the hand of the Lord is heavy upon me, when I have sold myself into a hard prison,[2] and am a severe judge against myself. If you are still my father (for I confess you have been hitherto) let your son feel it, that son whose filial affection has not grown cool to this day. I know, I know how difficult it is to wrest his club from the hand of Hercules, and I am on that account the more urgent, because I seek a difficult thing. But the more difficult it is the more earnestly do I entreat the bestowal of it. If

---

[1] This Andrew was well known and had been employed in many different businesses. His name is found subscribed to the original deeds of the Abbey of Chercamp (*Spicil.* Vol. ii. p. 329); and with S. Bernard he was a witness to the agreement made between King Louis and Argrimus, Archdeacon of Orleans (Duchesne Vol. iv. p. 764). In the transference of the Church of Vieux-Crecy A.D. 1122, to the Monastery of S. Martin des Champs, by Burchard Bishop of Meaux, there is amongst other things a donation made by Stephen, son of Roric, "in the presence of Count Theobald, and Andrew of Baudiment, who gave his approval as far as he was concerned." The same Andrew was present at a Council held at Troyes A.D. 1128. *Cf.* Ep. 284.

[2] *I.e.* of monastic seclusion and retreat.

I obtain it I shall confess myself a debtor for a great, a very great kindness. And I am not ignorant that it is more blessed to give than to receive (Acts xx. 35); but I yield to necessity, I go to meet dangers, I take counsel in my difficulties, and for the time being I either put aside or forget my selfishness. And so yielding to you, as is fitting, the more honourable place I take for myself the more modest; I show my modesty not only in being indecorously ready to receive, but also more importunate in asking. I ask, then, suppliantly, instantly, opportunely, importunately. For I do not ask anything which it does not become you to grant, or which will bring me shame afterwards for having accepted, even if it does not become me now to seek it in this way. For if you set free the poor man from the hand of the powerful in this you will benefit me very much, but most of all yourself. I have made known my wish, you know the affair, the afflicted now await the result to them.

LETTER CCXXVIII. (A.D. 1143.)

To Peter, Abbot of Cluny.

Bernard complains that he did not reply to him.[1]

To the Reverend father and lord PETER, by the grace of God Abbot of the Cluniacs, BERNARD, called Abbot of Clairvaux, sends his humble greetings.

1. I should wish to think that you are pleased to joke in your letter; if such is the fact, and if I ought not to see anything

[1] Manrique (*Annals* A.D. 1135 c. 3) thinks that this Letter was written in the year 1135; but the order of the Letters seems opposed to his view. And certainly if it be compared with the next Letter, which is Peter's answer to this, it will be seen directly that it was written after the disturbances about the election at Langres, which took place A.D. 1138, as was said above, ep. 164. For Peter the Venerable answers thus: "When will my sincere love for you be extinguished, or the warm affection of my heart be drowned by any rivulets of adverse rumour, since many waters of tithes have had no power to extinguish it, nor the violence of the stream of Langres to drown it?" Moreover, in the last part of the same Letter Peter mentions the translation of the Koran, afterwards dedicated by him to S. Bernard, which was finished A.D. 1143, as the Cluniac Library testifies, and to this year the Letter seems to belong.

unkind in what you say, then I allow that you are treating me well and like a friend. Do not wonder at this. For your sudden and unexpected condescension makes me doubtful about this. For it is not long ago, when writing to you, I saluted your Greatness with due reverence, and you answered me not a word. Not long before that I again wrote to you from Rome, and not even then did I get a single word in reply. Do you now wonder that when you lately returned from Spain I did not presume again to trouble you with my chatter? For if it is a fault not to have written for some cause or other, to have had no mind to write, nay, more, to have despised writing, you will surely not be altogether without blame. You see what I might urge with justice (since you require it of me); but I prefer to go and meet goodwill when returning than to delay its return while I try needlessly to excuse myself or to accuse another. I have merely said this so that I might not keep anything in my mind without giving it utterance, for this true friendship forbids. For the future, let all suspicion be now removed, for charity believeth all things (1 Cor. xiii. 7). I rejoice that you have been stirred to a recollection of our former friendship, and to recall the friend that you had wronged. Now that I am recalled I gladly return. I am happy to be recalled. Henceforward I remember no wrongs.[1] Here am I, now as then,

[1] We need not spend much time in investigating the wrongs mentioned here. For the context of both Letters, this and the following, shows plainly enough that the words are spoken in a pleasant and rhetorical way. I am aware that there had been some cause for dispute between the two saints, *e.g.*, the election at Langres (ep. 164) and the exemption of the Cistercians from paying tithes to the Cluniacs; but I can never admit that they deserve the name of injuries. As far as the tithes are concerned, the fact is this: Innocent, when in Gaul A.D. 1132, on learning the poverty of the Cistercians, gave them a precept freeing them from the payment of all tithes. Amongst others the Cluniacs protested against the exemption. Hence there was ground for the complaint which the Abbot Peter laid before Innocent first, then before Haimeric in moderate terms, and lastly before the heads of the Cistercian houses in general Chapter; and when he found that they were somewhat displeased at his action, in the next year he sent them a Letter of apology, by which brotherly love was repaired and kept inviolate. The outrage which was afterwards committed against the Cistercians by the monks of Gigny will be dealt with in the notes to ep. 283. For the rest, it seems desirable to have the Letter of Peter which was the occasion

the devoted servant of your Holiness. I give thanks that the lines are fallen to me in a pleasant place, inasmuch as I am again admitted to your intimacy, as you kindly write that I am. If by any chance I had grown lukewarm, as you complain, no doubt I should quickly become hot again when nourished by the warmth of your charity.

2. And now I must say that what you have been pleased to write I have received with outstretched hands. I have read it eagerly; I read it again with pleasure, and the oftener I read it the more pleasure it gives me. I must say that I like your pleasantry. For it is at once agreeable from its gaiety, and serious from its gravity. I do not know how it is that you manage to mingle grave and gay in such a way that your pleasantry does not savour of lightness, and, while you preserve your dignity, the pleasantness of your mirth is not lessened. Further, you so preserve your dignity that the saying of holy Job can be applied to you: *If I laughed on them they believed it not* (Job xxix. 24). Well, you see that I have replied, and I think that now I may rightly demand more than you promised. It is right that you should know how things are here. I have determined not to leave the monastery again except for the annual meeting of Abbots at Cîteaux. Here, supported by your prayers and good offices, I will wait for the few remaining days of my warfare, till my change comes. May God be gracious to me, and not withdraw from me your prayers or His mercy. I am broken in strength, and I have a valid excuse for not travelling about as I used to do. I will sit still and be silent, to see if perchance I may experience what from the fulness of his sweetness the holy Prophet says, *It is good that a man should both hope and quietly wait for the salvation of the Lord* (Lam. iii. 26). And,

of this being written: it may not be amiss, therefore, to include it in the list of S. Bernard's, that before all lovers of true Christian friendship, especially before Religious, there may be placed this most perfect example of the two friends, Bernard and Peter. Cardinal Baronius has so spoken of Peter as to pronounce him in "that holiness which worketh by love, no unworthy rival of Bernard." If further evidence of this is wanted see Peter's own works, lib. i. ep. 28, and lib. iv. ep. 46.

that you may not seem the only one to joke, I suppose that you will not again venture to chide me for my silence, and, after your manner, to call that sloth, which I think the Prophet Isaiah more fittingly and more properly calls the *cultivation of righteousness* (Isaiah xxxii. 17), about which you read in his Prophecy, where he says from the Lord: *In quietness and in confidence shall be your strength* (Isaiah xxx. 15). Commend me to the prayers of your sacred Convent of Cluny; salute it first from me, the servant of all, if you think fit.

LETTER CCXXIX. (A.D. 1143.)[1]

PETER THE VENERABLE, TO ABBOT BERNARD.

He courteously answers Bernard's letter, and at the same time explains the causes of the strife between the Cluniacs and Cistercians.

To him who is to be honoured with special veneration, to be embraced closely with the arms of entire affection, the inseparable guest of my heart, my Lord BERNARD, Abbot of Clairvaux, his brother PETER, humble Abbot of the Cluniacs, wishes the eternal salvation which he longs for.

1. Since I am found to be long in replying to the sweet and pleasant letter of my friend, to which I ought to have sent an answer directly with equal good will, your Holiness will perhaps wonder why I have not done so, and will, I am afraid, put it down to indolence or contempt. But do not think that it is either, for both are absent; for I have hardly ever been so glad to receive anything in the way of a letter, or so careful in reading it. The cause of my long silence was partly the bearer of it, who, when he came to Cluny, and did not find me there, though I was not very far away, being at Marigny,[2] neither brought it nor sent it on to me, but left it at Cluny. But I do not wish to accuse the good man; I believe that he was hindered from going to

[1] This is Ep. 16, B.v of Abbot Peter's own Letters.—[E.]
[2] Marigny sur Loire was a nunnery on the Loire, founded by S. Hugh, Abbot of Cluny.

me by some business which he had to do, or by the severity of the winter, which was then upon us. I, too, was kept in that place for a month, partly by the snow, partly by business, and returned home with difficulty at the beginning of Lent. Then at length I received your letter from the Sub-Prior, to whom it had been given. My heart was drawn to you immediately; and though my affection for you was great before, it was kindled into a flame by the loving breath that came through your letter, and no room was then left for coldness or lukewarmness. I was drawn, I say, and so drawn to you, that I did what I cannot recollect that I have before done, except to the Sacred Books, I kissed affectionately your letter as soon as I had read it. And then I read again to some of the brethren what I had before read to myself, and I exhorted them with all my heart to greater love for you. I would stir up those whom I can influence, and I wish I could influence all to imitate your charity; I always endeavour to do this. Then I laid it by, and placed it among the gold and silver which, after the custom handed down to me by my fathers, I am in the habit of carrying with me to distribute in alms. Nor was it unfitting. For your favour to me, your charity is precious to me above all gold and silver.

2. I wished to write to you on the next day all that was in my mind; but I was prevented by business which made other claims on me daily, nay, continuously, and I kept silence. My hard taskmaster, whom I had no power to resist, imposed silence on me, and the care of an infinite number of matters forced me to hold my peace not for one day, but for many. And so a fortnight passed by, then a whole month, then several months in succession, during which I was always making attempts to write but was not allowed by the said taskmaster. At length I broke the galling chain, and though with difficulty, I threw aside the yoke of my burden, and the sceptre of my tyrant, by writing stealthily. And lest I seem to labour too much in making excuse for my tardiness in replying I must say that you yourself have forced me to make my excuse when you

said, "It is not long since I wrote to you, and saluted your Crown[1] with fitting veneration, and you answered me not a word; and not long before I wrote to you from Rome, and not even then did I get a syllable. Do you now wonder that when you lately returned from Spain I did not presume to trouble you again with my chatter? But if it is a fault to have not written for some reason or other, to have been unwilling to write, not to say to have disdained to write, you will surely not be altogether without blame."

3. But what shall I say? Simply this: I would never make any excuse for the fault which you charge me with, if it had been from contempt that I had not answered your letter. For I admit that, if you had written first, I ought to have answered you; but as far as I can recollect, while you were at Rome I wrote first and you answered. It was not then my turn to write in answer, inasmuch I had been the first to write, but yours. Certainly I might have written in reply to your answer, but your answer was so full and completely satisfactory that it freed me from any necessity to write further. And if this is the state of the case, the fault that you speak of seems to be deserting me and looking towards you; for you have been endeavouring to lay blame on one that is blameless, and to lay on the shoulders of an unoffending brother other people's burdens, not to say your own. But to what you say about my having done the same thing on another occasion I have no answer, for I have no recollection of it. If by some chance it did happen I have no doubt that there was a reasonable cause, or if not I will make you my humble apologies. But you went on to say, "You see what I might urge with justice." I answer: At present, according to the reasons given above, justice rather makes for me, because no fault at all is found in me. Now, if I were not inclined to spare you, and if I were to apply to myself the name of an injured friend which you say you can claim, I should have good cause to exact a penalty for the wrong or injury that you have done me. But after my custom I spare you, and even though not asked, I freely forgive you everything. "I keep in

---

[1] "Your Greatness," p. 652.

mind," as you said, "no injuries." For this is but a fitting introduction to what I am going to say: I am about to endeavour to banish from the hearts of many their well-known feelings of resentment against each other, and I am going to do this not in jest, but in sober earnestness; and I intend to induce you to banish all such feelings. Let me be the first to extend forgiveness to everyone, and set the example of doing what I endeavour to press on others.

4. But perhaps you will say again, "I should wish to believe that you are pleased to joke?" Yes, I do please; but only with you. I do not jest like this with others. For with some, to pass the limits of dignified gravity is to run the risk of being thought frivolous; but I am not afraid of this from you; I seek after charity, lest haply I lose her. And, therefore, it is always pleasant for me to talk with you, and by friendly words to preserve the sweet honey of charity. I do my best to prevent myself being in the number of those brethren who hated Joseph in their hearts, *and could speak no peaceful word to him* (Gen. xxxvii. 4). Would that all your brethren and mine would do so (I do not speak boastfully), and would not deviate from the line of charity, by which alone after faith and the Sacrament of Baptism, they are entitled to the name of brethren, and by which they are united to each other in a close relationship; and that they would fear what the Apostle speaks of when he says, *Peril amongst false brethren* (2 Cor. xi. 26). Would that they would all do this, and would keep their heart from the deceitful thought, and their tongue from the bitter word, according to the Psalm which is so often in their mouth. What I have said seems to make large promises, and as if it were a preparation for great achievements. But lest the well-known verse, "What will this man, lavish in promises, produce worthy of so pretentious an opening?" (Horace, *Ars Poetica* v. 138) be applied to me, I must confess that I not only have no urgent cause for writing, but not even an important or moderately good one; still I am speaking of those things which worldly men think great and even most important, and from which the children of this world hope

to become great and powerful. Yet my cause *is* a great one, and so far surpassing all others, that by the Apostle it is called more excellent than all. *If you ask its name he calls it charity* (1 Cor. xii. 31 and xiii.).

5. This is my whole and sole cause of writing; I fully trust that I have it entirely as far as you are concerned, and I do not despair of seeing your brethren and mine preserve it towards each other, better than they have been wont to do, especially if you give your assistance to effect this. For as far as that charity goes which for many a year I have had stored up for you in the secret recesses of my heart, it seems to me that, as it is written, *many waters cannot quench it, nor the floods drown it* (Cant. viii. 7). This I think has often been proved in different cases. For when will my sincere love for you be ever quenched, or the warm affection of my heart be drowned by any rivulets of evil report, when neither the many waters of the tithe question could quench it, nor the floods of the troubles at Langres drown it. You know what I mean, and I only say this in order that your wisdom may be sure, when it recollects the proofs of my constant love for you in the past, that I am likely to be equally constant in the future. I feel sure of the same in you, and I trust that no power will ever banish me from the innermost depths of your heart. But since each of us is called a pastor; since our folds are filled with no small number of Christ's sheep; since to both the precept applies, *Be thou diligent to know well the countenance of the flock* (Prov. xxvii. 23), we have to see if our flock is known to us, if it is well, if it languishes, if it is feeble, if it is robust, if it is living or dead. For since the beloved disciple says, *He that loveth not abideth in death* (1 S. John iii. 14), why am I anxious about the weakness of my flock, when I see that it is already dead? For if he who loveth not abideth in death, in what death does he abide who hates? if he who loveth not abideth in death, in what death is he who is given to detraction? For what purpose do I say this?

6. I see that certain persons, as well from my folds as

yours, have engaged in deadly warfare against each other; and that those who ought to live in the house of the Lord as friends, have fallen from mutual charity. I see that they are of the family of the same Lord, soldiers of the same King, that they bear the same name of Christians, and are alike called monks. I perceive that they are bound to till their Master's field, not only by the yoke of a common faith, but beyond that by the yoke of the same monastic rule, and this under many different forms of toil. Yet, though, as I said, they are joined by a common name, united by the monastic profession, some hidden and accursed difference separates them, and splits up that sincere unity of hearts, to which they seem to have been called. And, O lamentable event! not to be worthily atoned for by any founts of tears, the haughty archangel, who was once cast down from heaven, has again seized heavenly places, and he, who could not establish his seat in the north, has strengthened it in the south,[1] that is, in the more splendid part of the sky. Truly it is so, he may boast that he has done so, when, after driving out Him who dwells in the heavens, whose abiding place was made, not for mutual hatred, but for brotherly concord, he lords it, after the fashion of a tyrant, over the minds of men whose profession is heavenly, whose example is conspicuous. And since the Stronger Man has come and overcome the strong man who had been long guarding his palace in peace; since the prince of this world was cast out; since his throne, who is the King of the children of pride, has been overturned even amongst Christian laymen; with what lamentations must we mourn, I pray you, if Satan, after having the throne of his wickedness overturned in others, should again erect it in the hearts of monks? God forbid that he, who is said to have been rendered so helpless by the Saviour as to suffer himself to be bound by His handmaidens, and to be a laughing stock to His servants, should mock at His servants and handmaidens, and bring them once more under vile bondage to him.

[1] See Letter 165, and note (p 500).—[F.]

7. But why do they oppose each other? why do they rail at each other? why are they consumed the one by the other? Let them bring forward the ground of their strife, and if they can bring any just cause of complaint against each other let it be ended by being entrusted to the decision of just arbitrators. What do you demand, I ask, my brother, from your brother? and to comprehend in two words all who are at variance, What do you demand, O Cluniac brother, from your Cistercian brother, and *vice versâ?* If it is cities, camps, farmhouses, farms, if the possession of any land whether small or great; if, in short, it is gold, silver, or any quantity or quality of money that the quarrel is about, come, I say, bring forward the claim. There are judges not of iniquity, but of equity ready to put an end at once to all strifes of this kind. Peace will easily be restored, and the wounds of charity healed, as soon as we know that such a separation of hearts has been brought about by these things or others like them. But I recollect that both of you have cast off all such things, that you have kept for yourselves no earthly goods, that, enriched with a blessed poverty, you have determined to follow the poverty of Christ. This, then, cannot be the ground of your quarrel. But I will not give over, I will not weary, I will not rest until I come to the bottom of the truth that I am in search of.

8. Perhaps the cause of your strife is the difference in your customs, in the observance of the monastic rule. But if this, dearly beloved, is the cause of so great an evil, it is, let me say it with the permission of both of you, very unreasonable, very childish and foolish. For does not that which is destitute of all reason, and whose soundness every wise man denies, seem to you unreasonable, childish, and foolish? For if a difference in customs, if manifold variety in an infinite number of things ought to rob the servants of Christ of mutual charity, what peace, or concord, or unity, or how much of the law of Christ will be left, not only to monks, but to any Christians, about which a great Apostle says, *Bear ye one another's burdens, and*

so fulfil the law of Christ? If, I say, the law of Christ, that is charity, is to be abandoned by all who follow different uses, it will simply be found nowhere any more. For when it shall have been rejected by all who follow a different custom it will be nowhere to be found. Has not, dearly beloved, the whole earth long since been filled with the Churches of Christ? And since the Churches which serve God in the same faith and the same charity are almost numberless, almost as great a variety of uses is found amongst them as there are churches. You will find this in the canticles, in the lections, in all the Church offices, in the different vestments; you will find it, too, in different fasts which are observed in addition to the authorized ones which cannot be changed; you will find it in all similar things, which according to differences of times, places, nations, and countries, have been instituted by the prelates of the Church, to whom, according to the Apostle, *it belongs to give orders in such things as they may see fit* (Rom. xiv. 5). Have all those churches abandoned charity because they have changed their custom? Will they cease to be Christians because they seem to differ in their uses? Will the great gift of peace be lost by all because each one works what is good in a way different from the rest? Not so thought Ambrose, a Doctor of the Church, in word and in life, who, speaking of the Saturday fast which he had seen kept at Rome, and which he had found was not observed at Milan when he was made Bishop, says: "When I am at Rome I observe the fast kept by the Church at Rome; when at Milan I follow the custom of its Church and do not fast" (Apud Aug. ep. 54). Hence, also, our father Augustine, in describing the devotion of his good mother, relates that she, according to the custom which she had seen observed in the African Churches, wished to offer her oblations at Milan contrary to the custom of the Churches of Italy, but was forbidden by Ambrose (S. Aug. Confess. lib. vi. c. 2).

9. But why labour this point? To no purpose is it to

surround what is so evident with manifold testimonies and examples, especially since neither in ancient times a difference in the time of observing Easter, nor in modern a well-known variation between Greek and Latin in the way of offering the Christian sacrifice, had any power to wound charity, or to produce any breach of unity. The Holy Fathers are witnesses to this, and their received writings which they left to the Church, that the East in former times kept Easter at one time, the West at another, the Angles in Britain at another, and the Scots at another. We, too, witness the same thing in our own time, for we see the Roman Church and the whole Latin race offer to God the life-giving sacrifice with unleavened bread; while the Greek Church and the greatest part of the East and barbarian nations who are Christians are said to sacrifice with leavened bread. But in spite of this neither ancients nor moderns have departed from mutual charity because of these well-known varieties of customs, for they found nothing in all this to wound faith or charity. But why do I say this? In order that, if your minds, brethren, have been alienated because of the variety in your uses, if they have grown weak in their love of peace and unity because of this or that custom handed down by the founders of the Churches, that by so venerable examples of such holy Fathers they may become one again, and after the way of the saints, who out of weakness were made strong, and became brave in the battle, may become too strong for any disease by shrinking from all weakening of charity.

10. But you will say: "Variety of uses must be understood in a different sense in the case of different Churches than in men of the same Order. If the customs of many Churches vary without any damage to faith or charity, it is nothing wonderful; but it is wonderful if men of the same purpose and profession do not preserve the same kind of rules." Is this all, dearly beloved, that divides you from each other? Is this the only blow to charity amongst yourselves? Is this the only thing which prevents the

children of peace from being at peace with each other? If even a layman *made for peace with those who hated peace* (Ps. cxx. 7), shall monk strive with monk in an accursed war? The child of the light loves the children of darkness to prevent the gift of peace being disturbed, and shall the child of the light fight against the child of the light? I refer this to the purpose, not to the monk. If, indeed, it is only this that is troubling your minds, if this is the sole cause of the wound of charity, it will be soon healed, if only there be no obstinacy. See, then, that love of your own opinion do not darken the light of your understanding, for no one deserves to attain to unity who does not seek her for herself, but rather seeks to have his own way. I therefore ask you to consider whether the cause of your disunion is a just one, without any desire to defend your own side or your own opinions, and when you find it to be an unjust one I ask you to become once more of one heart and of one soul. For each of you is fighting under the same rule, and under that particular rule each hopes to be able to attain to everlasting salvation. But if neither is to be disappointed of his hope I know not what place can now be left for discord, division, or reproaches.

11. For you said that it is a wonderful thing if men of the same purpose and profession do not observe the same kind of rules. My answer is: What does it matter if men of the same purpose and profession do not observe the same rules, if by their different observances they alike attain to the same salvation and everlasting life? What does it matter, what is the objection, if they come to the same Jerusalem which is above, which is the mother of us all, by a different path, if a different road leads to the same land, if the same life is attained by manifold ways? For if thou, O Cluniac, knewest that the Cistercian, or thou, O Cistercian, knewest that the Cluniac was making a mistake in the object that he had put before him, or if, according to the Scripture, you saw that he was proceeding to his ruin along a road which seemed to men to be right, you would be justified, I admit, in correcting or calling back your brother,

and even, if he refused to listen to you, in reproaching him and invoking God against him. Then, indeed, if you were to reproach him, to withstand him, to hate him, I would admit that you were judging justly, that you were acting rightly, especially when I hear a great prophet saying of such even to God, *Do not I hate them, O Lord, that hate Thee, and am not I grieved with those that rise up against Thee? Yea, I hate them right sore, even as though they were mine enemies* (Ps. cxxxix. 21, 22.) I should do more, I should rejoice that you were not a deaf hearer of the Scripture, which says: *Go, hasten thyself, rouse thy friend, give not sleep to thine eyes, nor slumber to thine eyelids* (Prov. vi. 3, 4.) And of another: *Cursed be he that keepeth back his sword from blood* (Jer. xlviii. 10). Then I would readily admit that you had just causes for hatred, and I myself, girt with the sword of zeal, would accompany you in your outgoings to subdue the enemies of God, and those who, according to the Apostle, *work a lie in hypocrisy* (1 Tim. iv. 2). But, as it is, I see that both of you are striving to rise from earth to heaven under the same rule, under different but yet holy observances, and so running by different courses for the same prize in order that you may obtain it; and so, it seems to me, you have no cause of anger, hatred, or reproach left you.

12. But you further ask me to prove what I have said, and to show how, under the same Rule, or profession of the same Rule, a monk can safely travel by diverse paths. I have an answer ready enough for this, and there is not wanting either authority or reason. Thou, O Cluniac, in thy way, thou, O Cistercian, in thine, canst alike travel happily along the road of God's commandments, and still more happily attain to the due end of thy course. And because I have already appealed to the authority which in such things is to be first consulted. in what follows I will show that reason is not absent, though she follow at a moderate distance.

13. But what is your objection, my brother? "I say that those who have professed the same rule do not observe

alike the commands of that rule." What you say is true, that in some chapters the commands of the same Rule are differently observed by the professed. But do not suppose that, therefore, monks of this class are to be blamed; do not for this dare to accuse them of unfaithfulness. Listen to a heavenly authority, that of the King of the heavens: *If thine eye be single, thy whole body shall be full of light* (S. Luke xi. 34.) Hear, too, the Apostle: *Let all your things be done with charity* (1 Cor. xvi. 14.) Hear, too, S. Augustine: "Have charity and do what you will." Hear, too, him who drew up your rule, or rather the Holy Spirit who inspired it: "Let the Abbot order and arrange everything so that souls may be saved; and whatever the brethren do, let them do it without murmuring" (Reg. S. Bened. c. 41.) What can be more clear, more open, more lucid? Does not the very flow of the words themselves show that they are altogether without cloud, and show to mortals the clear light of truth, without any intervening veil of clouds? Behold, the Heavenly Teacher says that all your body, my brother, depends for its light on the singleness of your eye; that is, that all your works must have purity of intention. After Him, the greatest doctor of the Church bids all your works to be done in charity; lo, the greatest instructor of the Church, after the Apostles, says that you may do what you will so long as charity remains; lo, your father Benedict himself, on whom you rely, orders the Abbot to direct all things so that souls may be saved, and that there may be no murmuring; and are you afraid for the salvation of those who follow different paths under the same Rule? Do you not see that those are safest from every danger whose precepts find their defence, according to the Rule itself, against every shade of variety or blame because of difference, in the intention of saving souls?

14. But now, that you may see that reason also is entirely on the side of the authorities above given, and clings to them inseparably, I must mention some points bearing on the question before us, in which some things are shown to have been changed because of the single eye, through love

unfeigned, and from the intention of saving souls. For when I have shown these I shall leave nothing, I think, for you to ask further, so far as this matter goes. For you use a single eye in not opening the gate of the cloister to a novice till after a year's probation; because, according to the words of the Apostle (1 S. John iv. 1) and of the Rule (Reg. S. Ben. c. 58), you test for the space of a year the spirit of the new-comer, whether it be of God. You use, too, the single eye when you admit a novice within the year from the fear that through so long delay he may return to his mire again, and to the detestable evil of his former life. You use, too, the single eye when you content yourself with two tunics, or two cowls, or with the addition of one or two garments of this sort, because you prefer to follow, if not the precept (Reg. S. Ben. c. 55), at all events the mind and intention of the founder of the Rule, than to add or assume other garments. You use, too, the single eye when you allow the use of a few skins, because you make provision for the sickly, the infirm, the delicate, for all who live in colder climates, so as to prevent their murmuring, or growing remiss, or having reasonable cause to retire from their purpose. You use, too, the single eye when you receive back all fugitives who have not fled three times, because you wish both to obey the words of the Rule (Reg. S. Ben. c. 29), and to deter foolish or unstable monks from repeated desertion, by fixing a limit beyond which there is no return. You use, too, the single eye when you receive back a monk who returns after deserting more than three times, from a fear lest by refusing forgiveness he be exposed to the enemy and perish, and so the wolf kill the wandering sheep, just as he is wont to carry off and scatter those within the fold.

15. You use, too, the single eye when you observe, without making any exception, all the usual fasts both in the summer and winter, from your wish to observe the rules imposed, and to bring forth more fruit from a longer abstinence. But, and I say it out of pure charity, I do not altogether recommend that fasts should be observed by

everyone during the octaves of Christmas, Epiphany, and the Purification, which in all respects are Lord's Days. You use, too, the single eye when you except from the ordinary observance of fasting days the days which I have just named, and every authorized feast day of twelve lections, from a desire to imitate the custom of nearly all Religious who so observe them, and thus you endeavour to honour the Lord Himself, the Apostles, and other saints. You use, too, the single eye in engaging in manual labour, according to the precept of the Rule (Reg. S. Ben. c. 48), from your wish both to obey the Rule and, by such holy exercises enjoined by monastic and apostolic commands, to avoid sloth, the enemy of the soul, as the same Rule says; and moreover, as far as you have opportunity, it is your wish to provide yourself with the necessaries of life, after the manner of the fathers of old. You use, too, the single eye in partly giving up this manual labour, for you may be placed, not in woods or in desert places, but in the midst of cities and camps, and be surrounded by people, and be unable, without more or less danger, to go backwards and forwards so often to your work through a promiscuous crowd of both sexes, and besides you often have not suitable places where you can engage in such works. But lest leisure, the foe of religious, find opportunity to harm you when you have nothing to do, either you do manual work when and where you can, or when you cannot, you make up for it by giving up the extra time to the Divine Offices, and so the evil spirit can claim for himself no empty corner in your heart, seeing that you fill up all your time with what holy pursuits are in your power.

16. You use, too, the single eye in reverencing Christ in every guest who comes or goes, with bowed head or with body prostrate on the ground, and in washing the feet of all, and so you do, as is fitting, all that you can to carry out carefully the good precept of hospitality, enjoined alike by the Gospel and the decrees of the Rule (Reg. S. Ben. c. 53), and you strive to win for yourself the reward due to such a proof of holy brotherly love. You use, too, the

single eye in not prostrating yourself before all guests, in not washing the feet of all, because it would be simply impossible for you to be always prostrating yourself before so great crowds of guests as are constantly coming and going, or to be always washing their feet, so much so that, even if you wished to be always engaged in such duties and were to leave out all the other offices of your Order, you would not have enough time. And because you see it is out of your power to do it, you omit it. What is necessary for the reception of guests you give them to the best of your power, and you show them all the honour in your power, but you excuse yourself from the above duties, which it is physically impossible for you to fulfil; but yet you do this in all singleness of eye. You use, too, the single eye in your wish that the Abbot's table should be always filled with guests and pilgrims, because you at once obey the Rule (Reg. S. Ben. c. 56) and show yourself hospitable to guests. You use, too, the single eye when you determine that the Abbot's table should not be always with the guests, but that he should have his meals always with the brethren, and by recalling him to the common table you thus apply a remedy to the profusion (to use a mild term) of many an Abbot who, when he has guests, is generous to himself but heedless of his brethren.

17. You use the single eye when, like Ezra, who restored the Law, or like the Maccabees, who raised up the temple of God which was in ruins, you labour to make good the great losses of the Monastic Order, and to repair the many rents in many monasteries and in their customs, and, while rejecting what is more of luxury than of necessity, you endeavour, after the manner of the old and original fervour, to banish the lukewarmness of our times. And you use the single eye when you so modify the commands both of the Order and of the Rule, that, according to the words of the same Rule (Reg. S. Ben. c. 64), what the strong want is not distasteful to the weak, as, *e.g.*, when he who cannot live on bread is allowed to have at least milk, so as to preserve life, and when he who has not breath enough to

obtain the prize set before him by running at great speed, is taught to win it at least by the slower walking pace, because he who returns to his country after a year is called as much an inhabitant of it as he who returns after a month. And I say this without meaning to prejudice the different kinds of toil of the wayfarers, because, according to the Apostle, *Every man shall receive his own reward according to his own labour* (1 Cor. iii. 8). You have S. Benedict himself as your authority in this, although, as he himself says, you are not bound to follow his written precepts when charity bids otherwise. Still you find pleasure in showing your devotion to so great a man by following his directions merely because they are his. You have him, too, as the authority for your bye-laws, inasmuch as he directs all his precepts to be carried out according to the rule of charity, and to be made subservient in some way or other to the salvation of souls. You have S. Maur also, his principal disciple, who was sent by him into Gaul, and is said to have altered many points in his rule, following the single eye of which I have said so much. You have, besides, very many fathers of monasteries after him, whose holy life and numerous miracles worked by them through the power of God show more clearly than daylight that they have been moved by the Spirit of God to modify the written words of the above-named Rule to suit times, places, and persons.

18. And what can I say more? If you go in a similar way through all the points on which there seems to be difference, you will find everywhere the single eye, which one will call charity, another the desire of saving souls; and you will see that in this way there is no difference, no discord, because all those points which seem to be differently treated become one through charity. To this I add what is yet evident to all, that there is no precept about such matters in the Rule, which has not conditions attached, and which is not left to the discretion of the Abbot. But even if it had been given imperatively, it could not in any way prejudice the single eye, *i.e.*, evangelical charity. For such precepts, as you know, belong to the class of things change-

able, and when charity bids, they are to be changed without any fear of transgressing. Nor in this respect ought those who profess the rule to be suspected of unfaithfulness to it; because this rule of the holy father depends on that sublime and general rule, from which and on which, according to the words of the Truth, *hang all the Law and the Prophets* (S. Matt. xxii. 40). But if the whole Law so hangs, then so does the monastic Rule. Therefore, a monk professing the rule of S. Benedict keeps it aright when he everywhere observes the law of charity, whether in obeying or in changing any of its articles.

19. Well, then, if this was the sole cause of your strife, brethren, does it not seem to you entirely excluded? Ought not the hearts of monks to be united again in brotherly concord when a single-eyed charity harmonizes all those differences which caused your discord? Does it not make many to be one, since it brings to their promised end, viz., their chief good, which is everlasting life, all who follow what good is under the one purpose of the Monastic Order, or of the same Rule, even though it be by different paths. Let there be then, O Jerusalem, peace in thy strength, that there may also follow abundance in thy towers. But lest, perchance, I be found of the number of those who say, *Peace, peace, when there is no peace* (Jer. vi. 14), let us see if there is still remaining any cause for quarrelling, lest a snake dart suddenly from its hiding place while we are asleep and off our guard, and sting some one of our brethren or yours while we are resting too carelessly.

20. For perhaps the different colours of your habits furnish an incentive to discord, and a manifold variety of garments produces a like difference in your minds. For, as I see too clearly, and as anyone can easily perceive, a black monk looks askance at a white monk when he happens to meet one; and a white monk cannot look a black one straight in the face. I have seen very many black monks, I will not say how often, who, when a white monk meets them, laugh at him as if he were a chimæra or a centaur, or some monster from a foreign country, and

signify their amazement in words or by some gesture of the body. On the other hand, I have seen white monks, who before had been talking loudly, and discussing with each other current events, suddenly become dumb on the advent of some black monk, and lay on themselves the necessity of silence, lest they should disclose their secrets to their enemies. I have seen, too, the tongues of both orders silent, but their eyes, hands, and feet eloquent, and I have seen them proclaiming very clearly by their gestures what they were unwilling to make known by words. I have seen the voice silent, the members talkative, and, by a perversion of the order of nature, men, who were taciturn before their fellow men, communicative to stones. On seeing such things I have often been reminded of the words of Solomon, who says of such men: *He winketh with his eyes, he striketh with his feet, he teacheth with his fingers; frowardness is in his heart, he deviseth mischief continually, he soweth discord* (Prov. vi. 13, 14). O wicked and stubborn device of the evil angel cast out by God! who, unwilling to lose eternal peace alone, gathers to him from wheresoever he can companions of his fall, and, that he may rejoice in a more glorious triumph, he endeavours by the violence of his wickedness to uproot the cedars and firs of the Paradise of God, where he once lived a happy citizen. He is grieved that the crown of heresies has fallen from his head, under which he was wont in early times to divide the Church of God; and seeing no way left to him to damage the faith, now that the Holy Spirit fills the whole earth with belief in it, he turns all his efforts to inflict a wound on mutual charity. For since he cannot now persuade Christians to become infidels, he tries with all his might to prevent them from loving each other. The sect of Arius, of Sabellius, of Novatian, of Donatus, of Pelagius, of the accursed Manes, older than them all, has now perished. Now the clouds of innumerable heresies which darkened the light of the faith have disappeared under the breath of the Spirit of God, and, every mist having been dispersed, have left us the clear light of day.

But a hurricane from the south has succeeded these, and is suddenly endeavouring to throw everything into confusion ; and, because the enemy knows that the faith has prevailed, he is trying to make good his earlier losses by injuring charity.

21. But, putting aside lamentation, I will bring back my pen to the matters that I began on. Why, O white monk, does the black colour of your brother's habit, not of his soul, seem hateful to you? Why, O black monk, does the white colour of your brother's habit, not of his soul, seem marvellous to you? Are not you both sheep of the Shepherd who says, *My sheep hear My voice, and I know them and they follow Me; and I give unto them eternal life, and they shall never perish, neither shall any man pluck them out of My hand* (S. John x. 27, 28)? And what shepherd, to say nothing of God, but what man ever quarrelled about the different colours of his sheep's wool? Who ever thought about it? Who ever thought that the black were more his sheep than the white, or the white than the black? Who ever cares whether they are black or white, so long as they are of the same flock? But see the wickedness of men, the innocence of the sheep. See the constancy of the brute creation to the nature first given them. See the perversity of nature in the rational creature? Did ever any white ram scorn a black one? Did ever any black ewe loathe a white one? Do they not fill the shepherd's folds in common, peacefully, without any disturbance, without any quarrel about the difference of their colour, without giving him any anxiety? Sometimes, indeed, one ram butts another with his horns, one ewe will thrust at another, but it is not any difference of colour that provokes them to fight, but the kindling of the hasty resentment which is natural to all animals. But now I see that man, being in honour, hath no understanding, but is more foolish than the beast ; and, what is more pitiful still, a monk cuts himself off from the unity of charity because of some variation of colour. Do not, my brother, do not, if you wish to be a sheep of Christ, quarrel about a difference of clothing, for

the Good Shepherd casts out of His fold none except him whom, not difference of colour, but a rupture of faith or charity separates from the flock of His sheep. He does not, I say, cut off anyone from His flock because of his colour. From widely-separated countries, from diverse religions, He has gathered together Jew and Gentile alike in the one fold of the Christian faith.

22. This, perhaps, has been taught you by the patience of the holy patriarch Jacob, who, without repining, allowed Laban to change his wages ten times. He has shown us how to make no difference between black and white or different kinds of cattle by showing the good disposition and care which a good shepherd shows for all parts of his many-coloured flock (Gen. xxx.). And the Apostle says, *In Christ Jesus neither circumcision availeth anything, nor uncircumcision, but a new creature* (Gal. vi. 15). And in another place, *Where there is neither Jew nor Gentile, circumcision nor uncircumcision, barbarian, Scythian, bond nor free, but Christ is all and in all* (Col. iii. 11). Who, then, can have so childish a mind as to think that it matters anything to salvation what the colour of different dresses is, or what diversity of customs there may be, as long as there is a new creature in Christ? But if it matters nothing to salvation, why does a difference of habit divide monks? Why does it breed schisms? Why separate their hearts? Why wound charity? There is no cause or reason for taking notice of it, much less for dividing, and still less for complaining of such things. You have, O white monk, a powerful defender enough of your habit in the single eye of your conscience. It has caused you to don a white cowl and tunic, to prevent the black monk supposing, through a long-existing custom, that no one can be a monk who is not dressed in black. Moreover, you have noticed, too, that an innumerable number of monks of this Order have become lukewarm, and, therefore, with praiseworthy intention you have endeavoured to stir them up to a fresh and greater fervour of monastic life by adopting an unusual colour for your habit. You too, [O black monk], in the same way have good authority for the black colour of your

habit in the long-standing custom handed down by your fathers. You feel yourselves more safe in following the old than in introducing what is new. Both of you can appeal to the words of the Rule (Reg. S. Ben. c. 55) as an unimpeachable authority for both colours. It enjoins monks not to quarrel about the colour or the thickness of their habits, but to use garments of that colour and quality which are most easily obtainable in the country where they are living. Let, then, the reason I have given be sufficient defence for your white garments, or perhaps some still stronger reason than I have found. Let, on the other hand, the authority of your fathers be the defender of your black habit. That authority is of equal force with any reason, and should not be reckoned as inferior by anyone who thinks aright.

23. And what farther shall I be able to adduce as setting an example in this matter? Can I bring anyone greater than S. Martin? The great Martin, monk and bishop, chose black as the colour of his garments, as we read in his life. "And when the beasts close to his side saw him enveloped in a black and flowing cloak, they retired terror-stricken to another place." That he was a monk is shown by his founding a monastery not far from Poictiers, another at Milan, and another for himself at Tours. You see that Martin was a monk, and that he wore black. But what does S. Jerome say about this in the letter that he wrote to Nepotian? He says, "Avoid alike black and white garments." This was meant to warn him to beware of pride and ostentation, not only in white garments, which men of the world then wore, but also in black, which professors of religion at that time were accustomed to use. About this, too, Paulinus, the famous Bishop of Nola, contemporary and intimate friend of the same Martin before mentioned, of Ambrose, Augustine, Jerome, and often named with praise by them and by Pope Gregory, in describing the journey of a noble lady who had lately been converted to the monastic life, speaks as follows in a letter addressed to Sulpicius Severus:—

"We saw the glory of the Lord in that journey of the mother and her sons; the same journey, indeed, but of very different degree of luxury. We saw her sitting upon a miserable hackney, beside which an ass would be thought valuable, with senators all around her, and following her, with all the pomp of this world that men of position and wealth could display, with horses in rich trappings, nodding plumes, gilded cars, and with many chariots filling and making resplendent the Appian Way. But the grace of Christian humility outshone these empty splendours. The rich were filled with wonder at our holy poverty, but our poverty laughed them to scorn. We saw the confusion worthy of the deity of this world, its purple, its silk, and golden furniture doing obeisance to worn-out and black garments. We blessed the Lord, Who exalteth the humble, filleth the hungry with good things, and sendeth the rich empty away." You see from this that not only in old times did men, but also women, in taking upon them the religious life wear black garments.

24. For if I may say what I think, it seems to me that those great fathers thought that black was more suitable to humility, repentance, and mourning, and since the whole monastic life ought especially to be given up to these things, they determined that the outward and inward should be united as closely as possible, the colour to the character, the dress to the virtues, for white garments have from of old represented glory rather than shame, joy more than sorrow. And this was shown more clearly to the Church, as is well known to all, by the Angel of the Resurrection, and by the Angels who acted as heralds of the ascending Lord, and by the Saviour Himself in the glory of His Transfiguration, when He showed Himself bright in white garments. Thence it was that that good and learned man Sidonius, Bishop of Clermont Ferrand, when ridiculing in bitter condemnation the faults of certain men, said, "They go in white to funerals, in black to weddings," declaring them to be so confused in their ideas as to pervert the usual order of things, and to go in wedding garb to funerals, and in funeral

to weddings. For those who observed the common custom of that age did not go in white to funerals, in black to weddings, but in white to weddings, in black to funerals, that white garments might agree with nuptial joy, black with funeral grief. When I was lately in Spain I saw and wondered at this old custom being still observed by all the Spaniards. For when a wife, husband, children, parent, any relation, or a friend dies, then the husband, wife, parents, children, relations, or friends at once lay aside their arms, their silk garments, their furs, their many-colcured and costly dresses, and wear nothing but sordid and black clothes. They also cut off their own hair and the tails of their horses, and stain themselves and their animals with black. With such marks of mourning and grief they bewail the dead that they have lost, and spend a year, at least, by the rule of society, in such public mourning.

25. By such authority and reason as this I defend you and your colour, black monk, but still I do not condemn the white monk for his colour. I praise you for not wishing to depart from the holy custom of your fathers; I praise him, too, for stirring up by this uncommon colour in dress his mind to more and more fervour of devotion. He to some degree separates himself, not from charity, which would be impious, but from the well-known lukewarmness of many of this Order. Since, then, you are under one Shepherd, Jesus Christ, since you dwell in one sheepfold of the Church, since you live by the same faith and hope in eternity, you, white monk, as well as you, black monk, why, to speak a little more severely, O foolish sheep, do you quarrel about the difference in your wool? Why do you proceed against each other for no reason, or for so foolish a one? Why for so childish a thing do you rend that first robe of charity? Why do you separate between your very dwellings? Why do you devour one another with the teeth of wolves rather than of sheep? Why do you rob each other and tear each other? See, take care, that this name of innocence by which you get your name of sheep do not prevent you from

being of those whom the great Shepherd will place on His right hand, and of whom He says Himself, *My sheep hear My voice, and I know them, and they follow Me, and I give unto them eternal life, and they shall never perish* (S. John x. 27, 28). But beware, lest it place you amongst those of whom it is said and sung, *Like sheep they are laid in the grave; death shall feed on them* (Ps. xlix. 14). Do you now see how foolish it is to dispute about a colour? How damnable to hate a brother for a colour? How wicked to calumniate a brother for a colour? If this were the sole cause of your discord, if this the sole ground for such a division, if, I say, this was the whole and sole cause of the monastic schism, now that its folly has been shown, shall not this old severance of hearts be repaired? —shall not the wounds of love be healed?—shall not evangelic peace return to the children of peace? Make agreement with peace, therefore, ye sons of peace, and enter into a perpetual covenant with her; if not, perchance at some time there may be directed against you that saying of the Prophet, *There is no peace, saith my God, to the wicked* (Isa. xlviii. 22). And now, thanks to God, I think that I have penetrated into the ancient causes and lurking-places of the hatreds of some men of our Order, and I do not suppose that I need now seek any farther for any remaining cause. And if I am right, you, O white monk, will no longer attack the black, nor you, black monk, the white, if you wish to obey the precepts of your Order, nor will you be moved from the state of a most exalted charity, in hostility to your brother, because of some difference in your customs or some variation in the colour of your habit.

26. But what have I said? How have I lost myself? Where is my understanding? How has the keenness of my sight become clouded over? I thought that I had found the whole ground of offence. I supposed that I had disclosed all the lurking-places of hatred. I was under the impression, as I said, that diversity of customs alone, that only variety of colours, the quality or quantity of clothes or of food had wounded charity among monks, and that this

alone was the cause of so great an evil. I saw the mote in my brother's eye, but I could not see the huge beam, a very oak, in my own eye. But now my eye has been purged, the sky is clear, and the sun in the meridian suffers nothing to lie hid, and I see what it is given me to say, with the leave of everyone, at all events of every good man. For whoever shall feel aggrieved will thereby confess that it has been said of him, as Jerome says. The sound part of the body does not shrink from the physician's hand, but that which quivers and withdraws itself from the finger that would touch it shows, without doubt, that disease is lurking within. What is it, then, that had escaped me?

27. Come, tell me (I will first address the man of my own Order), tell me, black monk; give glory to God, and lay bare whatever lies hid in the depths of your heart against your brother. Who, you say, can endure to have new men preferred to old, to have their intentions set before our actions, to have them regarded as more dear, our brethren as inferior? Who can see unmoved the world for the most part turn away from our older Order, and run after this new foundation, and look upon the well-trodden paths now abandoned, and crowds hurrying on the paths which till now were unknown? Who can bear to see the new preferred to the old, the younger to the older, white monks to black? This, black monk, is what you say. But you, white monk, what do you put forward? We, you say, are happy, because we are recommended by a system far more approved, because the world declares that we are more blessed than other monks, because our fame overshadows the reputation of others, our daylight their lantern, our sun their star. We are they who have restored religion which was lost, the Order which was dead; we are most justly they who condemn all half-hearted, lukewarm, and worldly monks; we prove the fresh fervour of our members to excel all others by our characters, our actions, our customs, our habit, all of which are different to others; and we have exposed to the world the tepidity of the older Orders. Now—now, we have the real secret cause, one far more

hostile to charity than the rest, which has destroyed the unity of your hearts, separated your houses from each other, and often, as the Prophet says, *sharpened your tongues like a sword* (Ps. cxl. 3) to calumnious or cursing words.

28. But let this deadly sword be met by the sword of the Divine Word, and if you are wise you will do all that you can to prevent the fruits that have been stored up with so much labour from being scattered by an empty breath of vain glory. O, loss accursed, and never to be lamented enough! If one hiss of the wicked serpent is to undo the pure continence of your long life, your unconquerable obedience, your unbroken fasts, your constant vigils, your heavy yoke of discipline, so many palms won by your patience, and, to sum up all, your great and numerous toils, both of the earthly and the heavenly life, stored up for so long against your reward in eternity, performed through the grace of God in you; if he is to empty you of everything at one breath, if the old dragon is to cause you to go empty before the sight of the Great Judge, then where is that which the Saviour said to his disciples when labouring under this disease, *I saw Satan as lightning fall from heaven?* (S. Luke x. 18). Where is that which he said in another place when a contention like this rose among them which of them should be the greater, *But ye shall not be so; but he that is greatest among you let him be as the younger, and he that is chief as he that doth serve?* (S. Luke xxii. 26). Where does that verse lie hidden from the eyes of our memory which *the High and Lofty One, of whose greatness,* the Psalmist says, *there is no end* (Ps. cxlv. 3), and Who, according to the Apostle, *is above all, God blessed for ever* (Rom. ix. 5), and Who, not preferring Himself to, or even equalizing Himself with, but submitting Himself to His servants, uttered, when He said, *But I am among you as he that serveth?* (S. Luke xxii. 27). The Apostle is rebuked for putting himself before his brother Apostle, and shall not the monk for preferring himself to his brother monk? Christ, the Master, puts the

greater under the lesser disciple, the superior under the inferior, and shall I, a Cluniac, endeavour to elevate myself above the Cistercian? Christ submits Himself to His disciples, and shall a Christian and a monk raise his neck, swollen with pride, above his brother, who is, perhaps, far better than he? Is majesty to abase itself, and infirmity to exalt itself? Is loftiness to humble itself, and the worm to be raised aloft? Is God to serve, and earth try to rule? And, my brother, how have you fallen from the height of your Rule, from whence you used to boast that you stooped! It bids "that the monk not only say in word that he is lower and viler than all, but that he believe it also inwardly in his heart" (Reg. S. Ben. c. 7). But why labour further? There is no need to say more to pious, wise, and learned men, and, as the proverb goes, to teach Minerva, or to bring trees to the wood, water to the rivers or the sea. The wisdom of you both sees and knows that it is impossible to please God without faith, and also without charity, and that no one, if he throw away humility, can by any efforts keep that charity. For pride of necessity steps into any place vacated by humility; where pride comes there immediately comes envy; where envy arises charity at once dies. For the envious man cannot love him whom he envies, nor can charity in any way remain in one who does not love.

29. Therefore, where there is no charity there is no humility, and where there is no humility there is no charity. This the Apostle declares most plainly when he says, *Charity envieth not, vaunteth not itself, is not puffed up*. And because she is not greedy of other's goods he goes on to say : *Seeketh not her own* (1 Cor. xiii. 45). Therefore, charity excludes all vain-glory, all ambition, all greediness, all avarice, nay, by charity, according to the Apostle, all iniquity is at once driven out. Now, if you wish to preserve this charity, which the Apostle says is the same as the law of Christ (Gal. vi. 2), my brother of Cluny, my brother of Cîteaux, if you wish to lay up for yourself by it great treasures in heaven, and to keep them when you have laid them up, do your utmost to drive from you all the causes,

not only of the departure of charity, not only of her destruction, but even of any injury, no matter how small. If they wish to return after you have driven them out, close the door of your heart against them, and hold fast charity and keep her as an ever present guest. Charity, if she be firmly held, will lift you to the Kingdom in the heavens, for by her sweetly irresistible force she brought down to earth the King of Heaven. The Apostle is a faithful witness of this when he says that because of His great love God sent His Son in the likeness of sinful flesh (Rom. viii. 3). You will rejoice evermore in charity before God, and your joy, as He Himself has promised, no one shall take from you, when God shall be all in all, when your long thirst shall be satisfied, when His glory shall be made manifest; when He shall appear and you will be like Him, and being united to Him for ever by this charity, you will see Him as He is.

30. Now at length let my pen come back to you, my dearest friend, to whom I send this letter. It began with you, and with you let it at last end. I call to witness my conscience that, as I said before, the sole cause of my writing is charity. My endeavour has been to fan it into a flame by the breath of our conference, and to force it to burst out into its wonted flames, if not into greater ones. It now remains for you, whom Divine Providence has given us to be the milk-white and strong column on which the edifice of the Monastic Order is supported, and to be, as it were a bright star, not only to the monks, but also to the whole Latin Church of our day, it now remains for you to throw your whole strength into this Divine work, and to prevent such great companies of one Name and one Order from quarrelling any further. I have always been zealous to commend to my brethren the holy monks of your congregation, and I would, if I could, unite them to each other in the bond of a perfect charity. I have never neglected to do this in public, in private, and in the great assemblies of our Order; and I have laboured to rub off the rust of passion and of quarrelsome zeal which is wont secretly to gnaw at our vitals.

31. Do you, too, labour hard, in proportion to the grace given you by God, in our common field; for no one since you in our time, it has been shown, has planted so usefully; and so with praiseworthy zeal and industry everything that is opposed to what is useful will be rooted up. Banish from their hearts by that eloquence which is from above, and which is set on fire by the Spirit of God, that childish rivalry, that back-biting, and instead of them, whether the brethren like it or not, sow the seeds of brotherly love. Let no diversity of custom, no difference of colours, any longer divide your flocks from ours; but let universal charity unite what is derived from the Divine Unity, repair what is decayed, join again what has been sundered, give life to what has been cut off. So is it fitting that there should be one heart and one soul (Acts iv. 32) in those who have one Lord, one Faith, one Baptism, who are contained in one Church, and who look for the same everlasting life of bliss. I have sent a morsel of crystallized salt to my friend who has no need of jewels, but to whom, as I have heard, its material use was once advantageous, and I thought that a special understanding of it was necessary as an introduction to what I have said above. For whatever the number and the value of the array of virtues on the table of the Eternal King, if they lack the salt of brotherly love they will be rejected as tasteless. But if they are seasoned with this salt the dainties are now acceptable, and will be received with them that offer them. For He Who in His law accepts no sacrifice without salt, shows that He is pleased with no gift of virtue which lacks this condiment.

LETTER CCXXX.

To the Bishops of Ostia, Tusculum, and Præneste.

Bernard warns them to do their duty in driving the wolves from the flock in the Diocese of Metz.[1]

God has raised you to an exalted position, in order that the more eminent the dignity you possess, the more you

[1] See Letter 178.

may use it for the good of His Church. Otherwise the great Father will put down from their seat the mighty whose usefulness has not been equal to the power that they have received. I do not think that you can be ignorant of how great loss the Spouse of Christ is suffering in the Diocese of Metz, though we here are the more horrified because we are nearer. See how great a wolf is daily endeavouring, not only by craft, but also by open assaults, to break through into the fold of Christ, and to scatter the sheep which have been brought together by the blood of Christ. And it is not of yesterday or the day before yesterday, but ever since the time that he was a little wolf he has not ceased with all his might to assail and to harass that flock of the Lord with robberies, fires, and murders. Therefore I, so far as in me lies, point out the wolf, urge on the dogs. What your duty is you will see. It is not my place to teach my teachers.

LETTER CCXXXI.

To the Same Three Bishops on Behalf of the Abbot of Lagny.[1]

He asserts the innocence of this Abbot.

1. I dare to say to you whatever comes uppermost. For if it behoved you to bear a little with my folly, your good-will will, no doubt, bear with my manner, for you are debtor both to the wise and to the foolish. And I say this not because I am thinking of thoughtlessly saying a word not pertinent to the matter, or of using levity, or taking pleasure in trifles, especially before you, who are seen to be pillars of the Church; but out of the abundance of the heart the

[1] Lagny was a place in the Diocese of Paris, standing on the Marne, where was a monastery founded by S. Fursey, with the help of Erchinoald, and restored by Heribert II., Count of Champagne. The Charter of King Robert is still extant in lib. vi. *de re dipl.*, n. 151. The Church of Lagny is described in the Letters of the general chapter of the Benedictine monks as " renowned and famous, formerly rich in holiness and piety."

mouth speaketh, and, when grief is urgent within, truth is impatient of repression, and bursts out into speech. For my feet, I tell you, had almost gone, my treadings had well-nigh slipped, because by what appears an accursed inversion of things wickedness so often overcomes wisdom. The ungodly are lifting their horn higher, the zeal of righteousness is being disarmed, and there is no one who will or can do good. The proud do wickedly on every side, and no one dares whisper against them. And I would that innocence were safe, and that righteousness were enough for its own defence. What sin has the Abbot of Lagny committed?[1] Is it that he is both good as a monk, and better as an abbot—that he is of good report and of better life? Or is it that he has adorned by his pity, and enriched with worldly goods, and increased in numbers of good brothers, the monastery over which he presides? Behold, this crime is laid to his charge. If it is a crime to have been approved by God and men, let him be lifted up and crucified. For heaven and earth are witnesses that it cannot be denied that he has been. If it is a crime to be hospitable, kind, sober, chaste, humble, let him deservedly come empty out of the hands of his enemies. For he is really all these, and in these he cannot be accused; the sanctity of his life and the glory of his renown prove him to be these.

2. But it is alleged against him that he refused to receive the messenger of my lord. That would certainly be a grave offence if it were so. The Abbot does not deny that the man who was sent into England, after being honourably entertained by him, asked to speak with him, but Humbert, the

[1] In the Charter of S. Martin des Champs we find Geoffrey given as Abbot of Lagny, A.D. 1122, in succession to Arnulf, who died A.D. 1106. In A.D. 1124 Ralph became Abbot of Lagny. For this see Hermann, a monk of Laon, lib. iii. De Mirac. B.V.M. c. 18, where he says that Theobald, Count of Champagne, by the advice of dom Norbert, placed a monk named Ralph, of the monastery of S. Nicholas, in the forest of Vosges, as Abbot over the wealthy Abbey of Lagny. He died A.D. 1148, and was succeeded by Godfrey. The Geoffrey mentioned in the Charter of S. Martin des Champs died A.D. 1162. We have two Letters of the general chapter of Black Monks against him, one to Adrian III., the other to Alexander III.

Provost, interposed, since the Abbot was getting ready to go out, and said that he, in the Abbot's place, would see the man. I leave you to determine if any want of respect was shown to the man, and whose fault it was. He is also accused of having taken a letter of my lord the Pope from Humbert by force and of having opened it; but the letter exists, still unopened and sealed; he did not lay hands on it, but Humbert, by the advice of Count Theobald[1] and myself, handed it to him of his own accord. The charge, therefore, is false. He is said also to have imprisoned some monks. That, too, is false. But if he did divide into different cells some who were mutinous and conspirators, lest they should do more harm by being thrown together, who that can judge rightly can possibly blame this? Then as to the charge that he has squandered and alienated the lands and goods of the Church and given them to his relations, sufficient reply was given before in the presence of the venerable Bishops of Soissons and Auxerre, and of Count Theobald, who acted as advocate of the monastery; and I give it again, that he gave to his own as to others, *i.e.*, according to the same scale and custom.

3. Moreover, since the beginning of the world, it was never heard that a mutinous, haughty, and ambitious monk merited from the apostolic See the privilege of his liberty. From the time of Judas Iscariot none has been found like him, to rise in this way against his master, and betray innocent blood. Happy is the master to whom the words of the prophet are common with the Master of all, *Mine own familiar friend in whom I trusted, who did also eat of my bread, hath laid great wait for me* (Ps. xli. 9). Before, indeed, you were lording it over the clergy against Peter the Apostle (1 S. Pet. v. 3), nay, against his co-apostle Paul, you were lording it over the faith of the whole earth (2 Cor. i. 23). But now you have added a new sin in

---

[1] Theobald the Great, Count of Champagne, advocate of Lagny, was buried at Lagny, and at his tomb his son, Count Henry, set up a [perpetual] light. Henry lived there some time, as appears from Suger's epp. No. 120. For Theobald see notes to ep. 37.

taking upon you too much against religion itself. What remains but that you should proceed to lord it over the holy angels themselves? Except that in this, the last Judas seems to have surpassed the first in craftiness and cunning, inasmuch as while all his fellow-disciples shuddered at the infamous deed of the one, the other has had the craft to entrap, not any undistinguished person, but the very leaders of the Apostles, to connive at, nay, even to favour his wickedness. I do not impute sin to my lord, from whom, being but man, [a decision] could be snatched by fraud, and I pray that God will not impute it. But God forbid that, when he knows the truth, the accursed and sacrilegious attempts of this evil man should prevail. And I would have written about this to my lord himself (Innocent) with my usual venturesomeness, if I had not perceived that he receives with less than his wonted favour whatever I write to him.[1] Do you, I beseech you, who are monks,[2] mourn the fortune of your master of S. Benedict, who, as you see, is in danger of being opposed on all sides; so will all the vigour of monastic discipline perish, if monks are to use the strong hand, and to lift up their horns against their abbots.

LETTER CCXXXII.

To the Same Bishops.

Against the Abbot of S. Theofred.

If those things which you hear about the Abbot of S. Theofred[3] are true, you cannot pass them over without danger to yourselves, both because of your office and your conscience. Conscience, I say, not only your own, but also of others. The things are likely, I believe them also to be true. For the bearer of this who also bears his testimony about these matters is trustworthy. You ask how I know all this? I hold a bundle of letters sent by holy men,

[1] See ep. 218.
[2] Viz., Alberic of Ostia, and Ymarus of Tusculum were Cluniacs; Stephen of Praeneste a Cistercian.
[3] A Benedictine, in the Diocese of Pau.

whom I know to be both holy and truthful, and they all alike contain as loud-tongued praises of the bearer as they do dreadful accusations of the abbot.

LETTER CCXXXIII.

To John, Abbot of Buzay, who had left his Abbey[1] and betaken himself to solitude.

Bernard kindly recalls him from his retirement.

To his beloved son JOHN, Brother BERNARD entreats that he walk in the Spirit, and not lay aside fear of the Lord.

1. I cannot say with what bitterness of soul, and sorrow of heart I write to you, dear John, now that I see that I gain nothing by all that I have written, and that my words have no effect upon you. I have written once and again, if I mistake not; and because of my sins my labour has brought me no answer. Now a third time I sow my seed, with prayer to Almighty God, that it may not return to me empty, but may prosper, do that for which I send it forth, and rejoice me at some time or other with the fruit of your obedience and salvation. If you listen to me, nay, rather, if God listen to me, I shall have gained my son. If not I will turn me again to my wonted arms, viz., prayers and tears, not against you, but for you. I have mourned, I still mourn, and draw deep sighs from the bottom of my heart for my offspring. Who will grant to me that you as my brother shall again suck the breasts of my mother? Who will recall you for me into that quietness of mind, that community of life, that fellowship of spirit, and tranquillity of conscience which once kept you fast bound to us?

2. And, if anything on my side is causing you loss or keeping you back, I ask you not to doubt that that report is false, which I hear you have been made to believe by

[1] A Cistercian Abbey in Brittany, in the Diocese of Nantes, a daughter of Clairvaux, founded A.D. 1135. See ep. 116.

some false tongues or other; viz., that I, without any reason or trial, was thinking of removing you from the care of the souls of your brethren that I had entrusted to you. This is not true; but in a word or two hear what is. Even if I had wished to do this, it would not have been lawful; and if it had been lawful (I speak on my conscience) I should never have wished it. This is the truth. If, then, this was the only reason why your heart has been turned, now that the truth has been made known, what remains but that you regain your wisdom, return to yourself, return to me, and moreover condemn yourself for your hastiness and thoughtless cruelty? For if one accursed suspicion had such power to alienate you, and cast you down headlong, how much more power now ought absolute certainty to have to set you up again, and bring you back to us! It would be disgraceful to you if you could be seduced by falsehood, and could not be brought back by truth. You may perhaps be forgiven for having yielded for a time to a disguised falsehood, but now that it has been found out and laid bare, it would be to your shame if you are not greatly angry at it, to say nothing of still giving it credence. Therefore, be angry and sin not, unless you wish me, or rather God, to be angry. For as to that which you have lost, it deserves our pity rather than our indignation. Of course you are a man, making your own way, like the whole human race, across this great and wide sea[1] wherein are things creeping innumerable. Who can boast that while on it he is never driven by winds, nor tossed by the waves? You know that you have been shipwrecked by them, that you have fallen amongst false brethren. I repeat it, this is the truth. You have been deceived, and a lying spirit in the mouth of false prophets has beguiled you.

3. But now falsehood has been dispersed by the bright beams of the risen truth. If, which God forbid, you still persist in your obstinacy, I will not in the meanwhile judge you; there is One that seeketh and judgeth. But I spare you, hiding my indignation, and delaying to come to you

---

[1] *I.e.*, of life.

with a rod. Further, I will endeavour, if I can, to draw you by compassion and a spirit of meekness; for I feel that I am more familiar with that, and I do not doubt that it will more easily gain you. I will not indeed delay to unsheath against you that sword which lies hidden in my well-nigh motherly breast, viz., a continuous sorrow in my heart, and frequent lamentations to God for you until you come back. But if, according to your hardness and impenitent heart, you turn aside all the blows of this sword so lovingly striking you, yet it cannot be but that at some time or other your soul will say, "I am wounded with love." For now it is not only truth, but also charity, which shall set me free. But what am I saying? How, unhappy that I am, how shall I be free when my heart is bleeding from the loss of my son? My affection shall not rest though no effect follow; my grief shall not be appeased; my tears shall not cease. I will show myself to you while I live like another Samuel; be not to me another Saul. I will pray you, I will pray for you, that you return. Come to me, come before I die, that I, who loved you in life, in death may not be separated from you.

LETTER CCXXXIV.

To Herbert, Abbot of S. Stephen of Dijon.

Bernard begs his forgiveness for a religious named John, who had attacked him in writing.

If brother John has said or written anything unbecoming against me, or in an unbecoming way,[1] it is not so much I whom he has injured as himself; for by writing in that way he rather betrays his own hastiness than proves me guilty of wrong; though even if he had in any point injured me it was not my intention to repay him with evil. And so looking to what becomes me rather than what he deserves, I ask and supplicate that you will also forgive the young

---

[1] This John was a regular Canon of the Church of S. Stephen of Dijon, where Herbert was abbot (see ep. 59). It does not appear what he wrote against Bernard.

man this fault, which seems to savour more of boastfulness than malice; on condition, however, that for the future he keep himself from writing or treating of matters which clearly are above him. For as plainly enough appears, in this little thing that he has been presumptuous enough to put forth, there was need of a maturer style and spirit. For you must see, even in this brief pamphlet, that the man either did not write what he thought, or did not think what he ought.

LETTER CCXXXV. (A.D. 1143.)

TO POPE CELESTINE IN THE CASE OF THE DISPUTED ELECTION AT YORK.[1]

Bernard begs the intervention of the Pope against the odious and Simoniacal intrusion at York.

1. It behoves you according to the righteousness which is of the law to raise up seed to your dead brother. This you will worthily fulfil if you maintain the good actions and

---

[1] The case is described by William of Newburgh (de Rebus Angl. lib. i. c. 17); by Francis Godwin (Lib. de Episc. Angl. on Ebor. n. 29); and by Roger Hoveden, in the last part of his Annals. The matter in brief is this: In A.D. 1140 Thurstan, Archbishop of York, died. There was a disputed election for his successor. Some voted for William, nephew of King Stephen, treasurer of the Church of York, others for Henry Murdach, Abbot of Fountains, a former disciple of S. Bernard's at Clairvaux. William was consecrated Bishop by Henry, Bishop of Winchester, but was refused the pall by the Pope when he applied for it. Stephen, indignant at the refusal, would not receive Henry, though confirmed by the Pontiff, and in possession of the pall. Moreover, the citizens followed the King, and refused to acknowledge Henry as their Bishop. At last, however, the King was won over, Henry was recognized by his diocese, and governed it for ten years, and finally died A.D. 1153 at Sherborne. In the meanwhile William was living with Henry of Winchester. But after the deaths of Eugenius and Bernard, on the death of Archbishop Henry, he went to Rome, and at length, by the help of Cardinal Gregory, he obtained from Anastasius, the successor of Eugenius, his confirmation and the pall. But he did not live long after it, as he died A.D. 1154, not without a suspicion of having been poisoned. Godwin says that he was placed in the roll of saints, and that many miracles were wrought at his tomb. But he also adds: "Let who will believe it; let him also remember that, holy as he may have been, he was certainly driven out from his See by Bernard, or, at all events, by his efforts." *Cf.* epp. 238-240, 252, 346 *et seq.* for this York election.

perfect the incomplete works of Pope Innocent, to whose place in the heritage of the Lord you have succeeded. You have a case before you in which you may do this. Is there anyone who knows not that the cause of the Church of York was settled by him? I wish that no one knew how the order which went from his lips has been executed. Who can prevent it from being told in Gath, from being published in the streets of Askelon? (2 Sam. i. 20). But to make a short story for one who is much occupied, let my Lord hear briefly what was said and what has so far been done. When the man who impiously sought his election to the primacy of the Church of York was accused of many faults the whole controversy was at length ordered to cease according to the testimony of the illustrious William,[1] Dean of the same Church, so that his ambition might fail of all its attempts unless the Dean should remove by his oath the charge of intrusion which, amongst other charges, was made against him. But this was done, not by way of sentence, but from mercy, for he himself had asked for it. Surely a most mild sentence, when he was charged with very many grievous faults, which he utterly refused to rebut. But it were well if matters had remained there, for even if justice was not satisfied, at all events the Church was set free from scandal. I do not speak of the remission of the sentence; that did no harm. But this indulgence, though too great, yet availed the adversary nothing, inasmuch as he was unable to carry out what he had himself come forward to promise, for the Dean, on whose support he seemed to reckon, failed him and refused to perjure himself. For when would a good man act as sponsor for a man whom common rumour and his well-known actions alike held up to detestation? What then happened? The one refused to swear, and the other is Bishop.

2. Oh! it is a matter to be kept from the knowledge of everyone, and, if it were possible, it should be condemned to perpetual silence. But that is too late. The triumph of

---

[1] He was called William of S. Barbara, and was afterwards Bishop of Durham.

the devil, alas! has become known to the world. The shouts of the uncircumcised mingle on all sides with the lamentations of good men, because wickedness seems to have overcome wisdom. The shame of our mother Church is pointed at by the finger. Our father Innocent still lives in you, though a worthless servant thinks him dead, and exposes and scoffs at that in him which decency would cover. If this was to be the end of it all, why was this most detestable cause dragged from so far to Rome, when it was more worthy of darkness and a corner? Why was so toilsome a journey over sea and land undertaken by many? Why were the religious summoned from the ends of the earth to accuse him, and why were the purses of Christ's poor drained by the expenses of the long journey? Could not so base and infamous a man have been made Bishop (with unwillingness and grief I say it) without Rome having to know the things at which England was horrified, and for which France abominated him? How much better would it have been if his case had never been brought before the Roman Curia, and if this horrible polluter of everything had never reached even its sacred threshold. How much more tolerable it would have been if the Apostolic see had never heard of this intolerable evil, which now, that it has been manifested, it tolerates. With what rashness was it brought about! The man was publicly spoken against, accused before the judge, not cleared—nay, convicted: and yet consecrated. Let him who after all this laid hands on him see whether I should not say, execrated,[1] rather than consecrated. For he will not deny that these things are so; he will not deny that he found them so stated in the Apostolic letters directed to him on the very subject. Some one, perhaps, may say that since sentence was not given he was not convicted. But I say that he confessed. For to escape judgment he of his own accord elected to have recourse to the testimony of William the

---

[1] This word *execrate* is similarly used as the antithesis to *consecrate* in ep. 166, n. 1, 223, n. 2, and in Duchesne, ep. 300, Vol. iv., which is a Letter of Drogo, Bishop-Elect of Lyons, to Louis the Younger.

Dean, and then since he failed him, what is this but giving judgment against himself, and being condemned by his own mouth?

3. Since these things are so, see, my lord and father, that your heart lean not to any work of wickedness, for, as the Prophet says, *As for such as turn aside to their crooked ways, the Lord shall lead them with the workers of iniquity* (Ps. cxxv. 5). Otherwise do you advise those unhappy Abbots whom the Apostolic command dragged to Rome for the purpose of accusing him, as well as the very numerous Religious in that diocese, that they are to obey him and receive the sacraments from a man twice intruded on them—first, by the King, secondly, by the legate? When he could not enter by the door he forced his way in with a silver axe, as they say, and so was impudently intruded by the legate into the sanctuary of God, against right and justice, against the command of the Supreme Pontiff, to the injury of the highest See and of the whole Roman Curia. If I mistake not, they will resign their posts rather than pay homage to this idol, unless your authority forcibly intervene. But with how much more holy zeal and how much more worthy of your apostleship would it be for you to draw the sword of Phinehas against the two who are so disgracefully committing fornication rather than to allow so many holy men to leave their posts, or to force them to remain against their consciences?

LETTER CCXXXVI. (A.D. 1143.)

To the whole Roman Curia, on the Same Subject.

To my lords and reverend fathers, the Bishops and Cardinals of the Curia, Brother BERNARD, Abbot of Clairvaux, health, and the assurance of his poor prayers.

1. What concerns all must be written to all. Nor am I afraid of being charged with presumption because, though I am least of all, I do not think that any injury done to the Roman Curia is no affair of mine. I am, I assure you, con-

tinually being consumed, so much so that I am even weary
of life. In the House of God I see dreadful things. And
since I have no power to correct them, I, at all events, bring
them before those whose business it is to correct them. If
they amend them, well. If not, I have liberated my soul :
you have no excuse for your sin. You are not unaware
that a sentence was pronounced by our lord, Pope Innocent
of good memory, with the general consent of the Roman
Curia and of yourselves, making void the election, or rather
the intrusion, of William of York, unless the other William,
who was at that time Dean, should deny on oath what was
charged against his namesake. And it did not escape you
that this was not a judicial sentence but one of mercy, and
undoubtedly so, because William had himself asked for
this. Would that that may be adhered to, and that what
has been done against it may not stand. For the one did
not swear, and the other sits in the chair, which I now call
a chair of pestilence. Who is there to send against this
fornication the sword of Phinehas, or to make Peter exercise his power, and with the breath of his lips slay the
wicked? Many are calling on me with all their heart to
urge you to punish this sacrilege as it deserves. Otherwise I am bound to tell you that there will be an exceeding
great scandal in the Church of God, and I am afraid that
the authority of the Roman See will receive heavy loss and
great damage, if punishment is not inflicted on the man
who has perverted its general sentence, and in such a way,
too, that others may fear to do the like.

2. What am I to say of his boast that he has secret
letters, truly letters of darkness? I would that they were
from the princes of darkness, and not from the princes of
the Apostles. Behold the children of the uncircumcised
have heard; they whisper it about that the Roman Curia,
after having given so outspoken a sentence, now sends
contrary letters privately. What am I to say to you? If
this grievous scandal which is scandalizing not only babes,
but also the mighty and the perfect, does not rouse you ; if
you have no compassion for the poor abbots whom the

Apostolic summons has dragged from the ends of the earth, if you feel no pity for the great and godly monasteries, which are threatened with destruction under the burden of this man, if (which I ought to have said first) zeal for the House of God is not eating you up, is the craft of so deadly a foe to be allowed so to prevail that the princes of the Church bear with equanimity her infamy and their own shame? What matters it though the man did obtain sacrilegious consecration? Surely it will be far more glorious to overthrow Simon when he has been elevated than to frustrate his efforts to rise. Moreover, what will you do for the religious men who do not see how with a safe conscience they can receive even the ordinary sacraments from the leprous hand? If I am not mistaken they will rather flee than join hands with death. They will prefer exile to eating things offered to idols. But if the Roman Curia compels them against their consciences to bend the knee to Baal, God will see it and judge. So, too, will that heavenly court in which no ambition can subvert judgment. Lastly, your son beseeches you by the bowels of mercy of our God that, if you have any zeal for God, you, as friends of God, will have pity on His Holy Church, and, as far as you can, prevent any countenance being given to so detestable an affair.

LETTER CCXXXVII. (A.D. 1145.)

To the whole Roman Curia, when they Chose the Abbot of S. Anastasius for Pope (Eugenius).[1]

Bernard expresses his surprise and apprehension at this election. He begs the attendance and faithful help of the Cardinals for the Pope Elect.

[1] Lucius II., successor of Celestine, died A.D. 1145, when Bernard, Abbot of S. Anastasius, at Rome, was made Pope under the title of Eugenius III. He had been a disciple of S. Bernard, and to him S. Bernard addressed his book *De Consideratione*. Ep. 344 was written by him to S. Bernard while he was still abbot; also when Pope he wrote the Letter prefixed to ep. 273. Ep. 475 was written on his death.

To the lords and reverend fathers, all the Cardinals and Bishops of the Curia, the son of their holiness wishes health.

1. May God forgive you what you have done! You have recalled to the world a man who was buried; you have again involved in cares and thrown amongst crowds a man who had fled from both. You have made the last first, and lo! his last state is more dangerous than the first. He was crucified to the world; through you he now lives again to the world, and you have chosen him to be lord of all, who had chosen to be a door-keeper in the house of his God. Why have you confounded the counsel of the poor? Why have you destroyed the resolve of one who was poor and needy and stricken in heart? He was running well. What made you block up his roads, turn aside his paths, and entangle his footsteps? He will fall among robbers just as though he were going down from Jerusalem, instead of ascending from Jericho. And so he who had powerfully shaken off from himself the hands of the devil, however violent the lusts of the flesh, and the glory of the world, could not yet escape from your hands. Did he leave Pisa only that he should be taken to Rome?[1] Did he, who shrank from being the second in command in one church, require the supreme command over the whole Church?

---

[1] Eugenius had formerly been vice-dominus of the Church of Pisa, and a MS. of Dunes quoted by Henriquez calls him Suffragan; he then became a disciple of S. Bernard, then Abbot of S. Anastasius, or of Trois Fontaines at Aquæ-Salviæ, near Rome. Contrary to the usual custom, the cardinals elected as a successor to Lucius, A.D. 1145, not a Cardinal, but an Abbot. And, therefore, Bernard expresses his wonder that one, who had found the office of vice-dominus of a single Church too heavy for him to bear, should have been called to govern the whole Church. We will briefly say what the office of vice-dominus (*Vidame*) was, for there are some Churches or Dioceses which still retain the title. At one time, indeed, each Bishop was bound to have a vice-dominus and a steward (*Distinct.* 89, cap. "Volumus"). And, therefore, S. Gregory the Great, writing to the sub-deacon Anthelm (lib. ix. ep. 66), says:—"We will that our Brother Paschasius appoint for himself a vice-dominus and a major-domo, whose duty it shall be to care, as far as possible, for any guests that may come, and to hear complaints which may arise, etc." The *Gloss*, on "Volumus and Vicedominus," then explains the word: "A steward of the episcopal property whose

2. What reason or counsel made you, when the supreme Pontiff was dead, rush upon a mere rustic, lay hands on him in his concealment, wrest from his hands the axe, pickaxe, or hoe, drag him to the palace, lift him to a throne, clothe him with purple[1] and fine linen, gird him with a sword to execute vengeance on nations, to rebuke peoples, to bind their kings in chains and their nobles with links of iron? Was there no wise and experienced man amongst you more fitted for such things? It certainly seems absurd that a man humble and ragged should be taken to preside over Kings, to rule Bishops, to dispose of kingdoms and empires. Is it ridiculous or miraculous? Certainly one of these. I do not deny, I do not doubt, that even this may have been the work of God, who alone worketh great marvels, especially when I hear constantly from the mouths of many that this has been done by the Lord. Nor do I forget either the judgments of God in olden time or the Scripture which tells us that by the will of God very many have been at different times called from a private, or even a rustic life, to rule His people. For example, to mention but one out of many, did He not choose His servant David in this way, and take him from the sheepfolds, from following the ewes great with young? So I say it may have happened by the good pleasure of God with our Eugenius.

3. Yet I am not sure; but I fear for my son, who is of delicate nature, and whose tender modesty is accustomed rather to leisure and quiet than to managing those things which are without: and it is to be feared that he will not execute the offices of his Apostleship with the dignity that is fitting. What sort of disposition do you think a man is likely to have who sees himself dragged into the midst from the depths of spiritual contemplation, and from the pleasing

duty it is to look after that property and to provide for guests." It adds: "Because a Bishop cannot manage such matters himself." What is said, then, about guests is to be referred to the Vice-dominus. But Filesacus (*Theol. Paris, ad tit. de Offic. Jud. Ordin.* lib. i. *Decret.* or on the sacred authority of Bishops) so distinguishes the two offices, that the steward's duty is to look after guests, and the Vice-dominus is to act as the deputy of the Bishop in hearing causes and suits.

[1] At that time the Pope was vested in a red cope (*Pet. Damian* lib. i. ep. 20).

solitude of the heart, and led like a sheep appointed to be slain to such strange and unwelcome duties. Unless the Lord support him with his hand he must, alas! be cast down and crushed under the unusual and excessive burden, which seems a heavy load for the shoulders of a giant, so to speak, or even of an angel. But it has now been done, and, as many say, from the Lord; it is your duty, therefore, dearly beloved, to anxiously help forward by your earnest efforts and faithful services what we see has been the work of your own hands. If there be any consolation in you, if any power of love in the Lord, if any godly pity, if any bowels of compassion, assist and co-operate with him in the work to which he has been called through you by God. Whatsoever things are true, whatsoever things are honest, whatsoever things are just, whatsoever things are pure, whatsoever things are lovely, whatsoever things are of good report, suggest them to him, urge him to them, do them with him; do this, and the God of peace shall be with you.

LETTER CCXXXVIII. (A.D. 1145.)

To Pope Eugenius: His First Letter.

Bernard at once congratulates and condoles with the newly-elevated Pope.

To his loving father and Lord, EUGENIUS, by the grace of God, supreme Pontiff, his humble servant BERNARD, called Abbot of Clairvaux, sends greeting.

1. We have heard in this our country, and it is on the tongues of all, what the Lord has done with respect to you. Till now I have forborne to write, I considered the matter in silence. For I expected to hear from you, and to be prevented with the blessings of sweetness. I was waiting for some faithful man to come from your side to tell me everything in order, what was done, by what means, and in what manner. I was waiting to see if by any chance one of my sons should return to soothe the grief of his father, and to say: *Joseph, thy son, is alive, and is ruler over all the land of Egypt* (Gen. xlv. 26). Hence it is that this letter is not of

free will, but of necessity, and is extorted by the requests of my friends, to whom I cannot deny the short remaining portion of my life. But as I have once begun, I will speak to my lord. For I dare not call you any longer my son, because the son has been changed into father and the father into son. He who came after me is preferred before me; but I feel no envy, because I am confident that what was lacking to me he will supply, who came not only after me, but also through me; for if you will let me say so, I begot you in one sense through the Gospel. What, then, is my hope and joy, and crown of rejoicing? Is it not you before God? A wise son is the glory of his father (Prov. x. 1). But henceforward you will not be called a son, but a new name will be given you which the mouth of the Lord has spoken (Is. lxii. 2). This change is of the right hand of the Most High, and many shall rejoice in this change. For as formerly Abram was changed to Abraham (Gen. xvii. 5), Jacob to Israel (Gen. xxxii. 28), and, to mention your predecessors, Simon was changed to Cephas (S. John i. 42), Saul to Paul (Acts xiii. 9), so my son Bernard, by what I hope is a joyous and beneficial translation, has been promoted to my Father Eugenius. This is the finger of God raising up the poor out of the dust, and lifting up the beggar from the dunghill, that he may sit with princes and may inherit the throne of glory.

2. It now remains that, since this change has taken place in you, the bride of your Lord who has been entrusted to your care may be changed for the better, and that no longer Sarai but Sarah[1] shall she be called (Gen. xvii. 15). Understand what I say; for God shall give you understanding. If you are the friend of the Bridegroom, do not say, "His beloved is my princess," but "His beloved is a princess." Claim nothing of hers as your own, except that for her, if need be, you ought to lay down your life. If Christ has sent you, you will feel that you have come not to be ministered unto, but to minister; and to minister not only of your substance, but, as I said before, your life itself. A true

---

[1] Sarai (שָׂרַי) = my princess, according to all the old commentators: whereas Sarah (שָׂרָה) = a princess.—[E.]

successor of Paul will say with Paul, *Not because we have dominion over your faith, but are helpers of your joy* (2 Cor. i. 23). The heir of Peter will listen to Peter, who says: *Neither as being lords over God's heritage, but being ensamples to the flock* (1 S. Peter v. 3). For by so doing it will no longer be as a handmaiden but as a freewoman, full of beauty, that the Bride will be admitted into the welcome embrace of her most glorious Bridegroom. By whom else if not by you is this freedom that is her due to be hoped for? By none, if you too (which God forbid), seek in the heritage of God the things which are your own, after having long ago learnt not to call anything your own which belongs to you, no, not even yourself.

3. Therefore, having such confidence in you as she seems to have had for a long time in none of your predecessors, the whole assembly of the saints everywhere rightly rejoices, and boasts herself in the Lord; and specially she whose womb bore you, and whose breasts you sucked. May I not, too, rejoice with them that do rejoice? Shall I not be one of the number of those who are glad? I rejoiced, but it was, I confess, with trembling. I rejoiced, but in the very moment of my rejoicing fear and trembling came upon me. For though I have laid aside the name of father, I have not laid aside a father's fear, or anxiety, least of all the affection and heart of a father. I look at the height and I fear a fall. I look at the height of your dignity, and I see the mouth of the abyss that lies beneath you. I notice the loftiness of your honour, and I shudder at the danger close at hand, because of that which is written: *Man being in honour hath no understanding* (Ps. xlix. 12). Which saying, I think, is to be referred rather to the cause than the time, so that we are to understand it to mean that when he is in honour he has no understanding, because the consciousness of his honour has swallowed up his understanding.

4. And, indeed, you had chosen to be a doorkeeper in the house of God, and to sit in the lowest room at his banquet, but it has pleased Him Who invited you to say: *Friend, come up higher* (S. Luke xiv. 10). And as you have

ascended on high, be not high-minded, but fear, lest perchance it happen to you to utter at last that piteous cry, *From the face of Thy indignation and wrath Thou hast lifted me up and cast me down* (Ps. cii. 10). You have obtained, it is true, a higher place, but not a safer; a loftier, not a more secure. Terrible, indeed, a terrible position is it. The place, I mean, where you are standing is holy ground, it is the place of Peter, it is the place of the Prince of the Apostles, where his feet have stood. It is the place of him whom the Lord made lord of His house, and chief of all His possession. And if you should turn aside from the way of the Lord, recollect that he was buried in the same place that he may be for a testimony against you. Deservedly was the Church entrusted to such a shepherd, to such a foster-father; for while she was still tender, still in her swaddling clothes, she was taught by his precept and educated by his example to tread under foot all earthly things, for he had kept his hands clean from every gift, and could say with pure heart and good conscience: *Silver and gold have I none* (Acts iii. 6). But enough of this.

5. The reason why I am writing to you before the time is this. The Bishop of Winchester[1] and the Archbishop of York do not walk with the same mind as the Archbishop of Canterbury; but they go contrary to him, and this is an old quarrel about the office of legate. But who is he, and who are they? Is not York[2] the same man who, while you were one of us, your brothers withstood to his face in your presence because he was to be blamed. But he has trusted to the multitude of his riches, and has obtained his way in his vanity. Yet it is certain that he has not entered into

---

[1] The Bishop of Winchester (A.D. 1129-1174) was Henry de Blois, nephew of King Henry, who had been formerly Abbot of Glastonbury; he was, therefore, naturally a supporter of his kinsman William. Theobald of Bec was at this time Archbishop of Canterbury; ep. 361 was written to him.

[2] The York trouble mentioned in ep. 235 had not yet been settled; for Serlo (*Monast. Anglic.* Vol. i. p. 747) says: "He was presiding over the Cathedral, and using the royal power against those who withstood him." Henry, Abbot of Fountains, and others summoned him before Eugenius, by whom he was deposed. His supporters sacked Fountains. See ep. 252.

the sheepfold by the door, but climbed in some other way. If he had been a shepherd he was one to love; if a hireling to be borne with; but, as it is, he is to be avoided and rejected as a thief and a robber. What shall I say about my lord of Winchester? The works which he does himself they bear testimony to him. Moreover, the Archbishop of Canterbury, whom they are opposing, is a man of true piety and of mild character. On his behalf, I ask that his righteousness may answer for him, and that their iniquity may be upon them, as it is written: *The righteousness of the righteous shall be upon him, and the wickedness of the wicked shall be upon him* (Ezek. xviii. 20). When you have an opportunity, recompense them after the works of their hands that they may know that there is a prophet in Israel.

6. Who will grant me to see before I die, the Church of God as in the days of old when the Apostles let down their nets for a draught, not of silver and gold, but of souls? How do I long that you may inherit the voice of him whose seat you have obtained! *Thy money perish with thee* (Acts viii. 20), he said. O voice of thunder! O voice of magnificence and power! at whose terror all who hate Sion are driven back and put to confusion. This voice your mother anxiously expects and demands from you; the children of your mother, both old and young, ask for it, sigh for it, in order that every plant which our heavenly Father has not planted may be uprooted by you. For you have been set over nations and kingdoms to uproot and destroy, to build and to plant. When they heard of your election many said: *Now is the axe laid to the root of the trees* (S. Matt. iii. 10). Many are still saying to themselves, "The flowers have appeared in our land, the time for purging is come, when the dead branches shall be cut away, so that those which remain may bring forth more fruit."

7. Be strong, then, and of a good courage; your hand is on the neck of your enemies. By constancy of mind and vigour of spirit show your right to the portion which the Almighty Father has given you above your brethren, which, too, he took from the Amorite with His sword and with His bow. Still, in all that you do, recollect that you are a man,

and keep before your eyes the fear of Him who takes away the spirit of princes. How many Roman Pontiffs have you seen with your own eyes carried off in a short time by death![1] Let your predecessors ever put you in mind of your own most sure and speedy death, and inform you of the short space you have to rule in, of the fewness of the days that you have to live. Amongst all the seductions of this transitory glory meditate constantly on your latter end, for, as you have succeeded others in the Apostolic See, so will you certainly follow them in death.

LETTER CCXXXIX. (A.D. 1145.)
To the Same.

Bernard urges upon him the deposition of William, Archbishop of York.

I am troublesome, I know, but I have a good excuse, viz., the Apostleship of Eugenius. They say that it is I, who am pope, not you, and all who have business come to me from every side. And amongst so great a number of friends there are some whom I cannot refuse to help without causing scandal, or even committing sin. And now I have another excuse no less pertinent in the goodness of

[1] It may be asked, and not improperly, what is the cause that the Roman Pontiffs retain their office for so short a time, that Peter is generally considered the only one to have reached 25 years; why a premature death takes off most of them in a few years, or months, or even days, when we see Emperors and Kings enjoying a much longer reign. The question is worthy of discussion. But who knoweth the mind of the Lord? I see that the same question was put by Pope Alexander to Peter Damian, and treated carefully by him (epp. lib. i. ep. 17). He says:—"You once asked me anxiously what seems to me the cause of the short life of Popes; why within so short a time their reign comes to an end; so much is this the rule that since the time of the Apostle Peter, who presided for about 25 years, no one of the Popes has attained to so long a term of office. Nay, in modern times, scarcely one has been raised to the dignity who has exceeded four or five years. And when I think of this a great amazement fills me; because this necessity seems to be laid on no one else in the world. But, as far as the mystery of the will of God is revealed to mortals, it seems to me that this is done to strike fear of death into the mind of man, and to show plainly, by extinguishing the glory of the head, how worthless is the glory of all temporal things; for since the first of men has to die within so short a time, each one is filled with fear, and provoked to make provision for his own

my cause. My pen is now directed against that idol at York, impelled by the very fact that though I have often aimed at him with this weapon, yet I have never stricken him through. And why is this? Perhaps because none of my darts was wielded like the sword of Jonathan, which never returned empty; but that was not the fault of the javelin but of him who hurls it. For it is evident that it has not been hurled with the necessary strength. And no wonder; for who save a son of the archers can shoot the arrows with a powerful hand? He who holds the place of Peter can at one blow destroy Ananias, at one blow Simon Magus. And to make what I say more plain, it is known to be the prerogative of the Roman Pontiff alone to peremptorily order the deposition of a Bishop, no doubt because, though many others have been called to a share of responsibility, yet he alone has the fulness of power. So, if I may be so bold as to say it, he alone is in fault, whenever a fault which deserves correction is not corrected, or is corrected with insufficient force. With what force the fault of the above-named intruder at York ought to be corrected, nay, destroyed as by a lightning stroke, I leave to your conscience. But I believe that what has not been done has been reserved for you, that in settling this scandal the Church of God, over which He has called you to preside, may see the fervour of your zeal, the power of your arm, and the wisdom of your mind; so that all people may fear the priest of the Lord, when they hear that the wisdom of God is in him to execute judgment.

end; and the human race, which is a tree, when it sees its topmost bough so soon perish, is smitten with a gust of fear, and trembles in its smallest branches." Damian gives the Popes a very short time in fixing four or five years as their limit, but, if the histories of the Popes be studied, they are, it seems to me, to be given even less than that. S. Bernard, therefore, well exhorts Eugenius in this Letter, to learn to consider his own death close at hand, by reflecting on the brief reigns of his predecessors.—[Mabillon's note.] Looking forward from this date, the only Popes who have exceeded twenty years' pontificate have been Alexander III. (1159-1181); Urban VIII. (1623-1644); Clement XI. (1700-1721); Pius VI. (1775-1799); Pius VII. (1800-1823); and Pius IX., who created a solitary exception to the rule which had obtained for his long line of predecessors, by a pontificate extending over thirty-two years (1846-1878).—[E.]

LETTER CCXL. (A.D. 1146.)

To the Same, on the Same Subject.

1. How much do I always desire to hear of you that by which God may be glorified, your ministry honoured, and my soul made joyful. This is why I rejoiced so greatly when I heard of your answer in the case of some who seemed to be filled with an extravagant ambition for the office of legate, and to hope for it with impudence, even more than I can say. And not only I but all who love your name rejoiced with exceeding great joy. Moreover, when I read your letter written in the cause of the Church of Rodez,[1] then was my mouth filled with laughter and my tongue with joy. Such things as these are worthy of your Apostleship, they honour the highest See, they are just what is becoming to the Bishop of the world. Whence, also, I bow my knees to the Author of your unique Primacy, that he will give you so to think and so to act in pulling up and planting, in destroying and building. In truth, you have been raised to this chair for the fall and rising again of many. Let those fall who stand to others' harm, let them fall; but let the worthy be raised. The axe is being laid to the root of the barren trees, the fruitful are being purged that they may bring forth more fruit. With the humble Eugenius at the head of all may the mighty be put down from their seat, and the humble exalted; let the hungry be filled with good things, and the rich sent empty away. Lately, for example, this was exemplified in the case of a certain poor bishop, to the delight of the whole earth.[2]

2. Come, then, let your holy zeal for religion cross over to that unhappy church on the other side of the sea, for it

---

[1] To depose an unworthy man who had been elected to that See.

[2] This poor Bishop, whose name is not given, is referred to again in *De Consideratione*, lib. iii. c. 3, where Eugenius is praised for furnishing him with the means to give, that he might not be considered as niggardly. He is there described as a Bishop from across the seas who wished to buy at Rome his bishopric, and was, perhaps, William of York.

is time to have pity on her. This vineyard of the Lord of hosts, this choice, this most beautiful vineyard is, alas! almost reduced to a wilderness, for a ravening wild beast is devouring it. Why do they say among the heathen "where is its God?" Where is he whom they have placed as guardian over the vineyards? Where is the hand that prunes, where is the knife of the gardener? How long is the ground to be cumbered with a useless tree, and the fruit choked? And certainly the time for purging it has come. Indeed, the man who was to make his peace,[1] by whose means he hoped to clear himself, testifies that there is more need of cutting off than of purging. Letters written by him to the legate of the Apostolic See are in existence, in which he openly asserts that there was an open intrusion, and denies the validity of the election. So therefore he finds that the witness that he had himself brought forward is his accuser. And these charges which are in the mouth of everyone would be enough to rightly deprive a knight of his military belt.

3. How, then, shall he be able to stand when you have many reasons for casting him down, and have moreover the will? I have read in your letters of your zeal for the Church, and I now ask you to show it. It is not my place to dictate to you as a wise man how you should proceed to overthrow him; there seems to be more than one way. Nor do I much care on which side the unfruitful tree falls, as long as it does fall. Still, I say that he who claims to be allowed to take possession on the ground that private letters have passed between him and the Pope, is he not a thief and a robber? Again, when he asserts that he had private letters authorizing his "*execration*," he says what is either true or false. If it is true, he is guilty of theft, and is an accuser of the Supreme Pontiff. If it is false, he ought to listen to the words, Hast thou killed and also taken possession? *For the mouth that lies slays the soul* (Wisd. i. 11). But God forbid that we should believe so great a man guilty of such duplicity, as by this man is alleged against him. If Innocent were here to answer for

---

[1] William, Dean of York.

himself he would no doubt say to him, "I gave sentence against you openly, and in secret have I said nothing."

LETTER CCXLI. (A.D. 1147.)
To Hildefonsus, Count of S. Eloy,[1] about the Heretic Henry.

He describes the impious teachings of the heretic Henry, successor of Peter de Bruys, and blames the Count for permitting such a man to teach undisturbed in his dominions.

1. How great are the evils which I have heard and known that the heretic Henry has done and is daily doing in the Churches of God! A ravening wolf in sheep's clothing is busy in your land, but by our Lord's direction *I know him by his fruits* (S. Matt. vii. 15, 16). The churches are without congregations, congregations without priests, priests without their due reverence, and, worst of all, Christians without Christ. Churches are regarded as synagogues, the sanctuary of God is said to have no sanctity, the sacraments are not thought to be sacred, feast days are deprived of their wonted solemnities. Men are dying in their sins, souls being dragged everywhere before the dread Tribunal, neither reconciled by repentance nor fortified by Holy Communion. The way of Christ is shut to the children of Christians, and they are not allowed to enter the way of salvation, although the Saviour lovingly calls on their behalf, *Suffer little children to come unto Me* (S. Matt.

---

[1] Query, *Eligii*, not *Egidii*.—[E.] Add "also of Toulouse." He was son of Raymund, Count of Toulouse, and Elvira; was born in the East (William of Tyre, *Bell. Sac.*, lib. x. c. 27), and baptized in the Jordan. The same author (lib. xvi. c. 28) also says of him, when speaking of his departure for the East: "There was at that time in the port of Acre the magnificent and illustrious Count of Toulouse, Anfossus (? Alphonsus) by name, son of the elder Count Raymond, whose exploits in the first expedition were worthy of his renown; a man famous by the name he bore, still more illustrious by his father's piety. When on his way to Jerusalem to give thanks to God for his safe arrival he put in at Caesarea, and ended his life there (as is reported) by poison given by an unknown hand." Further, the county of S. Eloy is a part of Gallia Narbonensis, named from the saint who once lived in it. The Count of S. Eloy calls himself Hildefonsus in a treaty of A.D. 1135, drawn up between him and Raymund, Count of Barcelona, where his wife is called Fardida.

xix. 14). Does God, then, who, as He has multiplied His mercy, has saved both man and beast, debar innocent little children alone from this His so great mercy? Why, I ask, why does he begrudge to little ones their Infant Saviour, who was born for them? This envy is of the devil. By this envy death entered into the whole world. Or does he suppose that little children have no need of a Saviour, because they are children? If so the great Lord was made small for no reason, to say nothing of His being scourged, spitted on, nailed to the cross, and put to death.

2. This man, who says and does things contrary to God, is not from God. Yet, O sad to say, he is listened to by many, and he has a following which believes in him. O, most unhappy people! The voice of one heretic has put to silence all the Prophets and Apostles, who in one spirit of truth have joined in calling together in the faith of Christ the Church out of all nations. Therefore the divine oracles have been deceived; the eyes and minds of all are deceived when they see fulfilled what they read was predicted. How certain is it rather that this man alone with a dull and altogether Jewish blindness, either does not see the truth which is manifest to everybody else, or envies its fulfilment, and so by some devilish art or other he has persuaded a stupid and foolish populace not to trust their own eyes in a plain matter of fact, and to believe that our ancestors were deceived, that their descendants are in error, that the whole world, even after Christ's blood has been shed, is going to perdition, and that the full riches of the mercy of God and His grace which saves the world have come to those only whom he is leading astray. And now, because of this, though in much weakness of body, I have set out on a journey to those parts[1] which this ravening wild beast is most laying waste, since there is none to resist him or to save them. Since he has been expelled from the whole of France for similar wickedness, he finds those parts alone opened to him where, under your protection, he is with all his might raging against the flock of Christ. How this is consistent with your good name I must leave you, as an

[1] See *Life*, B. iii. c. 6.

illustrious prince, to judge. Still it is no wonder if that crafty serpent has deceived you, since he has the form of godliness, though within he has denied its power.

3. But now hear who he is. He is an apostate; he was once a monk,[1] but has abandoned the religious habit, and has returned, like a dog to its vomit, to the abominations of the flesh and of the world. Being unable to live a life of shame among his kindred and those who knew him, or, rather, not being allowed to do so because of the greatness of his crime, he has girded up his loins, and has entered on a road of which he is ignorant, and has become a wanderer and a fugitive on the earth. When he began to go about begging he put a price on the Gospel (for he was well-educated), divided the word of God for sale, and preached the Gospel that he might earn his bread. If he was able to extract more than enough to live on from the more simple of the populace or from any of the matrons he would basely squander it at dice, or even on baser objects. Often, indeed, after being applauded by the people in the day, has this famous preacher been found at night with prostitutes, and sometimes even with married women. Ask, if you please, noble sir, why he left Lausanne, why Le Mans, why Poictiers, why Bordeaux, and there is no way of return to any of them open to him, because he has in all left foul traces behind him. Did you, pray, expect good fruit from such a tree? He makes the land in which he is to stink in the nostrils of the whole earth, because, according to the saying of the Lord, an evil tree cannot bring forth good fruit (S. Matt. vii. 18).

4. This, then, as I said, is the cause of my coming. Nor do I come of myself, but I am drawn thither alike by the summons and evil condition of the Church, to see if those thorns and their little seeds while they are little, can be rooted up from the land of my Lord, not by my hand, for I have no power, but by the hand of the holy Bishops with whom I am, and with the assistance of your strong

---

[1] Geoffrey (*Vita Bern.*, lib. iii. n. 16) calls this monk Henry (and Exord. Cister., referred to in lib. iii. c. 17 of the same life). The Acts of Hildebert, Bishop of Le Mans (*Analect.*, Vol. iii. p. 314) call him a hermit.

right-hand. Amongst whom the chief is the venerable Bishop of Ostia,[1] sent for this very purpose by the Apostolical See, a man who has done great things in Israel, and by whom the Almighty Lord has often given victory to His Church. It is your duty, illustrious Prince, to receive him honourably, as well as those with him; and also to take care according to the power given you from above that the great labour of these great men undertaken most of all for the salvation of you and yours be not rendered inefficacious and to no purpose.

LETTER CCXLII. (A.D. 1147.)

To the People of Toulouse after his return.

Bernard exhorts them not only to avoid heretics, but also to drive them away; also to exercise hospitality and not to listen to unknown preachers.

1. On the arrival of our dear brother and fellow-abbot Bernard[2] of Grandselve, I was glad and rejoiced greatly to hear what he told me of the constancy and sincerity of your faith in God, of the perseverance of your love, and of your devotion to me, of your zeal and hatred of heretics, so that every one of you is well able to say, "*Do not I hate them, O Lord, that hate Thee, and am not I grieved with those that rise up against Thee?* (Ps. cxxxix. 21). *I hate them with perfect hatred; I count them mine enemies.*" I thank God that my coming to you was not useless; and that my stay with you, though short, was not unfruitful. When I had made plain the truth not only by word, but also in power,[3] they were seen to be wolves who had come to you

---

[1] Alberic, mentioned in *Vita Bernardi*, lib. iii. n. 17, was born at Beauvais, became a Cluniac monk, was created Cardinal by Innocent, A.D. 1138, legate to England, then to Syria, and then to Gaul. Ep. 219 was written to him.

[2] Mabillon reads thus. But it is hardly doubtful that Abbot Bertrand is meant. MS. documents at Grandselve mention an Abbot of that name, from 1128 to 1148.—[E.]

[3] Refers to the wonderful miracles wrought by him (see *Vita*, lib. iii. c. 6). Even Berengarius recognizes them in his Apology for Abaelard: "Rumour has taken wings and carried the odour of your sanctity over the world, has proclaimed your merits, published your miracles," etc.

in sheep's clothing, and were eating up your people as though they were bread or as sheep appointed to be slain; the foxes which were spoiling your state, that most precious vineyard of the Lord, were seen; they were seen but not seized. Therefore, beloved, follow after them and seize them, and stop not till they utterly perish, and flee from all your territories, for it is not safe to sleep close to serpents. They sit lurking with the rich in secret places that they may slay the innocent. They are thieves and robbers (S. John x. 8), such as our Lord points out in the Gospel. They have themselves been subverted, and they are ready to subvert others, they utterly blemish your good name, and are corrupters of your faith. *Evil communications corrupt good manners* (1 Cor. xv. 33). The word of such, as the blessed Apostle says, *eats like a canker* (2 Tim. ii. 17).

2. Will anyone give me an opportunity to come to you once more? For my desire is, if in any way by the will of God I may be able, to see you again; though I am feeble and sick in body, I should think nothing of the labour since it would be for your exhortation and salvation. But in the meanwhile, beloved, so stand in the Lord as ye have begun, and as ye have heard of me. Obey your Bishops and the other rulers of the Church placed over you. Give diligence to show hospitality, for by this many have pleased God. Your father Abraham, through the holy care that he was wont to take in entertaining strangers, merited to receive Angels as his guests (Gen. xviii.). In the same way his nephew Lot, for similar devotion and pious custom in receiving them, was made to rejoice (Gen. xix.). And so do you, in like manner, receive not Angels, but the Lord of Angels, in the person of strangers, feed Him in the poor, clothe Him in the naked, visit Him in the sick, redeem Him in the captives. With such sacrifices God is well pleased, Who, at the judgment, will say: "*What you have done to one of the least of these My brethren, you have done to Me*" (S. Matt. xxv. 40).

3. I give you also the same advice which I gave you when I was with you, that you receive no strange or unknown

preacher, unless he be sent to preach by the Pope, or have permission from your Bishop. *How*, he says, *shall they preach unless they be sent?* (Rom. x. 15). These are they who put on the form of godliness, but within deny its power, who intermingle, like poison with honey, their profane novelties of terms and ideas with words from Heaven. Beware of them henceforward as pestilential, and know them to be ravening wolves in sheep's clothing. Let the bearer of this letter, the venerable Abbot of Grandselve, be kindly received by you, as also his house, which is also ours, having been lately handed over to us and our order by him, and specially affiliated to the church of Clairvaux. Show to us in the person of him and the saints with him how far you have profited by our admonitions in works of mercy, and give by your treatment of them a proof of your charity, and of the love which you have for me. Whatever you do for them, think it done for me. The grace of God and His peace be with you. Amen.

LETTER CCXLIII. (A.D. 1146.)
To the Romans when they Revolted against Pope Eugenius.[1]

At the instigation of Arnold of Brescia, the Romans tried to establish the ancient Republican liberty in place of the Pope's authority, leaving him only tithes and free-will offerings. Bernard reproves them sharply for ingratitude.

To the nobles and chief men, and to all the people of Rome, Brother BERNARD, called Abbot of Clairvaux, writes, desiring that they may eschew evil and do good.

1. My speech is to you, O great and famous people,

---

[1] *Cf. De Consideratione*, c. 2; Otto of Frisingen (*Chronic.*, lib. vii. o. 31; and *Gesta Frid.*, lib. ii. c. 20). The followers of Arnold are called heretics by Bonacursus, who classes them with the Cathari and Passagii, and accuses them of saying that Sacraments ministered by evil men avail nothing (*Spicil.*, Vol. iii. p. 85).

though I am mean and of no reputation, of small stature, and smaller influence. And, indeed, when I consider who I am that write, to whom I am writing, and, at the same time, how differently another may judge my action, I am held back by very shame. But it is a smaller thing to endure shame before men than to be condemned before God for silence, withholding of the truth, and concealment of righteousness. For He Himself says: *Tell my people their sins* (Is. lviii. 1). It will be, moreover, for a testimony to me before God if I shall be able to speak. *I have not hid Thy righteousness within my heart; I have declared Thy faithfulness and Thy salvation* (Ps. xl. 10). Therefore I am not afraid, though my modesty recoils from it, to write from afar to a glorious people, and by these letters from over the Alps from an obscure person, to warn the Romans of their danger and sin, if perchance they will listen to me and cease from their evil ways. Who knows whether they will be converted at the prayer of a poor man, though they will not give up their power for threats, nor for the whole armed force of the strong? Did not once in Babylon a whole people at the words of one person, and he a youth, return to a just judgment, after they had been seduced by old men, but unjust judges, and so innocent blood was saved on that day (Susannah i.)? So also now, though I am but a youth, and of no reputation, a youth, I mean, not by the small number of my years, but of my merits, yet God is able to give such power to my words that it may come to pass that a people which has been confessedly led astray may return to a better judgment. This, then, is my answer to those who may think that they ought to be angry with me or indignant at my interference.

2. If this is not enough, I add another consideration. The cause is common to all, and there is no distinction of small or great. There is pain in the head, and therefore it is not a matter of no concern to the smallest or the most extreme members of the body. Nor does it pass one by. This great pain, because it is so great, has reached even to me, though I am the least of all, and because it is of the

head it cannot but affect also the body, of which I am a member. When the head suffers, does not the tongue exclaim for all the members of the body that it, too, suffers with the head, and do they not all confess by it that the head is theirs, and its pain is theirs too? Suffer, me then, a little to bewail before you my grief, which is not only mine, but that of the whole Church. Is it not her voice which to-day is heard crying throughout the world: " My head suffers, my head is ill?" Is there any one Christian in the whole world, even though he be the last, who is not proud of this head, which has been exalted by the triumph, adorned by the blood of those two princes of the earth who bent their heads, the one to the axe, the other to the Cross?[1] And, therefore, any wrong done to the Apostles affects every Christian, and as their sound went out into all lands (Ps. xix. 4) so their wrong is felt by all everywhere, everywhere it is bewailed and wept.

3. What has made you, O Romans, offend the princes of the world, who are, too, your own special patrons? Why do you provoke against yourselves, by a madness which is as unbearable as irrational, the King of the Earth and the Lord of Heaven, by audaciously and sacrilegiously attacking the holy Apostolic See, which has been raised on high above all others by its sacred and regal privileges, and why are you striving to lessen its honour when, if need were, you should defend it alone against the world? Are you, O Romans, so foolish as not to judge and discern what is good, and, instead, to defile as much as you can the head of all as well as of yourselves, for which you should not shrink from laying down your own lives if necessity demanded it? Your fathers brought the world under the rule of your City; you are hastening to make your City the derision of the world. See, the heir of Peter has been driven by you from the seat and city of Peter. See, by your hands the Cardinals and Bishops, ministers of the Lord, have been robbed of their goods and houses. O dull and foolish people! O silly dove without heart! Was not he your

---

[1] *I.e.*, S. Peter and S. Paul: of whom the latter was beheaded, the former crucified, at Rome.—[E.]

head, and were not his eyes yours? What, then, is Rome now but a body deprived of its head, a face without eyes, a darkened countenance? Open, unhappy nation, open your eyes, and see your desolation even now close at hand. *How in a short time has her beauteous colour been changed* (Lam. iv. 1); how is she become as a widow, she that was great among the nations and *princess among the provinces* (Lam. i. 1).

4. But these are but the beginnings of evils, I fear worse. If you persist, are you not on the point of perishing? Return, return, O Shunamite! return to a better disposition;[1] recognize now, though it be late, the ills, the great ills, which you have suffered, or are still suffering. Bethink you for what cause and reason, by what agents, and to what uses you have, not long ago, squandered all the ornaments and revenues of all the churches belonging to you; think how, by impious hands, all the gold and silver which could be found on the altars or in the [form of] altar vessels, or in the sacred images themselves, has been stolen and carried off. Of all this how much do you now find in your purses? Further, the beauty of the house of God has irrecoverably perished. And what has made you now repeat this evil-doing, to call down on you again those evil days? What ampler gain or more sure hope is there now to rouse you? There is only this, that your latest doings are seen to be more heedless than the former, because then not only many of the common people, but also some of the clergy and princes in different parts of the world took your part in that schism. But now your hand is against all, and the hand of all against you. The whole world is wholly clear from your blood, except you yourself alone, and your children within you. Woe then to you now, O wretched people, and double woe, and this not now as before from foreign nations, not from the ferocity of barbarians, not from thousands of armed soldiers. Woe to you only from the face of your own people! Woe to you from your servants and friends, from civil war, from cruel searchings of heart, from the sufferings of your children.

[1] *Ad cor tuum.*

5. Do you now recognize that all are not peaceably disposed who are of your own house, nor all friendly who seem to be so? And even if we had known it before, we are now taught more plainly by your example the full truth of that saying of the Lord which He spake—that *a man's enemies shall be those of his own household* (S. Matt. x. 36). Woe to brother from the brother in his midst, and to children from their parents. Woe to them, not from the sword, but from lying lips and a deceitful tongue. How long will you so evilly encourage each other in your evil-doing? How long will you lay one another low with the swords of your lips, ruin one another, be consumed one by another? Assemble yourselves, ye scattered sheep, return to your pastures, and to the Shepherd and Bishop of your souls. Return, ye wanderers, to your first love. I say this not as an enemy to revile you, but as a friend to rebuke you. True friendship brings sometimes rebuke, never flattery.

6. But I add to it entreaty. For Christ's sake, I beseech you, be reconciled to God, be reconciled to your princes (I mean Peter and Paul), and to him their vicar and successor, Eugenius, whom you have driven from his house and home. Be reconciled to the princes of the world, lest haply the world begin to take up arms on their behalf against your folly. Know you not that when they are offended you can do nothing, that when they are favourable you have nothing whatever to fear? Under their protection you need not fear, O renowned city, home of the brave, for thousands of the people that set themselves round about you. Be reconciled, then, to them, and at the same time to the thousands of martyrs, who, indeed, are with you, but yet against you, because of the grievous sin which you have committed, and to which you obstinately cling. Be reconciled to the whole Church of the Saints, who are everywhere scandalized when they hear of your evil doings. Else will this very page be a witness against you. And the Apostles and Martyrs themselves will make a firm stand against those who have dishonoured them and deprived them of the glory of their labours. But let us all now alike hear an end of talking. I have pointed out what is right, pointed out beforehand to

you your danger, not concealed the truth, exhorted you to better things. There now remains, either that I be delighted by your speedy amendment, or grieve inconsolably at the sure knowledge of the righteous punishment ready to fall on you, that I wither and pine away for fear and looking after those things which shall come on the whole city.

LETTER CCXLIV. (A.D. 1146.)

To Conrad, King of the Romans.

He urges the King to defend the Papal authority against the rebellious Romans.

1. Never more sweetly, more harmoniously, or more closely could kingship and priesthood have been united or planted together than when they both alike met in the person of the Lord, since He was made for us out of both tribes according to the flesh, at once High Priest and King. And not only so, but he also mingled them and united them in His Body,[1] which is the whole Christian people, Himself being their Head; so that the Apostle calls this race of men, *A chosen generation, a royal priesthood* (1 S. Pet. ii. 9). In another Scripture are not all as many as were predestinated to life called kings and priests? (Rev. i. 6 and v. 10). Therefore, what God hath joined together let not man put asunder. What Divine authority has sanctioned let man's will be the more diligent to fulfil, and let those whom precepts have united be united in their minds. Let them help each other, defend each other, bear each other's burdens. The Wise Man says, *If a brother help his brother, both shall receive consolation* (Prov. xviii. 19). But shall they not both receive desolation if, which God forbid, they bite and devour each other? May my soul never come into the

---

[1] *Cf.* Suger, ep. 74: "Since it is agreed that the glory of the Body of Christ, which is the Church of God, consists in the indissoluble connection of royalty and priesthood, it is surely plain that he who provides for the one cares for the other; for that the earthly kingdom is rendered steadfast by the Church of God, and the Church of God profits by the earthly kingdom, is plainly recognized by all people of discernment." See John of Salisbury, ep. 44.

counsel of those who say that either the peace and liberty of the Churches is injurious to the Empire, or that the prosperity and exaltation of the Empire are harmful to the Churches. For God, the Founder of both, has not joined them for destruction, but for edification.

2. If you know this, how long do you continue to pass over their common reproach, their common wrongs? Is not Rome at once the Apostolic See and the capital of the Empire? To say nothing, then, of the Church, is it to the King's honour to hold in his hands a broken sceptre? I know not, indeed, what advice your wise men and the heads of your kingdom may give you on this matter, but I, speaking in my folly, will not keep back what I think. The Church of God has from the beginning down to the present time many times suffered tribulations, and many times been set free. Listen to what she says about herself in the Psalm, *Many a time have they fought against me from my youth up, but they have not prevailed against me. The sinners built upon my back, and made long their iniquity* (Ps. cxxix. 2, 3). The Lord, certainly, O King, will not now let the rod of sinners come into the lot of the righteous. The Lord's hand is not shortened or weakened that it cannot save. He will at this time again without doubt set free His Spouse, whom He redeemed with His own Blood, endowed with His Spirit, adorned with Heavenly gifts, and enriched none the less with earthly bounties. He will set her free, I repeat. He will set her free, but if by the hand of another, even the princes of the realm can see whether that would be to the King's honour or to the benefit of the kingdom. It would not be to either.

3. Therefore gird thee with thy sword upon thy thigh, O, most mighty, and let Cæsar restore to himself the things which are Cæsar's, and to God the things which are God's. It is well known that both are in the charge of Cæsar, viz., to guard his own crown and to defend the Church. One befits the King; the other the defender of the Church. The victory, I trust in God, is in your hands. The haughtiness and arrogance of the Romans are greater than their courage.

How is it? Would any Emperor or King, no matter how great and powerful, presume to offer such an insult at once to the Empire and the priesthood? But this accursed and turbulent people, which knows not how to measure its strength, to think of its object, to consider the issue, has in its folly had the audacity to attempt this great sacrilege. God forbid that popular violence and the rashness of the vulgar should for a moment be able to stand before the face of the King. I have become as a fool, in that, though a mean and unknown person, I have thrust myself like some great one into the counsels of such greatness and such wisdom, and in a matter, too, of such importance. But the more unknown and humble I am, the freer I am to say what charity suggests. And therefore I add also this in my folly: I do not suppose that anyone will, but if anyone should attempt to persuade you to anything else but what I have urged upon you, it is certain that either he does not love the King or has but little perception of what befits the royal majesty, or else he seeks his own advantage, and does not thoroughly care either for what is God's or for what is the King's.

LETTER CCXLV. (A.D. 1146.)
To Pope Eugenius, on Behalf of the Bishop of Orleans.[1]

He praises the zeal of the Pope in this matter.

Thus act always, I pray you. Always look at the petition,

[1] Helias. After the death of John, Bishop of Orleans, A.D. 1133, Hugh, the Dean, was chosen to succeed him. This is on the authority of Orderic (lib. xiii. on the year 1134), who writes as follows:—" After the aged John, Bishop of Orleans, had given up his Bishopric with his life, Hugh, the Dean, was elected to the vacant office; but returning from the King's Court he was attacked by desperadoes and died, thus leaving the Diocese to be for a long time tossed about without a ruler, like a ship on the sea without a rudder." This lasted till A.D. 1136, when Helias, after a protracted disagreement between the clergy and laity, was chosen by the unanimous vote of all. He was a monk and Abbot of S. Sulpicius of Bourges. Peter of Cluny (lib. i. ep. 11) calls him "a man full of piety, prudence, and learning." Peter wrote for his confirmation to Innocent, and he was consecrated by him in April, 1137. After some years, viz., in

not at the petitioner. The King's intercession for the
Bishop of Orleans was not listened to, yet he was not
offended, because his heart is in the hand of God. But
even if he had been, you would have had to bear it, lest
God should be offended, Who will be the more propitiated,
and more quickly give us deliverance from the evils that
we suffer and from our grief, if righteousness be held fast
and truth not given up. It is not easy to say how much my
heart is gladdened by such actions as these of yours, which
are daily being noised abroad, to the great joy of all. So
much for this. For the future, if anyone suggests to you
that more might be put upon me, know that my strength is
unequal to what I now bear. Inasmuch as you spare me
you will also spare yourself. I think that you know that it
is my determination not to leave my monastery again.[1] In
the matter of brother Balditius, though he is beloved by
and is useful to me, I have obeyed you without delay.
With regard to sending an Abbot to S. Anastasius,[2] if it
has not been done it shall be directly I know that it has
not. Further, as to sending someone else, as in your last
letter you said nothing about it, I did not presume to do it.
But this shall be done as quickly as you see fit to hasten it.
My lord of Auxerre and brother Balditius will give you an
answer about everything more at length and more plainly.
What Baldwin, Archbishop of Pisa, did in Sardinia in the
matter of the excommunication of the judge of Arvora, I
ask that you will uphold, ratified and unshaken by your
authority, because I believe that so good a man would not
have done this except justly. Lastly, let the judge of

1144, he was accused before Lucius II. of grievous crimes by the clergy of
Orleans, and when he could not clear himself, and when the Pope could not be
induced to show him favour, either by Peter (lib. v. epp. 19, 21, 27) or by King
Louis himself, he of his own accord resigned his See on the advice of S. Bernard,
A.D. 1146, when Eugenius had succeeded Lucius. It is, therefore, remarkable
that Alberic should say (Chron., A.D. 1149) that "Atto, Bishop of Troyes, and
the Bishop of Orleans were deposed in a council held at Rheims," when each of
his own free will resigned his office, as is clear in the case of the Bishop of
Orleans from this Letter, and in the case of Atto from the notes to ep. 23.

[1] See epp. 227, 228.
[2] Rualene (epp. 258, 259, 260) was sent.

Torre,[1] since he is said to be a good prince, find favour with you and receive a welcoming hand.

LETTER CCXLVI. (A.D. 1146.)

To the Same, on Behalf of the Same Bishop of Orleans, after his Deposition.

He commends to the Pope the Bishop of Orleans, who had voluntarily resigned his See.

1. It is now time for me to write, not as before, on behalf of a Bishop, but for a poor and lowly monk,[2] which is a more distressing task than if it were for one who is rich and in good position. Hence there is no room now for flattery, but only for mercy. Many wrote on his behalf to ask that he might remain Bishop, but this was too much to ask. I could not be induced to venture on that. But now if the affair is looked at more gently, humanity demands now, what before I avoided asking. The man had hope until now, and the reason of his hope was of this kind. He said: "The state of affairs has been greatly changed since the sentence that I should purge myself was pronounced against me. And, indeed, the sentence that I received was severe enough, and one that could hardly be fulfilled by the most innocent. But how can it now when everything has made it impossible? There is no Bishop at Nevers, nor yet even at Troyes. The Bishop of Auxerre has crossed the Alps. These three form a great part of the number of comprovincials by whom I was to purge myself. Those who can purge me are certainly not lacking, but the Bishops are either non-existent or absent. Can, then, that be rightly exacted from me which cannot be found? If the

---

[1] This seems to be Gunnar, once judge and tetrarch of Sardinia, who, coming to the grave of S. Martin, returned by way of Clairvaux, where, being welcomed by Bernard, he afterwards became a monk (Heribert, *De Mirac. Bern.*, lib. ii. c. 13).

[2] He was first Abbot of S. Sulpicius, then Bishop of Bourges, and then again a monk.

judge finds the case thus, is it wonderful if he relieve me from an impossible sentence? Or if it is not wholly impossible, he will, of his own accord, pass lightly over or not scrutinize too severely acts which are of small importance. Surely he wishes for mercy and not sacrifice. For what advantage is there in my blood that he should search out my iniquity and examine into my sin? But because he is kind and merciful, something he will forgive, something he will pass over, and will add somewhat of his own. He is the lord; is it not lawful for him to do what he will? Even if the Pope, as a man of apostolic gentleness and authority, does not care to supply me with an excuse, as, indeed, he need not, why should he not use the liberty he enjoys, and promptly let mercy triumph over justice?

2. When, then, this hope was allowed him in the midst of his fear, and not in vain, as it seemed to him and his friends, yet he gave way, and trusted himself entirely to my judgment. And in order that he might not trouble the Church too long with his case, on my advice he anticipated the end, and the descent of the axe, and resigned his bishopric. There is one source of consolation, most merciful father, which this noble and repentant man has in the midst of his sad fortune. Do you ask what that is? Certainly he does not exercise himself in great matters, nor in things too high for him. It is enough for him if by your indulgence he, who was once a bishop, may remain a priest ; if only the shield of your favour may be held before him to save him from the mark of infamy, and from being branded for ever with disgrace. A prayer, surely, that is worthy of being listened to. He does not ask this from pride, but lest he who was once so high should sink lower than the lowest. He will be contented with any position mid-way. Let him as he falls from on high stay himself on whatever honourable step he can lay hold of in his fall, and not descend to the lowest step of shame. He is young, of noble birth, has been placed in a high position, and yet he does not shrink from a lowly place, but from one of shame. Shall not even his humility gain him somewhat? The

impious Ahab humbled himself and was profited by it (1 Kings xxi. 27-29); and shall not humility bring its reward to one who is faithful and noble? Far be it from the highest See, and far from your holy mind, to despise a humble and contrite heart.

3. If I should say, "He has humbled himself, let him be lifted up," this would not be too rash or presumptuous for me to say for him; I should only be invoking a rule that you know (S. Matt. xxiii. 12). But as it is, I do not ask that he be lifted up, but that he be not trodden under foot, and that I be not disappointed of my hope. Nay, indeed, if we have received evil at the hand of the Lord, shall we not also receive good? For have you not the power to put down the mighty from their seat, and to exalt the humble and meek? Further, when we have received power, to prefer to use it against evil rather than for good, is to abuse it. Besides, he is worried by many debts, since he is now poor and needy. Let your authority order them to be paid from the episcopal revenues. It is hard to be at once deprived of honour, and to be burdened with a load of debts.

LETTER CCXLVII. (A.D. 1146.)

To the Same, for the Archbishop of Rheims.

Bernard is displeased at the severity shown towards the Archbishop of Rheims, in withdrawing from him the use of the pallium.

To his loving father and lord EUGENIUS, by the grace of God Supreme Pontiff, his humble servant BERNARD, Abbot of Clairvaux, sends humble greeting.

1. May God forgive you! What have you done? You have shamed the face of one of the most conscientious of men, and humiliated in the face of the Church one whose praise is in the Church. You have made all his adversaries to rejoice, but how many do you suppose you have grieved? There is no measure to the sympathy that he receives, be-

cause his friends are numberless. A man beloved by God
and men is suffering the punishment due to a great crime,
though it has not been brought home to him, nor confessed.
We hold, we feel, the zeal of Phinehas; the Israelite is
thrust through, but not with the Midianitish woman. It is
charged against him that he crowned the King,[1] but he does
not think that in so doing he has exceeded the tenor of his
privileges. It is objected against him that he knowingly
presumed to celebrate in a church lying under an interdict.
He denies it. In good time that will be brought to the

[1] I find that Louis the Younger was more than once crowned. The first time was during the lifetime of his father, when he received the crown from Innocent A.D. 1131, at Rheims. The second took place (Ordericus Vitalis says) at Bourges, A.D. 1138. He writes:—" In the year 1138 Louis King of France was crowned at Bourges on Christmas Day, and there was gathered together a large assembly of the nobles and of lesser men from all Gaul and Aquitaine, and from the surrounding countries. Thither assembled the metropolitans with their suffragans, thither came the consuls and other high personages to show their loyalty to the new king." Ordericus speaks of him as a " new king " because, on the death of his father, he was crowned King of Aquitaine. Here we see him crowned again by Samson, Archbishop of Rheims, before setting out for Jerusalem, perhaps that he might receive the oath of loyalty in solemn assembly before he left his vassals. Horst thinks that the place where this last ceremony took place was Chartres, where the question of the expedition to Jerusalem was discussed. But from the tenor of this Letter it is evident that this coronation took place at Bourges. The same thing is evident from the Letters of Eugenius, from which we see that Eugenius was under the impression that the church of Bourges, in which Samson had performed the ceremony, had been placed under an interdict. From this Letter, and from another of Ivo's to be quoted presently, it further appears that the Archbishop of Rheims contended that it was his prerogative to crown the king whenever the ceremony took place. This was denied by Peter of Bourges, and by Ivo of Chartres before him. But in this Letter S. Bernard does not deprive the Archbishop of Rheims of this prerogative, nay, he rather seems to admit it. Silvester II. mentions it in a bull sent to Arnulf, Archbishop of Rheims, whom he had suspended for a breach of good faith, and whom he restored A.D. 999 to his former dignity and all his rights. He says:—" We grant to you by the provisions of this edict permission to resume the ring and staff, and to discharge the office of Archbishop, and to enjoy after the usual manner all the insignia which belong to the metropolis of the holy Church of Rheims, to use the pall at the wonted solemnities, at the benediction of kings, and of your suffragan Bishops." And certainly it was most suitable, since the " most Christian Kings " had received the dignity of the royal priesthood from the blessed Remigius, Archbishop of Rheims, and also the pledge of their heavenly crown through their baptism and profession of the Christian religion, that they should give to his successors the right of consecrat-

test, and he be cleared. But be it so, let us suppose that all that his adversary has been allowed, or has cared, to say against him in his absence is true. Is it right that one whose other actions have been so praiseworthy should for this single excess be so hardly dealt with, so severely punished? To have exceeded this once only, might have been thought even a virtue, if the judgment on his action had proceeded from you and not from his enemies. What ought he to have done in such difficult circumstances? The day had been fixed, the court was solemnly assembled, the

ing and crowning kings; as for a like reason the Emperors gave it to the Archbishop of Mayence because of S. Boniface, the Kings of Spain to Toledo because of S. Eleutherius, the Kings of England to Canterbury because of S. Augustine; although, of course, this privilege of the Archbishop of Rheims was liable to be dispensed with by lawful authority as time and place might require. And I do not think that Ivo of Chartres meant anything more in his famous Letter 189, in which he defends the solemn coronation of Louis VI. by Daimbert, Archbishop of Sens. For elsewhere (ep. 48) he admits that this was the prerogative of the Church of Rheims; when writing to Pope Urban he says that that See " holds the king's diadem." And again in another Letter he protests that he does not begrudge it to Rheims, he does not oppose it, is not grieved if the Kings of France have such an affection for it, as to prefer to be crowned by it than by any other. But yet he defends the dispensation for what was done by Daimbert as a rightful one. "What we did," he says (ep. 189), "we did after wholesome deliberation and provident dispensation. There were certain men, troublers of the kingdom, who were eagerly on the watch for an opportunity to transfer the kingdom to another, or to diminish its dignity in no small degree." His assertion that that privilege was not based on reason, custom, or law, must not be taken too literally, for the tenor of his argument against custom is to show that " the Kings of France had not all been consecrated at Rheims, or by the Archbishops of Rheims," which is admitted. He seems to be directing all his efforts to deny, putting aside the question of a dispensation, that the consecration of kings must always take place at Rheims under pain of an anathema being incurred by anyone who for any reason should do otherwise, which seemed to be the contention of the representatives of Rheims in the matter. (*Cf.* Aimoin, *Continuation of Acts of the Franks*, lib. v. c. 50, and Hugh in *Chron.* Auxerre, A.D. 1154). At last, to prevent any future dispute, Louis VII., A.D. 1179, confirmed this prerogative of the Archbishop of Rheims by a solemn decree, and it was afterwards confirmed by Letters of Alexander and Innocent III. It is astonishing to us now what a value was then put on the use of the pall, which had been interdicted to Samson by the Pope; so much so that S. Bernard would rather that he himself was forbidden to celebrate mass than that the Archbishop should be deprived of the use of the pall. Moreover, S. Malachy did not hesitate, in order to obtain it, to cross twice from Ireland to Rome.

young King was there, and, above all, the business for which they had assembled was God's business, viz., the expedition to Jerusalem. All these things plainly forbade that the solemn crowning of the King should be put off, or that it should be deprived of the wonted masses, and of its due honour. Neither was it expedient for the Archbishop of Bourges to prevent this honour being shown to the King.

2. And since this is how the case stands, I think that it is not one without an opportunity for mercy, since great necessity can excuse any appearance of contumacy. Have you power to strike only, and not to heal? You know who said, *I will wound and I will heal* (Deut. xxxii. 39). Far be it from you not to use the words of Him Whose place you hold, especially His words of fatherly love. Therefore, for this time only let the arrow of Jonathan speed quickly back, and if need be let it be shot at me instead. I should think it more tolerable, I confess, for me to be forbidden to celebrate mass than for the Archbishop to be deprived of his pall. There is also another reason of no small weight which stands in the way of your godly severity here, and that is, that it may give great occasion of offence and irritation to your son, King Louis, since he will seem the whole cause of all this trouble; and this plainly is unadvisable just now, for the good work which under your exhortation he has set about zealously and earnestly may fail of a worthy ending if he does it while angry and offended. As to the rest, you have ordered, I have obeyed; and your authority has caused a ready obedience to be paid to the injunctions. I have declared and spoken, they are more than I can number. Cities and castles are made empty; and now they find with difficulty one man that seven women can lay hold of, so many widows are there everywhere, and their husbands still living.

LETTER CCXLVIII. (A.D. 1146.)

To the Same.

Bernard forewarns the Pontiff not to lend an ear to the Bishop of Seéz, who is endeavouring to be reinstated in his diocese.

1. It is not my custom, as it is with many, to use any preface, any roundabout phrases with you. I begin at once with the matter itself. A deceitful man is on his way to you, to deceive you, I believe, but I hope that he will not succeed. For this could not happen except with very great danger to many. It is always an evil to deceive anyone; it is commonly also an evil to be deceived by anyone. But it makes a difference who it is that is deceived, and in what he is deceived. The greater your power and dignity is, the more dangerous and more disgraceful is it to take any advantage of you, especially in ecclesiastical matters. For example, this deceitful fox of Seéz is craftily laying his snares for you, hoping by his craft to catch you, and you can imagine with what malignity he will rage against the vineyard of the Lord of hosts, no small part of which he has in a short time laid waste, if he is allowed to return to it fortified by your authority. Alas! what is left he will speedily devour. He who came a fox will return a lion, and he will no longer use cunning but cruelty against some of the clergy, as well as some of the laity. You must, then, be on your guard against his cunning, so that his violence may not break out a second time.

2. Be not moved by the piteous face of the man, his mean dress, his suppliant look, his downcast eyes, the humility of his words, nor yet by his crocodile's tears, running, they say, at will, and practised to further his lies. All these are but the appearance, and you know Who said, *Judge not according to the appearance* (S. John vii. 24). In such things as these consists the form of godliness, but not always its power. These are sheep's clothing, often put on, as the Lord warned us, by wolves for the greatest

destruction of the sheep. The sheep do not hide themselves, for the wolves come to them disguised (S. Matt. vii. 15). Thence it is that some of my friends, taken in by his falsehoods, have written on his behalf, not paying attention to what was wisely and truly said by the Wise Man, *There is one who wickedly humbles himself, and his inward parts are full of deceit* (Ecclus. xix. 23). Pay no attention, then, to his words, or to the gestures of his body; examine his deeds. By his fruits you will know him. Many grievous things are said of him; they will also be said against him if there is one that seeketh and judgeth. I am unwilling to tell you all that I have heard. For everything is not to be believed; but neither is everything to be disbelieved. I briefly mention one conjecture of mine; you will judge if there is anything in it. Why did he refuse the judges given him? If he objects to them personally, they were under no suspicion. If he objects to the place, it was in his own land, amongst his own kindred, where the whole matter could be investigated easily, and without trouble, at small expense, and without a long journey. We can clearly only conclude that he appealed to you as an expedient to escape from the great number of his accusers who would be unable to pursue him outside his native land because of the expense. We must thank the Bishop of Lisieux, whose zeal for the House of God has made him spare neither his purse nor his individual trouble. He is a good brother, whose desire it is to raise up seed to his dead brother.[1] Do you, too, thank him, because this diligent

[1] He skilfully applies the old and now antiquated command of God, that if a man died without children his brother should raise up seed to him, to Arnulf, Bishop of Lisieux; who by Letters to the Pope, and by his close attention, so preserved the rule of S. Augustine, which had been given by his brother John, Bishop of Seéz, to secular canons, and which had been allowed to be grievously neglected by his successor, that S. Bernard here happily remarks that he had raised up his brother's seed, which another's carelessness and license had well nigh choked. It is likely that he laboured in this matter for some twenty years, as appears from a Letter of his to Pope Alexander III., beginning, "There is one who," etc. John, the brother of Arnulf, died A.D. 1143, and was succeeded by Girard, the second of that name, formerly a secular canon, who from the above Letter to Arnulf seems to have been refused consecration as Bishop until he pro-

care of his will shed no small-lustre on your name, for by it the wicked is made manifest, and so overthrown, which is your glory.

LETTER CCXLIX. (A.D. 1145.)
To the Same.

He commends as worthy the Prior of Chaise Dieu, elected to the See of Valence.

If rarity gives value to things, nothing in the Church is more precious, nothing more to be wished for, than a good and useful pastor. Truly such is a rare bird. Accordingly, whenever such is found, and an occasion is given, immediately men's hands are laid upon him, and they strive with all their might, using every possible violence and act of wickedness to prevent his promotion and the good fruit that it promises. I have heard that in the Church of Valence the Prior of Chaise Dieu[1] has been elected by the vote of both clergy and laity. I should be greatly surprised if he were not a good and useful man in the work to which he has been called. Do you wish to know why I think so? Good men wish it, and one who pleases good men cannot but be good. And it is, it seems to me, no less a real proof of his goodness if he is displeasing to the bad in the neighbourhood. It becomes your holiness to confirm the election of these good men, lest if their choice be rejected you receive, by the efforts and conspiracy of the wicked, some other whom you would not wish.

LETTER CCL.
To Bernard,[2] Prior of Portes.

Bernard thinks that the refusal of the Pope to raise fessed the same Order himself. But, as the same Letter says, this Bishop was declared to have conceived the detestable desire of uprooting this plantation of regular canons. For this reason he is here alluded to by Bernard.

[1] On the death of John, Bishop of Valence, A.D. 1145, Orilbertus, Prior of Chaise Dieu, was elected, and this Letter, as well as ep. 270, was written on his behalf.

[2] The second of the name. He left the See of Belley A.D. 1142, and returned

Brother Noel on account of his youth to the Episcopate ought not to be resented by the brethren.

To the most reverend fathers and loving lords, BERNARD, Prior of Portes, and the saints with him, BERNARD, called Abbot of Clairvaux, sends greeting in the Lord.

1. From a passage in the reply of your Beatitude I find that I wrote something which made you think that I was troubled, and that you fear that not a little. But if so it is without cause. For there is no reason why you, most reverend fathers, should fear anything from your child who loves you in truth as friends and holds you as saints. Unless, perchance, you feared not me, but for me, with a fatherly love, because I seemed to you to be troubled without reason, or if with reason, more, perhaps, than I ought. I was troubled, I admit, not against you, but for you, and that but little. If this, too, was hastiness, then without hastiness I confess against myself my unrighteousness, and you will forgive the hastiness of my sin. Pardon me, such is my nature; the zeal of your house eats me up. I will not allow, so far as in me lies, such an example of sanctity to lose its lustre,[1] for God forbid that I should be afraid of its being corrupted. In exactly the same way in a beautiful body not only disease, but even a mole is distressing. Evidently the colour is not good if any one of the saints seems to be vexed at his lowly position; he is far from perfect if he does not rejoice and even glory in it. Moreover, for any imperfection to appear in one who purposes to aim at perfection is as a mole. This colour, then, in our Brother Noel displeased me. For even if he is pure in the sight of God; what then? We must also provide things honest in the sight of all men.

2. But you say, "It is we who were vexed, not he." We

to the Carthusian House at Portes, and there, before A.D. 1147, he succeeded Bernard, the first prior (see *note* to ep. 153). I cannot say with certainty that Noel here mentioned was called to preside after him over the Church of Bellay. William, at all events, succeeded Bernard, Antelm (or Nantelm) William. Antelm had been Prior of Portes, and ep. 234 (Duchesne) to Louis the younger seems to be about his promotion.

[1] *Decolorari.* See the next sentence but one.

come back to the same question. Again, I say what I think. I do not see why you should be vexed, unless you yourselves think that the matter is serious enough to be vexed about. Judge for yourselves whether this feeling was becoming to him, especially in newness of life. For before he took the vows, let me by his leave say it, this blot was seen in him, whether rightly must be left to his own conscience. And, perhaps, the Pope thought the same about him, since you say he has refused to confirm his election. I suppose that he was afraid of the tongues of traducers, and, therefore, withheld a too speedy promotion from a novice, lest slanderous tongues should say that this was the reward he aimed at when he took the cowl. But whatever the mind of the Pope may have been, whether this or something else, I must tell you that I knew nothing of his intention, lest anyone should say that it was done at my instigation. For, as far as I am concerned, it was my resolution that whenever I had an opportunity I would not only not hinder, but even with all my might, and, as they say, with both hands, help him whenever he should by the grace which is in him be in a position to bring forth fruit to God. Who will give me the happiness of seeing learned and holy men set over the Church of God as pastors, if not in all places, yet in many, or at all events in some? For what matters it if a youth declares that once he behaved in a youthful way? Old things are passed away, all things are become new. Shall I a second time rake up his buried vices when he has a second time been buried with Christ by the baptism of the wilderness [*i.e.*, monasticism]?[1]

3. I was very much displeased when I heard of the hard things which the Abbot of Chézy,[2] or he of Troyes, is said to have written to you, and when I have an opportunity I will tell him so, as far as I may consistently with charity

[1] Bernard evidently held with other Fathers that profession of the religious life was a second baptism. This is dwelt on at length in lib. *de Precepto et Dispensatione*, c. 17.

[2] Was this Simon, Abbot of Chézy, to whom ep. 263 was directed? His successor, Tes. (so his name is given abbreviated), is pointed to here, although we have no Letters of his against the Carthusians, but many in their favour.

and with the brotherly intimacy that exists between us. I thank God, who has enabled you not to be overcome with evil, but to overcome evil with good, inasmuch as you have not returned him evil for evil, or cursing for cursing. Further, you must know that the letters which you had before written to me against the above-named Abbots did not come to their knowledge by any efforts or wish of mine. But enough of these matters.

4. I must now forget not myself. My burdened conscience, and my life, which resembles some fabled monster, cry aloud to you. For I am a kind of chimæra of the age, acting neither as a clerk nor as a layman, for I have long since put off the life of a monk, but not the habit. I do not like to write to you what I daresay you have heard from others, what I am so busy about, what I am striving for, through what pitfalls my walk lies, down what precipices, I should rather say, I am hurled. If you have not heard, then I pray you to make inquiries, and according to what you hear, give me your counsel and the benefit of your prayers.

LETTER CCLI. (A.D. 1147.)
To Pope Eugenius.

Bernard prays him to pardon the monks of Baume, whom he had rightly punished, and to reconcile them with those of Autun.

To his loving father and lord, EUGENIUS, by the grace of God Supreme Pontiff, his humble servant BERNARD, called Abbot of Clairvaux, sends his humble greeting.

The monks of Baume have sinned grievously, but not with impunity.[1] To you, therefore, there are praise and

[1] We gather what this crime of the monks of Baume (in the Diocese of Besançon) was from two rescripts of Pope Eugenius, one to Humbert, Archbishop of Besançon, another to William or Guy, Count of Mâcon, in which he reduces Baume from an Abbey to a Priory, "because of its execrable and horrible wickedness, and its unheard of contempt of the Roman Church shown to its beloved master Osbert," as well as from Letters of William, Count of Mâcon, consenting to the degradation. The Letters of Eugenius were dated May 29th, 1147, Paris. They are in the Cluniac registry. However, Baume afterwards regained its title of Abbey.

thanksgiving due from the whole Church, because you have not kept silence, not passed it over, not been inactive. You rightly roused yourself; you struck, but it was to heal. But if my lord forgets to have mercy, and shuts up his pity in wrath, where will the healing come from? Therefore, I confidently wait for mercy after judgment, that I may sing to the Lord of mercy and judgment. I know well that you will not depart from the footsteps of Him whose vicar[1] you are, especially because he says: *If any man will serve Me let him follow Me* (S. John xii. 26). But the Prophet says of Him: *Who knoweth if God will turn, and pardon, and leave a blessing behind Him?* (Joel ii. 14). And this blessing I boldly ask from you who have come after Him. Besides, it is not right to destroy the innocent with the guilty. For those who did the evil have been removed. What remains but that those who remain may be saved? Why should not they who obeyed both you and your predecessor be saved? I speak with Paul, who said: *Put away from among yourselves that wicked person* (1 Cor. v. 13). Therefore, have pity on them; and let not the iniquity of the wicked prejudice the righteousness of the innocent. I say this because their cause comes before the presence of your majesty together with that of the monks of Autun, and they are afraid that the iniquity of these others may injure them. I beseech you most of all to strive for their harmony and peace; indeed, I wish well to both, and so I think it is expedient for both.

LETTER CCLII. (A.D. 1147.)

To the Same, about the Disputed Election at York.

Bernard begs him to cause the sentence of Pope Innocent against the Archbishop to be executed.

Ambition frustrated is furious, nay, it is desperate, even to madness. The man of perdition is running his head into

---

[1] The Supreme Pontiff is here called, not obscurely, Vicar of Christ; but in the old writers he was usually called Vicar of Peter, epp. 346, 183, of Peter and Paul, ep. 243.

the noose, and accelerating the sentence of condemnation that he has so long deserved. Truly, his sins are now manifest going before unto judgment. The accursed and thorn-bearing tree is anticipating the hand which is to cut it down, and calling down on itself the axe which was delaying to strike. Alas! how much more just would it have been if it had long ago fallen, rather than those saints whom, against right and justice, he has by his attacks cast down. For if he had not been standing he would never have overthrown those who were standing fast. And they who were standing to much more good than he have perished in their innocence, and for their innocence;[1] but their innocent blood will be required at the hands of those who, by giving this mischievous tree their secret support, have prevented its immediate downfall. The blood of the saints cries from the earth against them; the saints whose souls are in the hand of the Lord, and whom no torment of wickedness can touch. Still they were my children; they have been scattered abroad, and I get no consolation from words. And even if these could afford me any solace or remedy, yet they fail me because of my grief; sorrow shuts them in, sighs interrupt them. Yet, listen, or rather read, one last word which I can better write than speak. If he is still standing, alas! that I should say it, there is great fear that his standing is your fall; and his continued ill-doing, like an evil tree which cannot but bring forth evil fruit, will be deservedly imputed not to him, but to you.

[1] Bernard here speaks of the destruction of the Cistercian Abbey of Fountains by the supporters of William. Serlo the monk describes it at length in his history of the monastery (*Monast. Anglic.* Vol. i. p. 747), where he says that on the rejection of William by Eugenius, his supporters hastened to the monastery, whose Abbot, Henry, was William's rival, and plundered, burnt, and trampled down everything, without, however, causing any loss of life; Bernard, however, implies that some of the monks were slain. Serlo adds, that Henry the Abbot, when elected Archbishop, repaired to S. Bernard at Clairvaux, and from there went to meet Eugenius at Trèves, by whom he was consecrated and given the pall. He was at length, after much opposition, received by his diocese.

LETTER CCLIII. (A.D. 1150.)

To the Abbot of Prémontré.[1]

Bernard replies with gentleness to their bitter complaints against him, and reminds them of the benefits they have received from him.

1. I have read what you have heard of me, and I fear. For you write against me bitter things, but I hope with more severity than truth. What wrong have I done? Is it that I have ever loved your person, been kindly disposed to your Order, and helped it whenever I could? If you believe not my words, let my deeds be my witness. Indeed, my conscience tells me that I ought to have been commended by you. But since you have seen fit to speak and write against me, I will lend power to my words from the testimony of my actions. It goes, indeed, against the grain. I may seem to be boasting of my good deeds, and this is not seemly. But you compel me to act as a fool. Whenever have you or yours wanted my help and failed to receive it? In the very first place, the land of Prémontré, in which you are living, was formerly mine, and you had it as a gift from me.[2] For our brother Wido[3] (so the first

---

[1] This was Hugh, first disciple of Norbert, and his successor in the government of Prémontré. He had been Chaplain to the Bishop of Cambray. He is highly praised, not only in the life of S. Norbert, but also by his namesake, Hugh of S. Marianus, Chronicler of Auxerre, and by Hermann, a monk of Laon (*De Mirac. S. Mariæ*, B. iii. c. vi., viii., x.). Norbert also in many places is greatly extolled by the same author, and is even put before Bernard, both as the first founder of his Order, and also of the nuns of the same Order, who at that time were more than 10,000 in number.

[2] Authorities differ as to the origin of Prémontré. What Francis Alut, in his history of the family of Coucy (lib. ii. c. 19), says appears fabulous. Gordon, of the Society of Jesus, in his *Chronology*, A.D. 1116, says that this Order received its name from the site having been pointed out beforehand from heaven. But that the place was so called before S. Norbert's time is evident from his life (c. 17), where he is said to have chosen "a place utterly desert and removed from men, which used to be called Prémontré" (see also Hermann below). What S. Bernard says here about the ground being given by him seems at variance with the letters of foundation of Prémontré given in the name of Bartholomew, Bishop of Laon, in which the place in question is said to have belonged to the monks of S. Vincent, and to have been given by Bartholomew to S. Norbert. Bartholomew

inhabitants of the place called him) had given it to me through the Bishop. Next, it was principally through my efforts that the monks of Beaulieu[1] affiliated themselves to you. When King Baldwin was alive he gave me the place of the holy Samuel at Jerusalem,[2] and at the same time a

had received it first from Adelbero, Abbot of S. Vincent, whose grant was confirmed by his successor Seifred. Hermann, the monk (*Mirac. S. Mary of Laon*, lib. iii. c. 4), says the same. "When they came," he says, "to the above-named place, called Prémontré, they entered a church built there in honour of S. John Baptist, for the purpose of prayer. This was by permission of the monastery of S. Vincent of Laon." A late writer in his notes to the life of S. Norbert (c. 19), in commenting on this grant of S. Bernard's, says that he adheres to the statement that the site was given by the monks of S. Vincent at the hand of the Bishop Bartholomew. But though there were six hundred arguments against it, yet the word of S. Bernard himself ought to stand against them all; but if the matter be considered a little more carefully, these opposite statements are easily reconciled. For it is well-known that the monastery of Prémontré in its early days did not stand on the same spot on which S. Norbert had first placed it, but on another side of the mountain, to which his successor Hugh, to whom this Letter is addressed, had transferred it. Hermann himself, in the place quoted above, says the same thing, where he describes the foresight of S. Norbert in providing for the translation of the monastery, and again in c. 10, when he gives an account of the change. He says: "Hugh, seeing that the church (viz., S. John Baptist, which had been given by the monks of S. Vincent) was too small, and not able to hold the large numbers which now were filling the monastery, and which were daily increasing by the grace of God, knowing also that Norbert had provided by the Spirit that a larger church should be built on another part of the mountain, took counsel with his brethren, and when all the offices had been mapped out he asked the Bishop, Bartholomew, to come and lay the foundation-stone." The first site may have been given by the monks of S. Vincent, but what is there against the second having been given by S. Bernard, who had it from the hermit Wido? Two letters of Philip, Abbot of Bonne-Espérance, should also be read; this seems to be a reply to them.

[3] We read of Wido in the history of the monastery of Vicoigne, near Valenciennes (*Spicil.*, Vol. xii. p. 534), where Wido, or Guy, "a Breton by birth, a priest by office," is said to have lived at Prémontré at the time that Norbert went there, and to have given place to a greater than he, by retiring to Vicoigne, where he laid the foundations of a monastery which he put under the care of Walter of S. Martin at Laon, as Abbot.

[1] Beaulieu was a house of regular canons in the Diocese of Troyes, and was ceded to the Præmonstratensians A.D. 1140. Ep. 407 was written to Odo, Abbot of Beaulieu.

[2] Geoffrey, in Book iii., n. 22, of the *Life of S. Bernard*, says on this passage: "In short, like a fruitful vine he sent out his branches on every side, except that he refused to send his brethren to Jerusalem, although a place had been

thousand crowns with which to build; I gave you both the site and the money. Many know how hard I laboured that you might have the church of S. Paul at Verdun; and you enjoy the fruit of my labour. If you do not admit this fact against you, my letters to Pope Innocent of blessed memory are in existence, as true judges and living witnesses to the truth of what I say. Your brothers of Sept-Fontaines hold from me the place which they occupy,[1] which the first inhabitants called Francs-Vals.

2. For which of these acts do you wish to leave your friends? Are you not rewarding evil for good? For you threaten to break your compact,[2] to dismiss the peace that there is between us, to give up fellowship, to break our unity. But suppose that it is not for a good work that you stone me, but for injury done you, in that I received brother Robert, who was once of your Order, and gave him the monk's habit. I do not deny it; he is with us. But I thought that I sufficiently satisfied you about this when I truly told you by word of mouth, and not once only, the reason, method, and necessity of receiving him. But since you are not yet contented I shall not be displeased to repeat my former reply, as you do not hesitate to repeat the charge to which I had given my defence.

3. I never at any time urged brother Robert to leave you; nay, rather, for many years—not once, but often—I checked his desire to do so. Again, how can I be suspected of having enticed him from you when you have Magister Otho as the adviser and encourager of his withdrawal? If you do not know this, ask him. If I know the

offered him there, because of the dangers from the Saracens, and the unfavourable climate." *Of.* ep. 175 to the Patriarch of Jerusalem, who offered him a site, and ep 355, in which he commends the Præmonstratensians to the Queen of Jerusalem. For the monastery of S. Paul, see notes to ep. 178.

[1] Sept-Fontaines was in the Diocese of Langres, close to Mont-Clair.

[2] Manrique describes this agreement, which was entered into A.D. 1142 between the Cistercians and Præmonstratensians for the sake of peace, as fixing two leagues between their monasteries and one between their granges or farms. Hence Bernard says that the house of Basse-Font was outside the limits agreed on. It was situated in the Diocese of Troyes, and was founded A.D. 1143.

man well he will not deny it. I could also, perhaps, give you the names of others; many others, too, who had either turned to you or returned to you, whom you would not have now if I had not either persuaded or even compelled them to remain with you. But I spare you, not because I am short of matter, but because I am rich in modesty. I have known men within your walls who had been touched and converted by my preaching and disposed to join us, but who afterwards, on the solicitations of your members, altered their minds, and were received and kept in your order and habit. Then, again, their consciences began to prick them, and they wished to leave you, and would have done so, unless I make a mistake, if they had not been held back, not only by my refusal to receive them, but by my exhortations to remain where they were.

4. But since you wish it again, listen how it was that I received brother Robert. The Pope, on his own solicitation and that of his friends, enjoined it. He said that his request had been granted by you and also by his Abbot, so that no one might say that he extracted it from you by the Papal injunction. If you deny this, what is that to me? Let him see to it. If you think fit to charge the supreme and holy Pontiff with falsehood you must pardon me for thinking it impious not to believe so great holiness and not to obey so great majesty. Moreover, the venerable Abbot Gottschalk, who is one of your confraternity and had been specially named to you by the Pope to see to this matter, has clearly not denied that he had brought back from you both a free emancipation of the brother and your spontaneous avowal of it.

5. Again, in the matter of brother Fromund you have no ground for attacking me, since I did not receive him without the voluntary permission of his Abbot. And that you were not ignorant of this is shown by that bitter letter in which you bring a calumnious charge against me on the single point of the unexpected connivance of the Chapter, as if, indeed, that had been forbidden by our mutual agree-

ment, or as though the emancipation of a monk was the privilege of the Chapter and not of the Abbot alone.

6. You add as another complaint that I removed a house of your brethren at Basse-Font, although you omit to say that it was built outside the boundaries assigned you. I wish that before you condemned me you would ask the brothers themselves not only who removed it, but also the cause of its being removed. I do not think that they would have concealed the truth from you. But hear it now from me, and then, if you like, ask them. They had begun to build a place, where they placed some of their sisters, a long way from their Abbey, but close to two farmhouses of our house, and near the pastures where we feed our sheep. We asked them as friends, and as those who might be useful to them, not to sow the seeds of a scandal, and prepare a ground of quarrels to be left as a legacy both to their posterity and ours. But they, nevertheless, went on with the building. This was all the violence that I used, this was the way that I removed them. If to make a request is to use violence, then I am inexcusable.

7. As a matter of fact, which cannot be denied, the Bishop, who was indignant that they had ventured, without consulting him, to erect an oratory in his diocese, and a monastery on the land of the Church, and on the estate of his vassal, tried to put a stop, though in vain, to the work that they had begun. For they did not give it up even when forbidden to proceed. Afterwards, as I was passing through that district, I met the then Abbot of Basse-Font, who told me that they had stopped building. But I gathered from what he said that they had done this not so much on my account, but because of the Knight who seems to have given them the land, and who in many ways was harassing them so much that they complained bitterly of his treatment of them. But even if they had abandoned the work of their own accord, and from love of us, it would but have been becoming to their religion, and would have seemed perhaps a kindness to those who had some small claims on

them. I can only wonder where this complaint originated, for, if I mistake not, the Abbot ended this present life with devoted goodwill towards us, and his successor, who often consults me intimately about his needs, has never made any mention of this complaint, and, besides, I have since been very hospitably received in the same monastery, but I have never heard there from the Abbot or anyone else anything about it. Moreover, the Abbot was with us afterwards at Clairvaux, and also very recently when a chapter of your Order was held at Bar, whence came those letters of yours, which are rather calumnies than complaints; and yet I cannot recollect that either at the one place or the other, either by him or by you, was the slightest mention made of this matter.

8. You say, besides, that the monastery at Igny has burnt a little house of your brethren at Braine.[1] Do you call it a house? It was nothing but a hut of boughs which gave shelter to the brother whose duty it was to keep watch over the standing corn. Nor was it burnt by malice, as I am told on good authority, but because it was placed in a field of the brethren of Igny, and occupied land which had to be cultivated. In short, the house, as you call it, was hardly worth a penny; and I believe that such satisfaction has already been given to the Abbot of Braine that he makes no complaint, and has no ground for it either. But if not, I am ready to give every satisfaction as soon as you let me know. And so with regard to the Abbot of Long-Pont;[2] as soon as I heard of your complaint that he wished to build a cell within your lands I prohibited him, and, what is more, I believe that he desisted even from laying the foundations. But if not, it shall be done as soon as I know that it has not been done. You complain especially that our Abbot of Villars has been the means of an interdict

---

[1] Brena, or Braine, is a town on the Aisne, four leagues above Soissons; it had a famous Præmonstratensian Abbey, dedicated to S. Euodius. Igny, belonging to the Cistercians, in the Diocese of Rheims, was not far away. The Abbot of Igny was Humbert, to whom ep. 141 was written.

[2] The Abbey of Long-Pont, two leagues from Soissons, was Cistercian, as was Villars in Brabant, in the Diocese of Namur, where Fastred was then Abbot.

being placed on the Church of S. Foillan,[1] which belongs to your Order. But it would be more just if you were to complain of the incredible obstinacy of your brother and co-Abbot of the aforesaid house, rather than find fault with the punishment inflicted by the supreme Pontiff. I know for a certainty that the quarrelsomeness of the Abbot is strongly condemned by many of your brethren, so it is a great wonder that you do not also condemn it. And, therefore, I say to you that this is the cause of your indignation. Indeed, it is this man's covetousness or stubbornness which has brought the interdict on your brethren. It is a tedious business, and it would be difficult to set down all his subterfuges within the compass of a letter. Still, I will state in as few words as I can the cause of the interdict. After two or more agreements of peace, after a definite sentence issued by your abbots and ours, according to the determination of your Chapter, the Bishop of Cambray, in whose diocese the house of S. Foillan is well-known to be, was at length called in, and when he saw that the Abbot was obstinately bent on breaking through all agreements, he meant, as he said, to proceed against him by an ecclesiastical sentence. Then the Abbot, to gain time, appealed to the supreme Pontiff. The case came before him. And when he knew for a certainty, on the testimony of your own abbots, as well as of other religious, that the Abbot of S. Foillan not only refused to stand by any engagements, but that he also was withstanding a judicial sentence, he ordered the Church to be laid under an interdict until he should give satisfaction. At length, in the presence of the Bishop, who had received an order to pronounce the interdict, the lord (Abbot) of Cîteaux was asked by you, by the Abbot himself, and by us, to see that some form of peace was pro-

[1] The Abbey of the Irish S. Foillan (S. Foy), near Roeux, a town of Hainault, the place of his martyrdom, belonged to the Præmonstratensians. In addition to the other gifts of S. Bernard to this Order, add that of a site in the woodland of Ourthe, by Louis the Younger, "at the request of Bernard of happy memory, Abbot of Clairvaux." The Abbot of S. Marianus, of Auxerre, acknowledges this (in ep. 282, Duchesne).

vided, and this was gained by the entreaties both of your members and of yourselves. In the absence of the Abbot of Villars an agreement was drawn up, and the Bishop said that if the Abbot of S. Foillan would keep it he would refrain from publishing the interdict. However, when he had left the meeting he did not keep it, and what is more, that house which a judicial sentence and all the agreements drawn up had commanded to be pulled down, so much so that once even it had been destroyed, was again in the meanwhile, contrary to his promise and the judicial sentence, rebuilt; and this, I say, he held and still holds, and he has besides built another. Why should not the Bishop execute the order to issue the sentence of interdict which he had received from the Apostolic See, especially when the Abbot has been guilty of double-dealing? I, however, was still hoping to overcome evil with good, and I caused the sentence to be postponed till the Octave of Epiphany, in order to see in the meanwhile if the man would either determine to obey the sentence or observe some mode of compromise. And I hope that this may still happen; may the God of peace grant that our peace may rest upon him.

9. And since this is the true state of things you have no cause to complain of me; it rather seems that I might more justly complain of you. It only remains that you love those who love you, and especially endeavour to keep the unity of the spirit in the bond of peace. That is the bond between us and you, which has strengthened the cause of peace and charity, and no less beneficially for you, perhaps, than for us. You must decide if it is to be broken, it is certainly not expedient for you that it should be. And I do not think that it is in any way right for you to break it. For since the cause is common to us both it ought not to be prejudiced by the fault of an individual, even if those things were true which you say against me. But whatever you may do, brethren, I have made up my mind to love you always, even though my love is not returned. Let him who wishes to abandon his friend seek

occasion for it; my desire is, and always will be, not to give any of my friends a just cause to leave me, nor to look for it in another; for the one is the mark of a feigned, the other of an injured friendship. And since the prophet says that *it is a good thing to be joined together* (Is. xli. 7) you will be able to loosen, or even to cut off, yourselves, but not me. I will cling to you, even if you wish it not; I will cling to you, even if I do not wish it myself. Formerly I bound myself by the strong bond of charity unfeigned, which never faileth. When you quarrel I will be peaceful; and lest I give place to the devil, I will give place to the wrath of those who quarrel with me. I will be overcome by revilings, I will be overcome by kindnesses; I will help those who wish not for it, I will heap benefits on the ungrateful, and I will honour those who despise me. And now is my soul sorrowful because in some way I have offended you, and it will be sorrowful until your kindness relieve it. If you delay I will go and make excuses, I will keep knocking at your doors, I will be urgent opportunely, importunately, until I either merit or extort a blessing. The winter is more than half over, and I am still, to no purpose, it seems, waiting for my tunic.[1]

LETTER CCLIV. (A.D. 1136.)

To Warren,[2] Abbot of S. Mary of the Alps.

Bernard praises in this aged Abbot the zeal with which he undertakes the reformation of his house.

To his reverend father, worthy of all veneration, WARREN, Abbot of the Alps, and to all his brethren in the same place, Brother BERNARD, the servant of their holiness, desires that they may ever advance from good to better.

1. I find that to be true of you, my father, which I recollect that I have read in Holy Scripture: *When a man has been perfected, then only he begins* (Ecclus. xviii. 6).

---

[1] *I.e.,* charity.   [2] Or Guarine.

Rest is due to you in your old age, you have won your crown, and, lo! like some new soldier in Christ you are stirring up opposition to yourself afresh, you are provoking the adversary, and though a weary old man you are taking on you the part of the strong by compelling your old enemy to renew the conflict, and that in some degree against his will. For in relinquishing churches and ecclesiastical benefices under an inspiration from heaven, contrary to your usual custom and the traditions of your predecessors,[1] you are destroying synagogues of Satan, *i.e.*, cells under no parent house,[2] in which three or four brothers are wont to live with no rule and no discipline, and in banishing women from the monastery,[3] and in being more than ever vigilant in other good deeds of piety and sound learning, you are making the first and greatest sinner fulfil the verse: *He shall see it, and be wrath, he shall gnash with his teeth and consume away.* But what matters it? You, on the other hand, amid his confusion are solaced, and can sing to your God, *They that fear Thee shall see me, and rejoice because I have put my trust in Thy word* (Ps. cxix. 74). And there is no fear that the enemy will overcome one who has not yielded to old age. The mind is stronger than time, and even while the body is growing cold in death a holy zeal glows in the heart, and while the limbs grow helpless the vigour of the will remains unimpaired, and the ardent spirit feels not the weakness of the wrinkled flesh. And this is no wonder. For why should it fear the destruction of its old home when it sees a spiritual building daily rising on high and growing for eternity? *For we know that if this earthly house is dissolved we have a*

---

[1] *I.e.*, in relaxing discipline (see ep. 91).

[2] To scatter cells of this kind broadcast would be fatal to the observance of discipline; the rule could not be observed by so small a number. Ep. 400 calls them "obediences," so does ep. 150, n. 2.

[3] That is from the Church, for formerly in the Benedictine, as well as Cistercian houses, the rule was observed of not admitting even strange monks into the Church (*Orderic. Vit.*, lib. viii. p. 714). The Carthusians admitted religious only into the choir (*Guigo Statuta* cx.). For the interdiction of women from entering into Benedictine Churches see *Præfatio ad Sæcul.* i. n. 113, and *ad Sæc.* ii. n. 53.

building of God, an house not made with hands, eternal in the heavens (2 Cor. v. 1).

2. But someone will say, "What if a man is cut off by death before the spiritual building is finished?" I answer, that the perfect can advance no further. And he who is advancing shows by the very fact that he is advancing that he is not yet perfect. We can with all confidence give an unhesitating reply to that question. We will say, *He, being made perfect in a short time, fulfilled a long time* (Wisd. iv. 13). He who embraces eternity may well be said to embrace a long time. For has not he who passes into eternity fulfilled a long time? And, therefore, he rightly claims for himself a reward proportioned to the time he has spent here, if it be measured not by length of years, but by greatness of mind, that is, not by the flight of time, or number of days, but by devotion of the soul to God, or by its inextinguishable desire of ever advancing further. For he retains by virtue what he loses by time. Moreover, real virtue knows no end, is not bounded by time. Thence it is that the verse says, *Charity never faileth* (1 Cor. xiii. 8). And, again, *The patient abiding of the meek shall not perish for ever* (Ps. ix. 18); and, *The fear of the Lord is clean and abideth for ever* (Ps. xix. 9). The righteous never thinks that he has attained (Phil. iii. 13), he never says, *It is enough;* but he is always hungering and thirsting after righteousness, always striving as much as he can to be more righteous, always endeavouring with all his might to advance from good to better. For he gives himself up to the service of God, not, like a mercenary, for a year or for a fixed time, but for ever. Hear again the voice of the righteous as he says, *I will never forget Thy precepts, for with them Thou hast quickened me* (Ps. cxix. 93). It is not, then, for a time only. Therefore his righteousness remains, not for some little space, but for ever (Ps. cxii. 3). And so the everlasting hunger of the righteous deserves an everlasting satisfaction. And though he is made perfect in a short time, yet he is reckoned to have fulfilled a long time because of the endlessness of his virtue.

3. How, again, can shortness of time be a hindrance to the devotion of the good if it is not enough to excuse the obstinate wickedness of the lost? For, undoubtedly, the evil of an impenitent and obstinate mind, even though worked out in a short time, is visited with eternal punishment, because what was short in time, or in deed, was made up for by obstinacy of will; so much so, that if he were never to die he would never cease to wish to sin; nay, he would wish to live always that he might sin always. Therefore the same thing in another way can be said of him, *Being perfected in a short time, he fulfilled a long time,* inasmuch as he deserved to receive the reward of many ages, nay, of all ages, who never wished to change his mind. And so an unwearied desire for progress, and a ceaseless striving for perfection is reckoned to be perfection.

4. But if to be anxious to be perfect is to be perfect, evidently not to wish to go forward is to fall back. Where, then, are they who are wont to say, "It is enough for us, we do not wish to be better than our fathers?" O, monk! do you not wish to go forward? "No." Do you wish then to go back? "Certainly not." What do you wish, then? "I wish so to live, and to remain in what I have attained to, as never to suffer myself to become worse, nor wish myself to become better." Then you wish for what is impossible. For what is there that stands still in this world? And certainly of man it has been specially said, *He fleeth as a shadow, and never continueth in one stay* (Job xiv. 2). Again, did the Maker Himself of man and of the world stand still as long as He was seen on the earth and dwelt with men? On the testimony of Scripture, *He went about doing good and healing all* (Acts x. 38). He went about, then, not unfruitfully, not carelessly, not idly, not with slow foot, but as it was written of Him, *He rejoiced as a giant to run His course* (Ps. xix. 5). Moreover, no one catches a runner if he does not run himself. What avails it to follow Christ with the feet if we do not succeed in laying hold of Him with the hand? Therefore Paul said, *So run that ye may obtain* (1 Cor. ix. 24). Do you, O

Christian, place the goal of your course and of your race where Christ placed His. For however far you may have run, if you do not persevere *even unto death* (Phil ii. 8) you do not obtain the prize. The prize is Christ. But if while He runs you stop still, you do not make Christ yours, but you rather put Him at a distance, and you will have to fear what David speaks of when he says, *Lo! they that are far from Thee, O Lord, shall perish* (Ps. lxxiii. 27). And so, if to advance is to run, when you cease to advance you cease to run. And when you begin to leave off running, then you begin to go back. Hence, we plainly see that not to wish to advance is nothing but to go back.

5. Jacob saw a ladder, and on it angels, where none was seen sitting down or standing still, but all seemed either to ascend or descend (Gen. xxviii. 12); whence we are plainly given to understand that in the state of this mortal life no half way between going forward and going back can be found; but in the same way as our body is always either increasing or decreasing, so also must our spirit be either advancing or retreating. We must notice, however, that the spirit does not receive its increase or suffer its loss from the changes of the body. For in a robust and active body there always dwells a more effeminate and lukewarm soul; and, again, in a weak and infirm body a stronger and more vigorous soul flourishes. And this the Apostle testifies that he found true in his own case: *When I am weak*, he says, *then am I strong*. And he also gladly glories in his infirmities, *in order*, he says, *that the power of Christ may dwell in me* (2 Cor. xii. 9, 10).

6. And what I thus show by example I can also prove by sight, whilst in you, my father, is manifested to us the truth of the saying, *Though our outward man perish, yet the inward man is renewed day by day* (2 Cor. iv. 16). For whence springs your zeal to renew your Order if it is not from a renewed mind? So does a *good man out of the good treasure of his heart bring forth good things* (S. Matt. xii. 35). So does *a tree bring forth good fruit* (S. Matt. vii. 17). Your fruit is the first and purest. But

what tree but purity of heart bore it? Did ever an impure mind seek after and choose purity with such zeal for the monastic rule? Pure water does not flow from a muddy spring, nor does a pure thought from an unclean mind. It is undoubtedly from within that this delightful fount arises; and from that inward fulness there bursts forth that plenteous supply; so that which is beautiful in the mind is also pleasing in action.

7. Follow your father, my sons; be imitators of him, as he is of Christ. Say: *We will run in the savour of thy ointments* (Cant. i. 3). In truth, he is a good savour of Christ in every place (2 Cor. ii. 14). For to say nothing of you, who, being with him, perceive his fragrance around you, there has come to us, who are so far away, such a plenteous and pleasant odour from his zealous efforts, that it is to us most certainly an odour of life unto life. I think that in heavenly places also they have perceived this pleasant odour, and that they sing with more festive joy than usual: *Who is this that cometh out of the wilderness like a pillar of smoke perfumed with myrrh and frankincense, with all powders of the merchant?* (Cant. iii. 6). And again another: *Thy plants are an orchard of pomegranates with pleasant fruits* (Cant. iv. 13). If any of you does not hear this joyous strain in heaven he is envious. If any one does not perceive this odour, let him (by your leave I say it), let him imagine that it exists.

LETTER CCLV. (A.D. 1134.)

To Louis,[1] King of France.

Bernard advises the King not to hinder the assembling of a Council, which was become needful both for the Church and for the Realm.

To the most illustrious LOUIS, by the grace of God King of France, and to his beloved wife and children, his faithful servant, BERNARD, called Abbot of Clairvaux, wishes health from the King of kings and Lord of lords.

[1] Louis le Gros.

1. The kingdoms of the earth, and the rights of kingdoms remain, surely, sure and unharmed in obedience to their lords when they do not resist the ordinances and commandments of God. Why is my lord's anger kindled against the chosen of God whom his Highness also welcomed and chose for himself as father, for his son as Samuel? The royal indignation is in arms, not against foreigners, but against himself and his own house. It is no wonder if *the wrath of man worketh not the righteousness of God* (S. Jas. i. 20), when it makes you neither see the danger nor feel the loss to your own advantage, to your own honour and safety, although all can plainly see it. A council is called together.[1] How does this derogate from the honour of the King, or the good of the kingdom? There a ready and special devotion will be both felt and shown by the whole Church to your exalted position; especially because you were the first king, or among the first, to go to the defence of your mother Church in a most energetic and Christian spirit against the violence of those who were persecuting her. There well-deserved thanks will be given to you in glorious fashion by that large multitude, there will prayers be offered for you and yours by thousands of saints.

2. Beyond this, every one knows how necessary at the present juncture is an assembly of Bishops, except any one who is hard-hearted enough to pay no attention to the troubles of his mother Church. But, they say, heat is excessive, and our bodies are not of ice. It is true, but our hearts are frozen certainly, and that there is no one, as the Prophet says, *who is grieved for the affliction of Joseph* (Amos vi. 6). But of this at another time. Now I, who am the least in your kingdom in dignity, though not in loyalty, tell you that it is inexpedient for you to wish to hinder so great and so necessary a good. And there are not wanting either reasons by which I could make that plain to you, which are ready to my hand to bring before you if I

---

[1] Held at Pisa, A.D. 1134; the King forbade the French Bishops to go because of the great heat.

did not think that what I have said is enough for a wise man. Still, if anything has come from the severity of the apostolic power to make your Highness think that you have reason to be angry, your faithful servants, who support[1] you, will strive with all their might to have it in some way recalled, or moderated, as may be suitable to your honour. In the meanwhile, if I can do anything I will not omit it.

LETTER CCLVI. (A.D. 1146.)
To Pope Eugenius.

Bernard urges upon the Pope to come to the succour of the Eastern Church, and not to be discouraged at the loss of Edessa.

1. It is no light news which we have heard; it is very sad and grievous. And to whom is it sad? To whom is it not? The children of wrath alone do not see God's wrath, they do not mourn with those that mourn, but they rejoice and exult in the worst evils. Besides, the sorrow is common, because the cause is common to all. You have done well in praising the most righteous zeal of our Gallican Church, and in strengthening it by the authority of your letter. I must say that we must not in such a general and grievous matter act without zeal, much less timidly. I have read in some wise man or other: "He is not a brave man whose courage does not rise in the midst of difficulties" (Seneca, ep. 22 to Lucillus). But I say that one who is faithful may be trusted even more in disaster. The waters have come in even unto the soul of Christ, the apple of His eye has been touched. In this, the second Passion of Christ both the swords must be drawn which He allowed on the first occasion. And who should draw them but you? Both swords of Peter must be unsheathed as often as necessary, the one at his command, the other by his hand. And, indeed, of the one of which it seemed that he ought not to make use it was said: *Put up thy sword into its sheath.* Therefore that, too, was his, but not to be drawn by his own hand.

[1] Otherwise "cling to you," *adhærent.*

2. I think that now is the time, when necessity bids both be drawn in defence of the Eastern Church. You must not fall below the zeal of him whose place you occupy. What shall we say of one who holds the primacy and shrinks from its ministry? There is the voice of One crying, "I go to Jerusalem to be again crucified" (Hegesippus de Excid. lib. iii. c. 2). Though some be lukewarm, some deaf to those words, yet the successor of Peter may not neglect them. He himself will say, *Though all shall be offended yet will not I* (S. Matt. xxvi. 33). Nor will he be deterred by the losses of the former army, but will do his best to repair them. Is not man bound to do his duty, because God does what He pleases? I, for my part, as a faithful Christian, will hope for better things in place of such misfortunes, and will think it all joy that we are falling into divers temptations (S. Jas. i. 2). Truly we have eaten the bread of affliction, and have drunk of the wine of sorrow. Why, O friend of the Bridegroom, are you cast down, as though it were not that the kind and wise Bridegroom has, according to His custom, kept the good wine until now? Who knows if God will return and forgive, and leave a blessing behind Him? (Joel ii. 14). And certainly the Wisdom that is above is wont so to work, so to determine; I speak to a wise man. When has great good ever come to men which has not been preceded by great evil? For, to speak of nothing else, did not the death of the Saviour precede the supreme and unparalleled gift of our salvation?

3. Do thou, then, O friend of the Bridegroom, prove thyself a friend in His need. If thou lovest, as thou oughtest, Christ with all thy heart, with all thy soul, and with all thy strength, with that triple love of which thy predecessor was asked (S. John xxi. 15-17), then thou wilt withhold nothing, thou wilt leave nothing undone in this danger of His bride; but thou wilt devote to Her whatever strength thou hast, whatever zeal, whatever watchfulness, whatever authority, whatever power. A great danger demands a great effort. The foundation is shaken, and we must put forth all our strength as though the building were now ready to fall.

And these things I have said to you with full trust in you, as well as loyalty.

4. I suppose you have heard the news that at the assembly at Chartres,[1] by some strange caprice, I was chosen as general and leader of the expedition. Be assured that this was not of my seeking, and was and is against my will; and that, as I gauge my strength, it is altogether beyond my powers. Who am I that I should have charge of a camp and go out before the faces of armed men? Is there anything more inconsistent with my profession, even if I had the necessary strength and skill? But it is not my place to teach you wisdom; you know all these things. Only I implore you, by that love which you specially owe me, give me not over to the will of man, but, as is peculiarly incumbent on you, seek for counsel from God, and endeavour that His will may be done on earth as it is in Heaven.

LETTER CCLVII. (A.D. 1146.)

To the Same, for Brother Philip.

1. There is a matter which I do not mingle with other things,[2] because it affects others and troubles me, and needs more than usually urgent prayers on my part. Our brother Philip, when he exalted himself was humbled, when he humbled himself he was not exalted, as though the Lord had not spoken equally of both (S. Matt. xxiii. 12). There is rigour, but no relaxation. There is judgment, but without mercy. It cannot be denied that many have given this measure, but no one has ever wished this measure to be given to himself. But if with what measure we mete it shall be measured to us again (S. Matt. vii. 2), certainly he

---

[1] Held A.D. 1146. Respecting this, consult the Letters of Peter the Venerable, and of Suger.

[2] We gather from this that this Letter was sent with the one before to plead for Philip. We read of him in the Catalogue of the Priors of Clairvaux:— "Philip, who had been Bishop of Taranto, and was degraded at the time of the schism 'for supporting Anacletus,' came to Clairvaux, and, out of pity, was allowed to officiate as Deacon." Hence this Letter. He was Prior when S. Bernard died.

who shows no mercy will have judgment without mercy. Your Apostolic authority is capable of showing both righteous zeal and mercy. The honour of majesty, it is true, loves judgment; but God forbid that this should banish gentleness. That steward, too, whose praise is in the Gospel, chose to inflict loss on his Lord rather than not show mercy to his neighbour. For a hundred in one case he took eighty, in another fifty. And justly was he praised for preferring that his master should rather lose his goods than his men. And because he who so works is worthy of his reward, by one such deed he both kept them as his master's servants and made them his own friends (S. Luke xvi. 1-8).

2. But what am I doing? I seem to be arguing the case rather than offering my prayer. This is not good. If I go on saying such things I shall provoke judgment, not mercy. I have no more confidence in such arguments than in spiders' webs. *In vain is the net spread in the sight of any bird* (Prov. i. 17). I know how much more convincing arguments can be brought in reply, and especially by such ability as yours. Wherefore my weapons are the prayers of the poor, and in them I am rich. To these engines that tower of strength, no matter how impregnable else, must needs yield. The father of the poor, the lover of poverty, will not reject the prayers of the poor. Who are they? I am not alone, and even if I were I might presume still to make my petition. All your sons who are with me, and those who are not with me too, join me in this supplication. Who can number them? Of course brother Philip is excepted, who neither asks nor seeks that others should ask, and I do not know if he even wishes it; for, as far as he is concerned, he would rather be a door-keeper in the house of his God. But not even I ask only for the man, but on behalf of our Order, believing that a dispensation in this case will be highly beneficial to it.

LETTER CCLVIII. (A.D. 1145.)

To the Same, for Brother Rualene.[1]

Bernard begs that Brother Rualene, who had become Abbot of S. Anastasius, might be allowed to resign his post.

In truth, I find that our Brother Rualene has not yet learnt to acquiesce in his position, and I cannot hope that he ever will. Therefore, both for him and for me, there is need of a speedy remedy. I tell you that I am even consumed so long as he is made to offend. Do not be surprised at this; we are of one soul, except that I am the mother, he the son; for the name and authority of father I have yielded to you. That alone which could not be transferred, the affection which is torturing me, that remains to me still. *A mother cannot forget the child that she bore* (Is. xlix. 15). The sadness of my breast, and the grief of my heart for him, proclaim me his mother. You ask what I complain of? About myself I complain to you, about you I complain to myself. I, a cruel yet loving mother, spared not my own child, that I might purify my heart by loving obedience. I have offered a dear pledge of my bosom as a sacrifice, not of constraint, I admit, but willingly did I obey that will which constrains whom it will. But he thought not so. When constrained by me as well as by you he struggled, though in vain. Had I, then, any reason to fear that he would always resist so obstinately? It is the mark of a loving heart to yield to stubbornness which will not allow itself to be placed in its proper position. Besides, to hold one against his will to a position in which he was placed against his will is hard for him, beneficial to no one. Again, to occupy the ground and not to bring

[1] He had been Prior of Clairvaux, and after the election of Eugenius he was made Abbot of S. Anastasius, at Rome (see ep. 245). It is his absence which is lamented in ep. 43. Nicholas of Clairvaux was admitted by S. Bernard's influence most of all; he afterwards wrote several Letters in S. Bernard's name, and epp. 23 and 25 among them, which wrongly bear the title of Rivaulx instead of Rualene.

forth fruit is not good for the ground, and is not becoming to you or to me. No one, as blessed Ambrose says, does good under compulsion, even if what he does is good, because the spirit of fear avails nothing when the spirit of charity is absent (S. Ambr. in Ps. i.). And so I beseech you by the bowels of mercies of our God to show the love of a father and send back to his mother's breasts the child, while he lives, whose whole weakness is, perhaps, caused by his having been weaned too soon. It is better to suffer him to live than to divide him. What profit is there in his blood? One thing I know, and that is that it is not a father's or a mother's voice which says, *Let it be neither mine nor thine, but let it be divided* (1 Kings iii. 26). Perhaps you are not afraid of this, because you do not believe that it is likely to happen. But his letters and murmurings which frequently come to me fill me with fear of such an issue, for he is threatening to fly and to divide himself, or rather to tear himself asunder both from you and me.

LETTER CCLIX. (A.D. 1145.)
To the Same, for the Same.

Although I at one time wished what you wished me not to, your condescending gentleness provokes me now not only to wish, but to wish eagerly for what you do. It is your pleasure that Brother Rualene should be Abbot of S. Anastasius, and this had been my wish before, but because he was much opposed to it I gave way. Again, since your will does not concur with mine I again, as is right, give way and return to my first mind. We can make the experiment. What you ordered has been done, not because you ordered it, but because you wished it. The speedy execution of your command, of free will, and not grudgingly or of necessity, proves our obedience, and let my pen be examined as to my good-will. If I had not been content to execute your command should I not, according to the word of the Lord, have been an unprofitable servant in doing what I was bound to do? (S. Luke xvii. 10). But now, since I have acted with willingness also, I am no longer a servant but a son.

LETTER CCLX. (A.D. 1145.)
To Abbot Rualene.

Bernard sympathizes with Rualene in his unhappiness, but declares that he must remain at his post.

Your absence, my dear Rualene, has affected me enough, and more than enough, but I am far more troubled to hear of your sadness. For I seem to myself to lament more properly for you than for our losing or being deprived of you, although that loss is by no means small, and causes no small discomfort, since it is for so dear a son, so useful a brother, so necessary a fellow-helper. But the more vividly I call to mind your loveableness, the more deeply do I sympathize with your grief, holding your discomfort of more importance than my loss, and being more distressed at it. But I have not been negligent, not been idle, not held my peace, and have tempted God in this matter, almost even to the point of angering the supreme and holy Pontiff, that in some way or other, even though it were to my own danger, I might be allowed to recall you. But since I have so far failed in all my plans and efforts for you, I have at last, from very weariness, given way to higher judgment, and yielding to power, am forced to be content with what I can get, since I cannot have what I would. Do you, too, my dear brother, greatly longed for, be strong in the Lord, and do not kick against the pricks, lest when you are hurt, very many, who greatly love you in the Lord, be equally hurt. Spare yourself, spare me, who from love of you have not spared myself. But the rather put on strength, trusting and knowing that your strength is the joy of your Lord. Put on the joy of salvation that I, too, rejoice in your joy, and may give thanks and praise to God, who loves a cheerful giver, for your peace of mind, and for my own comfort in you.

LETTER CCLXI.

To Pope Eugenius.

Bernard prays the Pope to absolve the Abbot of S. Urbain, who had been subjected to censure.

One of the Knights of the Temple wished to become a monk of our Order, and found amongst us some to join him in his wish. But since they dared not, contrary to Rules, receive him within their walls, they took him secretly to a certain Abbey which is called Vaux,[1] telling and suggesting to the Abbot to cause to be given to the man a black habit of some other Order of monks, and then they would receive him and give him ours. And so it was done. The matter became known to me, and was brought by me before the Chapter, and by the decision of the Chapter that brother was expelled. But the Templars, not content with this, brought letters from your Majesty to the Bishop of Châlons by which he was to suspend the Abbot of S. Urbain, who had given the soldier the habit, from entering the Church till he should have presented himself before you. Thence it is that the Abbot of Vaux, at whose request he did this without suspecting anything wrong, was forced in great trouble of mind to send to implore your mercy the brother who bears this letter, in order that he who was entangled by him might by him be set free, if that is to say he as well as we, your children, may win this boon from your Paternity.

LETTER CCLXII.

To the Same, for the Monks of S. Marie-sur-Meuse.[2]

I cannot but again support the Bishop of Rheims in his petition, especially since it is one which deserves to be

[1] It is uncertain whether this Abbey, which belonged to the Cistercians, was actually within the Diocese of Châlons, or close to it. It had a monastery dedicated to S. Urbanus, mentioned below, built A.D. 865 by Herchenraus, Bishop of Châlons (Heric, the monk, de Mirac. S. German. Auxerre, c. 14).

[2] The Cistercian codex has the heading, "On behalf of Samson, Archbishop of Rheims." But the meaning is the same, for the Letter was written at the request

listened to. I pray, therefore, and earnestly supplicate on behalf of the poor monks of S. Marie-sur-Meuse, that they may be quickly set free from the oppression under which they suffer, and that by your powerful hand the injuries and accusations of the malignant may be warded off from them; of these the bearer of this letter will inform you. It is for this that these poor men have sent messengers from afar to cry to you. And what answer you should send back by them you may learn from the righteousness and poverty of these men who love you, and from the honour due to the above Bishop, who has intervened on their behalf, and who loves you not a little.

LETTER CCLXIII.

To the Bishop of Soissons, for the Abbot of Chézy.[1]

I besought you, when I might, perhaps, have enjoined you, and I thought that my prayer had been granted. But since I find that it has not, it seems that I shall not have now to ask simply and in common with others, but to cry aloud. For I cannot bear a refusal, lightly or with equanimity, and hitherto I have not met with one. Do, then, what you ought; do what you are wont to do; for custom has made you my debtor; do it, I repeat, if not because you are asked, yet because you are enjoined. Return, therefore, to judgment, for it does not seem just that the Abbot of Chézy, who is a pious man, a friend of mine, and your son, should lose the rights of his monastery because of a word spoken by him incautiously and inconsiderately, and without the assent of his church. And

of Samson, on behalf of the monks of the famous monastery of S. Mary on the Meuse, in the Diocese of Rheims, under the Benedictine Congregation of S. Vito. There is nothing about this letter in the Chronicle of *S.M.* sur M., *Spiscil.* Vol. iv.

[1] *I.e.*, Simon, see ep. 293. The Letter is best headed to Joscelyn, Bishop of Soissons, in whose Diocese the Cistercian abbey of Chézy was. Perhaps we must take it that the deposition of this Simon is what is spoken of in lib. ii. ep. 14 of Peter of Celles.

although his accuser sticks obstinately to that word, being one who has no confidence in the righteousness of his cause, it ought not, I think, to prevent the Abbot from receiving a just decision; especially when those by whose dissimulation the matter has been brought before you know very well that he did not mean what he said, nay, rather was opposed to it. I hope that you will not be put out with me because of this, nor be vexed. May God so rejoice your soul, and may He so preserve you free from all troubled feelings, O father, greatly to be loved and honoured, as by all the servants of Christ, so in particular by me.

LETTER CCLXIV. (A.D. 1149.)
Peter, Abbot of Cluny, to Bernard, Abbot of Clairvaux.

He expresses his friendship towards Bernard, and asks that a monk named Nicholas may be sent to him.

To Bernard, Abbot of Clairvaux, the strong and splendid pillar of the monastic order, nay, of the whole Church of God, Peter, the humble Abbot of Cluny, wishes the salvation which God has promised to those that love Him.

If it were allowed me, if the Providence of God did not forbid it, if man's path through life were in his own power, I should have preferred to be united by an indissoluble bond to your dear and blessed self, rather than reign anywhere, or be a prince amongst men. Ought not your dwelling, which is pleasing not only to men, but to the angels themselves, to be preferred by me before all earthly kingdoms? If I were to say that you were a fellow-citizen with them, though hope has not yet passed into possession, by the mercy of God I shall not be found a liar. If it had been given me to be here with you, even to my last breath, it would, perhaps, be given me after death to be for ever where you might be. Whither should I run save after you, drawn by the savour of your ointments? But since this is not given always I wish that it could be, at all events, given often. And since even this cannot be, I wish at least that I could often see those sent by you. And since this also happens but seldom, I wish next that your Holiness in the person of your messenger, Nicholas, who loves you, would come and stay with me till the Octave of the Lord;[1] and in this request I think your heart partly joins my heart wholly. I shall see you, holy brother, in him, I shall hear of you through him, and I will entrust to him whatever I wish to make known secretly to your wisdom. To your holy soul, and to all the Saints who serve Almighty God under your rule, I commend myself and mine with all possible prayer, with all possible devotion.

LETTER CCLXV. (A.D. 1149.)
To Peter, Abbot of Cluny (Reply to the above).

He disclaims praises as being unworthy.

What are you doing, my dear friend? You are praising a sinner, you are beatifying a wretched man. You must now pray that I may not be led into error. I shall certainly be led into it, if I begin to be ignorant of myself from the delight I might take in your praises. That did well-nigh happen to me when I saw the letters of your Beatitude which beatified me. How happy should I now be if words could effect it! Still let me call myself happy, not, however, because of my own merit, but your good-will. I am happy in being loved by you, and in loving you. However, I do not think that this sweet morsel which you offer me ought to be swallowed whole, nor, as they say, even admitted even into the mouth. You wonder why, perhaps. Because I cannot see anything in myself which makes me worthy of love, especially such as yours. I know, too, that a righteous man will never wish to be loved more than is right. Would that I could as easily imitate as admire so great an example of humility! Would that I might enjoy what I so greatly long for, your holy conversation—I do not say always, I do not say often, but even once in a year!

[1] *I.e.*, of Christmas.—[E.]

I think that I should never return from it empty. It would not be in vain that I beheld a model of virtue, a perfection of discipline, a mirror of sanctity. Nor would it be fruitless for one to see with the eye of faith how well you have learnt from Christ what I have not yet learnt—his meekness and lowliness of heart. But if I go on to do to you what I complain that you have done to me, though I speak the truth, yet I shall not agree with the law of truth, which says, *What you do not wish done to yourself do not to another* (Tob. iv. 15). And in answer to the little request with which you ended your letter I have to say that the brother whom you asked me to send you is not just now with me, but with the Bishop of Auxerre, and he is so ill that I am told that he cannot yet come to us without the greatest risk.

LETTER CCLXVI. (A.D. 1151.)

To Suger, Abbot of S. Denys,[1] to Comfort Him on His Death-Bed.

Bernard encourages him to meet death bravely, and expresses a great desire to see him before he dies.

To his dear and intimate friend SUGER, by the grace of God Abbot of S. Denys, Brother BERNARD wishes the glory which is within and the grace which cometh down from above.

[1] Suger's death took place A.D. 1152, as the Chronicle of S. Denys records as follows:—" This was the last year of Abbot Suger, of happy memory. But no one is excepted from the necessity of death. When he began to be troubled with the illness from which he died he was carried by the hands of the brethren, and at his own request taken into the Chapter-room. There, after edifying words, he threw himself with tears and lamentation at the feet of each monk, and asked humbly that for love's sake they would forgive him if he had injured them directly or by his negligence. This request all the brethren most readily granted with sincere affection and with much shedding of tears. The venerable father passed away while reciting the Lord's Prayer and Creed on the 13th January, in the 70th year of his age, in the 29th of his rule over the Abbey. Six Bishops and many Abbots and the most Christian King Louis were present at his funeral. The King, from the fulness of his heart and heedless of his Royal dignity, wept bitterly while he was being buried." The inscription over

1. Fear not, O man of God, to put off that man which is of the earth, which weighs you down to the earth and tries to sink you to hell. He it is that vexes, burdens, attacks you. him was simply " Here lies Abbot Suger "—short indeed, but Suger's name was sufficient description of him. Robert of Hereford highly praises him in ep. 216, amongst Suger's remains. Francis Chifflet has published a very beautiful eulogy of him, composed by Simon Chèvre-d'Or, a canon of S. Victor of Paris. It runs thus :—

"The Church's flower is dead—her gem, her crown, her pillar,
Her banner, shield, and helm, her light and pride.
Abbot Suger, the pattern of uprightness and justice,
Respected for his piety, pious though in high repute,
High souled, wise, and eloquent, generous, upright,
At councils present in body, but in mind self controlled.
The King his kingdom ruled by him with prudence great,
And thus the King's Viceroy was changed into his King.
And while the King long years spent over sea
The realm he ruled, discharging the duties of the King.
He joined two things which no one else has joined—
Approved himself to men, was good in sight of God.
He added by his own glory to the reputation of an Abbey already famous,
He reformed its abuses, and increased the number of its members.
Epiphany's seventh light him bereft of light,
The true Epiphany gave true light to the hero."

A lengthy and elegant eulogy of him was written by the Fathers of the Congregation of S. Maur with golden letters on a sheet of brass. See also notes to epp. 78 and 369. On the receipt of the Letter of S. Bernard Suger wrote for the last time, and sent him the following Letter, thanking him for giving him comfort in his last moments, and commending himself to his prayers :—

"To his loving lord and venerable father BERNARD, by the grace of God Abbot of Clairvaux, SUGER, till now a humble servant of S. Denys, wishes salvation and love unfeigned.

"You have visited me with your letter; may the Dayspring from on high visit you. You have sent to me, a miserable sinner, your presents—nay, rather, splendid gifts—a precious cloth, bread of your blessing, letters of consolation, in which are contained good words, holy words, words flowing with milk and honey; in my last moments you have given me comfort. But if I could have seen your angelic face but once before my departure I should depart with greater safety from this miserable world. Be assured that if I had merited to live here for a thousand years or more I should not care to remain unless it were the good pleasure of God. My trust is not in works of righteousness, but in the mercy of God alone, which He always shows to them that put their trust in Him; to Him with all my heart I long to return. And therefore I devoutly commend my soul into your hands, that by your prayers and those of your sacred congregations it may win the divine mercy. I humbly ask the prayers of your Holiness" (Vol. i. *Anecd.*, R. P. Edm. Martene).

What have you to do with earthly coverings, who art about to go to heaven to be clad with the robe of glory? It is near, but it will not be given to one that is clothed. It is able to clothe you, but not if you are already clothed upon. Be not distressed, then—nay, rejoice to be found naked and unclothed. God Himself wishes man to be clothed, but only when He is naked and unclothed. The man of God, then, will not return to God unless that which is of the earth first return to the earth, for these two are at enmity with each other, and there will be no peace till they are separated. And if peace do come it will not be the peace of the Lord nor with the Lord. You are not one of those who say, *Peace, when there is no peace* (Ezek. xiii. 10). The peace which passeth all understanding awaits you, the righteous wait for this peace to be given you, the joy of your Lord awaits you.

2. And I, my dearest friend, greatly long to see you once more that I may receive a dying man's blessing. But since it is not in man's power to choose his path I dare not, since I cannot be certain, promise certainly to come, but though I do not at present see how I can, I shall do all that I can to come. Perhaps I may come, perhaps I may not; but whichever it is I have loved you from the first, I will love you without end. I say with all confidence that I cannot lose one so loved to the end. He is not lost to me, but he goes before, for my soul clings to his with a force which nothing can destroy, and is united by a bond which can never be broken. Only forget not me when you arrive where I hope to follow you, so that it may be granted me to come quickly to you. In the meanwhile never think that the sweetness of the thought of you can ever leave me, though the loss of your presence leave us grieving. Yet we must not doubt the power of God to give you even now to our prayers and to preserve you to us who have such need of you.

LETTER CCLXVII.

To the Abbot of Cluny.

Your son, Brother Gaucher, has also become ours according to the rule, *All mine are thine, and thine are mine* (S. John xvii. 10). Let him be not less loved because he is common to us both, but, if possible, let him be more loved and held in greater favour; as he is mine because yours, so let him be yours because mine.

LETTER CCLXVIII.

To Pope Eugenius.

Bernard warns him of the promotion of a certain unworthy person which had been surreptitiously made.

Let others fear your majesty and scarce come with trembling lips and fingers, by long windings and many turnings, to the business in hand. I, however, only look to your good and your honour, and, therefore, plainly and openly state my case, and am not afraid to say, as though to one of ourselves, without any hesitation or circumlocution, what it is necessary for the Apostolic See to do. I say without any hesitation that you have been grievously imposed upon. Who has induced you to thrust into an ecclesiastical dignity a man stamped with ambition, convicted of it, and condemned because of it? As though it were not enough by itself that the man, should have wished to heap honours on himself! Is he not the same man that Bishop Lambert,[1] of holy memory, caught in detestable wickednesses which his ambition had urged him to, and whom he, therefore, solemnly degraded, not only from the rank that he then held, but also, as was fitting, from hope of all future promotion? You are simply revoking his sentence. And because of the anxiety of the

[1] He was Bishop of Angoulême after Gerard. In this diocese was the Benedictine monastery of the Crown. Lambert is praised in *Vita Bernardi*, lib. iv. n. 29.

holy brethren of "The Crown," who call to you for this, because of the respect due to the holy and learned Bishop, who was the prime mover in this matter, and also for conscience sake (conscience, I say, your own, not another's), there only remains that to satisfy my own conscience, I remind you of the saying, *Be angry and sin not* (Ps. iv. 5). For you sin if you are not angry with the man that suggested such a fraud and stole from you such an unworthy sentence.

LETTER CCLXIX.
To the Same.

Bernard begs the Pope to regard as null and of no value a letter obtained from him by surprise.

The serpent beguiled me. The crafty, chameleon-coloured man, destitute of righteousness, afraid of an interview, the enemy of his own conscience, guilty of a wrong done to his brother, got from me unawares letters in his own favour through the Bishop of Beauvais.[1] For what is there that I would not do for him? If you do not wish to burden my conscience beyond measure let this cunning man gain nothing by his imposition, and let him not by any letters oppress the innocent. And not even this will satisfy me, if this most malignant pilferer and most greedy extortioner is not made to suffer the punishment that he deserves.

LETTER CCLXX. (A.D. 1151.)
To the Same.

Bernard writes on behalf of the Prior of Chartreux against certain malcontents. He reports the death of the Abbot of Citeaux and recommends his successor.

1. Our tempters neither slumber nor sleep. They have laid their snares in the desert, even as they but lately

[1] Arnulph of Maïole most likely (see ep. 278).

persecuted openly in the mountains. The Carthusians have been put to confusion.[1] They have been put to confusion and made to stagger like a drunken man, and all their wisdom has been well-nigh swallowed up. Know, my lord, that an enemy hath done this, and is still doing it. He still has confidence that the fruits of their holiness will fall into his mouth. He has chosen them as his food, as you know well. He has raised up traitors against those whom he could not drive out himself, and by their means he attacks them with domestic and civil war. From the first founding of the place and of the Order it has never been heard that anyone who went away was to be taken back without giving satisfaction.

[1] The author of the French *Life of S. Bernard* (lib. vi. c. 10) has stated the cause of this as given in the *Life of S. Anthelm*, or Nanthelm, who was firstly Prior of the Great Chartreux and then Bishop of Bellay. It is there said, " For when the new Prior, Anthelm, was endeavouring, whenever the ancient strictness of the Order had received any loss, to have it reformed according to the original constitutions, he strove to call back, that they might bear better fruit, whomsoever he saw negligent or rebellious, by kindly admonitions, by words and threats, by precepts also, and rebukes. But if anyone refused to amend, and was evidently obstinate, he did not hesitate to expel him from the society of the brethren. There were some who spurned his wholesome instructions because they were great in their own eyes, men of a malicious disposition, and prone to strife, who did not scruple to withstand him. But he refused to submit to their arrogance, and expelled them from the monastery that they might not disturb the peace of the rest." Some of them, as we can readily believe, fled to Eugenius, got absolution, and were sent back without any penance being imposed on them. It is of this that S. Bernard complains that " it had not been heard from the foundation of the place that anyone who left should be received back without giving satisfaction." Manrique (Annals, A.D. 1151, c. 2) assigns another cause from the Letters of Peter the Venerable (B. vi. n. 12), viz., the strife which, when Hugh, Bishop of Grenoble, was translated to the Archbishopric of Vienne, arose, A.D. 1151, on the occasion of the new election between the different Carthusian monasteries, Chartreux, Durbuy, Portes de Mailly, Selve, and Anvers. Some said " that the man elected ought not to be made Bishop," and they wanted to have the case tried judicially. Others, on the other hand, declared that " it was not their business to go to law, but only to say what they thought, not to have recourse to the tribunals to plead." But since in this last matter it is an altercation between the monasteries, which is the question, not a rebellion of the monks, which Bernard implies in this Letter, this must be referred rather to the first. We refer them to the year 1151, because they happened a little after the death of Rainauld, Abbot of Citeaux, as appears from the Letter. He died December 15th, A.D. 1150, as Manrique proves from the Cistercian Martyrology on the year 1151, c. i.

Those who did wrong in leaving have done worse in their return, inasmuch as they have added treachery to their misdoing. What do you think, Holy Father, that they are likely to do, who went out with transgression, and came back in pride? And now their pride is ever going higher (Ps. lxxiv. 23). They exult in their evil doing, they insult those who suffer wrong. They have conquered, they are triumphing. The Prior is now no longer Prior. "When the wicked is lifted up the poor is consumed." He even wishes to leave the Order, for he cannot bear to see its destruction. And he would have left ere now if he could have left alone. And the Prior must be a good man, for I hear from good men that those on whose advice he leans are good.

2. Do you see, most gracious father, how you have been imposed on? Shall not the author of this deception receive what he deserves? If I know you well, he will bear his judgment, whoever he is. They came to you in sheep's clothing, and their sacred habit deceived you, for you are but a man. But now that the fraud has been discovered, let your zeal show itself, and boldly do its duty against the wicked. Let not your soul come into their council, let the counsel of Ahithophel be confounded. Watch over yourself. To be imposed on through ignorance, and to let zeal sleep are not alike in their guilt. Ignorance is the excuse for the one, negligence makes the other inexcusable. He will, perhaps, take another ground, and try to persuade you of something else. Let his iniquity lie against himself and not against my lord, for the truth of the case is as I have stated it. Nothing is pleasanter, nothing more just in your judgments, than when an occasion of this sort presents itself, when a man is endeavouring to injure others, that he should fall into the pit that he himself made, and that *his mischief should come upon his own head, and his wickedness fall on his own pate* (Ps. vii. 16, 17). The zeal of the Lord will do this. And the Prior will again be made Prior, I hope, so that iniquity may not altogether boast itself; else (and this is no empty fear) the Order will not long remain safe if the Prior be not restored to his office. May

God give you the grace to receive this as a father, and to give a good answer for our comfort, for we have been greatly harassed and afflicted beyond our strength.

3. My Lord Abbot of Citeaux[1] has gone from us, to the great loss of the Order. And now we have as head in his place, Goswin, Abbot of Bonneval. Let it be your pleasure to strengthen him with letters from the Apostolic See, and by your favour to confirm his election. You know him, and there is no need to commend him to you, for his life and the wisdom given him by God are a sufficient recommendation. My lord of Valence is better, and when he is able he performs good works. Besides, all lovers of good love him, and he them. From this his goodness is plain. It is yours to love and cherish such men. Your son is more feeble than usual, his life is ebbing drop by drop, perhaps because he is not worthy of being killed at a blow, and so coming quickly to life.

LETTER CCLXXI. (A.D. 1151.)

To Theobald, Count of Champagne.

Bernard warns him that he ought not to advance his young son to dignities in the Church.

You know how much I love you, but how much God knows better than you. I do not doubt also that for the sake of God I am beloved by you. And if I should offend Him you ought no longer to love me, for God would not be on my side. For who am I that so great a prince as you should care for one so small as I, unless it is that you believe God to be in me? Therefore to offend Him will not be good for you. And this I shall certainly do, if I do what you ask. For I am not unaware that honours and ecclesiastical dignities are the due of those who have both the will and the power to administer them worthily, and for God. Moreover, you must know that it is neither right for you, nor safe for me, that those should be acquired for your little

---
[1] Reynold died A.D. 1151, and was succeeded by Goswin, Abbot of Bonneval.

boy by my prayers, or by yours.[1] And, moreover, in most churches it is unlawful even for an adult to hold pluralities, except under dispensation given, either because of some great necessity of the Church, or great individual benefit. Wherefore, if this reply seem to you ungracious, and you are determined to carry out what you have in your mind, spare me in this matter, for, unless I mistake, you can easily obtain what you want by yourself and by your other friends. And so you will none the less gain what you wish, and I shall not have sinned. Assuredly, I wish well in all things to our little William,[2] but, above all, that he may have the favour of God. Thence it is that I am unwilling that he should have anything against the law of God, lest he lose God's favour. And if another wish differently, I am unwilling that he should gain it through me, lest I, too, lose God. But when he wants anything which he can have according to God's will, I will prove myself a friend, and, if need be, will not withhold my efforts. I need not labour much to excuse my righteous dealing before a lover of righteousness. Please excuse me to your Countess,[3] in accordance with this reply of mine.

[1] We must notice and admire in this Letter the signal virtue, zeal, and constancy of the Saint, who, in a matter which he felt was contrary to the interests of the Church and to his own conscience, refused to comply with the request of a great prince like Theobald, to whom he was greatly indebted as a liberal benefactor to Clairvaux. Bernard (ep. 42 n. 25) complains bitterly that boys are promoted to ecclesiastical dignities because of their high birth, and that pluralities are allowed. It is extant among his tractates, the second in order, Vol. ii.

[2] This was the fourth son of Theobald; he was raised first to the See of Chartres, then to Sens, then to Rheims, and finally was made Cardinal and Legate of the Roman Church in Gaul. He consecrated his nephew, Philip Augustus; it was to gratify him that Alexander III. confirmed to the See of Rheims the right of consecrating the French King. Pet. Cell. writes of him (ep. 5 lib. 1); Peter of Blois, epp. 28 and 122, and others.

[3] This was Matilda, daughter of Count Engelbert, brother of the Bishop of Ratisbon, as appears from the *Life of Norbert*, c. 32, where we read: "Norbert took the legate of Count Theobald to Ratisbon. For the Bishop of that State was of noble birth, and his brother was the powerful Count Engelbert, who had some grown up unmarried daughters, one of whom, Matilda by name (Orderic sub finem lib. 13) was espoused to Count Theobald."

LETTER CCLXXII. (A.D. 1152.)

To the Bishop of Laon.[1]

Bernard presses him to show pious liberality.

I am yours. If you know this, nay, because you know it, the bearer of this can be effectually and surely reconciled by me to you, and through you to everyone else that he may have offended. Otherwise you offend one whom you admit to be your friend, and this, surely, you dare not do. Since you first became a Bishop till now, I have received no blessing from you, neither purse, nor scrip, nor sandals for the feet.

A LETTER OF POPE EUGENIUS TO THE CISTERCIAN CHAPTER.

(To which Ep. CCLXXIII. was an Answer).

EUGENIUS, Bishop, servant of the servants of God, to his beloved children G.,[2] and all the Abbots assembled at Cîteaux, in the Name of the Lord, health and Apostolic benediction.

1. We should much like, dearly beloved, to be present in person at the meeting of your holy brotherhood, because, as we walk with you in the unity of the Holy Spirit, so would we discuss together His life-giving power, and His advances in the soul. But since we have been, by the Divine will, placed in the midst of the ocean to guide the ark of the Church, and as we are tossed about by a succession of raging storms, so that we have to do, not what we would wish, but what we wish not; and as we are tied by the duties of the government entrusted to us, and cannot, therefore, turn our steps wheresoever we will, we come to

---

[1] This was Walter of S. Maurice, formerly Abbot of S. Martin at Laon, who, A.D. 1151, was appointed to succeed the pious Bishop Bartholomew, who, after an episcopate of 33 years, retired to the Cistercian Abbey of Foigny, which he had himself founded. There is extant a beautiful Letter of his to Samson, Archbishop of Rheims, in which from his retreat at Foigny he clears himself from the accusation of having wasted the goods of the Church at Laon.

[2] Goswin, fifth Abbot of Cîteaux.

you in spirit and by letter, and, so far as is possible, are present in your assembly in charity and earnest desire for you; we desire, indeed, and pray you with our whole heart to be of one mind with us, and to implore by your common prayers a greater gift of God's grace for us. Though stationed on the top of a mountain, and beaten by the winds that blow from every quarter, yet we hope by God's help to be able to withstand the tempest, if we merit to obtain God's help through your prayers. But that we may be able to have confidence that your prayers for us are heard, and that we may obtain by your intercessions what we cannot obtain by our merits, we wish you of your charity, in those things which belong to God, such as the obedience due to the Order, and the maintenance of discipline, to be anxiously looking forward to those things which are before, neglecting what is behind, so that no cloud may show itself in your works, to prevent your prayers at any time from rising to the throne of God.

2. And, therefore, as you come together, dearly beloved, take common counsel to correct whatever amongst some of you needs correction, and to enact whatever may need enactment for the salvation of souls and the good of your Order, because *he who despises little things, by little and little decays* (Ecclus. xix. 1), and do not leave uncorrected any lesser faults you may find among yourselves. For to no purpose are the gates of the city guarded if a single opening is left to the enemy, as the Scripture says, *A leak neglected is as bad as a violent wind,* and *You have escaped great perils; see that you do not perish on the beach.* Look, I beseech you, to the ancient fathers who founded our sacred Order, and notice how they left the world, despised all earthly things, let the dead bury their dead, fled into solitude, and sat with Mary at the feet of Jesus (S. Luke x. 39), while others were busying themselves in their various ministries; and so the further they had fled from Egypt the more copious showers of heavenly manna did they receive. They truly went forth from their land and from their kindred; they forgat their own people and

their father's house; and since their King greatly desired their beauty He made them to increase into a great nation, and He sent out their shoots to the ends of the earth, so that the brightness of their charity filled the whole body of the Church, and the woman of Zarephath (1 Kings xvii. 10-16) at their words filled numberless vessels with the little oil which she had in a cruse. Truly they received the first fruits of the Spirit, and their pleasant ointment has run down even to us.

3. See, then, in thought and deed that you do not fall below their virtues, but that you be in the bough what you were in the seed, and bring forth the same seed and fruit as did they from whom you received your life. Take notice how they whose lamps are extinguished desire to receive oil from you, and how many, who have become filthy by wallowing, like sows, in their own mire, ask to be placed under your rule and to be commended to your prayers, that they may receive grace from above. And since the children of this world are always endeavouring to drag you against your will into obedience to them, and sometimes wish to call you from the quiet of contemplation and the silence of the desert to take part in their affairs, recall to your memory the institutions of your fathers, and, looking upon them as examples for all time, prefer to be *doorkeepers in the house of God than to dwell in the tents of ungodliness* (Ps. lxxxiv. 11). And because you have nothing which you did not receive, think of the goodness of the Lord, of your own unworthiness, so as to follow in the footsteps of Him who said, *When ye have done all that is commanded you, say we are unprofitable servants* (S. Luke xvii. 10). If you have received diversities of tongues, grace for working healings, knowledge of prophesying, if your words are more fragrant than the most costly ointments, if the world honours you and takes pleasure in running in the odour of your ointments, it is all nothing but the work of Him who says, *My Father worketh hitherto, and I work* (S. John v. 17).

LETTER CCLXXIII. (A.D. 1150.)

To Pope Eugenius.

Bernard thanks the Pope for the affectionate letter he had sent to the Chapter of Cîteaux.

To his loving father and lord, EUGENIUS, by the grace of God Supreme Pontiff, Brother BERNARD, called Abbot of Clairvaux, sends humble greeting.

1. The voice of the turtle has been heard in our Chapter; we have exulted and rejoiced. Your words are pure, burning with zeal, prudent and discerning. The spirit of life breathes in your letters, a spirit mighty, thundering, chiding, and provoking us with a godly jealousy. I cannot say which pleased me most, your graciousness or our benefit; the condescension of your majesty, or the exaltation of our humility; the sharpness of your severity, or the soothing sweetness of your fatherly love. Those amongst us who in any small degree were hungering after righteousness were refreshed; those who cared little for it were moved; those who cared nothing were confounded.[1] I beseech you to act in this way always. That care which you are bound to take for all, is not to be withdrawn, nay, rather it is the more anxiously to be given to those whose special due it is. Charity is kind and can spread itself abroad, but not diminish aught. Let her call together others, then, but let it be in our company. It specially becomes your Apostleship to cherish all who can say with the Apostles, *Lo! we have left all and followed Thee* (S. Matt. xix. 27). They ought not to be left who have left themselves. They are the Lord's little ones, and put their trust in Him; they will not be abandoned by a faithful and wise servant, least of all by Him to whom the whole has been entrusted. This little flock is a part of the whole, little, indeed, but, unless I am mistaken, they have merited to

---

[1] These three classes are found in every Order, no matter how holy it may be, and chaff will never be wanting in the Lord's threshing-floor. See Sermon 3 on the Ascension; Sermon on the Dedication of a Church, n. 3; Sermon 30, "*de Diversis*," n. 1; and Sermon 46, on Canticles, n. 6.

have God for their Father, and they will receive a crown of glory from the hand of their Lord, and a diadem from Him in the Kingdom of their God. For they do not think it robbery to be heirs of God, and joint heirs with Christ. They have heard the words: *Fear not little flock, it is your Father's good pleasure to give you the kingdom* (S. Luke. xii. 32). Enough of this.

2. The Abbot of Trois-Fontaines[1] had been planted well beside the streams of waters. But I am afraid that a good tree bringing forth good fruit may, when taken up, bring forth none. I have sometimes seen a vine fruitful when first planted, then barren. I have seen a tree when well planted flourish, and when transplanted wither away. And, therefore, if you do not send him back to me you will wound my feelings grievously, for we are one heart and one soul. As long as that heart is divided, each part must necessarily be stained with its own blood. How shall I, having lost the prop of my old age, be able to bear alone the burden which

---

[1] This Hugh, to whom the following Letter was written, was Abbot of Trois-Fontaines, in Champagne, not of S. Anastasius, at Trois-Fontaines, near Rome, whatever Wion, Ciaconius, and others may say to the contrary. In the first place, the name of "Three Fountains," especially at that time, is restricted to the Abbey in Champagne, as appears from S. Bernard's life, and from the heading of ep. 69 to the Abbot of Trois-Fontaines, while the monastery at Rome was wont to be called after the name of S. Anastasius, as is proved by the inscription of ep. 345, "to the Brethren of S. Anastasius." In the second place, Rualène, who had been Prior of Clairvaux, was then Abbot of S. Anastasius, as is seen from epp. 245, 258, and the two following, as well as from ep. 43 of Nicholas of Clairvaux, to Rualène, Abbot of S. Anastasius. Besides this, the next Letter of S. Bernard's (274) is directed to "Hugh, Abbot of Trois-Fontaines, when he was at Rome," which clearly implies that his monastery was at some little distance from Rome. Moreover, Bernard in this Letter, 273, tells Eugenius that he is inconvenienced because Hugh had been summoned to Rome, doubtless to be made Cardinal; and he adds that he will suffer great loss if he is not sent back to him. This Hugh, then, was an Abbot in Gaul. Lastly, from ep. 274, it appears that Bernard, who was then in Gaul, was present to take part in the election of a successor to Hugh. Again, Hugh, A.D. 1150, was made by Eugenius, in the third creation, Cardinal-Bishop of Ostia, and at the same time Ciaconius says two other monks of Clairvaux were raised to the same dignity, whose names were Henry and Roland; it then happened that Velletri was united to Ostia because of the small population of the latter. Hugh is mentioned again in epp. 274, 287, 290, 296, 306, and 307.

we found it heavy to bear together? If my trouble is of little account let the no small loss of the whole Order touch you, and do not wish, from the hope of some uncertain good, to bring about in the meanwhile evils that are certain. But if, finally, you determine to keep him, I beseech you, hold him in great esteem, and lift up your hands to God that He would vouchsafe to provide that house with a suitable man in his place. As to the rest, I earnestly ask for a speedy answer from your Benignity, and one of deed, not word, to those matters concerning the whole Order, and the other businesses which I thought it good to entrust to the above-named Abbot to convey to you.

LETTER CCLXXIV. (A.D. 1151.)

To Hugh, Abbot of Trois-Fontaines, when he was at Rome.

Bernard regrets to have recommended the nephew of the Bishop of Auxerre.

I am sorry that I wrote on behalf of that youth, and I wish, if possible, my prayer to be recalled, for by it I seem to have approved the decision of my friend[1] about the office of provost conferred by him, and badly assigned, too. And this I do not approve, nor have ever done so. But I was induced, I admit, by the great affection with which I was bound to the youth's uncle, an affection very great indeed, but in this case not spiritual enough. I was urged on, too, by my sorrow for his recent death. I may seem to have acted carelessly, but I would rather be thought by my lord to have written too hastily than be suspected before God of having been guilty of falsehood. Although indeed, it would be no excuse even if I had written with caution and foresight, for I knew for a certainty that his two predecessors had ordered it otherwise, and had confirmed it otherwise by their authority. But if you have any influence with him you will do a good work if you can restore her

[1] Hugh, Bishop of Auxerre.

privileges to the Church, and give force to those privileges. Would that we could purge the holy Bishop from this blot on his line, and provide for the youth in other ways.

LETTER CCLXXV. (A.D. 1151.)
To Pope Eugenius, about the Election of a Bishop at Auxerre.

He makes the Pope aware of the bad faith which had been shown in this election.

When I first wrote to you about the church at Auxerre I had heard of the first election, but not of the second. And lo! just as if I were a prophet, the scandal which I suspected has followed, and the fear which I feared has come. Recollect what took place at Nevers,[1] and see if it is not in like manner, by a very similar artifice, by double-dealing. and, as they say, with the very same person as promoter, that a second election has now been ventured on: when, after one candidate was nominated, both were rejected, and finally a third, whom they wished to elect. craftily brought forward. They sent to me to ask me to write to you on their behalf, and I thought it good to send a brother from my side, to learn something more certain about both actions, and to acquaint me with the facts. When he had entered the church, and made diligent inquiries about everything, he found on the testimony of all who had come together that there were on that side none of the presbyters except one, viz., Hugh, the brother of Brother Geoffrey,[2] and none of the deacons except Stephen only; I must except, of course, those officials of the church who had been the chief agents in the

---

[1] This is repeated at the end of the next Letter. He refers to the disturbances which took place at the election of Raymond, Bishop of Nevers. *Cf.* ep. 246.

[2] He seems to have been the candidate of the turbulent party; but at length the election of Alan was accepted. He was Abbot of the Cistercian monastery of La Rivour, in the Diocese of Troyes, and wrote a short life of S. Bernard. In the Acts of the Bishops of Auxerre the See is said to have been vacant for a year. See ep. 280 and 282, etc., and De Consideratione, lib. iii. n. 11.

matter, the precentor, the archdeacon, and, as it seemed, the treasurer, for he was not himself present at the time. Further, he found that there were on the other side, besides others of the lower order, nine deacons and eleven presbyters. The twelfth, who is also arch-priest, declared that he had not subscribed, and would not subscribe, for either side, although he was in favour of the first. The above-named Hugh held the seal of the church,[1] a man not of peace, but of discord, and one who in giving his account paid more attention to his own wishes than to the truth. So the matter stands. And with my usual presumption I say one thing: wickedness ought not to be allowed to boast itself, it is unseemly for wisdom to be deceived, inexpedient for a church to have its functions longer suspended.

LETTER CCLXXVI. (A.D. 1151.)
To the Same, after the Death of the Bishop of Auxerre.

He informs the Pope of a strange will made by the Bishop.

1. I have a point to mention, which I would have brought before you earlier, if I had known what I now know. There is a man who has made Israel to sin. He, I mean, who, when the holy Bishop[2] was somewhat dull and confused in the presence of death, made him die almost intestate. For on the suggestion and entreaty of Stephen he left to his nephew according to the flesh, a young man, and a secular, incapable of being of service to the Church, almost all that he had got together for the episcopal table, and left little or nothing for the poor and the churches. They say that he has left him seven churches, tithes, and the meadows in the Bishop's own forest, besides, which is a blot on all religion, of his moveables, all his vessels of gold, and his

---
[1] It appears from this that the Bishop and the Cathedral of Auxerre had different seals.
[2] That is Hugh, who, from being first Abbot of Pontigny, became Bishop of Auxerre. He died Oct. 10, A.D. 1151.

own equipages, and since these would not be enough to enable him to complete a journey to you to get these bequests confirmed, they say that he has left orders for the equipages of a monastery to be handed over to him. There are some, indeed, who think that the Bishop knew nothing of these bequests, but that Stephen did all and set his seal to what he liked, and it is very likely; for only last year, when the Bishop was, as was thought, at the point of death, they made him give a church to this same nephew; but when he afterwards recovered he declared, as I have found out. that he knew nothing of having made the donation. Again, who can believe that a holy and spiritual man, if he had his understanding, and was in his right mind, would have made a will like this? What man of the world is there who would say that this was the will of a priest? Is this the disposition of that sober and spiritual man who adjudges all things and is himself judged by none? Who in heaven or in earth would not sit in judgment on him if this is to remain so?

2. Do thou, then, O servant of God who holdest the sword of Peter, cut off this shameful confusion from religion, this scandal from the Church, this crime from the Bishop, and from all spiritually-minded men who loved him in the spirit and not according to the flesh, and take bitterness and grief from your own heart. Arise, Phinehas, stand and make propitiation that the plague may cease. Stand, I say, inflexible against flesh and blood, the battering ram by which undoubtedly the children of this world attempt to shake the wall of your constancy. You will show true affection for the uncle if in a matter of this kind you oppose the nephew.

3. Know this also, that the holy men, the Dean of S. Peter at Auxerre and the Prior of S. Eusebius, acting for himself as well as for the Abbot of S. Laurence, when ready to set out to you to lay before you the first election of the Church of Auxerre, were prevented by the opposite party through the Count of Nevers,[1] and deterred from coming.

---

[1] William IV., who succeeded his father on his retirement to Chartreux, A.D. 1147. *Cf.* ep. 280 and note.

Indeed, the Count himself summoned them to him, and commanded them not to think of it, and prohibited them with grievous and open threatenings, and this the Prior made known to me and complained of by the above-named abbot, and his brother according to the flesh, and by the Dean sent to us about this same matter, and he asks me by them to bring it before you. I said before, and I repeat it, recollect what took place at Nevers. The law is sometimes best observed when something is done contrary to law. Those who discourse wisely about your Keys, place the one in discretion, but the other in power.

LETTER CCLXXVII. (A.D. 1146.)

To the Same, on behalf of the Abbot of Cluny.[1]

He asks that the Abbot of Cluny may be received honourably and kindly.

It seems a foolish thing to write to you on behalf of the Abbot of Cluny, and to seem to wish to act as patron for a man whom all wish to have as their patron. But I write, not because it is necessary for him, but to satisfy my own affection for him; my own, I say, not another's, for as I cannot be with him in person I follow my friend on his journey by letter. Who shall separate us? Neither the height of the Alps, nor the cold of the snows, nor the length of the journey. And now I am present with him to help him by my letters. He shall never be without me. I am a

---

[1] S. Bernard gave this Letter commendatory to Peter the Venerable, who was going to Eugenius to receive some mark of honour at his hands. He mentions this journey in lib. ii., *De Miraculis*, c. 25, where he says: "In the first year of the Pontificate of Pope Eugenius I went to Rome to see both him and our common mother the Roman Church." And again, writing to Bernard (lib. vi., ep. 46), he says: "I saw him (that is, Eugenius) at Rome in the first year of his Pontificate." It was on this journey that he was stripped of his goods by the Marquis Opizon on his way through Italy. He recovered everything, however, afterwards by the help of the men of Placentia. (See lib. vi., ep. 44.) He paid another visit to Eugenius, however, A.D. 1151, and in a Letter to S. Bernard bears witness to the kindness of his reception, and Bernard's good offices on this occasion.

debtor to his worth, by which I have been counted worthy to be admitted to such a degree of grace. But grace itself has freed me from the debt, for necessity has passed into will. Honour the man as one who is truly an honourable member of Christ; unless I am mistaken he is a vessel for honour, full of grace and truth, filled with all good works. Send him back with joy, that he may rejoice very many by his return. Hold him worthy of more grace, as indeed he is, so that when he returns we may all receive of his fulness. If he asks anything of you in the name of the Lord Jesus he ought not to meet with any difficulty. For if you do not know it, let me say that he it is who is always stretching out a helping hand to the poor of our Order; he cheerfully and frequently distributes for food the goods of his church, as far as he can by the consent of his brethren. Notice why I say "in the Name of Jesus." For if, as I suspect and fear, he seeks to be set free from the government of his Order, who that knows him can think that he asks in the name of Jesus? I am mistaken if he is not oppressed by fear more than usual, if he has not become better than himself since you saw him. Moreover, almost from the time that he entered on his office he is known to have improved the Order in many ways, *e.g.*, in the observance of fasting and of silence, and in the care he takes for precious and curious vestments.

LETTER CCLXXVIII. (A.D. 1150.)

To the Same, for the Bishop of Beauvais.[1]

There is no need that one should teach you how worthy is the Bishop of Beauvais, your son, to obtain his petitions. He himself will easily enough persuade your fatherly affec-

---
[1] Henry, brother of Louis the Younger, and afterwards Archbishop of Rheims. *Cf.* epp. 269, 305, and 307. Honorius II. took him at the hand of his father Louis for the service of God, for which see his Letter (in *Spicil.*, Vol. iii. p. 150), where there is another following it of King Louis' to the Apostolic Legate about giving this same Henry a prebend in the Church of Pontoise. He was Abbot of S. Mary at Etampes, and also Archdeacon of Orleans.

tion what it is meet and right to do. Still I plead for him. He is a devoted young man, fit to be honoured by his father's favour, and the righteous zeal which he displays for his church should be not only approved, but also assisted. So will he daily become more devoted, more fervent, and more strong, as he feels that the vexations and tribulations which are always harassing his church[1] from evil men are directly lessened by the unfailing help of your right hand. I ask, too, that the petition of Arnulph of Maïole be granted. Master G.—, this is the messenger's name, will tell you what it is. As to the petition of the Abbess of the Paraclete,[2] you can ascertain for yourself if it is a fitting one, and if it is fitting to grant it.

[1] This comes out in two Letters of Anselm to Urban II. (lib. ii., epp. 33 and 34). See also ep. 87 for what Ivo, Bishop of Chartres, says of the state of the Church of Beauvais. He says: "The said Church of Beauvais has so long given up the practice of having good pastors that it seems the proper thing for it to have bad ones, and wrong to choose good ones," etc.

[2] This was Heloise, once the wife of Peter Abaelard, then a nun, then Abbess of the nunnery at Argenteuil on the Seine, which flows through the Diocese of Paris. In the year 1127 the monks of S. Denys, after a long interval, resumed possession of this house, having proved their right from an old charter, which gave it them under the gift of Hermenric, and Numma, his wife. For Theodrada, wife of Charlemagne, had placed there a Sisterhood, which was ejected on its rejecting the monastic discipline. Shortly before, as was said above, Peter Abaelard, with the consent of the Abbot of S. Denys, had retired into solitude in the environs of Troyes, where he had built and dedicated, first of all to the Holy Trinity, an oratory made of reeds, rushes, straw, and flags interwoven. He afterwards gave it the invocation of the Paraclete, because there at last he thought, after his many troubles, he had found some comfort. This place he afterwards handed over to Heloise. Some call Heloise Helwida, and Hugh Metellus wrote her two Letters under this name. "To Helwida, venerable Abbess of the Paraclete. Rumour tells me that you have surpassed your sex, by your words and verses, and, what is better than all, how you have overcome the weakness of woman," etc. Bernard once visited her, and gave her some exhortation (*Abael.*, ep. v.).

LETTER CCLXXIX. (A.D. 1152.)

To Count Henry.

He entreats the Count to enforce restitution for an injury.

The Abbot of Châtillon,[1] a man of piety, when setting out for Rome, committed all his goods to the custody of me under God. And lo! the servants of Simon de Belfort have stolen his pigs. I would rather that they had taken mine. I require them at your hands. The Prince of the Kings of the earth has made you a prince on the earth, in order that under Him, and for Him, you may cherish the good, restrain the evil, defend the poor, help them to right that suffer wrong. If you do these things you do the work of a prince, and my hope is that God will extend and establish your power. If you do them not, it is to be feared that He will take from you the honour and power which you seem to have.

LETTER CCLXXX. (*Circa* A.D. 1152.)

To Pope Eugenius about the Trouble at Auxerre.

Bernard complains that the Pope's decision in this matter has been disregarded.

1. You do well in strengthening one who is weak-hearted, and comforting one who is weary of the time that he has yet to spend here, by so often listening to him graciously.

---

[1] Baldwin, to whom Letter 401 was written, was afterwards Bishop of Noyon (ep. 402). The Abbey of Châtillon here alluded to was without doubt the house of regular Augustinian canons on the Seine, in the Diocese of Langres, where Bernard received his earliest education, and which he turned from a secular into a regular Order: it was not the Neustrian Châtillon, as some wrongly think. Châtillon, of which this Baldwin was Abbot, was not far from Clairvaux, so close indeed that the Abbot, when about to set out for Rome, entrusted his goods to Bernard's care. Moreover, Belfort, which from the context of this Letter was not far from Châtillon, was situated on the river Voire, which flows into the Aube below Clairvaux, and the town of Bar-sur-Aube. In the ancient records of Châtillon of Langres Baldwin, moreover, is reckoned as second Abbot, after Aldon, the first.

I, indeed, do not deserve it, but it becomes you. Do not suppose that I take any pleasure in abusing your kindness so as to use it merely to get my own way; my conscience is my witness that I am ready to accept as gladly what you think it right to refuse as what you grant. I like to have my wishes gratified, as every man does, but not if they are opposed to righteousness, prejudicial to the truth, or displeasing to you. I say this lest you should think either that I do not notice a kindness, or that I have no gratitude for it. Now let your Holiness hear what the case demands. As far as I am concerned the loss is very small, and such as can be easily repaired. I think that there is no medicine better suited to allay the stings of my conscience than insults and revilings. It is certainly not for myself that I am moved, being as I am a man of no worth, deserving shame and contempt. But if ever the injuries of the wicked touch the anointed of the Lord my patience, I confess, gives way, and almost all my meekness disappears. Have I ever sought from my lord the ordering of Churches, the disposing of Bishoprics, the making of Bishops? A fitting instrument truly should I be, an ant dragging a waggon. You wished the promotion of a man against whom not even those who wished otherwise could find a word to say.

2. The decision of your good pleasure was made known to all whom it concerned. It was publicly announced, but so far we are deprived of any fruit or benefit from it. You ask who is the cause of this? It is the man of your peace in whom you trusted. He is a man to whom religion is hateful, to whom wisdom is burdensome, righteousness terrible, who has no scruples to prevent him from disclosing his master's secret, and nullifying his decree. It is no wonder, then, that he was not ashamed to show himself in his true colours. He has yielded to his own envy and malice, and, therefore, he is not likely to show much consideration for you. I have been put to shame, but what matters that? I do not shrink from the shame which zeal has allied to obedience. The cup, indeed, has not passed from me, but

through me it has passed on to you. When the decision
that you have given is affronted, not to say perverted, it
must be evident to everyone that it is the author rather
than the promulgator that is affected. Ought the promotion to have been rendered uncertain of a man
against whom no ill could be said?[1] One of two things is
certain: either the word which I have testified has gone
out of your lips will stand fast, or I shall be thought a liar,
as, indeed, I am now. But it will be better and more
worthy of your Apostleship that he who has been powerful
in iniquity should not boast himself in his wickedness.

3. Your command has been in part obeyed, and by the
greater part. It was entrusted to three; one scorns it, two
uphold it. What remains, then, but that your voice should
supply what is wanting? And you may do this safely. You
have nothing to fear from the offence of those of whom the
Lord says, *Let them alone, they are blind leaders of the*

---

[1] On the death of Hugh, Bishop of Auxerre, A.D. 1151, "when the clergy wished, according to custom, to choose another Bishop," says Bernard (*De Consid.*, lib. iii. c. 2), "a certain youth interposed with an appeal and forbade the election to go forward till he had been to Rome and returned. He did not, however, carry out this appeal. For when he saw that he was scorned for having appealed without any reason, he held a meeting of all whom he could get to support him, and had himself elected on the third day after the election had been held by the others" (ep. 275). Eugenius, on hearing of this, entrusted the decision to three arbitrators, of whom Bernard was one. S. Bernard and one of the others agreed, the third dissented, and hence S. Bernard asks Eugenius in this Letter to supply what is wanting. The Bishop-elect seems to have been Alan, who at length succeeded Hugh. The "Book of Burials" of Clairvaux thus speaks of him: "To the right of Godfrey, formerly Bishop of Langres, near the Choir, lies Alan, Bishop of Auxerre, who was educated as a boy in a Church in a famous town of Flanders, called Lille, and took the religious habit under S. Bernard at Clairvaux. He was afterwards made first Abbot of the monastery called La Rivour, over which he presided for twelve years, and by the help of God left it enriched with members and goods. In the last year of the life of B. Bernard he was unanimously elected Bishop of Auxerre. He showed great hospitality to the many religious who visited his houses, and at length, after having occupied his See for thirteen years, he resigned it by the permission of the Pope and retired to Clairvaux. He died 14th Oct., A.D. 1181." When his election is spoken of as having been unanimous we must understand that finally all the votes were given to him, as, indeed, S. Bernard says (ep. 282) to King Louis.

blind (S. Matt. xv. 14). For the rest, the people, the better part of the clergy, the King himself, and the whole Church of the Saints will rejoice. You have shown this age many good works of the grace which has been given you. But nothing will redound more to your glory than this action. I bear my testimony against them, that they have nominated many to offices in the Church, not because they love religion, but because they wish to see it weak, so that there may be none to restrain their wickedness, or have strength to repel force by force, and so that they need not fear the power of those whose holiness they hate. The Count of Nevers[1] does not walk in the steps of his father; he is opposed to this man, as well as to every good man. He is a foe to the lands and goods of the Churches, like a lion ravening for his prey. He is ready to receive even a Saracen or a Jew, if he may be free from this man, who is the only one who seems to have the ability and power to withstand his wickedness and cunning. Hence it is that he has silenced many of the clergy by threats and open charges, to prevent the opposite side from glorying in their numbers.

4. And to say briefly what I think, if you think it worth while for the monasteries in that diocese to be impoverished, the Churches to be down-trodden, religion to be held up to scorn, the episcopal See itself, whose goods and possessions he particularly covets, to be reduced to slavery, then let not the man of Regny[2] by any means rule as bishop.

[1] This Count of Nevers was William IV. (ep. 276), whom we read of as having conferred many benefits on many churches, for he restored to the church of Vézelai the goods which his father had taken from it. He gave a free gift of lands to the church at Pontigny, and, to mention no more, he honoured the church of S. Germanus, at Auxerre, with his favour, and there he has his tomb in the chapter-room, although he had chosen to be buried in the graveyard. His father, whose ways he is said not to follow, was William III., a man full of piety and religion, of whom Hugh, the monk, speaks as follows:—" In the year 1147 William, Count of Nevers, resigning his throne, and despising all earthly honour, sought Chartreux, and spent his last days with God in the most humble poverty, and within a year of his conversion happily ended his life."

[2] This is said in irony, if, at least, we are to understand it of Alan, to whom Bernard applies this name, perhaps, because he was born in the village of Regny,

Where is now the spirit which you showed in the York affair? Shall not he who has attempted a like crime feel the same spirit? I hear that he is coming to you in the spirit of him who stirred up the Curia against me to see if he can accomplish the same object. Let me remind you again of the business of the Bishop of Lund. The charge of bribery has now been removed, and nothing remains to be done but what was to have been done. And let me add this: To have a chancellor who is good, just, and of good repute is no small part of the Apostolic dignity, no mean support to the Apostolic administration, no despicable guardian of the Apostolic conscience. An evil appointment is always pernicious, and after long deliberation even disgraceful.

LETTER CCLXXXI.

To Abbot Bruno of Chiarravalle.[1]

He reproves Bruno for writing passionately and imprudently.

Doest thou well to be thus angry? I think not. Your own words condemn you, for they have not been calmly considered, but uttered in haste and anger. For a calm judgment reasons thus, *Better are the wounds of a friend than the kisses of an enemy* (Prov. xxvii. 6). "But," you say, "I am beaten for nothing." Well, suppose that you are. Still, none the less, if my words wound you they show my loving anxiety for you. The little that I said breathes of the solicitude of a father. And so, if you have

or Reninghe, in Belgium, not far from Yprès. The "Book of Burials" of Clairvaux, cited above, implies that he was called "of Lille," as he everywhere is, from the place of his education, and not of his birth. For he cannot be named from the monastery of Regny, since he was taken from Clairvaux to be Abbot of La Rivour, and then elected to the Bishopric of Auxerre. It is possible, however, that in the second election at Auxerre a monk of Regny was chosen, for whom S. Bernard writes here, and that on the opposition of so many Alan was at length chosen at a third election.

[1] The older editions give Clairvaux, but the better MSS. give Chiarravalle. The latter was a famous Cistercian Abbey near Milan. See ep. 134.

done no wrong, I have not injured you. Your own conscience acquits you. If you have, then it is against you rather than against me that anger should arise. You complain that I did not believe you, just as if you had ever said a single word to me on the matter. But suppose that I did believe him who complained of you. How was I to believe or disbelieve you when you said nothing? Do what you said you would. Pay what you owe as soon as you can, lest perhaps scandal arise amongst us, if not amongst others about us. But think well of me, and of all who think well of you, and who do not disbelieve you, as you say passionately, not knowing what you say. These words are my own; they express my affection for you.

LETTER CCLXXXII. (A.D. 1152.)

TO LOUIS, KING OF THE FRENCH, ON BEHALF OF THE BISHOP-ELECT OF AUXERRE.

He begs the King not to oppose the Bishop-Elect.

1. Have I ever wished for the honour of the King and the good of his kingdom to be in any way lessened? God knows, and your own conscience, I trust, will reply. Take care lest those who are disturbing the election do not rather do you harm, lest we have in the churches men who seem to serve the King, but who rather serve themselves out of the Church's revenues. I intervened in the election at Auxerre. All was harmony, because the clergy, who before this had taken opposite sides, now at length, by the mercy of God, had come to an unanimous agreement. I know the Bishop-Elect well; I bear testimony to him that he is a good man. Moreover, I believe that no one was present in that assembly who had any doubt about your assent, for your assent was contained in the letter that you had written. Who could have imagined that your first assent was not enough and that another must be asked for, especially when no second election had taken place since you wrote? Is it necessary to seek the approbation of the

King as many times as the clergy happen to disagree? This is neither according to reason nor custom. For example, you will perhaps recollect that in the Church of Soissons the clergy disagreed as often as they met together to elect a Bishop, and separated without finishing the business, and yet I do not suppose that, having once obtained your assent, they sought it every time that they assembled.

2. So, my lord King, you have no ground for disannulling the elections that have taken place, when it is evident that you had given your assent to their being held. But there are some who are troubling you and are striving to trouble the Churches, seeking their own profit, and, what is more serious, endeavouring with diabolical zeal to break the mutual goodwill and affection which exist between the Supreme Pontiff and the King's Excellency. May God forbid it. They will bear their judgment, whoever they are, and the King will always act like a good King, as he has hitherto done. And so see that more welcome instructions are issued, so that the Church, which has been so long harassed and afflicted, may no longer sit in sadness. Let the King entertain no suspicion about the person elected, for either I am much mistaken or he will be faithful, and the King will be well pleased with him. I trust in the Lord that you will not sadden the hearts of the multitude of saints in that diocese and of me, your servant, who, to speak the truth, have never borne anything at your hands so distressing as this will be if you persist in your present intention, which may God avert.

LETTER CCLXXXIII. (A.D. 1150.)
To Pope Eugenius, on behalf of the Monks of Moiremont.[1]

He begs the Pope to intervene to settle a dispute which had arisen.

[1] The Cistercian MSS. have the heading, "On behalf of the brethren of Moiremont." Some MSS. "For the brethren": the editions "for those of Gigny." But it is all the same, for this Letter was written against the monks of Gigny and for the brethren of Moiremont. For when Innocent gave

At Cluny I met the monks of Gigny in the hope of peace, for which we have worked hard, but without success, for the only result of our four days' labour was the destruction of our hopes. According to the instructions contained in your letters, the reparation of the losses and the restitution of the goods removed were demanded, but in vain. It seemed a great demand to them, because they had done great injury, inasmuch as the worth of the losses was reckoned at more than 30,000 solidi. Indeed, not to go into details, our abbey was totally destroyed. Since the loss had been so heavy I was prepared to forego much of it, but they offered so little that the venerable Abbot of Cluny, who was labouring with more zeal than success for the purpose of peace, did not think it worthy of acceptance. And so no agreement was come to, because so ridiculously small an amount was offered in reparation. What they said was this: "Some evil-disposed persons amongst us have done this evil. What is that to us? Let them see to it." But this is absurd. It was well known in the whole neighbourhood that this great misdeed had been perpetrated by men belonging to the Church, that some monks also had been present, and that all had consented to

---

to the Cistercians exemption from paying tithes he greatly incensed the Cluniacs (as was said in the notes to ep. 228), and especially the Cluniac house of Gigny, in the county of Burgundy, against their neighbours, the Cistercians of Moiremont, both of whom were in the province of Lyons. To such a pitch did their resentment go that they did not hesitate to destroy the house of the brethren of Moiremont, and when Eugenius heard of this he wrote a stern Letter to Peter the Venerable, bidding him see that as soon as possible satisfaction was given to the Cistercians for their losses, and denouncing severe punishment against the guilty monks if this were not done. He also gave the Archbishop of Lyons power to use ecclesiastical censures against them if the losses were not made good within twenty days. S. Bernard and Peter the Venerable met at Cluny to settle the matter. For four days they discussed it, and found the loss to be computed at more than 30,000 solidi. But as the monks of Gigny were tardy in obeying the sentence Bernard signified their tardiness to Eugenius in this Letter. After the death of Bernard an arrangement about the tithes was come to between the monks of both places, A.D. 1155. But though we have no record of compensation having been given by the monks of Gigny, yet the munificence of Peter the Venerable is recorded in giving to the Cistercians what had been left at Cluny by Baroni, a sub-deacon of Rome. See epp. 388 and 389.

it. For up to the present I have not heard of even one who has opposed the evil-doers. Lastly, the Abbot of the Order himself openly rebuked and condemned shufflers of this sort by declaring that what was known to have been lost through the Church was with justice demanded at the Church's hand. Your decision is now awaited in this matter, which, as it has been sufficiently proved, cannot be set right except by a strong hand.

LETTER CCLXXXIV. (*Circa* A.D. 1151.)

To Pope Eugenius, on behalf of the Archbishop of Rheims and other Persons.

My lord, Samson, Archbishop of Rheims, lives in the house of the great Father as a vessel made to honour. If you know this, preserve his honour, and the honour of his church. If I know the man well, the more you honour him, the more by him and in him will God be honoured. The Bishop of Arras[1] is a simple and upright man, and one who up to the present has refused promotion, so that there is no need for him to be humbled by another, lest he lose his authority, and so his usefulness. If you think him worthy, give him this authority, because he will never have it of his own seeking, being one who is, as far as he is concerned, content with his lowly position. There is one who opposes himself, and is puffed up, and there is need of a Bishop to humble him, and it will be not less beneficial to the man himself. To resist the proud and to give grace to the humble is what your Lord delights to do, and you have heard Him saying: *If any man serve Me, let him follow Me* (S. John xii. 26). The Abbot of Ancourt[2] is a good

---

[1] Godeschalc (see epp. 214 and 253) succeeded, A.D. 1150, Alvisus, mentioned in epp. 65 and 395. The dispute alluded to here seems to have been with Guerric, Abbot of S. Vedast, to whom Eugenius wrote "that he should promise in writing obedience to Godeschalc for those things which he held from the church of Arras."

[2] This was a house of regular Canons of S. Augustine, near Bapaume. It is variously written in the MSS.

man, let him be rewarded according to his goodness. Let him be listened to when speaking of his necessities, and let not an apostate be heard against him. The Dean of Bethune, by the wish of his Bishop, and the assent of the advocate for his church, has determined to set on foot a good work in the same church, and it is well that it should be confirmed by your authority. In the same way I plead for the Deans of Soissons and Cambray, that they may obtain their requests. I have been in perils amongst false brethren, and many letters have been forged, and fraudulently sealed with my seal, and have gone forth into many different hands, and my chief fear is that this treachery may have reached even to you. This is why I am forced to discontinue the use of my former seal,[1] and to use this new one, which you notice is fresh, containing both my device and my name. Do not accept the other seal as mine for the future, except in the case of the Bishop of Claremont, to whom I gave a letter sealed with that seal before I had this one made.

LETTER CCLXXXV. (*Circa* A.D. 1153.)

TO THE SAME, ON BEHALF OF ODO,[2] ABBOT OF S. DENYS.

He recommends this Abbot to the Pope, and declares him innocent of the accusations brought against him.

1. I should not hesitate to write on behalf of the church of S. Denys, and for Odo, its Abbot, even if no one else would.

---

[1] From this it is plain that what William, the third Cistercian Abbot of the name, says in a Letter to Theobald, Count of Champagne, is not true, viz., that a seal of the Abbot of Buzay, recently discovered, was spurious, because on it was engraved the name of the Abbot, when, as he said, no Order ever had its Abbot's name engraved on its seal. Certainly, in a document of Bernard himself, written to settle a strife between the monasteries of S. Geneviève and S. Victor, the seal of Bernard was appended with his name and effigy, holding in his right hand a book and in his left a pastoral staff. See Letter of M. Deville (Vol. ii. p. 457.)

[2] Odo, who was formerly a monk of S. Denys, near Paris, then Abbot of S. Cornelius, at Compiègne, was chosen to succeed Suger as Abbot of S. Denys, A.D. 1151. For his ordination and merits see epp. Suger, 156 *et srq.*, especially

The cause is a good one, and doubtful on neither account: the church is a famous one, and the Abbot is of good report. The one is known to the world, the other to us, his neighbours. Add to this, that both he and the church have a special claim on you. And because of all this, as I have said, if need were I should not be ashamed to write for them, even though I were alone. But as it is, others are writing as well as I, who would not be disbelieved even if I did not write. They are men who have often treated of this matter. They know what the Abbot has done, and what they know they say. My prayers for him may go forth with confidence when supported by such indubitable testimonies. With confidence I solicit and entreat you to take some thought for the property of yours which he holds, which has been wickedly attacked, and grievously harassed. I ask you, I beseech you, lift your hand, stretch out your arm, and cover him with your shield. Let the sword of Peter defend the patrimony of Peter.

2. In vain have men risen against him; his reputation is his sufficient excuse, nay, the universal esteem in which he is held is his commendation. They are good sons, forsooth, who, prying too curiously into the secrets of their father, have dreamt of some crimes or other which no one else has discovered. Those who hear of this sudden and unexpected change stand amazed. They are ashamed, because nothing of this sort had ever before been said of Odo. The Abbot of S. Denys cannot be said to be hid under a bushel. He stands on a candlestick, and however much he may wish it, he cannot hide what he is. His light, and so his smoke, must be seen by all. Why have these men turned on him their lynx eyes, seeing what no one else has ever yet been able to see? Their charge, I confess, seems to me suspicious. What makes me more incredible is the fact that one of their number is a man named Raymond, who, they say, is the head of this wickedness that they have attempted:

ep. 162, which is one of Baldwin, Bishop of Noyon, who, writing to Eugenius, says that he was "a religious and energetic man," duly elected, and blessed by himself.

whom I have found loquacious enough face to face, but secretly a back-biter, ambitious to excess, currying favour by his flatteries, wholly set on deceit, and no less on causing confusion. I have marked the wolf under the sheep's clothing, or by certain signs I have pointed him out, so that now he may either be afraid to bite, or be powerless to do harm.

LETTER CCLXXXVI. (A.D. 1153.)

To the Same, on behalf of the Same.

If secret calumnies and craft have prevailed against the Abbot of S. Denys, I am clean from his blood, for I wrote before against his bitter foes. But what accusation do they bring against the man? Is it not a fact that they cannot find whereof to accuse him? And if they have good grounds for accusing, how is it that he is acquitted by all his neighbours who are of a right conversation? He is accused of having incurred many debts, of having mortgaged his lands, and wasted his goods, as though all this could not have happened from necessary and good causes. An assembly of that Church gave me an account of all these things, and testified through a trustworthy person that things are not as they have been reported to you. Nevertheless, let an inquiry be held, for in matters of this kind we place more confidence in what we see than in any oath; and if things are found to be as his accusers maliciously state, no matter how it came about, then let not the Abbot be excused. If they are not so, then let not these informers gain anything by their falsehood. They charge him with the death of a certain man; if he cannot clear himself let him die. And yet anyone can see how unlikely it is that he should have handed over to death a man whom but a little before he had rescued from it. How can these men have the audacity to insinuate such charges into your mind, when they have seen and known the zeal of the Abbot in freeing those who before had committed homicide, and in punishing those who had avenged the blood of a relation?

Lastly, if you had known them well, it would be enough to make you disbelieve any unsupported statement of theirs. May God help your Holiness, that the deceitful tongue may not avail anything against the Abbot's innocence.

LETTER CCLXXXVII. (A.D. 1153.)

To the Bishop of Ostia,[1] on behalf of the Same Abbot.

My lord, the Abbot of S. Denys is being accused by the wicked, but by all the good men in his Church and neighbourhood he is excused. I ask your Christian love for him the more earnestly because my esteem for him has been and still is very great. Befriend him with your kindness, if not because he is a friend of mine, yet, at all events, because the charges brought against him are neither true, nor likely. If he is burdened with debts, then the necessity of the time is evidently the cause of it, although his debts are nothing like the amount stated. As to the alienation of his lands, the charge is easily proved to be false. For I suppose that not even his enemies themselves can possibly suspect him of the death of G—; inasmuch as he kept this same G— and all his companions in shelter from their enemies, and with much labour snatched them from the very jaws of death. For all this, and because especially I know of the underhand dealing of Raymond, I earnestly beg you to vindicate with all care the innocence of the Abbot.

LETTER CCLXXXVIII. (A.D. 1153.)

To his Uncle Andrew, a Knight of the Temple.

Bernard deplores the unhappy issue of the Crusade.

1. The letter which you lately sent me found me lying in bed. I received it with open hands, joyfully, read and re-read it, but should have been more joyful could I have

---

[1] Hugh. See epp. 273, 274, 290, 296, 306.

seen you yourself. I read in it of your desire to see me, and of your fear because of the danger threatening the land which the Lord honoured by His presence, the State which He consecrated by His own blood. Woe to our princes!¹ In the Lord's land they did no good, in their own, to which they returned with all speed, they practise incredible mischief, and they are not grieved for the affliction of Joseph. They are mighty to do evil, but good they cannot do. But I trust that the Lord will not reject His people, and will not cast away His inheritance. Moreover, the right hand of the Lord will yet execute power, and His arm will help Him, that all may know that it is better to trust in the Lord than to put any confidence in princes. You do well to compare yourself to an ant. For what else are we children of men, who are born of the earth, always labouring after useless and empty things ? What profit is there to a man for all his labour wherewith he labours under the sun? Let us, therefore, climb up above the sun, and let our conversation be in heaven ; let us in mind go before thither whether we shall one day follow in body. There, my dear Andrew, is the fruit of your labour, there is your reward. You are warring under the sun, but it is for One who sits above the sun. Let us who fight here expect from Him our largesse. The reward of our warfare is not of the earth, is not from beneath ; its prize is from afar, and from the utmost land. Under the sun is want, above the sun abundance. *Good measure, pressed down, and shaken together and running over, shall men give into our bosom* (S. Luke vi. 38).

2. You wish to see me; and you say that the gratification of

---

[1] This is to be understood of the unfortunate expedition to the East. For ambition, quarrels, and rivalry between the Christian leaders of that holy expedition broke their strength and frustrated their undertaking, so Bernard says (*De Consid.* lib. ii. c. 1), and so says Otto of Frisingen, an eye-witness, in his *de Gest Frider.* lib. i. c. 78, where, after relating the great disasters that fell on the Christian army, he adds : " Yet, notwithstanding such reverses, the haughtiness of the Kings to each other that had sprung up did not cease." See Emilius on Louis VII., where, treating of the siege of Damascus, he says that it would have been taken if it had not been saved by the ambition of the Christian leaders. See also Sigonius *de Reg. Ital.* lib. xi., and *De Consid.* lib. ii. c. 1.

your wish depends on me. For you hint that you wait for an order from me to come. What shall I say to you? I both wish for you to come, and yet fear your coming. So placed between wishing and not wishing, I am in a strait between two, and which to choose I know not. On one side is the wish to satisfy what is at once your own desire and mine; on the other, the doubt whether I ought not to believe rather the common report of you, which says that you are so necessary to the land that no small disaster is likely to happen if you leave it. And so what I dare not command I yet wish for, viz., that I may see you before I die. You can see and know better than I if you can anyhow come without loss and reproach to the country. And it might be that your coming would not be altogether unprofitable. Perhaps, with God's blessing, some would be induced to accompany you on your return to support the Church of God, since you are known and beloved by all. God can bring it to pass that you, too, can say with holy Jacob, *With my staff I passed over this Jordan, and, lo! I return with three bands* (Gen. xxxii. 10). One thing, I say, if you do come, do not delay, lest, perchance, you come and find me not. For I am now ready to be offered, and I do not think that I have much more time to spend on earth. Who will give me the happiness of being somewhat refreshed before I depart hence, with your sweet and gladsome presence? I have written to the Queen as you wished, and I rejoice in the good report which you give of her. Salute in the Lord your Master and brethren of the Temple, likewise those of the Hospital. Salute also all who are shut up, and all the Saints to whom you have an opportunity of speaking, and commend me to their prayers. Be instead of me to them. I hear that our Gerard,[1] who spent some time in our house, has now been made Bishop; him, too, I salute most warmly with great affection.

---

[1] Was this the Gerard, Bishop of Bethlehem, of whom William of Tyre speaks in the beginning of his 17th Book under the year 1146, and again at the end under the year 1152? or was he Bishop of Sidon?

LETTER CCLXXXIX. (*Circa* A.D. 1153.)

To the Queen of Jerusalem.

Bernard instructs her how she should behave if she would be an honourable widow before God and queen before men.

To his beloved daughter in Christ, MILISENDIS,[1] Queen of Jerusalem, BERNARD, called Abbot of Clairvaux, wishes mercy from God our Saviour.

1. I wonder why I have not seen any letter from you for so long a time, and have not had your usual salutations. I cannot forget your old affection for me, which I have ofttimes put to the proof. I have heard, I confess, some evil reports of you; and although I do not altogether believe them, yet I am grieved that, whether they are true or false, your good fame should be so compromised. But my dear Uncle Andrew has written, and I cannot disbelieve him in anything; he gives me a better account of you; he says how peaceably and meekly you bear yourself, how wisely you rule yourself and yours by the advice of wise men, how you love the brethren of the Temple, and cherish them, with what foresight and wisdom, according to the measure given you by God, you meet with sound counsels and aids the dangers threatening the Holy Land. These are the actions that become a brave woman, a lowly widow, an exalted queen. For though you are a queen, it is no disgrace to be a widow, and if you had wished it you would not be one. I think that it is your glory, especially among Christians, to live no less as a widow than a queen. One is of succession, the other of virtue; one of birth, the other of the gift of God; that came by good fortune, this by a brave spirit. The honour is twofold, one according to the world, the other according to God, but each from God. Nor

---

[1] Milisendis, or Melusina, was daughter of Baldwin, the second Latin King of Jerusalem. He was succeeded by his son-in-law, Fulk, husband of this Milisendis, who was thrown on his head from his horse while hunting, and died after three days, A.D. 1142. Ep. 206, 354, and 355 were written to her. Her sister, Ivera, was a nun (*Will. of Tyre*, lib. xv. *sub finem*).

let the honour of widowhood seem to you small, about which the Apostle says, *Honour widows which are widows indeed* (1 Tim. v. 3).

2. You certainly have before you a second familiar piece of advice in the wholesome words of the Apostle, who teaches you to "provide things honest not only in the sight of God, but also in the sight of men" (2 Cor. viii. 21). In the sight of God, as a widow: in the sight of men, as a queen. Recollect that you are a queen, and that your good deeds cannot lie in obscurity under a bushel. They are on a candlestick that they may be seen of all. Recollect that you are a widow, and that you have not now to please your husband, but to please God alone. Happy are you if you place your Saviour as a wall before you for a guard to your conscience, and a bulwark to repel infamy. Happy, I say, if like one desolate and a widow you entrust yourself wholly to God, for Him to rule you. Else, if you are not well ruled you do not rule well. The Queen of the South came to hear the wisdom of Solomon, that she might learn to be ruled, and so to rule. And behold! *a Greater than Solomon is here* (S. Matt. xii. 42). I speak of Jesus, and Him crucified. Commit yourself to Him to rule you, to be taught by Him how you ought to rule. Learn as a widow, *for He is meek and lowly of heart* (S. Matt. xi. 29); learn as a queen, because *he judges the poor with righteousness, and reproves with equity for the meek of the earth* (Is. xi. 4). Therefore, when you think of your dignity, forget not your widowhood, because (to say to you plainly what I think) you cannot be a good queen if you are not a good widow. You ask how a good widow is to be known. From the words of the Apostle: *If she have brought up children, if she have lodged strangers, if she have washed the Saints' feet, if she have relieved the afflicted, if she have diligently followed every good work* (1 Tim. v. 10). If thou doest these things, happy art thou, and well will it be with thee. May the Lord bless you out of Sion, my daughter renowned in the Lord, worthy of all veneration. My admonition has been sent first; I shall

now expect a reply to follow. I have given you the occasion, and will admit of no excuse, if our friendship is not renewed by your sending me frequently for the future words and letters of friendship.

LETTER CCXC. (A.D. 1152.)

To the Bishop of Ostia about Cardinal Jordan.[1]

Bernard describes the Legate of the Holy See, and what disgraceful traces he had everywhere left behind him.

Your legate has passed from nation to nation and from one kingdom to another people, leaving with us foul and horrid traces everywhere. From the foot of the Alps and the Kingdom of the Teutons this Apostolic man has gone about in every direction through nearly all the churches of France and Normandy, as far as Rouen, and he has filled them not with the Gospel, but with sacrilege. He is said to have done disgraceful things, to have carried off spoils from churches, to have promoted, when he could, boys to ecclesiastical honours with no other qualifications than their beautiful faces, and, where he could not, to have wished to do it. Many bribed him not to come to them. He exacted and extorted money by his messengers from those to whom he could not go. In the schools, the courts, the very streets, he has made himself a proverb. Seculars, religious, all speak ill of him. The poor, and the monks, and the clergy all complain of him. It is the men, too, of his own profession who are loudest in expressing their abhorrence of his reputation and his life. He has this report, too, both from those within and those without. Not so did John Paperon,[2] not so he whose praise is in the Churches, as of

[1] The legate spoken of here was Jordan Orsino, and was sent, A.D. 1151, as legate into Germany to the Emperor Conrad.

[2] John Paperon or Papyrion, A.D. 1152, on the testimony of John Hagustald, "set out for Ireland, and distributed four palls to their respective Sees, and taught that nation the law of marriage to which they had been strangers." Up to that time the Irish Bishops consecrated their own Bishops. See Gerald, *Topog. Hib.* c. 17.

one who honours his ministry everywhere. Read this letter to my lord. Let him see what is to be done with such a man; I have freed my soul. Yet I say, with my usual rashness, that it will be good for him to purge his court, and so free his conscience. I had determined to say nothing about this, but the venerable Prior of Mont Dieu [1] impelled me to this, and inspired me to write. Know, too, that I have said less than is openly talked of in public.

LETTER CCXCI.

To Pope Eugenius for the Church of S. Eugendus [2] in the Jura.

If what is said is true, and it is not wholly to be rejected, the famous monastery of S. Eugendus, formerly renowned for its wealth and piety, is ready to perish. I grieve to see houses belonging to it, which are near us and known to you, partly destroyed already, and partly being destroyed daily. What we see in the members we have heard by report is worse even in the head. But why should I give you an account now of these evils which are numberless? The bearer of this, a monk of the same monastery, and the Prior Archegaud, a man long known to me for his worth, and beloved for his piety, will be able to tell you what they know more fully than I do, although not everything. For who could do this? The evils are so many and so great that it is a wonder if they do not compel the apostolic axe to lift itself and strike, even though it be hiding itself and sleeping. I have liberated my soul, but it is not enough, unless the monastery be also liberated. Its life and death are in your hands.

[1] Gervase was then Prior of Mont Dieu, a Carthusian foundation in the Diocese of Rheims, founded, A.D. 1136, by Odo, Abbot of S. Remigius. It seems from this passage that Gervase, as well as the monastery, enjoyed the esteem of Bernard.

[2] It was formerly named after Augendus, who was a holy Abbot of the renowned monastery of Condé, built by S. Romanus on the mountains of Jura. He gave to it the name of S. Eugendus, which was afterwards changed into S. Claudius. It was in the Diocese of Lyons.

LETTER CCXCII.

To a Certain Secular.

Bernard reproves him for dissuading a novice named Peter, his relative, from taking the vows.

1. Though unknown to me by face, yet you are not by fame, for I have gathered that you are a wise man, and one held in honour by the world. My beloved son Peter, to whom you seem to be well known and to be in some degree related, has wished me to write to you, or rather reply to you. For you wrote to him, and I wish that you had written what was honourable to yourself and expedient for him. You did not so. You ventured to dissuade a new soldier of Christ from the service of his Lord. I tell you that there is one that seeketh and judgeth. Were not your own sins enough for you that you must involve yourself in those of others, and, again, as far as you could, recall to his sins a youth who was penitent, and so, according to your hardness and impenitent heart, keep up for yourself wrath against the day of wrath? Was it not enough that the devil himself tempts him, but you must help that tempter, you, a Christian, his leader, and his familiar friend? You, indeed, have played the part to him of another serpent, but he has not acted as a second Eve. He was moved by what you said, but not overturned. He was founded on a firm rock.

2. Nevertheless, I do not pay you back in your own coin, but I overcome evil with good. I pray for you, I wish for you better things, and I write better things. In the first place, as you are said to be a wise man, I send you to a wise man in order that what is said of you may be more true. He says, *Do not prevent him who can do good, and, if you can, do good yourself* (Prov. iii. 27). You have now time in which to do good. But how long will you have it? Consider how little time you have to live, especially now that you are old. Life is a vapour that cometh forth for a brief space and is quickly dispersed. If you are wise you will know whether that curse is coming on you, *I have seen*

the foolish firmly rooted, and straightway I cursed his beauty (Job v. 3). Well did he who was truly wise call the fool falsely-wise, knowing that the wisdom of this world is foolishness with God (1. Cor. iii. 19). O that thou wert wise, and didst understand and provide for thy latter end (Deut. xxxii. 29). That thou wert wise in the things of God, understood what the things of this world are, and provided for the things beneath the earth! Surely you would fly from the things beneath, you would yearn for the things above, you would spurn the things which make for evil. My mind, or rather my spirit, prompts me to say many things to you about the salvation of your soul, but until I see by your answer how you take this, I will add nothing further, lest I become burdensome to one to whom I wish for the future to be a friend, and, if he will let me, a helper in the way of salvation. I salute your wife, beloved by me in Christ, although she has done nothing to merit this affection.

LETTER CCXCIII. (*Circa* A.D. 1150.)

To Peter, Abbot of Moustier la Celle,[1] on behalf of a Monk of Chézy, who had changed over to Clairvaux.

To the cause of your writing I thus reply. I think that the annoyance of my lord of Chézy is not more annoying to anyone than to myself. But I suppose that you know that a long time ago, by his own wish and precept, that monk was made mine, and that he promised obedience to

---

[1] Petrus Cellensis is better known by having been Abbot of Cella, a monastery in the suburbs of Troyes, than from having been Abbot of S. Remigius, or even Bishop of Chartres. He wrote two Letters to the monks of Chézy, which are epp. 14 and 15, lib. ii. Nothing is known of this monk, except that his name seems to have been Adam, from two Letters written in his name to Peter of Cella by Nicholas of Clairvaux, in which Peter is congratulated on the reformation of his monastery. It was this Peter who defended the memory of S. Bernard, and his opinion about the Conception of the Blessed Mary, against the attacks of another Nicholas (ep. 174 note). He says that he was a disciple of S. Bernard in lib. lx. ep. 8 to the Cistercian Chapter (see also ep. 263).

me, and that I undertook the charge of him. It is not easy to recollect how often since then I have opposed his desire to come to me, and sent him back when he came. Only now at last has he come and remained, but against my will, and I can in no way persuade him to return. He said, indeed, that if I sent him away he would go away altogether and never return. But not even so had he my consent; nay, he entered even against my advice. But having entered so, my conscience would not let me reject him, nor can I now do so, inasmuch as he was before put under my care, as I said, and I shall have to give account of him. For a long time, I confess, had I passed over this danger to my conscience, lest I should annoy the good abbot; and I would have still have passed it over, if the monk would have in any way listened to my advice. But since this is the state of things, it is yours to console the abbot, to blot out his sadness, to make my excuse to him for this reasonable cause. Lastly, he himself, as you know, is in a state of uncertainty, and has often thought of leaving his house.[1] But if he wished now to carry out what he has meditated I would not stand in his way, because I know that he remains in the house not without great anxiety.

LETTER CCXCIV. (*Circa* A.D. 1150.)

TO POPE EUGENIUS, ON BEHALF OF THE BISHOP OF LE MANS.

He recommends the Bishop and others to the Pope.

The Bishop of Le Mans is here.[2] If you do not know him let me say that he is a man of whose truth and honesty no one has any doubt, except those who do not know him well. From his youth up he has been known and beloved by me for his well-known virtues, as well as for the other

[1] Ep. 15 of Peter of Cella to the monk of Chézy, lib. ii., alludes to this: "As long as you can retain with you your father, who is also ours; do not think of another." This must be understood of Simon, who finally, on the death of Bernard, retired to Clairvaux. See above on ep. 263.

[2] William of Passavant, formerly Archdeacon of Rheims.

good points in his character. If any slander against him has been brought before you, holy Father, either I am deceived, or the slanderer has lied to his own harm. Hear the Bishop, and dismiss him in the fulness of your favour. I have been deceived if he has not been well placed. I ask that the Abbot of Vendôme, who is specially devoted to you,[1] may find special favour with you, and that his reasonable request may be obtained without difficulty. The Bishop of Angers is sending a messenger, seeking something at your hands, both by himself and through one, and I ask that he may be heard for his righteousness, and that a lying slanderer may not be heard against him. It is fitting that you who live for all should have power for all according to their merits.

LETTER CCXCV. (*Circa* A.D. 1150.)

To Cardinal Henry,[2] for the Same Bishop.

I write to you as if to myself, and this every time that I write to you. For where you are, there I hope to be, for I love you as myself. If you love me as much, or, I should say, because you love me, see that my lord of Le Mans, as far as you can, does not have to return disappointed in any way. Otherwise I shall be disappointed too, for I love him for his uprightness, and I wish him to be loved by you.

LETTER CCXCVI. (*Circa* A.D. 1150.)

To the Bishop of Ostia, for the Same.

A certain cleric is said to have gained the ear of my lord, and to have brought a charge against his own Bishop, who

---

[1] So he said also of Odo, Abbot of S. Denys: "His Church and himself are specially devoted to you," doubtless because both the Abbey of S. Denys, and that of Vendôme, over which Robert then was, are directly under the power and jurisdiction of the Roman Pontiff.

[2] Otherwise "to Cardinal Helias." Ernald speaks of him in lib. i. of his *Life of S. Bernard*, whose monk he had been at Clairvaux. His title was of SS. Nereus and Achilles. A Letter of his is extant in Vol. iii., *Biblioth. Cisterc.*, p. 239, about the due election of Alexander III.

is a friend of mine, to satisfy his own greed. If you have any regard for me, or rather for the righteousness of God, take care that this malignant slanderer gain nothing by his falsehood, and let not the innocent Bishop, my faithful friend, take any harm.

LETTER CCXCVII.

To the Abbot of Montier Ramey,[1] on behalf of a Fugitive Monk.

The bearer of this was lately, at my request, admitted into your society, but prompted by folly and carelessness he threw off the sacred habit, and left you. But he is now, it seems, penitent, and wishes to return, and humbly begs to be received again; and I, too, beg the same thing for him, that for the love of God and of me you will not refuse admission and the habit to one who is now penitent.

LETTER CCXCVIII. (A.D. 1151.)

To Pope Eugenius, about Nicholas.

Nicholas[2] has gone out from us because he was not of us, but he has left behind him foul footprints. I long ago knew

---

[1] Guido, to whom ep. 398 was written.

[2] This is the Nicholas of whom Peter of Cluny made so much, as we see in his Letters. From a monk of Montier Ramey, in the Diocese of Troyes, he became a Cistercian, and Bernard's secretary. He was a powerful writer, and only second to Bernard himself. His Letters are extant in the Cologne edition of the Library of the Fathers, edited by John Picard, of S. Victor, at Paris. But he was a traitor, and for a long time concealed his wolf's disposition under sheep's clothing, and at length manifested his hypocrisy. For it was not once only that he fraudulently used Bernard's seal; and when his fraud was discovered he took to flight. It is commonly reported that he fled into England, on the account of there being a certain Nicholas a monk of S. Albans, in Hertfordshire, who attacked the opinion of S. Bernard on the Conception of the Blessed Virgin after Bernard's death. It was not, then, without cause that Bernard wrote to Eugenius that he was in peril among false brethren. But since Peter of Cella, who undertook to defend S. Bernard (lib. vi. ep. 23, and lib. ix. ep. 9), calls him English, and indicates that he is well-known to him, and his friend, and as it

what he was, but I had been waiting either for God to convert him or for him to show himself a Judas. This he has done. Besides books, silver, and much gold, there were found on him when he left three seals, one his own, one the prior's, the third mine, and that not a very old one, but the new one which I had been forced to use because of his treachery and secret frauds. This is why I wrote to you, I recollect, without giving my name, because I was in perils among false brethren. Who can say to how many people he wrote what he chose under my name, and without my knowledge? Who will give me the satisfaction of seeing your Curia thoroughly purged of the dregs of his lies, and of seeing that the innocence of those with me is sufficient to excuse us to those who have been circumvented and prevented by his lies? It was partly proved, and partly he confessed, that he had written to you more than once in this underhand way. The earth is stained by his disgraceful deeds, and they have become proverbial amongst all; I refrain from polluting with them my lips and your ears. He boasts that he will come to you, and that he has friends in the Curia. If he does come, remember Arnold of Brescia; he is a greater sinner than Arnold. No one better deserves life-long imprisonment, no fitter sentence could be pronounced against him than one of perpetual silence.

is agreed that the other was a Gaul, and familiarly known to and beloved by Peter of Cella, as is plain from the Letters that they interchanged, we must come to the conclusion that they were not the same person. To say nothing else, his style is not so biting, but is too courteous to let us think that he could have addressed Peter of Cella so outrageously as Peter complains that Nicholas, the Englishman, had done (lib. ix. ep. 9). But Nicholas passed over from the monastery of Montier Ramey to Clairvaux in S. Bernard's absence, A.D. 1146, when certainly Eugenius was Pope, as is seen from ep. 7, which he wrote to the monks of Clairvaux before his admission. But he fled A.D. 1151, no doubt after the election at Grenoble, about which see notes to ep. 270; and, indeed, he is found to have written his name to ep. 389, where that election is dealt with.

LETTER CCXCIX. (*Circa* A.D. 1150.)

To the Count of Angoulême, on behalf of the Monks of S. Amand de Boisse.[1]

He complains of the heavy exactions from his brethren by the Count.

Do not think it strange of me if I regard as excessive the rent-charge which you demand of our brethren for the domain of Boisse, since we are not accustomed to pay anything like that amount. We have founded many Abbeys, and none of them has been rendered liable to such heavy dues. But as this is your absolute will, and as God more willingly accepts a voluntary offering than a forced one, I will ratify the agreement which my brethren have made with you, until God shall inspire you with a more indulgent spirit towards us, as I do not despair that He will do. In the meantime honour them with your affection and favour, give them your protection and support; there is no better means of enabling you to appear with confidence before the tribunal of Christ than to have the poor for your friends and intercessors.

LETTER CCC.

To the Countess of Blois.[2]

He consoles the Countess for the excesses of her son,

---

[1] In the first Lyons edition of the Letters of S. Bernard, in 1494, reads *Comiti Angelberto* (perhaps the same who is spoken of in Letter 123) *pro fratribus de Bruria*. In another edition, 1530, *Comiti Engelberto pro fratribus de Bruxia*. In another at Lyons in 1520, and in all following, except one, it stands as given in the text. The authors of our age prefer this subscription, asserting that William, surnamed Taillefer, Count of Angoulême, granted to the Cistercians in 1143 a spot situated in the territory of Boisse, where was situated the Benedictine Abbey of S. Amand, founded by Count Arnald in the tenth century. But these last having protested against the grant made to the Cistercians, Bernard, for the sake of peace, gave it up in 1153; but on the condition, says Picard, that the monks of S. Amand should repay sixty silver marks to those of Clairvaux for the buildings which they had raised and other things acquired by them in that place.

[2] Matilda of Flanders, the wife of Theobald the Great, Count of Champagne. Bernard seems to have comforted the Countess not with a vain hope, but rather

which he imputes to his age, and encourages her to hope for a better future for him ; he advises her to treat him with kindness and indulgence, rather than with harshness.

If your son has ever fallen into any unsuitable conduct towards you I greatly regret it ; and deplore the excess of the son as well as the injury to the mother ; but after all his conduct is excusable in a young man. For the faults of youth find both their cause and their excuse in the heedlessness of that age. Do you not know that *the thoughts and imaginations of man's heart are given to evil from his youth?* (Gen. viii. 21). Console yourself in the hope that there will be a change in him for the better by the merits and alms of his father.[1]

Because of this you must be more and more earnest in your prayers and vows to God for him ; for although he may not show all the filial affection and respect at all times that he should, yet a mother ought never to forget her motherly affection, nor, indeed, is she able to do so. *Can a woman forget the son of her womb? And if she,* He says, *should forget, yet I will not forget thee* (Isaiah xlix. 15). Let us entreat and lament before God ; as for me, I have good hope that He will in His mercy cause a young man of such excellent qualities to endeavour to imitate his father's noble character. Treat with him, then, in a spirit of gentleness and with affectionate intentions : because he will thus be better induced to good actions than if he is exasperated with reproaches and reprimands. In this way I feel sure that both your heart and mine will equally be gladdened in with a prophecy. For I find that she bore to Theobald four sons ; Henry, Count of Blois, who succeeded his father in 1151 ; Theobald, Dapifer, successively of Louis the Younger and Philip Augustus, in which charge he succeeded Ralph, Count of Vermandois; Stephen, afterwards a monk of the Chartreuse ; and, finally, William, who is mentioned in Letter 271, for the promotion of whom to Church dignities while yet a boy Bernard refuses to make interest. Bernard seems in this Letter to speak of Henry, the first of these, who on his return from Syria, inflated with his succession to his father's power, allowed himself to fall into some excesses, easily to be understood at his age. Letter 279 is to him.

[1] This was Theobald the Great, for whom see the Notes to Letter 37. The Life not only of Bernard, but also of Norbert, speak of his alms-giving and other good deeds. See also Letter 416.

a short time by the happy change which will take place in him. You will not doubt that I desire as fervently as you to see him return to a better mind. Would that I may find him always towards everyone such as I have always found him towards myself; for I do not think that he has ever refused to yield to any wish of mine; may the Lord recompense it to him! But you may believe that, as you have frequently requested, I have remonstrated with him, and I will continue to do so whenever the occasion shall offer.

LETTER CCCI. (*Circa* A.D. 1149.)
TO SANCHIA, SISTER OF THE EMPEROR OF SPAIN.[1]

He begs her to use her influence to close a controversy which had arisen with some other monks about the reception of a certain monastery among them.

1. As relates to the reception of the monastery of Tholdanos, you know that what has been done was not done by

[1] This was Alfonso of Castile and Leon, King or Emperor, for the Kings of that date loved to be honoured with the latter title. He was frequently called " the Good "; Sanchia, his sister, was much attracted towards S. Bernard, and had founded in 1147 in the Diocese of Palencia a Cistercian monastery called S. Peter d'Espina. S. Bernard sent thither a colony of monks under the charge of his brother Nivard. A little time afterwards the black monks of the monastery of Tholdanos, in the kingdom of Leon, recently founded by the Infanta Elvira, detached themselves from the monks of Caracetta, upon which they were dependent, and put themselves under the authority of the Cistercians. Immediately the monks of Caracetta protested, and begged Sanchia to use all her influence with S. Bernard. What was the issue of this affair will be seen from an ancient document which Manrique has published in his *Annals* under the year 1148, c. 8. It reads thus : " After the death of Dom Florentius, the Abbot Ferdinand, Abbot of Tholdanos, declared himself without reason against the Convent of Caracetta, and led by a spirit of rebellion, betook himself to the house of Clairvaux. The Lady Sanchia, the Queen, who held the monastery of Caracetta in much affection, was displeased at this, and wrote to the Abbot and community of Clairvaux not to receive the before-mentioned Abbot in an illicit manner. The Abbot of Clairvaux yielded to the wishes of the Queen, refused to receive the Abbot Ferdinand, unless he should obtain the licence of the Abbot of Caracetta for his admission. As he was never able to obtain this he died without being a monk either at Clairvaux or Caracetta."

Nevertheless, some years afterwards this monastery passed under the rule of Citeaux.

me, since I was absent and knew nothing of what was going on. That it was done by my brethren I do not deny, but they took care to surround it in every respect with precautions, taking the advice of many persons of piety, assuring themselves of the consent and assistance of the Bishop of the Diocese, and having acted only on the request of a noble lady who had founded that house upon her own lands; and in no respect was it done secretly. They supposed that they were able to accept freely what the foundress offered to them spontaneously, declaring it free and independent of any other religious house, and it was even said that she had the written proofs of his in her hands. But as you inform me that the monks of Caracetta complain that in this matter their rights have been injured, and as, instead of following the advice of Solomon, who says to them, *Do not hinder him who desires to do well, and do well thyself if thou art able* (Prov. iii. 27), they opposed themselves under these circumstances to us in this good work, and since it does not become the servants of God to strive (2 Tim. ii. 24), my conclusion is to put back the whole matter into your hands, that you may set at rest, by your action and authority, a calumny altogether, as they say, unfounded and unjust, and that for the glory of God and the health of your own soul you may restore calm and peace to an Order established in the Church.

2. For my brother Nivard, who praises your bounty much, advises me to put entire confidence in you on this occasion, as well, because of your especial goodwill for our Order, as because of the promise which you have had the goodness to make to him. I cannot suppose that our opponents will refuse to submit themselves to your salutary warnings or advice. If, however, they should do so it will be necessary to commit the judgment in this matter to the two Bishops in whose dioceses the places in question are situated, so that the whole controversy between them may be terminated. Whatsoever they shall have determined or agreed upon by mutual consent it will be your part to ratify and see executed. If you fear God, do not suffer that

so good a work should be hindered, nor that the wish of that pious lady should be frustrated, nor that those religious should be deprived of the fruit of their devotion, nor, finally, that God should be defrauded of an offering so acceptable to Him as that of an Order reformed.[1]

I entreat you also to show your maternal affection for your new foundation. I mean the house of Espína. Let those brethren, sustained by your generosity, continue in the service of God according to the Rule of their Order.

LETTER CCCII. (A.D. 1153.)

To the Legates[2] of the Holy See, on behalf of the Archbishop of Mayence.

He commends to them the cause of the Archbishop, who was oppressed by his adversaries.

To my Lords and reverend Fathers, Legates of the Holy See, the son and servant of their Holiness, BERNARD, called Abbot of Clairvaux, wishes health, and that through all

---

[1] Lambert Deschamps, author of the edition of 1520, remarks in the margin upon this passage "that even in the time of S. Bernard mention was made of a reform of the monasteries."

[2] Baronius speaks thus, under the year 1153, of this Legation: "In the same year Pope Eugenius sent a Legation into Germany to judge the Archbishop of Mayence. For this duty were chosen the Presbyter Bernard and the Deacon Gregory," etc. Bernard was the Prior of the regular Canons of the Lateran, when he was made Cardinal-Presbyter with the title of S. Clement, in 1145, by Pope Eugenius. As for Gregory, he is believed to be the same who was made Cardinal, with the title of S. Angelo, by Pope Innocent in 1137. Bishop Conrad, who wrote a Chronicle of Mayence a hundred years later, says that Archbishop Henry was deposed, and lays all the fault upon a certain Arnold, who had betrayed him; but Dodechin, in his Appendix to *Marianus* in *Canonicos*, imputes the deposition of the Archbishop to the Legates, whom the Chancellor Arnold had succeeded in corrupting by means of money. Nevertheless, Otto of Freisingen, who was present, asserts that he was justly deposed (*De Vit. Frid.* ii. 9).

To the same Henry Letter 365 was written.

However this may have been, Henry after his deposition retired into Saxony, and a little time after made a happy and pious death in a Cistercian Convent.

things they may please God and bring forth worthy fruits of their mission.

Although far removed in body, I am closely united with you by affection and goodwill; and I desire and pray that your acts and intentions may be directed in everything to justice and right. Having then learned that the unfortunate Archbishop of Mayence has been cited to appear before you in order to reply to the accusations of his adversaries, I have taken upon me to make an appeal to your goodness on his behalf. I believe that you will honour your ministry if, as far as justice allows, you support this feeble and tottering wall by the shoulders of your authority; and that you will not permit the bruised reed to be broken nor the smoking flax to be quenched, as far as in you lies. Let him feel, I entreat you, that my intercession has been of service to him; and let him not be utterly lost by that simplicity of soul, because of which he is said to have been entrapped by false brethren, rather than discovered in any action rendering him worthy of deposition.

LETTER CCCIII.

To Louis the Younger, King of France.

Bernard advises the King how he ought to act in the cause of a certain Breton seigneur, who was adulterous and excommunicated.

If by the promise to absolve him from the excommunication which he has incurred, it would be possible to determine that seigneur from Brittany to send away the adulteress, permitting her to enjoy the lands which her father has left her according to the division which she has made with her brother; although she is unworthy of any such concession, perhaps it ought not to be refused, so that you may by this means obtain the support and aid of a powerful seigneur. Otherwise it is not the advice of your humble and faithful servant that either land should be granted to a stranger, or your favour accorded to a man excommunicated and incestuous: lest (which may God avert) you may one day hear the words applied to you: *When thou sawest a thief thou consentedst unto him, and hast been partaker with the adulterers* (Ps. l. 18). Yet I would not advise precipitate action, or a sudden breach with the man. Action should be taken through some faithful and prudent agent, by whom, if possible, he may be led on, and time gained. If he will not listen to any proposal and remains obstinate, you may have confidence in the Lord that he will not prevail; since justice will be on your side and will be a powerful aid. I know not whether the Bishop[1] of that district would be a fit and suitable person for this purpose: not that he is not faithful to you, for he is, on the contrary, most loyal; but on account of his position towards that seigneur, who detests him, and would not, I fear, have any confidence in him. He is, however, prepared to do everything in your service, which, with the will of God, might be in his power. If he should make any more private suggestion to you as from me you will know that it comes from me, and please to receive it as from my mouth. For he is a man whom I love much and in whom I have considerable confidence; you also may, I believe, safely confide to him whatever you think proper.

LETTER CCCIV. (A.D. 1153.)
To the Same.

Bernard thanks the King for the interest that he takes in his health, and says some words in favour of the King's brother Robert.

The letter which your Highness has deigned to send to me has rejoiced my soul: may God, who has inspired you with this good thought, recompense you also with a similar joy. What am I, or what is my father's house, that your royal Majesty should trouble about my life or my death?

---

[1] He refers here, perhaps, to John, Bishop of Aleth or S. Malo, who had been a monk at Cîteaux, and to whom Peter de Celle wrote many Letters. (Book i. Letter 15 and following.)

But since you do me the honour to inquire respecting my health I may reply that I am somewhat better, and, I believe, out of danger, though I am still very weak. I take this opportunity to inform you that Lord Robert, your brother, has done me the honour and kindness to visit me during my sickness; he has spoken to me in a manner that has filled me with joy and better hope on his behalf. Remember to show him some affection; I promise you that he will give you satisfaction, if his actions answer to his words. Have the kindness to express to him your satisfaction at knowing that he is willing henceforth to rule his conduct according to the advice which I have given him, and that of good men. I have not my seal at hand, but I hope that he who reads this will recognize my style, because I have myself dictated[1] this.

LETTER CCCV. (A.D. 1153.)

To Pope Eugenius.

Bernard recommends to the Pope the cause of the Bishop of Beauvais, who is detained by just causes from travelling to Rome.

The Bishop of Beauvais,[2] your son (whom I might also call mine if it were not presumption on my part thus to speak), having been summoned to your presence, would have come willingly, being strong in the justice of his cause, and confiding in your fatherly favour. But I have detained him, and have had much difficulty in so doing, so desirous was he to see your face. What made me wish to keep him back was chiefly (among other good reasons) that I was doubtful what was your wish in respect of him. Besides, without speaking of many other considerations

[1] That is, *I have written*; as may be gathered from the words themselves. In this sense also the same word *dictavi* is used in other epistles, *e.g.*, 85, n. 4, and in Letters 307, 310. But *dicto* is used in a different sense from *scribo* in Letters 89 and 90, n. 1.

[2] This was Henry, brother of the King of France, Louis the Younger, who is mentioned in Letter 278. See Letter 307. Bernard gives him the name of Son, and in the following Letter calls him *your brother* because he had been a monk at Clairvaux, as may be seen in the *Life*, iv. 15. See the notes on Letter 307.

which opposed themselves to his departure, he and his brother, the King, do not walk together in one mind, and it would not be altogether safe for him to be long absent from his diocese. Do not ask me on which side is the wrong: it is not for me to bring a charge against anyone; it is sufficient for me to excuse the Bishop. I have seen him in the King's presence, showing to him every mark of submission and respect, and that to no purpose. However, you may be sure that whatever he may have to fear and whatever may happen in his absence, he will come to you without delay whenever he shall have learned that you desire him to do so. His person and his interests are in your hands. Nor has he so acted in the post committed to him that he should not be able to count on your goodwill. Therefore he has sent this person in his place, well knowing that he might act towards you as towards a father. Would it please you to know what orders have been given to him? To do nothing without your direction, and to follow in all respects your wishes, to which he wholly commits himself. And he is confident that you will do better for him than act merely as his judge, but that you will be his support, his strength, and his protector. If it should please you to commit the cause to the judgment of the Lord Archbishop of Rheims, I believe it would be speedily terminated with the help of God, especially if the right of Appeal was taken away from each party.

LETTER CCCVI. (A.D. 1151.)

To the Bishop of Ostia,[1] for the election of Thorold, Abbot of Trois-Fontaines.

He justifies himself from the reproach which Hugo had thrown upon him of having named Thorold as Abbot of Trois-Fontaines, in preference to a certain monk named

[1] He was named Hugo, and had been Abbot of Trois-Fontaines in Champagne, as we learn from Letters 273 and 274. This was why, after he had become Cardinal, he took a special interest in that Abbey.

Nicholas, whom Hugo had intended for that post. He also explains the election of Robert as Abbot of a newly-founded monastery.

1. Woe to the world because of offences (S. Matt. xviii. 7). Do I offend you? am I an offence unto you? Who could believe that such a thing could happen except those to whom the unity of feeling, and mutual affection, in which we have walked in the house of God together, is altogether unknown? What a sudden and lamentable change for me! He who used to support me now prepares to oppress me; and the very person who used to defend me now frightens me with threats, and accuses me of prevarication and even of blasphemy! Our first parents were not punished for their only fault, although a grave one, until they had been questioned and convicted: the Ninevites had time given them for penitence (Jonah iii. 10), and the people of Sodom were punished not merely after hearing, but also after sight of their sins (Gen. xix. 16). But how differently my judge acts with me, no doubt because I am so much more contemptible than these! I am not thought worthy of being placed on my defence, of being invited to justify myself, to render a reason, of having opportunity given me for reply. I am judged without being summoned, and condemned without being convicted.

2. But now listen, if you will be so good, to my excuse, and if it does not seem sufficient to you, it is at all events a true one. You had wished that Brother Nicholas should be substituted for yourself in your post, and I remember well that I did not disagree with you. You and I were thus completely agreed, and because we were so, I thought and said that there could be no difficulty in thus settling the matter. That it was not so settled was owing to necessity and not to any duplicity on my part. The matter was variously taken by others, and caused discord. Do I say *discord?* It was rather *concord;* for all the electors were found to be so completely agreed in disagreeing to the plan which we had determined upon, that not even one

monk or lay-brother, except two or three who were your countrymen, was willing to give consent to our plan. Nevertheless, I tried by many arguments, now entreating, now threatening, to bring about the resolution we desired, but they withstood me with as much agreement as obstinacy. I might have been able to use force, but this I omitted to do, and I pray God to spare me, as I spared that monk for whom we were interested, in not casting into the midst of such a storm and of so many rebellious spirits a man humble, timid, and inclined to avoid the weight of the charge attempted to be laid upon him. For without speaking of all those outside duties in which you yourself have had experience of him, all the other duties of this charge seem to be beyond his strength. Therefore, permitting him to go forth from his monastery with those who were of like mind with himself, I have put him at the head of a house which will be so much more easy for him to govern, as he will be seconded by my own monks in the performance of the work. For it is a place newly founded by my own brethren, and very near to me, so that I can frequently visit it. Of all the Abbots who were in a condition to occupy your post, I did not venture to propose any, since I had not your approval; and Brother Robert, in default of a better person, seemed to me more fitted than anyone else for it. I proposed him, then: when the reply came from you, and by your judgment he was shut out from it. Why should I prolong the story? They accepted the man, who, as I learn, displeases your Holiness.

3. Nor is the cause unknown, as I am told you declare loudly that he is a man of bad character, and that because of his crimes he was expelled from the monastery[1] over which he had before presided. It may have been the case;

---

[1] This was the Abbey of Fountains in England, over which after Maurice, a monk named Thorold, or Thurold, presided as Abbot " for two years, acting greatly by his own arbitrary authority, and presuming to do some things against the advice and direction of the venerable Archbishop, with whom he speedily disagreed. Wherefore, by the order of the holy Father Bernard, he resigned his office and returned to Rivaulx, from which he had been taken" (*Serlo, Hist. Fontan., Mon. Ang.* i. p. 748).

but as far as I am competent to be a witness, I declare before God and his Angels that I have never, up to this time, heard anything of that kind respecting him. Not even his Archbishop,[1] when he was making every effort to obtain his removal, ever signified to me by letter or messenger, anything to that effect. Can you possibly believe, that if it had been otherwise, I should be a supporter of disorder or turpitude? If your Excellence thought thus of me I do not know how the long friendship with which you have honoured me up to this day, and the great kindness which you have never ceased to show me could at all be justified. And what could you say or think of the Archbishop, who had put at the head of a house of which he had himself been superior, a man of such a character of which, if it were a matter of long and public notoriety, he could not have been ignorant? As for me, God forbid that I should in the least suspect of such conduct a man of such high character and office. It is true that he who had promoted the man to be Abbot, himself removed him. I do not deny it. For what reason he did so is a matter that only concerns himself. But he is known to have displeased many by so doing, and has been accused of not observing either reason, rule, or custom in that removal. The Archbishop acted simply according to his own pleasure, and in order not to cause him annoyance, this Abbot at my entreaty gave place to wrath, and retired from his place in peace.

4. One thing I must say. From the time that he entered into this house[2] no one has remarked in him (and this is the testimony of all) anything which would render him unworthy of the post to which he was elevated. He lived

---

[1] The Archbishop of York, Henry Murdach, an Englishman by birth, and previously a monk at Clairvaux. It is to him that Letter 106 is addressed. He also had been Abbot of Fountains, as may be seen by the Letter cited, and in the notes to Letter 321.

[2] He had then quitted Rivaulx, to take up his abode at Clairvaux. As to his learning, Serlo speaks of it in these terms:—" He was a man unusually versed in sacred literature, and equally well instructed in the liberal arts."

without disagreement with anyone; besides this, he is versed in literature and theology, he is of pleasant demeanour and appearance, and affable in speech. It is true that he was too short a time with us to make these testimonies quite irrefutable. This I confess. He will perhaps do well, and perhaps badly. I distrust all that I do, and am unable to foresee what will come of any step I take. Since then I am not fully assured, I am unable to express positive certainty to you. It is done, and what is done cannot be undone. If I had been a prophet it is certain that I should have avoided to give to a friend cause of offence, to trouble the mind of a saint, to give scandal to a Bishop. What do you wish that I should do, since I was obliged by necessity to act, and to act according to regular order?

5. This is my excuse. If it is sufficient, let the ill-feeling be taken away from between us; if not, I will endure your judgment, of whatever character it may be. It would be painful to me to destroy so quickly with my own hand what I have built up, unless some convenient opportunity should offer, which, perhaps, in course of time, may be the case. But if you wish to depose him the power is in your hands; you will find in me no resistance. Why should I oppose myself to a torrent? Unjustly I have not acted. If I seem to have acted foolishly it is in your power at once to correct my folly, or, if you think the case requires, even to punish it. Yet I add that if I am dealt with piously and christianly, a righteous man will correct me in mercy, and if he shall reprimand me will not in anger disgrace me before others. Here you have my position, unless I have given you some fresh offence, even in this letter. For, although your indignation against me has become known to me by others and not by yourself, yet I have guarded myself from replying in a similar manner, but have preferred to complain to you of yourself in these lines. For the rest I bless God, who has Himself deprived me before my death of this consolation which He had bestowed, and which, perhaps, I enjoyed with too great pleasure, namely,

the favour of my lord[1] and now yours, so that I might learn, even by my own experience, not to rest my hope upon man.

LETTER CCCVII. (A.D. 1153.)
To the Same.

He defends the Bishop of Beauvais against unfavourable reports. He relates in what extremely poor health he is; and what had happened to the Archbishop of Lyons.

1. I write to you in great haste, and consequently with less care, because the traveller who is to convey this is hastening his departure. It is a wonderful coincidence, but a very convenient one. Brother G. Fulcher has just arrived with your letter and that of my lord almost at the same moment as the stranger who bears this; by the providential care, no doubt, of God that I might have a means for replying to you at once; which otherwise I might not have been able to do, however much I wished, with sufficient quickness. As you placed first what concerned the Bishop of Beauvais, so I begin with this in my reply. You know that he is a free agent, his life and character are not in my power, but in that of the State. If he acts sometimes otherwise than he ought, or is becoming to him, I am able to lament it, but however much I may wish to correct it, that is not in my power. But yet I ought to say to you that up to the present I have had no occasion to remark that he absents himself frequently from his diocese; nor have I ever heard that this is the case. His brother Robert has come to him, and now is staying with him. I have not yet heard that he has committed, or led the Bishop to commit, any action disgraceful or criminal, and it would be very wonderful if any such had reached you while it was unknown to me. I will do all in my power to persuade

---

[1] Viz., of Pope Eugenius, who had become alienated from S. Bernard, as had also Innocent II. See Letter 218. So difficult is it to retain the favour of the great, however distinguished be the services rendered to them, without the sacrifice of truth!

him as you wish, to resign his See, if ever I have a fitting and reasonable opportunity. I should already have done so if I had been able without offending the Bishop, and if I had not feared to see him replaced by some one still more useless in the Diocese. He came himself to see me in Lent, prepared to go to Rome on account of a certain appeal; and he would have done so if I had not dissuaded him. The motive of my dissuasion was this, that it did not seem to me that the purpose which called him to Rome, or the people by whom he was accompanied, were such as were becoming to the person of a young man who was a Bishop. Yet he still proposes to set out at a convenient season. He is your brother; you ought to have consideration for him, so that his adversaries may not prevail against him. I could wish that you had written to him rather than to me, and given him a brotherly warning respecting the reports which have reached you about his conduct.[1]

[1] Henry, the son of Louis le Gros, and brother of Louis the Younger, Kings of France, being then Bishop of Beauvais, did not enjoy, it appears, a very good reputation with the Pope. Wherefore Bernard replies that he lamented the errors of the Bishop, if there were any, but was quite unable to amend them.

In the *Life*, B. iv. c. 3, is recorded how S. Bernard had predicted that it would not be long before this young man was converted, and embraced a religious life. Following Baronius in his Chronology, we have placed that event in 1149. It appears certain that it was in this year he was made Bishop of Beauvais, as Sirmondus remarks.

The date of 1161 for his election to this See by Henriquez is then far from the truth.

He became Archbishop of Rheims in 1163.

It was quite against his own will that he was promoted to the Episcopate, as is shown by many of his Letters. S. Bernard himself was uneasy on account of his premature elevation, and thought that Peter, Abbot of Cluny, ought to be consulted, as may be seen in his *Letters* (B. v. L. 8). There is a Letter of the same Henry, written to Suger, Abbot of S. Denys, in *Gallia Christiana*, in Episc. Belvac.

Another, written to the Abbot of Cluny, which we add to this note, we suspect to have been dictated by Bernard himself, or, at least, composed in imitation of Bernard. It is not improbable that it was the former, since Bernard wrote many times for other persons, even for Bishops. If it is not by him it cannot be denied that it is imitated from his writings. Compare the beginning with Letter 236, and the latter part with Letter 16.

"To the most reverend of fathers and the most dear of friends, Dom PETER, Abbot of Cluny, Brother HENRY, by the will or the permission of God Bishop-

2. I have felt that you were anxious about the state of my health. It is true what you have heard. I have been sick even to death,[1] but for the present I am in a measure restored. But I feel that it is not for long, for the state of weakness in which I am passes all belief. This I say, however, without pretending to set bounds to the Providence of God, which is able to recall even the dead to life. Kindly let my reply in this matter be not only to yourself, but also to my lord, for whom I earnestly pray. Be so good also as to associate with yourself the Bishop of Frascati, to express to him in my name, and with the fullest devotedness in your power, my best thanks for his extreme condescension and anxiety about my health.

3. As to what has happened to the Archbishop of Lyons,[2] this is the truth. He had set out on a journey, with an honourable suite, as became an Archbishop, and much

<small>Elect of Beauvais, offers his own self and all that he is able to do. May Almighty God forgive you what you have done. You have recalled to men a man who was buried, and by your advice, which has been too well confided in, I find myself exposed and resting on a terrible sea of cares, so that the lofty height of honour claims me again. In my ignorance my soul is troubled because of the chariots of Aminadab, which I have undertaken to rule, while I have need of being ruled myself, and not to rule others. They have put my hands to brave deeds when I have need of bravery. I am made a watchman to the House of Israel while I have not the needful prudence. I am become a debtor to the wise and to the unwise, for which I need righteousness, and am sent to be a preacher to the people of God, for which I have need of temperance, lest perhaps when I have preached to others I should myself (which may God forbid) be a castaway. But what are those things and what am I, or where are they and what am I? . . . . But in whatever manner this be done, and whatever issue the Lord our God give to the matter, I am none the less one of your followers, and entirely prepared to render you all the services that you may deign to demand of me. Receive me as your servant, your friend, your son, and associate me by a lasting bond to the holy community over which you preside by the grace of God, as one of its members, a monk in its bosom, for I do not wish to call myself here by my title of Bishop."—[*Note of Horst.*] I think that this Letter was not written by Bernard, but rather by Nicolas of Clairvaux, his secretary, who has written many other Letters under the name of Henry, and particularly the thirteenth, to Peter the Venerable, and the twenty-sixth, to Hugo of Compiègne.—[*Note of Mabillon.*]

It is clearly not by S. Bernard.—[E.]

[1] Geoffrey cites these words in the *Life*, B. v. n. 3.

[2] Heraclius.</small>

money; but when he was scarcely beyond his own limits, lo! he fell into an ambuscade of his enemies. What would a man of his impetuosity of character do? To pass on was impossible; to retreat and give up his journey seemed to him less tolerable than any captivity. Part of his people he sent back, part he caused to scatter; he disembarrassed himself of most of the money he had brought with him, retaining only sufficient to meet the cost of his journey with the few followers which he kept with him. What more? He went forward with only three or four attendants, he himself, nevertheless, being dressed as a servant; mixed up his troop with the promiscuous crowd of travellers, as one of them, and so reached Saint-Eloi.[1] There finding himself ill, he was conducted to Montpellier; where he remained a considerable time, and spent on physicians all the money he had, and more.

LETTER CCCVIII. (A.D. 1153.)

To Alfonso, King of Portugal.

Bernard replies that he has done his best to comply with the King's request, and he predicts that in a short time his brother, who was then engaged in the warfare of earth, would pass over into that of Heaven.

To Alfonso, the illustrious King of Portugal, Bernard, called Abbot of Clairvaux, desires all that the prayer of a sinner can obtain for him.

I have received with extreme joy the letter and greeting of your Highness, and am glad in Him who sendeth health unto Jacob. What I have done in this matter will be shown by the event, and you yourself will be able to appreciate it by that means; you will see with what zeal and ardour I have wished to respond to your commands, and to the exigency of the case. Peter,[2] the brother of your

---

[1] See notes to Letter 241.

[2] This Peter, brother of Alfonso, King of Portugal, was one of those young men who were passionately fond of tournaments, and whom (it is said) S. Bernard prepared for conversion by a draught of beer, which he blessed when

Highness, a meritorious and accomplished Prince, has made me acquainted with your wishes. After having crossed France with his men-at-arms, he is now carrying on war in Lorraine, but he will not be long before he is a combatant in the armies of the Lord. My son, Brother Roland, brings to you a letter bearing the liberality of the Holy See. I commend him to you, also the Brothers of my Order dwelling in your realm, and, lastly, myself.

LETTER CCCIX.[1] (A.D. 1153.)
To Pope Eugenius.

He praises Abbot Suger and recommends his deputies to the Pope.

To his very dear father and lord EUGENIUS, by the grace of God supreme Pontiff, Brother BERNARD, called Abbot of Clairvaux, wishes health and offers his humble homage.

If in our Gallican Church there is any vessel capable of doing honour to the palace of the Great King; if the Lord counts among us a second David, coming in and going out at His command (1 Sam. xxii. 14); in my judgment it is no other than the venerable Abbot of S. Denys. I know that great man perfectly; if he is faithful and prudent in temporal things he is not less fervent and humble in spiritual things; and is equally without blame (which is a very difficult thing indeed) in the management of both. Before the King he behaves as one of the Court of Rome,

giving it to him. Concerning this see the *Life*, B. i. c. ii. n. 55. What directions Alfonso had sent to Bernard about him appear in the Letter from that King to that Saint, which Henriquez prints in his Menology under May 9. This is the subject of it: After having defeated the Moors, Alfonso had assumed the title of King, which was offered by his subjects, but the King of Castile refused his consent unless a certain tribute was paid to him in return for the concession. He requested of S. Bernard, in this Letter, to obtain for him the title of King from the Pope, preferring, if it were necessary to pay tribute to someone, to pay it to S. Peter, or to the Holy See, than to a neighbouring and jealous Prince. See Letter 419.

[1] This Letter is numbered 361 in the Royal Edition; Duchesne has placed it at the head of the Letters of Suger, where is added also the reply of Eugenius. See Letter 7 of that Collection.

and when in the church before God as one of the Court of Heaven. I request and entreat you to receive kindly the messages of so good a man, and to reply to him as becomes you, and as he is worthy of receiving, in good and friendly words, full of familiarity and affection, of goodness and favour; for you may be quite sure that to show special love and honour to his person is a sure means of doing honour to your own office and ministry.

LETTER CCCX. (A.D. 1153.)

To Arnold of Chartres, Abbot of Bonneval.[1]

Bernard was almost at the point of death, when he addressed to his friend this letter, which was the last he ever wrote.

I have received the marks of your affection with gratitude, I cannot say in pleasure, my sufferings are too great

---

[1] Many modern writers, among them Horst, Charles de Visch, and the author of a *Life of S. Bernard* in French, do not share the opinion of Trithemius, Bellarmine and many others, but distinguish this Arnold from the author of the second *Life of S. Bernard*, to whom they give the name of Bernard and the title of Abbot, not of Bonneval or Bonnevaux in Poitou or Rouergue, but of Bonneval or Bonnevaux, a Cistercian house in the Diocese of Vienne in Dauphiny.

They adduce still another Arnold, Abbot of Bonneval, a Benedictine house in the Pays Chartrain, and to whom was addressed this Letter.

But all these great writers will permit me to say that all these Arnolds are only one and the same person. For as regards the difference in the two names, we see that the author of the second *Life* is written Ernald in the very ancient MS. of Corbie, by which name our Arnold of Chartres is designated by Arnulf, Bishop of Lisieux, in his Letters to him.

But, putting aside this controversy about the name, it is certain that the second book of the *Life* was written while Godfrey, Bishop of Langres, was still living. For he writes (c. v. n. 29): "Godfrey, Prior of the same house, his relative both in the flesh and in the spirit . . . became afterwards Bishop of Langres, where he continues to this day, going out and coming in in all good reputation." That was written before 1161, in which year Godfrey, resigning his See, "returned to Clairvaux, to the embrace of his Rachel," as the *Chronicle of Clairvaux* records. The same register mentions his death on the 8th Nov., 1164. And from the foundation of Bonneval in Dauphiné, in 1117 up to the year 1180 no Abbot named Bernard is found to have ruled that house. The first Abbot was S. John from 1118 to 1138; then Gozevin, who was succeeded, in 1151, for that; still, what I endure seems to me tolerable in comparison with what I feel when obliged to take food. Sleep has departed from me, so that I suffer without intermission through the exhaustion of nature. All my ailments resolve themselves into a great weakness of stomach, which has to be supported frequently day and night with very small quantities of liquid food; for I am entirely unable to bear anything solid. It is not without excessive suffering that it endures the little that is given to me, but still worse is feared, if it should be entirely without any at all. A drop more than is absolutely needful, however, causes me extreme pain. My feet and ankles are swollen as if I were dropsical. In the midst of all this, for I ought not to hide anything from you of the state of a friend for whom you are anxious, as to the inward man I may declare (but I speak as a fool) that the spirit is vigorous, though the flesh is weak. Pray our Saviour, who willeth not the death of a sinner, that He will not put off my departure, which is fully seasonable, and that He will guard me when I pass away. Give diligence to strengthen by your prayers a poor, humble soul, bare and devoid of all merit, that the crafty enemy may not find place, to seize me and inflict a mortal wound. I wished, notwithstanding the state in which I am, to write these few words, that you may recognize, on seeing the handwriting you know so well, how much I love you. But I should have preferred to reply to a letter from you than to write the first.

by Rainald of Citeaux. After him came Peter; then in 1171 Hugo of happy memory. He was still Abbot of Bonneval at his death in 1180. Where, then, is to be placed an Abbot Bernard who wrote the *Life* before 1164, as we have shown above it must have been written? Our argument rests on the *Annals* of Manrique.

But besides, it is evident to every attentive reader of the preface to Book II. of the *Life* that it was not written by a Cistercian. We conclude, then, that the author of Book II., and that friend to whom S. Bernard wrote this Letter just before his death, was Arnold or Ernald, Abbot of Bonneval in the Pays Chartrain.

LETTER CCCXI.[1] (*Circa* A.D. 1125.)

To Haimeric, the Chancellor.

He sharply chides those envious persons who are opposing the efforts of the good, and takes occasion to urge Haimeric to a sedulous care for the good of the Church.

To the illustrious lord HAIMERIC, Chancellor of the Holy Roman See, HUGO, Abbot of Pontigny, and BERNARD of Clairvaux send greeting, in the hope that their conduct in the house of God may ever be such as it ought to be.

1. The good which Bishops seek to gain is, as we believe, the gain of Christ, since their business is properly the cause of God. Let those, therefore, who see for God make commom cause with them. If anyone hangs back let him hear what the Lord says : *He that is not with Me is against Me* (S. Matt. xii. 30). There is no middle course. Either they will follow the advice of the Apostle, who says to them, *Quench not the Spirit* (1 Thess. v. 19), or they will certainly hear, as the Jews did, *Ye do always resist the Holy Ghost* (Acts vii. 51), and, as the Prophet said, *Woe unto them that call evil good and good evil, that rejoice when they commit sin and exalt over wickedness* (Isaiah v. 20, and Prov. ii. 14). They will not be able to rejoice also in good, nor can the righteous man, for his righteousness, and the sinner in his evil desires be praised together by the same lips. And yet what is there strange in it if the good thing, which is an odour of life to the good, should be an odour of death to the wicked ? Do we not know that He who is the source and origin of all good was born for the ruin of many as for the resurrection of many, and for a sign that is everywhere spoken against? (S. Luke ii. 34, and Isaiah viii. 14). Even to-day to how many is the Saviour found *a stone of stumbling and a rock of offence* (Isaiah viii. 14). And yet those are not wanting who say with willing heart, *He is our peace, who hath made both one* (Ephes. ii. 14). He to whom the Peace Himself is a

[1] Formerly numbered 313. That which was before No. 311 is now No. 374.

stumbling-block, what peace can there be for him? Or he for whom the Saviour Himself is the cause of condemnation, in whom can he hope to be saved? It is written, *In his house* (without doubt that of the righteous man) *shall be wealth and riches* (Ps. cxii. 3), and he explains what he means by *wealth and riches*, for he adds, *And his righteousness endureth for ever*, and in truth there is no glory, no riches to be compared with the righteousness of the conscience of the just. But what is it that the unrighteous loses? If Paul boasts of the riches in his heart, saying, *Our rejoicing is this, the testimony of our conscience* (2 Cor. i. 12), who is injured thereby? Yet the Prophet assures us that *the sinner shall see it and be grieved* (Ps. cxii. 10). What perversity! These riches are in nowise like those of the earth, which cannot be acquired without others being deprived of them. Why, then, art thou angry, who hast lost nothing? or why dost thou envy good things to good men, and those good things which thou dost not care to acquire for thyself? Is it not like the dog in the fable, who forbad to others the hay which he was not able to eat? But although thou mayest gnash with thy teeth and consume away, yet the work of God cannot be undone. Whether you will or no, the righteous shall see it and rejoice, and all the wicked shall keep silence.

2. But all this only concerns those who can be suspected. But to you we say this: use well the talent committed to you, and you shall receive the recompense. What profit is it, wrapped in a napkin, when one day it will be required again with usury? While we have time, why do we neglect to make use of it? It is true that in your office it is always the time to seek diligently the interests of piety; but especially is the present moment favourable for indulging a holy avarice; you have only to be diligent in using the treasure of the Lord which He has put into your hands to this end. Otherwise, *if wisdom be unused, or a treasure unknown, what usefulness is there in either?* (Ecclus. xx. 32). It is said that you are disposed, as well by your own desire, as by

the duty of your office, to do good unto all men; as you are *specially bound to do to those of the household of faith* (Gal. vi. 10). That command of the Apostle is general, yet we may venture to be so bold as to remind you that it is a special privilege of your office and ministry. Unless perhaps (which we do not in the least think) you hold more to the position itself than to the honour of fulfilling its duties. Indeed, since there is scarcely any good work or supposed good work in the whole world which does not pass at some time or other through the hands of the Chancellor of Rome, which is not submitted to his judgment, shaped by his advice, strengthened by his good will, and assisted by his help; and what can be more fitting than that it should devolve upon him to take action when anything in these various projects is either incomplete or wrongly directed, especially as the glory of all holy and praiseworthy enterprises is sure to redound upon him? Thus, as we have said, the man who fills that post is either the most happy of men, or the most miserable; as he is, by his position, either always a sharer in every good work, or its enemy: and justly, therefore, the entire praise or blame, according to the issue of each, and his zeal in regard to it, will fall upon him. Blessed, then, is he who shall be able to say unto the Lord: *I am a companion of all them that fear Thee, and keep Thy precepts* (Ps. cxix. 63).

3. But what are we doing? While we have taken in hand to speak to you of your obligations we have almost forgotten that we are pouring these observations into ears most fully occupied. We trust, however, that we shall not seem needlessly intrusive: not that we claim the least right to speak to you as we have done, but that we have present to our mind that you have deigned to be the first to solicit by your gifts the friendship of such humble persons as ourselves. We hold this as a remarkable sign of your condescension and piety that your Excellency, being so great a person and busied with such important affairs, should have thought it worth while to salute such obscure and humble persons as ourselves, and even to honour us with presents.

May God Himself recompense you, and give you the spiritual gold, which is wisdom, in exchange for the material gold, which you have bestowed upon us, so that not only we may rejoice in your gift, but you also in the reward which shall be returned to you. Adieu.

LETTER CCCXII. (A.D. 1130.)

To Raynald,[1] Archbishop of Rheims.

Bernard thanks him for a letter which he had received from him.

To the most reverend father and lord R., by the grace of God Archbishop of Rheims, Brother BERNARD, of Clairvaux, wishes health and whatever the prayers of a sinner can effect on his behalf.

I thank the Lord who has inspired you with the thought of consoling me with a letter from your hand. I am, indeed, well enough able to return letter for letter, but when shall I ever be able to acquit myself to you of the debt of gratitude which you have placed me under by the goodness that you have shown towards me, in encouraging me by the sweetness of your blessing, in rousing me by your exhortations, and honouring me with your salutation? Assuredly there never was anyone less worthy than I of the names that you bestow upon me, or less worthy to be known to you; but the less I am worthy the more I am grateful to you. It is true, though, that when you act thus you act as becomes you, and as recognizing that you are debtor to the unwise as well as to the wise. You say to me that the reputation of which the report has come to your Excellency has moved you to this condescension towards so humble a person as myself; but this is, indeed, not only too flattering, but also dangerous to me. It is, however, a very

---

[1] This Letter is new; the former, No. 312, is now 398. Raynald, or Reginald, second Archbishop of Rheims of that name, occupied that See from 1124 to 1139, according to our calculation, and died on the 13th of January of the latter year, as we have noted upon Letter 170.

happy and agreeable thing for me that a breath of reputation, though it be only like an empty puff of wind, should have moved a priest of the Most High of such high rank to have such kind feeling toward me, before even I had merited to come to his personal knowledge. The monk who is the bearer of this letter will tell your Holiness with respect to my coming to you why I have not come at the present time, and at what time I should be able to come. He will reply also with faithfulness to any other questions that it may please you to put to him with respect to me; it is for that purpose that I have sent him, while waiting until I shall be able to come to you myself.

LETTER CCCXIII. (A.D. 1132.)

To Geoffrey, Abbot of S. Mary at York.[1]

Bernard recommends him not to hinder those who wished to enter a religious Order more austere; and declares that those should be regarded as apostates, who, after having thus removed, fall back to their former manner of life.

To the venerable Dom Geoffrey, Abbot of the Church of S. Mary at York,[2] Brother Bernard, Abbot of Clairvaux, sends salutation in our Lord.

1. It has pleased your Reverence to write and consult so humble a person as myself on some doubtful questions. But I am afraid to give any decisive answer; and hesitate the more to do so, inasmuch as if men with the purest intentions are unable to discern the minds of their nearest companions, they are still less able to discern the secret designs of the Divine Will. Again, I am afraid in so speaking to wound those who do not share my opinion; and this is certain to happen with those unsatisfied souls who only seek to justify their conclusion in their own eyes by a cloud of incoherent and obscure reasonings. But yet

---

[1] This was formerly numbered 371, the former No 313 is now No. 311. The subject depends upon that of Letter 94.

[2] Benedictine.

their conscience itself is the avenger of this voluntary darkness: because at the same time that they strive to delude themselves with regard to that they have done, the truth of the matter comes back to them in the shape of remorse which wounds and preys upon them. Of such a character was the gnawing remorse from which the Psalmist prays of God to be delivered, saying: *Bring my soul out of prison that I may praise Thy name* (Ps. cxlii. 7). If, then, I do not reply to your questions in a manner as satisfactory as you would wish, or if I do not dare to express myself as fully as I might, do not, Reverend sir, suppose that it is from a studied artfulness. Your letter begins by complaints upon the painful position in which the departure of a certain number of your monks has placed your old age, since they have quitted you only to embrace a manner of life stricter and more secure. It seems to me that in this case you ought rather to be afraid that your sorrow is the sorrow of this world which worketh death.

2. For if there is any reason at all in the opinion of men, it is a thing not to be lamented if a man ever endeavours to devote himself with greater strictness to the practice of the law of his Creator. And we indeed should be acting not merely not holily, but even without ordinary fatherly care and interest, if we should envy the advances made by our sons. If, then, you wish, as I suppose, chiefly to make your profit of one good counsel out of a thousand, not only should you strive to prevent those who still remain with you under a mitigated rule, from falling into a lower state through their relaxations; but also you should be, as says the prophet, *the first to bring bread* (Is. xxi. 14), the first to favour the design of those, who, fearing that the health of their souls would suffer if they remained longer in a house of less severity, aspire to observe their profession in all its purity. On the first you ought to lavish the greatest care lest they grow careless to their spiritual loss; but to the second you ought to show every kind of goodwill, that they may attain to the crown. For those who meditate continually in their heart on the means of

rising higher are those who *go from strength to strength;* they merit *to behold the Lord of Lords in Sion,* and that the more surely because they are consumed with a fervent zeal to adhere to Him by a more holy and perfect life (Ps. lxxxiv. 5, 7).

3. As for the monks Gervase and Ralph, whose withdrawal Archbishop Thurstan, like a true father and a worthy Bishop, had sanctioned, and to which you, as you yourself declare, had consented, I am sure that, far from erring, they would have done well to have remained firm in that more perfect path of purity to which they had ascended, and to have persevered in it laudably. It is evident to me, nevertheless, that if they wished to regain the path of purity from which they have rashly descended, they would be deserving of very great praise for that proof of Christian valour, as soldiers who return to the fight contend the more bravely for the victory, that they had for a moment shamefully fled from the battle field. You, indeed, are quite able, I believe, to recall the permission you had given, but the judgment of the Almighty cannot be thus rendered of no effect. You allow that their life would afterwards be a more holy one; but you say that they would not be able to support its rigour, on account of the delicacy of their constitution, or of ties of relationship impossible to break. To this you add, that their presence is necessary to you; and therefore you urge me to say, whether they may not without fault remain in a house which they have not been able to quit without offence.

4. To this I reply, that there are different kinds of offences; that carnal affections ought to be entirely cut off for the sake of Christ, that the Gospel loudly declares, and one passage in the Scripture repeats after another, that temporal advantages and enjoyments are to be abandoned for the salvation of the soul; and that to be ignorant of this is a fault so gross as to be almost heretical. But I am not certain whether such a return as you speak of could be made without fault needing punishment. Certainly, it would expose them to evident peril, and a fall almost

certain, because it is presuming on the mercy of God against His justice, and to set up the one against the other. The Scripture says: *Be not without fear to add sin to sin and say not, His mercy is great* (Ecclus. v. 5, 6). For it is a bad kind of discretion that makes the less important consideration preponderate over the more important, and tries to put the worse in the same line with the better.

5. Lastly, you protest vehemently against the name of apostates being applied to these men if they should return to their own monastery, and endeavour to discharge the sacred rules of their profession. As for me, I reply, it is not my business to condemn them. *The Lord knoweth them that are His* (2 Tim. ii. 19). *Everyone shall bear his own burden* (Gal. vi. 5). He whom the darkness does not comprehend shall manifest Himself as the Lord in the day of judgment, and *the sinner shall be taken in the work of his own hands* (Ps. ix. 16). Each person may judge himself as leniently as he will; as for me I will say what I think about myself. I, Bernard, if after I had passed over by my own free will from a good state to a better, from a dangerous condition to one more secure, I had, by a culpable change of will, presumed to go back again to what I had left, should have feared not only that I was an apostate, but that I was also unfit for the kingdom of God. This also S. Gregory says: 'Whosoever has proposed to himself a higher good is no longer free to follow one which is lower. For it is written: *No man putting his hand to the plough and looking back is fit for the Kingdom of God* (S. Luke ix. 62). And such is the man who, having embraced a higher life, falls back again on one who is lower (*Pastor.* iii. 28.) As to a certain excommunication on which you desire to open a discussion in your letter, it appears to me that it would profit you nothing to discuss that question, and that it is not my business to decide it. You know that the law refuses to judge anyone until he has been first heard: and it is always rash to deliver judgment on an absent person.

LETTER CCCXIV. (A.D. 1134.)

To Pope Innocent.[1]

Bernard, having reconciled the Milanese to the Church, had set out at the command of Innocent to endeavour to restore peace among the other cities of Lombardy, first proceeding to Pavia and Cremona. But not succeeding with the Cremonese, he acquaints the Pope with their obstinacy, and he advises that the very severe sentence which was being prepared against the Archbishop of Milan should be for a while suspended.

To his very dear father and lord, Supreme Pontiff, INNOCENT, Brother BERNARD sends his humble homage.

1. The Cremonese are hardened, their worldly prosperity is their ruin. On the other hand, the Milanese think lightly of others, their self-confidence deceives them. These, who put their hope in their war chariots and their horses, have frustrated my endeavours, and rendered my labour useless. I was sadly departing when behold the great consolation with which you favoured me: so that although my tribulations for Christ abound, yet my consolations, through him, abound also. I have received your wished-for letter, which brings sweetness to my soul in the news of your safety, of the successes of our friends, and the reverses of our enemies. Unfortunately the end of the letter tempered the joy which I had felt on reading the first part. For whom would not your indignation cause to tremble? I confess that it is just, and therefore fear it the more. Yet I would say that that which has not yet been done should indeed be done, but at the fit time which God will point out. You will then be equally free to do what you propose, and it will perhaps not be equally dangerous. To act at the present time is alas! to destroy utterly all that God by an extraordinary stroke of His grace has accomplished in this city, and which has cost so

---

[1] Formerly No. 318. That Letter which was numbered 314 is now 390. This Letter relates to the same affair as Letters 131, 132, and 133.

much care and labour to you and your assistants.[1] It will be strange if such a proceeding is pleasing to Him who, as we read, exalts mercy over justice (James ii. 13.) But oh! that unhappy Bishop who, having been translated from a kind of earthly paradise to Ur of the Chaldees, finds himself become a brother to dragons, and a friend[2] of ostriches. What can he do? He wishes to obey, and behold the beasts of Ephesus gnash their teeth upon him. He wishes to dissimulate prudently for the moment, and incurs all the harshness of your far more formidable indignation. There are difficulties for him everywhere, unless he should find it his better course to be without a see, than without a lord: and should hold, as it becomes him to do, the favour of the Pope, as of greater value than the See of Milan. Have you any doubt of his attachment? If any one has been so malicious as to persuade you to suspect him, he shows himself really less loyal than the suspected person, since in his envy he has blackened with his faithless tongue, the good name of a prelate of such high reputation. Have consideration, good Father, for your faithful servant, have consideration for work which is so new, for a plant which has not had time to take root; have consideration for people who are attaching themselves to you, and do not efface the memory of those very benefits, which, as you yourself most truly declare, you have bestowed upon them. Remember, pious Pontiff, those words of your Lord: *Behold these three years I come seeking fruit upon this fig tree, and find none* (S. Luke xiii. 7). But you have waited for scarcely three months, and yet you are preparing the axe. If you had waited three years, you would have followed even in the fourth, as a faithful servant should, the example of your Master. Let us then say:

[1] These were Guy of Pisa and Matthew of Albano; they had been sent by Innocent to the inhabitants of Milan as legates of the Holy See, with Bernard, as we see in Letter 131.

[2] I imagine that there is here a reference to Ribald, who had been elected and confirmed Archbishop of Milan, in the place of Anselm, who had been driven from his See, as we learn in Letter 131.

Let it alone this year also; perhaps during that time the ground may be trenched with the spade of penitence, and enriched with tears, and it may be that He who has given you this sterile ground of the hearts of the Milanese to cultivate, will enable it to bring forth the fruit which you desire.

LETTER CCCXV. (*Circa* A.D. 1134.)[1]

To Matilda, Queen of England.[2]

Bernard begs her to receive favourably a request already presented to her on behalf of the monks of La Chapelle.[3]

To the illustrious lady and beloved daughter in Christ (which I say in affection, not of presumption), MATILDA, by the grace of God Queen of England, BERNARD wishes health.

It is not, I trust, a matter of surprise to you if I presume somewhat in addressing your Highness. I am not alone in thinking, what indeed all are aware of, that you have some kindness towards me, and that I have in some degree your favour. Because of which I have a request to make on behalf of a certain friend of mine, the venerable Abbot of La Chapelle,[3] who has asked me to remind you of a certain tithe which I have already asked from you at Boulogne, if you are kind enough to remember, and which request you then, with your accustomed kindness,[4] favourably entertained. But because what I then asked has not yet been carried out, I write to pray you that it may at length be

---

[1] Formerly No. 344; the former No. 315 is now 341.

[2] This was Matilda, daughter of Malcolm III., King of Scotland; wife of the Emperor Henry V., and afterwards of Henry I. of England. She had, by the latter, Henry II., of whom Bernard speaks at the end of this Letter, which was written before the death of Henry I. There was another Matilda, daughter of Fulk, Count of Anjou, who married William, son of Henry I. Her husband perished by shipwreck; when she took the veil at Fontevraud and became Abbess of that house. Peter de Celles wrote a Letter to her (B. i. n. 10).

[3] A house of the Benedictine Order, in the diocese of Boulogne.

[4] Matilda had such esteem and affection for Bernard, that when she was at Boulogne, she went out of the town on foot to meet him. See *Life* B. iv. n. 6.

effectually done. Let me beg that you will take good care for me of the son whom you have borne: because I also, if it will not displease the King, claim some portion in him. Adieu.

LETTER CCCXVI. (*Circa* A.D. 1135.)[1]

To Henry, Archbishop of Sens, and Haimeric, the Chancellor.

He begs them not to oppose a certain nobleman in possession of Church property who proposed to restore this to certain religious.

It is a good work for a layman to be willing to give up abbeys or ecclesiastical benefices which he possesses contrary to the canons, but when he is willing to transfer them for the use of servants of God the good is doubled. But as these resignations cannot be carried out except by the consent of the Bishop of the Diocese, it follows that a Bishop would commit a double evil by refusing this assent or a double good by giving it. What a certain knight asks of you in this matter, this you ought to have asked of him. For you, surely, cannot believe that a sanctuary of God is better as the family possession of a man of war than in that of the saints of God. If such be your view, it will be strange if all who hear do not wonder at you. Avoid this, I pray you, lest the sons of the uncircumcised should hear and rejoice. Suppose that you are able to take the captive Abbey from the hands of the powerful, and to re-establish it in its rights, which I do not at all suppose. What heir and successor, I ask, would you prefer to choose? A soldier who would do service for it in the armies of the King, or a monk who would intercede for their sins? Do, therefore, what is just, what is worthy of you, what is agreeable to God, and to all good men; what, finally, if there were no other reason, I should confidently demand of you for the sake of your affection for me.

[1] Formerly No. 375; the former No. 316 is now 356.

LETTER CCCXVII. (A.D. 1138.)[1]

To his Prior, Godfrey.[2]

The schism being extinct and peace concluded, Bernard announces to him his return with the least possible delay.

To Brother GODFREY, Brother BERNARD health.

On the very day of the octave of Pentecost, God has filled up the cup of my desire in giving unity to the Church and peace to Rome. On that day all the supporters of Peter Leonis came to prostrate themselves together at the feet of the Pope, and to take an oath of fidelity to him, and become his liege men. The schismatic clergy also, together with the idol[3] whom they had set up, knelt at the feet of the lord Pope to promise him obedience with all the formalities, and there was great joy among the people. For some time past I felt certain that events would not long delay to take this turn; it is that which has kept me so long here, and if it had been otherwise I should long since have returned to you. At present there is nothing to detain me here. I am doing what you have earnestly urged upon me; I am turning "I will come," into "I come." For behold I come quickly, and my reward is with me, the victory of Christ and the peace of the Church. The messenger whom I sent to you left Rome on the Friday after that day. Therefore, when I return I shall come with gladness bearing sheaves of peace. These are, indeed, pleasant words, but the facts are still pleasanter. So pleasant are they and glorious that whosoever does not rejoice in them must be either foolish or wicked. Farewell.

[1] Formerly No. 320; the former No. 317 is now No. 357.

[2] In Letter 143 Bernard calls him *very dear*. He afterwards became Bishop of Langres, as we have seen upon Letter 364. Pérard has preserved his Letter on p. 122; in the year 41 he completed the second year of his Episcopate.

[3] This was the anti-Pope Victor, whom the party of Anacletus had chosen as his successor.

LETTER CCCXVIII. (*Circa* A.D. 1138.)[1]

To Pope Innocent.

He represents to the Pope the distress of the Church of Rheims, and desires speedy help from him.

To his very dear father and lord, INNOCENT, supreme Pontiff, Brother BERNARD, called Abbot of Clairvaux, health and his humble homage.

The Church of Rheims is on the point of ruin. That glorious city is overwhelmed with disgrace: she cries to the passers-by that there is no sorrow like unto her sorrow. For without are fightings, within fears. And, indeed, there are fightings within also, for her own sons fight against her, nor has she a spouse to set her free: her only hope is in you; it is only Innocent who can wipe the tears from her cheeks. But how long, my lord, must she wait before she is covered with the shield of your protection? How long shall she be trodden under foot, and you not arrive to her assistance? Behold, the King has yielded, and his anger has already sunk into silence. What then remains but that the afflicted Church should be sustained by your apostolic arm, and her wounds tended and healed? The first thing to be done, in my opinion, is to hasten the election of a Bishop, lest the presumption of the people of Rheims should scatter what still remains, if the popular disorder be not checked with a high hand. If this election be made according to the prescribed forms, I trust that God will give a good issue by His grace in other matters also.

LETTER CCCXIX. (*Circa* A.D. 1138.)[2]

To Thurstan, Archbishop of York.

He advises and begs him not to resign his See: but if there are good reasons for his doing so, and the Pope sanctions it, he should seek a religious house of strict observance for his place of retreat.

[1] Formerly No. 329; the former No. 318 is now No. 314.
[2] Formerly No. 372; the former 319 is now No. 399.

LETTER CCCXIX.

To the Reverend father and lord THURSTAN, by the grace of God Archbishop of York, BERNARD, called Abbot of Clairvaux, wishes health in the present life and in the future life eternal.

1. I praise you for desiring quiet, and that you long to rest in peace in the Lord. But those reasons which you allege for laying down your pastoral charge seem to me insufficient: unless (which I do not believe, and may God forbid) you have some mortal sin to reproach yourself with, or permission has been given you by the supreme Pontiff to resign.[1] You have not forgotten, I am sure, that rule of the Apostle: *Art thou bound unto a wife? seek not to be loosed* (1 Cor. vii. 27). By an engagement, such as you say you have taken, a Bishop is not bound any farther than that he should persevere in the ministry to which he has been called.

2. It seems, then, to me, without attempting to impose my advice upon you to the prejudice of any that is wiser, that you should continue to hold the office that you have now, and should exhibit in a Bishop the humble dress and the holiness of life of a monk.[2] However, if some secret

---

[1] Bernard here recognizes two legitimate reasons in a Bishop for laying down his charge: the necessity for doing penance on account of some great crime, and the permission of the Pope. At one time Bishops were reduced to the rank of simple priests on account of capital crimes, for instance on account of fornication, theft, perjury, and homicide; but it seems after these words of Bernard, that there was some other mortal sin which rendered it necessary for a Bishop to resign and retire into a monastery in order to do penance for it. This Letter appears to have been written a little before the death of Thurstan, which Ordericus places in 1139 (B. xiii. p. 119, where he speaks of him as brother of Andin, Bishop of Evreux). To the same Thurstan were written Letters 195 and 235.

[2] It was not permitted to monks, when they became Bishops, to change their former habit and manner of living (Read *Præfat.* ii., *Sæcul.* iv. n. 178, *sqq. et.* 189). But how many things have changed since that time! Read a sermon of Abaelard on S. John the Baptist, p. 966! The conviction spread in many minds that the life of a Bishop, as it then existed, was incompatible with the practice of monastic rules; and many monks who were elected to the Episcopate refused altogether to accept it. Such was Guy, Abbot of Clairvaux, who, having been elected to the See of Rheims, at the death of Archbishop William, constantly refused to accept it for that very reason (Baluz, *Miscell.* Vol. ii. p. 247).

motive makes it a duty for you to lay down your charge, or if the Pope indulges your wish for quiet, I advise you, according to my humble lights, not to let any degree of hardship in food or clothing, nor any extremity of poverty deter you from entering some religious house where you may hope to find the most strict observance. Although you must remember in houses of this kind, though everything is sacrificed to the soul, yet this must be so done that due account is taken of age or of weakness. As I am entirely devoted to you, I pray God most earnestly to inspire you to whatever course of action may be for the best; and to enable you so to carry the burden and heat of the day that you may receive in the evening the denarius of the parable impressed with the image of the King.

LETTER CCCXX. (A.D. 1138.)[1]

To Alexander,[2] Prior of Fountains, and to his Brethren at the Same Place.

Bernard urges upon him that the election of a new Abbot should be made with unanimous accord.

To his most dear brethren in Christ, ALEXANDER, the Prior, and the whole community of Fountains, Brother BERNARD, called Abbot of Clairvaux, health and his humble prayers.

1. Your venerable Father has perfected his course in a blessed end, and has fallen asleep in the Lord. But I, as at all times I think of you with the anxious care and tenderness of a father, so am specially careful on your

[1] Formerly No. 381; the former No. 320 is now 317.

[2] He was brother of Richard, second Abbot of that name, of the Abbey of Fountains, in England. He came to end his days in peace at Clairvaux (*Serlo, Monast. Anglican.* V. i. p. 854, where he is speaking of Kirkstall Abbey, or Mount S. Mary, in the neighbourhood of York). Of this place Alexander was instituted as first Abbot in 1147, Henry Murdach, to whom the following Letter is addressed, being then Archbishop. Another Alexander, also an Englishman, was Abbot of Fontaines, in the Diocese of Tours. Respecting Fountains Abbey in England, see on Letters 235 and 252.

account at the present time, when this great necessity lies upon you. Wherefore, also, I should have sent to you long since if I had not been waiting to do so with more fitness and advantage when the venerable Abbot Henry[1] had terminated certain affairs which had hindered him from coming sooner. It is upon him that I had reckoned from the beginning as being most worthy of this mission, and most suited to acquit himself of it well. Him, therefore, dearly beloved brethren, receive with that honour and affection of which he is worthy, and listen to him in all things as to myself; and, indeed, much more, as he excels me both in prudence and merit. I have given to him full powers, whether for the election of your Abbot, or for making ordinances, or for introducing reforms which he may think good to do into your house, and into those[2] which depend upon it. I have given him for travelling companion Brother William, who is my very dear son.

2. And now I entreat you, as my beloved sons, to be all of one mind in the election of your new Abbot; that there may be no divisions among you, but that you may with one mind and one mouth glorify God. For He is not a God of dissension, but of peace. Wherefore, also, it is in peace that His abode is placed, and He says, *He who gathereth not with me scattereth* (S. Luke xi. 23). Let this be far from those who dwell in the school of Christ, under the leading of the Holy Spirit, nor let them give opportunity to the enemy to rejoice in glory over their dissension. For by this they both put their own souls in peril, lose the entire fruit of their penitence, endanger the good repute of our Order, and cause the name of Christ to be blasphemed on account of those by whom it should be most glorified. On the contrary, choose with one voice for

---

[1] Henry Murdach, then Abbot of Vauclair. The following Letter is addressed to him; he was then occupied with a controversy, which grew very hot, between the monks of Vauclair and Cuissy (See *Herman de Laon*, Book iii. c. 16). Henry had for his opponent in this discussion Luke, the Abbot of Cuissy, to whom Letter 79 is addressed.

[2] Upon Fountains Abbey depended Newminster, in the Diocese of Carlisle; Kirkstall and Louth Park in that of Lincoln.

yourselves, as becomes saints and servants of Christ, and as I fully trust that you will do, a fit pastor over your souls, in company with the venerable Abbots of Rievaulx and of Vauclair, whose advice I wish you to follow in all things as my own.

LETTER CCCXXI. (A.D. 1138.)[1]

TO HENRY MURDACH,[2] FIRST ABBOT OF VAUCLAIR, THEN OF FOUNTAINS, AND FINALLY ARCHBISHOP OF YORK.

He orders Henry not to refuse his election to the Abbacy of Fountains.

To his dearest brother and co-Abbot HENRY, Brother BERNARD, called Abbot of Clairvaux, sends greeting and the assurance of his prayers.

I enjoin you, my brother Henry, not to refuse the election of our brethren at Fountains, with the advice of the venerable Abbot of Rievaulx, if it shall have fallen upon you; but to yield to it in charity. I give this precept, I assure you, unwillingly, knowing that by your absence I shall be deprived of a great consolation. But I do not dare to oppose myself to a unanimous choice, for I believe that God speaks by the conclusions which a number of Religious come to with one consent; as I have read in the Gospel, *Wheresoever two or three are gathered together in my Name, there am I in the midst of them* (S. Matt. xviii. 20). Take courage, therefore, my dear brother; receive their promises of obedience, and watch over them, as the shepherd of their souls. Do not fear on account of the house which you have already undertaken to rule. For I, please

---

[1] Formerly No. 382; the former No. 321 is now 345.

[2] This Henry was English by birth; it is to him that Letter 106 is addressed. At first he was a monk at Clairvaux; thence he was sent, in 1135, with twelve other monks, to found the Abbey of Vauclair in the Diocese of Laon. He presided over this until 1138, when he was translated to the Abbacy of Fountains, and accepted it at the advice and bidding of S. Bernard, as these Letters show. He became Archbishop of York in 1147, and died in 1153, on the 14th October, according to the necrology of Vauclair.

God, will provide for it a faithful administrator; for it is very near to me. Nor do you make any difficulty on account of the Bishop;[1] depend upon me to arrange the matter with him.

LETTER CCCXXII.[2] (*Circa* A.D. 1138.)

To Hugo, a Novice, who afterwards became Abbot of Bonneval.[3]

Bernard praises his design of becoming a Religious; he forewarns him against temptations, and exhorts him to perseverance.

To his very dear son in Christ, HUGO, who has become a new creature in Christ, Brother BERNARD, called Abbot of Clairvaux, sends greeting, and desires that he may be made strong in the Lord.

1. The news of your conversion has given me joy and gladness. Why should not that be a cause of rejoicing to men, when it is so even to angels? Already the day is observed as a festival, it resounds with songs of praise and giving of thanks. A young man of high birth, delicately brought up, has overcome the enemy, despised the world, sacrificed his body, renounced the affections of his relatives, and burst the confining nets, which riches had spread around his wings. From when did you obtain this wisdom, O my son? For I do not find so great wisdom in the aged men of the world,[4] who, according to, or rather in spite of the word of the Apostle (1 Tim. vi. 9), have only one desire to be rich in this world, though they fall into temptation and into the snare of the devil. No, the wisdom of our dear Hugo is not from this world but from heaven. I

---

[1] Bartholomew, Bishop of Laon.

[2] Formerly No. 351; the former No. 322 is now No. 363.

[3] This was an Abbey in the Diocese of Besancon. Later on Hugo became its Abbot, and showed himself a very pious man, and worthy nephew of S. Hugo, Bishop of Grenoble, of whom mention is made in the *Life of S. Bernard*, B. iv. n. 40.

[4] *Babylonis.*

confess, O Father, that Thou hast hidden these things from the wise, and hast revealed it to a child. As for you, my son, be not ungrateful for the goodness of the Saviour to you. Lay aside the disposition of a child; or rather, be a child in malice, but not in wisdom (1 Cor. xiv. 20). Let not the austerity of our Order affright your tender age. Remember that the rougher thistle makes the softer web;[1] a severe life makes a good conscience. The sweetness of Christ shall make itself known to you, and the meal of the prophet shall render palatable the bitter and nauseous pottage (2 Kings iv. 39). If you feel the piercings of temptations, look up to the brazen serpent raised upon the pole, and draw life from the wounds, or rather from the bosom of the Crucified. He shall be to you kind as a mother, and you shall be to Him dear as a son; the nails which fasten Him to the Cross shall, as it were, pierce your hands and feet as they have pierced His.

2. But *a man's enemies shall be those of his own household* (Micah vii. 6, and S. Matt. x. 36). They are those who really love, not you, but the enjoyment which they have from you, otherwise they would have joy to hear you say, *If ye loved Me ye would rejoice, because I go to My Father* (S. John xiv. 28). "If your father," says S. Jerome, "lay across the threshold to prevent your passing; if your mother, dishevelled, should appeal to you by the bosom whence you were nourished; if your young nephew should hang upon your neck to stop you, trample under foot father and mother, and hasten without a tear to the banner of the Cross. The highest stretch of filial duty it is to be cruel for the sake of Christ" (epis. i. *ad Heliodor.*). Do not be influenced by the tears of demented relatives, who mourn to see that you, from having been a child of hell, have become a child of God. Alas! why do these unhappy people cherish an affection so violent, so cruel, and so unjust? *Evil communications corrupt good manners* (1 Cor. xv. 33). Wherefore avoid as much as possible, my son, conversa-

---

[1] Apparently a reference to the custom of using the head of the teazle thistle to render smooth and even the surface of velvet and cloth.—TRANS.

tions with guests, because these leave the mind empty and the ears full. Learn to pray to God; to lift up to Him your heart as well as your hands. Learn in all your needs to lift suppliant eyes towards heaven, and to bring upon you the pitying look of the Father of mercies. It would be an impiety to believe that God will shut up His bowels of compassion from you, and remain deaf to your groans and cries. For the rest remember that you ought to be docile to the directions of your spiritual fathers as if they were precepts from the Divine majesty. Follow that rule of conduct, and you shall have life. Follow it, and the blessing of God shall come upon you, and for every single thing which you have given up you shall receive a hundredfold, even in the present life. Distrust also the spirit that persuades you not to do this too hastily, and that this matter should be deferred to a more mature age. Rather trust Him who said, *It is good for a man that he should have borne the yoke from his youth. He sitteth alone and keepeth silence because he has borne it upon him* (Lam. iii. 27, 28). Farewell, and study perseverance, to which virtue alone the crown is due.

LETTER CCCXXIII. (A.D. 1139.)[1]

To Pope Innocent.

Bernard defends the Archbishop of Trèves against the Abbot of S. Maximin.[2]

1. How often have I experienced, my lord, your kindly feeling and affection towards me! And now I am in hopes of having a new proof of it under the present circumstances. By no means would I dare to request anything which I thought was contrary to the will of God and to your honour. But as I am persuaded that this petition which I am about to present to you is both reasonable and honourable, I have considerable confidence that my prayers will not return to

---

[1] A new Letter. The former No. 323 is now No. 365.
[2] See Letters 179, 180.

me void, especially as my petition is to a father for his son, and to Innocent on behalf of an innocent person. It is not necessary that I should remind you in detail how faithfully the Archbishop of Trèves has loved and upheld the honour of the Apostolic See and the peace of the Roman Church from his youth; how carefully and immoveably he has adhered to it in time of tribulation, and for it has borne the burden and heat of the day while others were sitting in the shade; and how steadily and courageously he has maintained before kings and princes the defence of his brethren; for all these things are certainly present to your mind. But furthermore, to speak of what I know, and testify what I have seen, how prudently and wisely has he extricated the goods and revenues of the Church out of the hands of strangers, how kindly and liberally has he imparted from his own means for the public good, and especially for that of the servants of God; with what diligence and circumspection has he guarded his own reputation from lying lips and from the deceitful tongue!

2. What then, in him, has displeased your Paternity? Was it that he freed the Abbey of S. Maximin from the royal power and subjected it to that of the Church? or was it that he did not accept for Abbot that man who, as it is said, desired to be a general before he was a soldier; that is, to be an Abbot before he was a monk? But if it was this, or some other matter, that displeased you in him, it would have been not unworthy of a kindly Father to bear in mind the Archbishop's affection of long standing towards him, to excuse with kindness a fault, and to let the memory of many good services win indulgence for a man who is praiseworthy in many respects, if to be blamed in a few. But now, my lord, you have lifted up the right hand of those who oppress him, and made all his enemies to rejoice. It is a subject of wonder in the eyes of many on what reputation for virtue or goodness of life a man is placed in the position to rule over souls, who has given so little heed to his own. For how can he rule others who has not known how to be ruled himself? How can he venture to

be in the position of a superior, who has not himself learned to submit, or to require the obedience from others, which he himself has not rendered to those above him? *If any man has not known how to rule over his own house,* says the Teacher of the Gentiles, *how shall he be capable of taking care of the Church of God?* (1 Tim. iii. 5). More than this: such as is the father, such are also the sons; have they not had the cruelty, in fact, to lacerate their mother by their favouring of dissensions and schisms? and concerning their character and manner of life it is more decent to be silent than to say anything. But I do not make these statements as taking upon me to judge the servants of another, who stand or fall to their own loss; but because I know that if the wretched designs of those men should succeed, that young men averse to obedience will break off the yoke of discipline from their necks, so as to become wanderers and vagabonds upon the earth, according to the example given to them by these. And if their design does not wholly succeed they will be able, at least, to boast themselves that they have been able to maintain resistance to their prelates. Alas! how many persons, and those of consideration, who suppose that they have some ground to count on your protection, will find their hope and confidence altogether uprooted, if the first blast of the tempest which threatens a son once so beloved shall drive him from your heart, and from the consolation of your sympathy.

3. If, then, blessed father, there is any hearing for my entreaties with your Excellence, I respectfully beg of you, I whose affection is for yourself rather than for your favours, that you would not abandon, now when it is your day of prosperity, a man who has remained firm to you in your day of trial; and that you would not suffer his authority to be weakened in any respect; for he may reasonably hope that from you it will receive enlargement, not suffer decrease. Otherwise, if contrary to the general hope, and in spite of the merits of the man, it shall prove that strangers are allowed to rob him of the fruits of his labours, that his good deeds are repaid with evil, and his good will

·with hatred; he, indeed, alone, will receive a wound from a hand at which he did not expect it, but many will resent his persecution. May the Spirit of Truth, who proceedeth from the Father, teach you to separate the light from the darkness in all your actions, so that you may know how to reject the evil and to choose the good.

LETTER CCCXXIV. (A.D. 1139.)[1]

To Robert,[2] Abbot of Dunes.

Bernard suggests the thought of the future union of their souls, and also bodies, in the Resurrection, as the solace of their absence from each other.

To his brother and very dear friend, Abbot ROBERT, Brother BERNARD, of Clairvaux, sends assurance of devoted friendship.

You were late made known to me, my dear Robert, and speedily taken away. But I am consoled by this fact, that it is only in the body that we are separated, and that in soul you are always with me. Yet how could I bear even this with resignation, if it were not in the cause of God Himself? But a time shall, shall come, when we shall be restored to each other, and when we shall each of us rejoice in the other as in himself; we shall be in each other's presence with each part of our being, nor fear to be thereafter in any way divided. He who is now the cause of our temporary separation shall be then the bond of our close union. He shall be present without ceasing to each of us, and shall render us constantly present to each other. I salute all your sons, whom I regard as mine also, and entreat that they will pray for me.

[1] Formerly No. 336; the former No. 324 is now No. 382.
[2] It was this Robert who succeeded Bernard as Abbot of Clairvaux, having been named by him as his successor when dying. The Belgians call the hills or mounds of white sand thrown up by the sea, *Dunes*. This was a monastery founded by S. Bernard, near Furnes, in Belgium, and was in a very flourishing condition; but the renewal of the wooden piles which hindered the advance of the sands was neglected "through the calamities of war," and the buildings being completely overwhelmed the convent was removed to Bruges.

LETTER CCCXXV.[1] (*Circa* A.D. 1139.)

TO THE SAME, RESPECTING THE NOVICE IDIER.

Bernard advises, in answer to his inquiry, what course should be taken with a novice of difficult character, named Idier.

To his very dear brother and co-Abbot, ROBERT, of Dunes, Brother BERNARD, called Abbot of Clairvaux, wishes health.

On the subject of the religious whom you have mentioned to me, and whom you believe will be not only useless, but also a burden to the community, without speaking of secret defects, such as you suspect, I will give you such counsel as I should act on myself were I in your place. After what you have told me, it seems to me that during his probation he has shown himself neither worthy nor capable of being rendered so, and that, therefore, you are able with a good conscience to put away an evil person from among you. If, however, it pleases your charity to exalt mercy above judgment, you are able to allow him to remain in your house as long as you shall see fit, but without permitting him to take the vows. But I dissuade you most strongly from receiving him to profession whilst he is in this condition; and let him be subjected to a new probation if perchance he should show any sign of becoming that which he ought to be. If not, use resolutely your power of expulsion, so that one diseased sheep may not infect the entire flock.

LETTER CCCXXVI.[2] (*Circa* A.D. 1139.)

FROM ABBOT WILLIAM TO GEOFFREY, BISHOP OF CHARTRES, AND TO BERNARD, ABBOT OF CLAIRVAUX.[3]

Abbot William begs them to defend the cause of God

[1] Formerly No. 337; the former No. 325 is now No. 395.

[2] Formerly No. 391; the former No. 326 is now No. 400.

[3] This Letter was prefixed by way of preface to the disputation of the same William, Abbot of S. Thierry at Rheims, with Abaelard, which is printed in Vol.

and of the Church against Peter Abaelard, and cites several of his erroneous propositions.

To the Reverend Lords and Fathers in Christ, GEOFFREY, Bishop of Chartres, and BERNARD, Abbot of Clairvaux, health and prosperity.

1. I am filled with confusion before you, my lords and fathers, as God knows, by finding myself constrained to draw your attention to a subject of grave necessity, and relating to the common interest of the Church. But as you and others to whom it belongs to speak keep silence, I, though a very humble person, venture to address you. For I see the faith on which rests our common hope gravely and dangerously compromised, no one resisting or objecting; and yet Christ consecrated it for us with His Blood, and the Apostles and martyrs strove for it even until death, the holy doctors defended it with the greatest labour and industry, and handed it down even to our depraved times whole and incorrupt. I reflect on this with great regret, and am obliged by my inward distress and sorrow to speak at least a few words on behalf of that for which, if it were needful, I should wish even to lay down my life. Nor are these attacks made on doctrines of small importance, but on the faith of the Holy Trinity, on the Person of the Mediator, the Holy Spirit, the grace of God, on the sacrament of our common redemption. For Peter Abaelard is again teaching and publishing novelties; his books cross the seas, pass the Alps; new speculations concerning the doctrines of the faith, and new dogmas are spread throughout provinces and realms, are openly preached and freely defended; it is even said that they have partisans in the Curia of Rome. I say to you that your silence is dangerous, as well for yourselves as for the Church of God. We are regarding it as a matter of no account that the Faith is being corrupted, although it is for the Faith that we have renounced our own selves, and in order that we may not be

iv. of the *Bibliotheca Cisterciensis*. It is apparent from the first lines of this Letter that it was written before all those of Bernard against Abaelard, and therefore before the year 1140.

attacked we do not fear to offend God. I say to you that this evil is as yet only in process of birth; unless it be dealt with beforehand, it will burst out into a basilisk, nor will it be easy to find an enchanter who can prevail against it. Give your attention, therefore, to what I have to relate.

2. A little while ago I read by accident a certain treatise of that man, entitled, *Theologia of Peter Abaelard*. I confess that the title made me curious to read it. I have two copies containing almost the same, except that the one may be a little more lengthy than the other. In it I found certain statements by which I was greatly shocked; I have taken notes of them, and subjoined my reasons for objection. These I have sent you, with the books themselves, so that you may judge whether I was right in my disapproval. And since my disapproval was founded on the unheard-of novelties of phrase which he applies to matters of faith, as well as to the novel senses which he puts upon received terms, and since I had no one to whom I might pour out my suspicions, I have found no one but yourselves to whom I might turn, and upon whom I might call in the cause of God and of the whole Latin Church. For you even that man fears and pays respect to. If you shut your eyes, whom will he have any fear of? And since he says what he does even now, what will he not say when he has no critic to fear? Almost all of the great masters of theology have been taken from the Church by death.[1] An enemy belonging to our own house, as it were, burst in upon the empty territory of the Church, and arrogated to himself the sole right of teaching within it. He proceeds in treating of the Holy Scripture, as he is accustomed to do in dialectics; he brings in his own devices, his recurring novelties; he makes himself a critic of the Faith, and not a disciple; an improver of it, instead of a follower.

[1] Hugo Metellus, in his fourth Letter to Pope Innocent against the same Abaelard, expresses himself in a very similar way: " After the death of Anselm of Laon, and of William, of Champeaux, it seemed that the light of the word of God failed upon the earth," etc.

3. These, then, are the propositions collected from his works which I have thought it advisable to submit to you:—
1. He defines Faith as an opinion about things that are not seen.
2. That the names of the Father, Son, and Holy Ghost are improper in God, but only serve for a description of the fulness of the Supreme Good.
3. That the Father is all Power; the Son, a certain Power; but the Holy Ghost, not a Power.
4. That the Holy Spirit is not of the substance of the Father and the Son, as the Son is of the substance of the Father.
5. That the Holy Spirit is the soul of the world (*anima mundi*).
6. That we are able both to will and to act rightly by the power of our free will alone, without the help of Divine grace.
7. That it was not in order to free us from the yoke of the devil that Christ assumed flesh and suffered death.
8. That Jesus Christ, who is God and Man, is not one of the Three Persons in the Trinity.
9. That in the Sacrament of the Altar the form of the earlier substance remains in the air.
10. That the devil inspires his suggestions into men by physical means.
11. That what we derive from Adam is not the fault of original sin, but the punishment of it.
12. That there is no sin, except in consenting to sin, and in contempt of God.
13. That no sin is committed in concupiscence, or by delectation, or by ignorance; there is no sin in these, but only a fact of nature.

4. These are the propositions, collected out of the books of Abaelard, which I considered I ought in the first place to put under your eyes; both to arouse your zeal, and to convince you that I have not been disturbed without reason. These, and others which depend upon them, I shall attempt,

with the help of Him in whose hands are both we and our discourses, to remark upon at greater length; and I shall regard it as of small account to displease you by my style, provided that I satisfy you in the statement of my faith. I hope, too, if I can by any means show that I have rightly formed an unfavourable opinion of these propositions, to carry you also with me in so doing; so that you will not shrink from sacrificing, in order to save the head, if need be, the foot (as we may call that man), the hand, or even the eye. For I have both loved him, and would wish still to love him, God is my witness; but in this cause no one shall ever [gain partiality from me as being] neighbour or friend. Now that the evil has become so patent, and presses itself upon public notice, it is no longer a question of private warning or correction. For there are, as I hear, some other treatises of his besides, of which the names are *Sic et Non, Scito te ipsum,* and some others, about which I fear that their doctrines may be as monstrous as their titles are strange; but, as I am told, they hate the light, and cannot be found even when sought for.

But to return to our subject . . . etc.

LETTER CCCXXVII.[1] (*Circa* A.D. 1139.)

REPLY OF BERNARD TO ABBOT WILLIAM.

Bernard praises the treatise written against Peter Abaelard, and promises to confer with him after Easter.

To his very dear WILLIAM, Brother BERNARD.

In my judgment, your indignation was both just and necessary. And your treatise, which refutes and belabours the mouth of them who speak unrighteousness, shows that it is not an empty indignation either. I have not yet had the time to read it with the attention that you require, but have only run through it in haste; nevertheless, I like it much, and think it a powerful instrument for the destruction

---

[1] Formerly No. 392; the former No. 327 is now No. 339.

of that unhappy teaching. But as you well know, I do not rely entirely on my own judgment, especially in such weighty matters; and I think it will be worth while, when a time of meeting can be arranged, for you and me to meet at some convenient place and discuss all these matters. I think this cannot be done before Easter, if we are to give ourselves without distraction to earnest prayer, as this holy time requires. For the present, then, suffer me to keep silence still for a while upon all these questions, of which the greater number, not to say all, are entirely new to me.[1] But God is able in His great power to bestow upon me the wisdom and the light which you shall ask for me in your prayers. Farewell.

LETTER CCCXXVIII.[2] (*Circa* A.D. 1140.)
To the Roman Pontiff.[3]

Against the person elected Bishop of Rodez.

Hitherto I have not hesitated to write to you in season and out of season, at the request of my friends: but now, the interests of the Christian religion would forbid me to be silent, even if I wished to be so. *Cursed be he*, says the Prophet, *who keepeth back his sword from blood* (Jer. xlviii. 10) [when he ought to strike]. To-day malice is profiting, the desires of evil men prosper, and there is no one to oppose them, no one who rises up to defend the rampart of the house of Israel. Even in your days most

---

[1] It is clear from this that it was William who was among the first to call attention to the errors of Abaelard; which, indeed, William himself virtually asserts in the previous Letter, where he complains of the silence of Geoffrey and Bernard.

[2] A new Letter; the former No. 328 is now No. 339.

[3] This Letter was placed immediately after that of a certain A. *To the Abbot of Kieti*, and inscribed *To the Same*. But it appears from the Letter itself, which treats also of an election of a successor to Adhemar, Bishop of Rodez, that it is also from the hand of Bernard, and was addressed to Pope Innocent or Pope Eugenius. In Letter 240, n. 1, Bernard congratulates Eugenius on having finished the matter of the Church of Rodez, by deposing, as it seems, an unworthy person who had been elected Bishop, about whom this and the following Letter is written.

corrupt men have made violent efforts[1] to climb up into the most holy places: they have stricken hands with death, and made a covenant with hell. Why then this patience? The clergy of Rodez[2] have elected a man for Bishop who is consentient with their vices; and have not been ashamed, it is said, to conceal the truth even from your eyes, both as to the business of the election and as to the person elected. That man, chosen not by God, but by men, has many witnesses of the infamous life he has led, none at all of his repentance and change of life; and in plain fact, it is more decent to be silent concerning him than to speak. God forbid that such wicked men should, under your pontificate, be promoted, and that one should be set for a shepherd of souls, who values at nought the shedding of the blood of Christ, and the price of his own soul's redemption. What to them is a cunning insinuation of injury and suppression of their appeal, if they can thus ingratiate themselves with the Curia, and interest them in their cause? Do not believe the word of falsehood: for, according to the statement of people of veracity, as there was no appeal, so no suppression of it could have followed. It is important that you should sanction with the weight of your authority what the Bishop[3] has done at the advice of the Religious. I wish at the same time to commend more and more the same Archbishop to you: and I should neither wish to ask this, nor to be heard by you, if he was not one who respects and discharges diligently his function.

[1] *Manibus et pedibus.*
[2] *Rutilenses.* But we ought to read *Rutinenses*, as we find from the following Letter. Rutila was a monastery in the Diocese of Treves. See *Life*, B. iv. n. 47.
[3] *I.e.*, the Archbishop of Bourges, of which See the Bishop of Rodez was a suffragan.

LETTER CCCXXIX.[1] (*Circa* A.D. 1140.)

TO THE BISHOP OF LIMOGES.

Against the same person, who had been elected to the See of Rodez.

The words which I shall speak to you, I speak not in my own behalf, nor in them do I seek any advantage of my own. The life of man is very short: as long as you are Bishop of Limoges, strive to do honour to your office, by letting us see your good works. I have the consolation of knowing that you have been entrusted by his lordship, the Pope, with the matter of the election of the Bishop of Cahors[2] with full power to decide it canonically without appeal. See, then, what an opportunity you have in this to manifest to the Church how wise a course has been taken by the Pontiff; an opportunity that will be realized if only there is in you the fear of God, a love of justice, and a strict adherence to the canons. As to the Church of Rodez. there is a question debated—whether that church shall receive a true pastor, a Bishop of souls, a successor to Christ, one, I say, who shall raise up offspring to his brother deceased. Who shall be regarded as fit for this? Shall it be one whom his life has defiled, whom his own conscience accuses, whose reputation is a scandal?—a man who has sunk from abbey to abbey, or rather from one depth to another, and who has not scrupled to violate the virgins to whom he had himself given the veil? Would that be taking heed of the precept of the Apostle, *A bishop must be blameless, as the steward of God* (Tit. i. 7). Do not, then, act in contradiction with yourself, saying one thing and doing another, but let your actions respond constantly to your words, so that the words may not be applied to you, *Their own tongues shall be turned against them* (Ps. lxiv. 8). See, the matter is in your hand. But keep your

[1] A new Letter; the former No. 329. is now No. 318.

[2] *Catinensis* [*Catania*] in the text. It should perhaps be read *Caturcensis*; for this Letter can scarcely relate to any other city. If so, then this passage seems to refer to the election of Raymond, whom, in consequence, William de la Croix wrongly erases from the list of Bishops of Cahors.

own soul free from stains, nor make yourself liable for the offences of another. With you it will rest to uphold or to annul his election; but in taking the latter course you will make your hands holy to the Lord.

LETTER CCCXXX.[1] (A.D. 1140.)
To Pope Innocent.
Against Peter Abaelard.

To his very dear father and lord INNOCENT, BERNARD, called Abbot of Clairvaux, sends humble homage.

The Spouse of Christ weeps bitterly in the night. Her cheeks are bedewed with tears, and there is not one to console her of those to whom she is dear. That Shunammite, my lord, is committed to your care during the days of her pilgrimage, and while her Spouse delays His coming. To no one will she confide her injuries and her troubles so unreservedly as to the friend of her Spouse. Because you love Him you are always prepared to listen to her complaints in time of trouble. And among all the various kinds of enemies with whom the Church is surrounded, as a city among thorns, there are none whose attacks are more persistent and more dangerous than those whom she has borne in her bosom and nourished at her breast. It is they, and such as they, who have drawn forth the exceeding bitter cry, *My lovers and my friends draw near and stand against me to take away my life* (Ps. xxxviii. 11, 12). There is none more powerful to injure than an enemy of our own household. We may judge of this from the treacherous attachment of Absalom, and from the kiss of Judas. Other foundation for our faith can no man lay than that which is laid (1 Cor. iii. 11). Now in France there is being fabricated a new faith which does not look at virtues and vices from the point of view of morals, at Sacraments with the eye of faith, which reasons about the Holy Trinity itself in a way far from simple or reverent, and arrives at conclusions other than the

[1] A new Letter. The former No. 330 is now No. 349.

truth we have received. Magister Peter and Arnold, of whose evil influence you have cleared Italy, have *Stood up and taken counsel together against the Lord and against His Anointed.* Scale is joined to scale, so that not a breath can come between them. They are corrupt, and become abominable in their pursuits. With the leaven of their corruption they corrupt the faith of the simple, pervert the rules of morals, and soil the whiteness of the Church's robe. Like him who changes himself into the similitude of an angel of light, they have a form of piety, but without its power. They are adorned like a decorated sanctuary that they may privily shoot at them that are of a right disposition. Scarcely have we ceased to hear the roaring of Peter Leonis occupying the seat of Simon Peter than we are threatened by Peter the dragon[1] assailing the faith of Simon Peter. The one persecuted the Church of God openly, as a ravening lion, but the other, as a dragon, lurks in hiding places that he may murder the innocent. But Thou, Lord God, will bring down the high looks of the proud; Thou wilt tread under Thy feet both lion and dragon. The one did evil as long as he lived, but death put an end to his malice; but the other, committing his new dogmas to writing, provides for the transmission of his poison to future generations. In short, to describe this theologian in few words, he distinguishes with Arius degrees and inequalities in the Trinity; with Pelagius he prefers free will to grace; with Nestorius he divides Christ in excluding His humanity from union with the Trinity. But in all these things he boasts that he has opened the fountains of knowledge to the cardinals and ecclesiastics of the Curia; that his books are in the hands of the Romans, his maxims in their hearts, so that he takes those by whom he ought to be judged and condemned to be the protectors of his error. With what intention, with what effrontery can you [I ask him], who art the persecutor of the faith, appeal to the protection of its defender, and with what unabashed boldness can you, the insulter of the Church, dare to look in the face the friend of the Church's

---

[1] Draconis.

Bridegroom? If the care of my brethren and the weak state of my health did not keep me here, how greatly should I wish to behold the friend of the Bridegroom exerting himself zealously in defence of the Church, in the absence of her Spouse! Can I possibly endure the wounds of the Church when I could not bear in silence the injuries done to my lord [the Pope]? Do thou, then, most dear father, cease to withhold thy help from her. Rise up in her defence; gird thee with thy sword. For already, through the overflowing of iniquity, the love of many waxes cold, and unless you put to your hand I foresee the day when the Spouse of Christ will go forth and follow strange paths, and be led astray by false pastors.

LETTER CCCXXXI.[1] (A.D. 1140.)

To Cardinal Stephen, Bishop of Palestrina.

On the Same Subject.

To the venerable lord and very dear father S . . ., by the grace of God Bishop of Palestrina, Brother BERNARD, Abbot of Clairvaux, health and that he may be strengthened to act firmly in the Lord.

I impart to you the distresses and complaints of the Spouse of Christ with the more confidence, because I am well aware that you are the friend of the Bridegroom, and rejoice greatly because of his voice. If I have rightly known your inward disposition, I am confident that the Lord may count on you, since you seek not your own interests, but those of Jesus Christ.

The life, the character, and the books already published of Peter Abaelard show him to be a persecutor of the Catholic faith and the enemy of the cross of Christ. He is a monk in outward appearance, but within he is a heretic, having nothing of the monk beyond the name and the habit. He opens the old cisterns and the dried-up pools of the heretics that the ox and the ass may fall therein. He

---

[1] A new Letter; the former No. 331 is now No. 350.

had been long silent, but while he kept silence in Brittany he conceived sorrow, and now in France he has brought forth iniquity. The serpent of many coils has come forth from his cavern, and, like the Hydra, produces seven heads for one that has been struck off. A single one was lopped off, a single heresy of that man, at Soissons, but in its place seven, or it may be more, heresies have appeared, of which I have and send you a copy. Scarcely has he separated his young and unskilled scholars from the rudiments of dialectic than he introduces them, who are as yet barely able to comprehend the first elements of the faith, to the mystery of the holy Trinity, the holy of holies, the very chamber of the King, and even to Him who makes darkness His dwelling-place. In short, our new theologian distinguishes with Arius degrees and inequalities in the Trinity, with Pelagius prefers free will to grace, with Nestorius he divides Christ in excluding His Humanity from union with the Trinity. Proceeding thus through almost all the Sacraments and sacred doctrines, he touches on each with the utmost boldness, and treats each in a most blameable manner. Besides this, he boasts that he has imbued the Curia at Rome with the infection of his novelties; that his books and his opinions have made their way into the hands and the minds of Romans, and that those by whom he ought to be judged and condemned are the protectors of his erroneous teaching. May God keep guard over His Church, for which He gave His life, so as to present her to Himself without spot or wrinkle; and may He so order that perpetual silence may be imposed upon that man, whose mouth is filled only with cursing, and bitterness, and woe.

LETTER CCCXXXII.[1] (A.D. 1140.)

To Cardinal G . . .

Also against Peter Abaelard.

To the venerable lord and most dear father G . . .,

[1] A new Letter; the former No. 332 is now No. 367.

LETTER CCCXXXII.

Cardinal of the holy Roman Church, BERNARD, Abbot of Clairvaux, desires the spirit of counsel and might.

I cannot hold my peace respecting the injuries done to Christ, the difficulties and troubles of the Church, the misery and complaints of the poor. We are fallen upon perilous times. We have doctors prone to flattery, and scholars who close their ears to the truth and turn aside unto fables. We have in France Peter Abaelard, a monk, who lives without rule; a prelate, who has no spiritual charge; an abbot without an abbey, who disputes with boys and converses with women. In his books he provides for his followers secret waters and bread eaten in secret, while in his oral discourses he leads them to profane novelties of phrase and of meaning. He approaches to the thick darkness in which God is, not alone, as did Moses, but with the numerous crowd of his disciples. Along the streets and in the open spaces people dispute about the Catholic Faith, about the childbearing of the Virgin, about the Sacrament of the Altar, about the incomprehensible mystery of the holy Trinity. We have ceased to hear the roaring of Peter Leonis only to hear the hissing of Peter Draconis. But thou, O Lord Jesu, shalt bring down the high looks of the proud, Thou shalt tread under foot both lion and dragon. The one did harm but as long as he lived, and when his life ended, so did his mischief, but the other is making provision for preserving his poison to the harm of generations yet to come. He has put upon record with pen and ink his poisonous novelties; I have procured his books, and send them to you that you may judge of the author from his works. You will see that this theologian distinguishes with Arius grades and inequalities in the Trinity, that with Pelagius he prefers free will to grace, that with Nestorius he divides Christ in excluding His Humanity from the Trinity. These are but a few things out of many. Will there be no one among you who laments this attack upon Christ, who loves righteousness and hates iniquity? If the mouth that speaks perverse things be not stopped, let Him see to it and judge, who alone considers our distress and trouble.

LETTER CCCXXXIII.[1] (A.D. 1140.)

To Cardinal G . . .[2]

To his venerable friend G . . ., Cardinal-deacon under the title of SS. Sergius and Bacchus, BERNARD, Abbot of Clairvaux, wishes health and joy.

It used to be your custom to rise before me as often as I entered the Curia, and I trust that you will do so now. Do not think that I am merely in joke, for there is a serious matter to be decided. At this very moment I present myself before the Curia, if not in person, at least in the cause which is referred thither. As you were accustomed to rise to greet me, so rise to greet my cause, or rather, that of Christ; for it is His, and it is His truth which is in question. Rise, or rather start up in wrath, against the man who disputes about the faith in order to destroy the faith, and contradicts the law in words of the law ; whose hand is against every man, and the hands of all against him. This is Peter Abaelard, who writes, dogmatizes, and disputes, deciding exactly as he pleases, upon morals, upon the Sacraments, yea, concerning the Father, the Son, and the Holy Spirit. After having disturbed and troubled the Church, he presents himself before the Curia, not to offer excuses for his errors, but to defend them. If you are a true son of the Church, defend her now who has borne you and nourished.

LETTER CCCXXXIV.[3] (A.D. 1140.)

To Guy, of Pisa.[4]

Against the same Abaelard.

To GUY, Abbot of Pisa, BERNARD, Abbot of Clairvaux, wishes a sound mind in a sound body.

[1] A new Letter; the former No. 333 is now No. 386.
[2] This was Gregorius Tarquinius, Cardinal-deacon of SS. Sergius and Bacchus, who was created by Callistus II.
[3] A new Letter; the former No. 334 is now No. 362.
[4] Guy Moricot de Vico, a Pisan, created by Pope Innocent Cardinal under the title of SS. Cosmas and Damian.

I know that you have so much affection for me (as I for you) that I should with great confidence entrust to you my dearest interests; but it is with more confidence still that I entrust to you those of Jesus Christ, who is to be loved far more than I. The cause is Christ's, since Christ Himself is in question, and the truth is in peril. The garments of Christ are being divided, when the Sacraments of the Church are rent in pieces; but His seamless robe is entire, which is woven from the top throughout. For this tunic is the unity of the Church, which does not admit of cutting or division. Man is not capable of dividing that which has been compacted from above, and made firm by the Holy Spirit. Though heretics sharpen their tongues like serpents, though they arm themselves with the sharpest weapons of the intellect, in order that they may disturb the peace of the Church; yet though they are the gates of hell, they shall not prevail against her. If you are truly her son, if you recognize the bosom which bore you, do not desert your mother in her peril, do not withdraw your support in the time of tribulation. Magister Peter has recourse to the Curia, that the authority of the Apostolic See may serve him as a wall and a rampart to protect the errors which he has taught and written, and in which he has impugned the Catholic Faith.

LETTER CCCXXXV.[1] (A.D. 1140).

To a Certain Cardinal Presbyter.[2]

Also against Peter Abelard.

To the CARDINAL PRESBYTER, BERNARD, Abbot of Clairvaux, wishes health and happiness in the Lord.

Let no one despise your youth. It is not white hairs nor weight of years that is required by the Lord, but maturity

---

[1] A new Letter; the former No. 335 is now No. 368.

[2] Edward Martene remarks upon this: "Letter 335, which in the editions is inscribed: *To a certain Cardinal Presbyter*, is in the Vedastine MS. addressed by name to the Cardinal Peter." (*Amplis. Collect. Vet. Script. et Monument.*, p. 745.)

of mind and a blameless life. Neither Jeremiah nor Daniel feared nor trembled, though both of them were young men, before old men disgraced by vice, though heavy with the weight of ill-spent days. And I might rightly, perhaps, treat as disgraced that man, who tried to corrupt the beauty of the Church, and to stain the purity of the Faith. That is Peter Abaelard, who disputes and defines as he chooses, and differently from accepted tradition, upon matters of faith, upon the Sacraments, and the mystery of the holy Trinity. Now, after having disturbed the Church and thrown it into confusion, he presents himself to the Curia, not that he may make amends for the mischief he has done, but because he relies upon the crafty subterfuges that he has at his command to conceal his errors. It is now that those who know themselves to be the Church's sons will stand firmly in her defence.

LETTER CCCXXXVI.[1] (A.D. 1140.)

To A Certain Abbot.[2]

On the Same Subject.

To his very dear brother and co-Abbot, Brother BERNARD, Abbot of Clairvaux, wishes a zeal for the Lord according to knowledge.

It must needs be that offences come, so that those who are approved may be made manifest. If any one is the Lord's servant, let him take the Lord's side, for His cause is now in question. The truth is attacked; the vestments of Christ are torn in pieces, the Sacraments of the Church divided. From the sole of the foot to the crown of the head, the well-being of the Church is compromised, and the simple faith of believers ridiculed; the lion is on the point of arising from his lair against the Church that he may make a prey of the nations. Already Peter Abaelard

[1] A new Letter; the former No. 336 is now No. 324.
[2] This was perhaps an Italian Abbot named Bernard, whom S. Bernard had sent to Rome. See Letters 343 and 344.

goes before Antichrist to prepare his ways, speaking differently from tradition with respect to matters of faith, of the Sacraments, and of the Father, the Son, and the Holy Ghost. He writes, teaches, and disputes; and his words tend to the subversion of the hearers. With Arius he distinguishes degrees and inequalities in the Trinity; with Pelagius he prefers free will to grace; with Nestorius he divides Christ, by excluding His Humanity from the fellowship of the Trinity. But in all these things he boasts that he has won over the Roman Church to his side; that the Romans have received his books and his opinions into their hands and hearts; and that those by whom he ought to be judged and condemned have taken upon them his defence. May the Lord look upon it, and judge, if the mouth of that man who speaketh unrighteousness be not speedily closed. The bearer of this will explain to you the details at greater length.

LETTER CCCXXXVII.[1] (A.D. 1140.)

To Pope Innocent, in the name of the Bishops of France.[2]

The Bishops of Gaul explain to the Pontiff what had been done in the case of Peter Abaelard, who had challenged Bernard to a discussion in Synod; but being unwilling to make answer to the specific charges of heresy made against him, had appealed to the Apostolic See.

[1] Formerly No. 370; the former No. 337 is now No. 325.

[2] In the Vatican MS. numbered 662, this Letter is placed next after No. 189, with the title *The Bishops of France to Pope Innocent*; where by the word France is understood the metropolitan province of Sens. Hence in Letter 161, the voice of the blood of Archembald, subdean of Orleans, is said to cry from the earth of France to Pope Innocent; and Letter 126, n. 4, distinguishes France from Burgundy. Nevertheless, even at that time a great part of Belgica Secunda* was included under the name of France.—[*Mabillon's Note.*]

* This was the northern of the two provinces into which Belgica was divided soon after B.C. 44. It may roughly be said to be the district between the Rhine, the Scheldt, the Moselle, and the Sea. It was generally known as Germania Secunda.—[E.]

LETTER CCCXXXVII.

To the most reverend father and lord INNOCENT, by the grace of God supreme Pontiff, HENRY, Archbishop of Sens, GEOFFREY, Bishop of Chartres, and servant[1] of the holy apostolic See, ELIAS, Bishop of Orleans, HUGO, Bishop of Auxerre, ATTO, Bishop of Troyes, MANASSES, Bishop of Meaux, send the assurance of their earnest prayers and due obedience.

1. As it is certain that those things which are established by the Apostolic authority are considered settled, so that they cannot be interfered with or altered by the objections or bad motives of any one, we have thought it proper, most holy Father, to make you aware of all that took place at our meeting lately, in order that your Serenity may deign to approve and permanently confirm by your judgment and authority what we, with the help of many pious and learned persons, have thought fit to do. Therefore, since throughout almost the whole of France, in towns, villages, and castles, by scholars not only within the schools, but in the roads and public places, disputes are carried on about the holy Trinity and the Nature of God; and that not only among learned or passably instructed persons, but among children even and simple and ignorant persons; and besides all this, many propositions are put forth by these disputants, not less contrary to reason than to the Catholic Faith, and to the doctrine of the holy Fathers; and since, though frequently warned by those who thought more justly on these matters that they should lay aside those foolish fancies (*ineptias*), those persons showed themselves more ardent still; and, relying on the authority of their master, Peter Abaelard, and especially upon his book entitled *Theologia,* as also of other treatises of his of a similar kind, persisted more and more in sustaining and defending these dangerous novelties, to the detriment of many souls; we, though distressed and alarmed, as were many others, at this state of things, were fearful to meddle with these [difficult] questions.

---

[1] That is, *legate*. Geoffrey used to call himself by this name through modesty, as we see in the Cartulary of S. Stephen at Dreux. The legates of the Holy See were frequently called its vicars.

2. But the lord Abbot of Clairvaux, who had frequently heard from various persons of these matters, happened also to meet with a copy of the previously mentioned book of Magister Peter, called his *Theologia*, and of other books of his, and having read them attentively, thought it incumbent on him to meet the author, and to admonish him, at first in private, and then, according to the precept of the Gospel taking with him two or three witnesses, invited him in a kind and friendly manner both to restrain his hearers from occupying themselves with such questions, and also that he should correct his books. Many of his scholars, also, the Abbot exhorted to cease from reading, and to reject those writings full of poison; also to refrain from, and be on their guard, against doctrine which injured the Catholic faith. Magister Peter was enraged at this, and scarcely able to restrain his anger; nor did he desist from frequent demands until we had written to the Abbot of Clairvaux upon the matter, and fixed a day, viz., that of the octave of Pentecost, on which he should appear before us at Sens. Thither Magister Peter professed himself willing to come prepared to defend and prove the propositions which the Abbot had as aforesaid blamed as partaking of heresy. But the Abbot on his side would neither promise to appear on the appointed day, nor to accept the argument before us against Peter. But as in the interval the latter had begun nevertheless to call together his followers from all sides, and to entreat them to be present at the disputation which was about to take place between himself and the Abbot of Clairvaux, so as by their presence to support his opinions and his system; the Abbot, to whom this became known, fearing that his absence might be made an occasion for unthinking persons as well as for the partisans of error, to regard all the opinions, or rather all the fancies of their master as being more certain than they really were; and touched with the fervour of a holy zeal, or rather kindled by the fire of the Holy Spirit, presented himself before us on the very day which had been named to him, although he had not at all engaged to do so. On that day, in fact,

being the octave of Pentecost, all our brethren the Suffragan Bishops of our province had assembled to us in the town of Sens to contribute by their presence to the honour and reverence paid to the holy relics, of which we proposed to make an exposition to the people in our cathedral church.

3. In the presence, then, of the glorious King of France, Louis, of the pious William, Count of Nevers, of the lord Archbishop of Rheims with certain of his suffragans, of us also and all our suffragans, except those of Paris and Nevers, of a great number of Abbots as pious as wise, and of clergy well instructed, the lord Abbot of Clairvaux and Magister Peter, with his supporters, respectively appeared.[1] To speak briefly, the lord Abbot brought before us the book *Theologia*, written by Magister Peter, and pointed out from this book various propositions, which he stigmatized as absurd, or even as plainly heretical, in order that Magister Peter might either deny that he had written them, or, if he accepted the authorship, might either justify or correct them. But Magister Peter appeared to be at a loss what to do; and, in order to make a way of escape, refused to reply, although he had a free hearing given to him, a safe place, and impartial judges; but appealing to your hearing in person, most holy Father, he left the assembly with all his supporters.

4. But we, although that appeal seemed to us not canonical, yet out of respect to the Apostolic See, we abstained from pronouncing any judgment against him personally. But as to his errors in doctrine, which had infected many, and had penetrated into the deepest recesses of not a few hearts, we had condemned them the day before Abaelard made his appeal, after having read and reread them in public audience, and having heard them plainly and undoubtedly proved to be heretical, both by convincing

[1] All the historians, with Hugo, Chronographer of S. Marianus, place this ceremony in 1140; but they do not mention the exposition (*relevatio*) of the relics, nor does the Chronicle of S. Peter Vivus. In treating of this synod, Otto, Bishop of Frisingen, says that Theobald Count Palatine, with other nobles, was present there (*de Gestis Frider.*, B. i. c. 48).

reasonings and by authorities cited from S. Augustine and other Fathers by the Abbot of Clairvaux. And because they draw many to most hurtful and evidently destructive error, we beg, most just Father, unanimously and with the utmost earnestness, that you would condemn with a perpetual judgment, by your authority, both them and all persons who obstinately and contentiously maintain them. And as for the before-mentioned Peter, if your Reverence would impose silence upon him, would suspend altogether his powers of lecturing and writing, and would condemn his books as being without doubt filled with erroneous teaching, you would thus root up the thorns and briars from the field of the Church, and would enable a joyful harvest to increase in flower and fruit for Christ. We transmit to you, Reverend Father, the list of certain propositions which we have condemned, that by these extracts you may the more easily form an idea of the remainder of the work.

LETTER CCCXXXVIII.[1] (A.D. 1140.)

To Haimeric, Cardinal and Chancellor.

He urges that Peter Abaelard, having been convicted of heresy, ought not to find the abodes of the Cardinals and the Roman Curia open to him as a refuge.

To his illustrious and very intimate friend HAIMERIC, Cardinal-deacon and Chancellor of the holy Roman Church, BERNARD, Abbot of Clairvaux, desires that he may act wisely before God and before men.

1. I have both heard of the opinions of Magister Peter Abaelard, and I have seen his books. I have remarked his words, I have taken note of the hidden senses (*mysteria*) of them, and found them to be mysteries of iniquity. This divine contradicts the Law in the very words of the Law. He casts that which is holy to the dogs, and pearls

[1] Formerly No. 369; the former No. 338 is now No. 401. See Letter 187 and those following it; also the Notes.

before swine; he corrupts the faith of the simple, defiles the purity of the Church. It is said that "the vase will long preserve the odour with which it has once been imbued."[1] His book had passed through the fire, and was brought into a place of refreshment. The enemy of the Church reposes in the bosom of the Church, the persecutor of the faith finds in it an asylum. He was utterly conquered. Let him not rise again (it is said) who has invaded the couch of his father and defiled it! Now that man has dishonoured the Church, and infected with his vices the minds of the simple. He endeavours to scrutinize by the light of his reason alone, the mysteries which are apprehended by the pious mind only by the intuition of faith: the faith of the pious, which believes and does not discuss. But that man holds even God in suspicion, nor is willing to believe anything unless he shall have first considered it by reason. Though the Prophet says, *If you will not believe, ye shall not understand* (Is. vii. 9, lxx. version), that man blames spontaneous faith as mere credulity, making an ill use of that saying of Solomon: *He that is hasty to give credit is light-minded* (Ecclus. xix. 4). He blames, then, the B.V. Mary for believing without hesitation the word of the angel which announced to her: *Behold, thou shalt conceive and bear a Son* (S. Luke i. 31). Let him blame also him who at the last hour, almost the last moment, of life, believed the words spoken to him by One who was dying likewise: *To-day thou shalt be with Me in Paradise* (S. Luke xxiii. 43); and let him reserve his praise for those, the hardness of whose hearts merited the reproach spoken of them: *O fools, and slow of heart to believe all that the prophets have spoken* (S. Luke xxiv. 25), and commend also the slowness of belief in him, to whom it was said: *Because thou hast not believed My words, thou shalt be dumb and not able to speak* (S. Luke i. 20).

2. Finally, in order to abbreviate a multitude of observations into the strait limits of a letter, I will say shortly, that

---

[1] Horace, Epp. b. i. ep. ii. v. 69, 70.

this admirable Doctor with Arius distinguishes degrees and inequalities in the Trinity; with Pelagius prefers free will to grace; with Nestorius divides Christ by excluding His Humanity from the fellowship of the Trinity. But in all these matters he boasts that he has opened the fountains of knowledge to the Cardinals and ecclesiastics of the Curia; that his books are in the hands, and his opinions in the minds, of the Romans; and he relies on those persons, by whom he ought to be judged and condemned, being a protection to him. Hyacinth[1] has shown me much ill-will, but has done me no harm; simply because he was unable. This I endure with equanimity, since he spares not Rome, nor the Curia, nor even the person of the Pope. What else I have seen and heard, my dear Nicholas, who is equally devoted to you as to me, will tell you better by word of mouth.

LETTER CCCXXXIX.[2] (*Circa* A.D. 1140.)
To Pope Innocent.

Bernard maintains the innocence of Alvisus,[3] Bishop of Arras, against his calumniators.

To his very dear father and lord, INNOCENT, by the grace of God supreme Pontiff, BERNARD, called Abbot of Clairvaux, offers respectful homage.

It is a thing neither new nor wonderful that the mind of man should be able to be both deceived and deceiving. But as this is a double evil, and each part of it has to be guarded against, the Angel of great wisdom has suggested to you a safeguard against either danger, when he says, *Be ye wise as serpents, and harmless as doves* (S. Matt. x. 16). Prudence will prevent your being deceived, and simplicity will prevent your deceiving others. The monks of Marchiennes[4] have come to present themselves before you, in

---
[1] See Letter 189, and Note.
[2] Formerly No. 327; the former No. 339 is now No. 402.
[3] ? Aloysius or Alois.—[E.]
[4] Marchiennes was a Benedictine Abbey, situated at Scarpe, in the Diocese of Tournay. It was founded in the seventh century by S. Rictruda.

a spirit of falseness and error, against the Lord, and against His anointed. They have made a false accusation against the Bishop of Arras, whose life and conversation is in good report in every place. Who are they, to bite reputations as dogs, who call good evil, and give light the name of darkness? Who are they, who against the law curse the deaf and put a stumbling block before the blind? (Lev. xix. 14). Wherefore, my lord, are you angry with your son and do you give joy and gladness to his enemies? Have you forgotten that warning of the Apostle, *Believe not every spirit, but try the spirits whether they are of God* (1 S. John iv. 1). I trust in the Lord, that He will confound their projects: and by making the truth appear, put falsehood to flight, and turn their deception against themselves. I have heard with my own ears how faithfully and firmly he spoke in defence of the Roman Church in the presence of the King and his nobles. He proposes, in the innocence of his heart, to go on the day when he is summoned, to present himself before you: but in the meantime, he has sent before him his Archdeacon, who is the bearer of this letter, and whose person and character I commend to your kindness.

I learn also that the Abbot of S. Vedast[1] is coming to have an interview with you: he is one who is an enemy to himself, and no less to his Religious and to his Abbey: he has undertaken only the bare name of Abbot, since he seeks his own interests, not those of Jesus Christ. As for the Religious G—, who accompanies him, all that can be said is that he is a worthy son of such a father: he spares neither his reputation nor his conscience; so that he is become the derision of his entire neighbourhood. May the Spirit of truth grant you to divide the light from the darkness, to advance the good and to repress the evil.

[1] This was Walter, who was succeeded in 1147 by Guerin, of whom mention is made in Letter 284. *Gallia Christiana* states in his honour that Pope Innocent did not make any decree against him.

LETTER CCCXL.[1] (*Circa* A.D. 1140.)

To the same Pope Innocent.

On behalf of the Bishop of Angers.

To his very dear father and lord, INNOCENT, by the grace of God supreme Pontiff, BERNARD, Abbot of Clairvaux, sends his respectful homage.

The Bishop of Angers[2] is worn out by his age as also by the labours and perils he has endured: who can look upon him with an indifferent eye, that is not destitute of sensibility, and even of any human feeling? As for me, I am not able, without feeling myself deeply moved, to look at this aged man, to whom but a single reproach could be addressed, whose life and whose learning render him venerable. I am ignorant of what has passed between him and the Abbey with which he is at variance, and I do not presume to write anything respecting a matter I am not acquainted with. But if it shall appear that he has fulfilled his engagements, I suppose that there is no other course to be taken than to restore him to your favour and to the exercise of his functions.

LETTER CCCXLI.[3] (*Circa* A.D. 1140.)

To Malachi, Archbishop of Ireland.

Bernard receives with thanks the letter and the staff, and welcomes the monks sent by him. He recommends Malachi to have an abode prepared fit for Religious: and commends himself to his prayers.

To the venerable lord and most blessed father MALACHI, by the grace of God Archbishop of the Irish[4] and Legate of

---

[1] A new Letter; the former No. 340 is now No. 403.
[2] Ulger, to whom Letter 200 is written.
[3] Formerly No. 315; the former No. 341 is now No. 385.
[4] Usher brings forward this Letter among Irish precedents, where he shows against John Picard, that the Bishops of Armagh were styled Archbishops, and exercised metropolitan power, before they began to receive the pallium, which

the Apostolic See, Brother BERNARD, called Abbot of Clairvaux, desires that he may find grace in the Lord.

1. Among the multitude of my anxieties and heartfelt cares, which distract my mind by their multitude, the brethren which have come to me from a distant land, in order that they may [learn to] serve the Lord, your letter, and the staff which you have sent me, have consoled me much: the letter as a pledge of your kindly feeling towards me; the staff to sustain my body, which is bowed down by infirmity; the brethren to serve God in the spirit of humility. All I have accepted with pleasure; all equally work together for good. As to your desire that I should send you two Religious to assist you in choosing a fit place of settlement,[1] I have thought it expedient not to send you these before the others, but to wait until Christ be more fully formed in them, until they shall be entirely equipped for the wars of the Lord. When then they shall have become instructed in the school of the Holy Ghost and endued with virtue from on high, then at length your sons shall return to their father, that they may sing the Lord's song in their own land, and not any longer in a foreign country.

2. In the meantime do you, according to the wisdom which has been bestowed upon you by the Lord, make choice of a place of settlement for them, separated from the tumults of the world, according to the principles of choice which you have seen acted upon with us. For the time is at hand when, with the grace of God helping, I shall be able to send you back new men, instead of those clothed with the old man whom you entrusted to me. May the Lord be

---

was first given in 1150. Usher is surprised at the title of Archbishop being given to Malachi, who had resigned his Archbishopric several years before, to undertake the administration of the Diocese of the Dunes (*Life*, c. 14). Bernard, however, calls him by that title probably because of his former dignity; but in following Letters he styles him only Bishop.

[1] Later the Abbey of Mellifont (Dioc. Armagh) was thus chosen, and founded in 1141. The first Abbot was named Christian, who is mentioned in Letter 357, n. 3. Respecting this Abbey, see *Acts of S. Malachi*, *Life of S. Bernard*, and *Duchesne*, Tome iv. ep. 254.

blessed for ever, of whose gift it comes that your sons have become also mine; and that from the trees planted by your preaching and watered by my exhortation, God has given increase. I pray your Holiness to apply yourself to the preaching of the Word of God, that you may give to your flock the knowledge of salvation. You lie under a twofold obligation to do this; from your quality as Bishop, and your delegation from the Holy See. For the rest, since in many things we offend all (S. James iii. 2), and being placed among men of this world, we frequently contract much of the dust of the world; I commend myself to your prayers and those of your brethren, that Jesus Christ, who is Himself the fountain of holiness, who once said to Peter, *If I wash thee not, thou hast no part with Me* (S. John xiii. 8), would deign to wash me, and to cleanse me in the waters of His mercy. And, indeed, I not only earnestly entreat this of you, but require it as in some sense the payment of a debt, since I do not cease to call upon the Lord for you, if the prayer of a sinner is of any avail. Farewell in the Lord.

LETTER CCCXLII.[1] (A.D. 1140.)

To Joscelyn, Bishop of Soissons.

Bernard begs him to appease the King, who was displeased with the Archbishop of Bordeaux.

To the venerable lord and very dear father, JOSCELYN, by the grace of God Bishop of Soissons, BERNARD, Abbot of Clairvaux, sends greeting, and desires that he may find grace with the Lord.

1. It is an injury to the Realm and the nobles of it if the plans of the King are proclaimed of his own hasty motion, and made public without mature consideration. But it pleases me much to see that the King trusts you, and confides in you; for I know that you are zealous for the Sovereign and the realm with a godly zeal, and I know also

[1] A new Letter; the former No. 342 is now No. 383.

that you have the qualities of a good adviser for him. Both order and reason require, in fact, that in a Royal counsellor should be united in a similar degree devotedness and prudence. Everything depends upon this for him; with these two qualities he cannot fail to be a sound adviser and to direct with wisdom the enterprises of the King. But if either his devotedness makes default in prudence, or his prudence in devotedness, when he performs his duty as counsellor, then woe to the land whose King shall be a child! May my soul never come into the counsel of those who, either though they love me, are not prudent; or being prudent, love me not. For so Adam, that unhappy one, fell from his rights of immortality, for having yielded to the counsel of the sinful; of Eve who, though she loved him, was not prudent; and of the serpent, who was prudent, but loved him not.

2. Why is it that my lord the King endeavours to draw the Archbishop of Bordeaux[1] into a dispute without any reason? Is that done by your advice? May God keep you from doing such a thing, and me from thinking it possible. For what harm has that man done? Is it that he consecrated, according as he was free to do, by the Canons, a Bishop[2] elected by those of Poictiers with a unanimous voice, without opposition? or that he did not snatch from the poor and from the Churches of Poictiers, from the mouths of the hungry, so to speak, the money which a dying man had left them? Lo, their blood is required at his hand. If it is a fault to have given a pastor to wandering sheep, to have refrained from despoiling the widow and the orphan, to have maintained intact the privileges of the Apostolic See, then he cannot be accused. O, ill-judged judgment, in which righteousness is taken for wrong and innocence is counted as guilt! Look to yourselves, you who are Bishops.

---

[1] It was Geoffrey Loratorio (de Loroux) to whom Letter 125 was written, when he was not yet Archbishop.

[2] This was Grimoard, elected in 1140, but Louis VII. refused for some time to ratify the choice. He had been Abbot of S. Mary des Allois.

Your interests are in question when your neighbour's wall takes fire (Horace, *Epist.* i. 18, 84).

3. However this may be, since you, my lord, approach the King more nearly than others, and you count for much in the transaction of his business, it is your duty to use all your influence with the King on behalf of your brethren, so that his anger should not be altogether inflamed. I declare to you that you have to do with a resolute man, powerful in speech and action, who will not readily be driven from his right. He enjoys great influence in that district. If there should be any dispute, many would side with him in his grievances. See, then, to it, that no one throws oil on the fire. Let the flame be extinguished before it has had time to light up a conflagration:

For it is too late to use a remedy when by long delays the disease has grown strong (Ovid, *de Remed. Amor.* 91, 92).

LETTER CCCXLIII.[1] (A.D. 1140.)

FROM ABBOT BERNARD, OF ITALY, TO POPE INNOCENT.

He complains that in the Abbey of S. Saviour all things are not as the Pope had promised.

To the dearly-beloved and longed-for father, INNOCENT, by the grace of God supreme Pontiff, his servant BERNARD sends greeting and the prayers of the poor.

I am in deep perplexity; for on the one side modesty requires me to be silent, and on the other necessity obliges me to speak. I shall speak, therefore, to my lord, I who am but dust and ashes; but I shall speak in the bitterness of my soul. I complain, my lord, of you, but it is to yourself; my complaint is made in strict secrecy, but the cause of my complaint is only too manifest. I did as you commanded; I came to the monastery of S. Saviour,[2] as you

---

[1] A new Letter; the former No. 343 is now No. 384.

[2] This monastery existed still in the time of Mabillon, about eight miles from the Abbey of Farfa, on which it depended. It served as a country house for the monks of Farfa, who retired there during the heats of summer. See Letter 184, and its Notes.

bade in your letter to your servant, our father.[1] What has become now of your promises and of my hopes? I have passed through fire and through water; and unless the Lord had helped me, the water would perhaps have swallowed me up. I have been afflicted by dangers of waters and of robbers, in cities, in solitude, on the land and in the sea; nor was there any to help me. All these things came upon me: nor was even then the end. By your letter, my lord, I was drawn from the bosom of my father, and, at your mere bidding, leaving my father and my brethren, I hastened to obey your will. By your letter I was torn from the bosom of my mother, and deprived of her consolations: driven forth from an abode of happiness; and that I might not return thither, you, my lord, have opposed to me a flaming sword, which turns every way. My crown has fallen from my head, and my songs of gladness have turned to lamentation. How could I, my lord, sing the Lord's song in a strange land? How much more sweetly and safely did my soul rejoice herself in the abode and bosom of my mother? Now, I so run as one in uncertainty; I so fight as one that beateth the air: but for this, my lord, your promise is to blame, which I believe to be full of grace and truth. But now, since the winter has departed and the bad season is over, if it shall please my lord, allow me to leave this place, and to seek where I may find rest for my feet: since hitherto snow and hail, ice and storms have prevented my so doing. It seems most cruel and most inhuman to deprive of his wish him[2] who loved me before he knew me, who has shown himself to me a father so tender that he would have torn out his own eyes and given them to me had it been possible. My King and my God, whose kingdom was not of this world, had not where to lay His head: would that the world would drive us out also and oblige us to wander in deserts, in mountains, in caves, and dens of the earth!

[1] S. Bernard.
[2] This was Atenulf, Abbot of Farfa, respecting whom see below.

LETTER CCCXLIV.[1] (A.D. 1140.)

From the Same Bernard to Saint Bernard.

He complains of the Prelature which had been forced upon him.

To the venerable lord and dearly-loved P—,[2] Abbot of Clairvaux, his son B— sends greeting, and prays that he may have the unction which teaches all things.

As often as I recall that day of misery and calamity, on which I was torn from your consoling bosom, I am more inclined to weep than to write anything. If the eloquence of my prayers equalled the abundance of my tears, I should easily be able to make you realize how miserable and deserted I am. When I apply my mind to reflecting upon it, and my hand to the pen, my grief is renewed. The extreme bitterness of my soul returns to me as I write; and I am troubled by the remembrance of that unhappy day, on which my foolish and unworthy self was placed in a position of eminence. I do not, my lord, blame your action, nor the motive of your action, which is believed to have been pointed out by the finger of God; but I lament a little the unhappiness of my lot. For, behold, after I was driven away from the sight of thine eyes, my life was worn away in grief, and my days in mourning. Woe is me! I have lost sight of the pattern on which I tried to fashion myself, the mirror of what I ought to be, the light of my eyes! No longer does that sweet voice sound in my ears, nor that kindly and pleasant face, which used to blush at my faults, appear before my eyes. Wherefore, my lord, has my hope been frustrated, and the desire of my heart denied me? My life has been cut off as the thread of an unfinished web,

---

[1] A new Letter; the former No. 344 is now No. 315.

[2] That is to say Father (*Pater*), namely, Bernard, for it appears clear that this Letter was written to S. Bernard, and by that Bernard who at a later period became Abbot of S. Anastasius at Aquæ Salviæ, near Rome, and at length Pope under the name of Eugenius III. The preceding Letter is also his, and likewise Letter 428. All these appeared at first under the name of S. Bernard.

and broken off short as a plant yet shooting up. That unhappy sentiment is fulfilled in me which you quoted upon the Song of Songs, and which I now read in the book of experience, *Man, being in honour, hath no understanding* (Ps. xlix. 12). For I did not sufficiently understand when I was in Clairvaux that I was in a place of happiness among the trees of Paradise, and therefore I held that Delectable Land as of no account. I ask of you, my lord, why you thought fit to determine this lot for me, why you set me as a leader and a teacher of others, and a chief over your people? Was it my career in the world? But that was foul. Was it my life in the cloister? But that was lukewarm and backward. Why, then, when I was little in mine own eyes, have I been made the head of a tribe in Israel? Wherefore, when I was not myself clean from secret sins, have you not spared to make your servant responsible for those of others? What can a man do whom sorrow for the past renders unhappy, the responsibilities of the present weigh down, and the thought of the future renders fearful? Overburdened with grief and affliction, I presume, my lord regretted and longed for, to say this to you alone, because my wound was received from a hand the least expected. But, my lord, to speak of this place to which you have sent me, I have run as if uncertainly, I have fought as if beating the air. For the lord Pope, on whose letter I was sent forth, has not yet fulfilled his promise to confirm the donation of this place, and what is taking place at this moment is a proof of this. The Lord Abbot of Farfa[1] welcomed me at my coming with great joy, and received your sons with the utmost gladness, so that, if it were possible, he would have plucked out his own eyes, and have given them to me. In this one respect alone is he to be blamed and corrected by you, that he goes only too far, exceeding not only his own promises, but even our wishes. As this letter is already so long, I am able to say nothing

[1] *Fars.*, but read *Farfensis*. This was Atenulf; he had asked for monks from S. Bernard. See *Life*, B. iii. c. 7, n. 23.

shorter, nothing truer about my inner life, than that I am wasting my time.[1]

LETTER CCCXLV.[2] (A.D. 1140.)

To the Brethren of S. Anastasius.

He commends their zeal in, and strict observance of, the Religious life. And yet he disapproves of their too great readiness to have recourse to the art of medicine in their maladies.

To my very dear sons in Christ, the monks of S. Anastasius, I, Brother BERNARD, called Abbot of Clairvaux, wish health, and give the assurance of my earnest prayers.

1. God in heaven is my witness how greatly I long after you all in the bowels of Jesus Christ; insomuch that I should have greatly desired to see you, if the thing had been possible, not only on your account, but also on my own. What a joy and solace it would be for me to embrace you, who are my own flesh and blood, my joy and my crown. But since that is not yet permitted to me (for I firmly trust that in the mercy of God it will be permitted, and that the day will come when I shall behold you, and my heart shall rejoice, and my joy no one shall take from me), in the meantime it is a great joy and consolation to me to receive the good report concerning you, which has come to me from my very dear brother and co-abbot, the venerable Bernard, your abbot. I congratulate you much on the satisfaction which is given to him by your love for the discipline and Rule of the Order, by your obedience and voluntary poverty, for which, without doubt, a rich reward is laid up for you in heaven. Wherefore I bid you, and earnestly entreat you, my dearly beloved brethren, so to persevere, and so to stand fast in the Lord, carefully keeping the observance of the Order, that the Order may keep you,

---

[1] *Lit. laterem lavo.* A proverbial saying used by Terence in the sense of *to waste* time.—[E.]

[2] Formerly No. 321; the former No. 345 is now No. 321.

carefully preserving the unity of the Spirit in the bond of peace (Eph. iv. 3), and having one for the other, and especially for your superiors, that humble charity which is the bond of perfection (Coloss. iii. 14). Follow humility before all things, and peace above all things, because of the Spirit of God who dwells in you, and who *rests only upon him who is of a peaceful and humble spirit* (Is. lxvi. 2).

2. But there is one thing, indeed, which your venerable father asks me about, which I can in no wise approve. And I believe also that I am right, and have the Spirit of God in the matter. I know, indeed, that the district in which you live is unhealthy, and that many of you labour under infirmities; but remember him who said: *I will even glory in my infirmities, that the power of Christ may dwell in me;* and, *When I am weak, then am I strong* (2 Cor. xii. 9, 10). I sympathize, therefore, really and truly with your infirmities of body; but what is much more to be feared and avoided is infirmities of soul. And it is not only not in agreement with your vow as religious to have recourse to medicines for the body, but it is not even really conducive to health.[1] It is certainly permitted to poor religious to make use sometimes of simples of little value; and this is frequently done. But to purchase drugs, to call in mediciners, and to take their potions and remedies, this is neither becoming to the rigour of our vow nor befits the honour and purity of our Order. For we know that *those who live in the flesh cannot please God* (Rom. viii. 8). *Spiritual things are to be compared with spiritual* (1 Cor.

[1] This doctrine seems somewhat strange to us; but, at least, this passage, compared with another in Serm. 50 *in Cantica*, ought to restrain monks, who profess to hold their flesh in hatred, from having recourse with too much eagerness to the medical art, but that they should rather follow the example of the ancient monks, who had recourse to the advice of medical men sometimes, but only to learn from them the means of regulating their food and manner of life (as we see in the *Life of Pachomius*, c. i., issued by Palemon). It is evident that the Cistercians allowed their religious to make use of medicines, from Letter 405, and from Herbert, B. iii., c. 15; nor does Bernard in this Letter deny it, but he wishes (those who could procure them) to content themselves with local herbs and productions of the garden, instead of drugs supplied by mediciners.

ii. 13), that our potion may be that of humility, and that we may cry with our whole heart: *Heal my soul, O Lord, for I have sinned against Thee* (Ps. xli. 4). This health, dearest brethren, do ye strive for; follow this, preserve this, for vain is the health given by men.

LETTER CCCXLVI.[1] (*Circa* A.D. 1141.)
To the Lord Pope Innocent.

He urges the Pope not to favour the cause of the Archbishop of York, as it was unjust.

To his very dear lord and father, INNOCENT, by the grace of God supreme Pontiff, BERNARD, called Abbot of Clairvaux, sends his humble duty.

Since *there are many called, but few chosen* (S. Matt. xx. 16), it is no great reason for putting faith in a doubtful matter, or thinking it praiseworthy, that it is praised by many people. The Archbishop of York, concerning whom I have often written to your Holiness, has come to you. He is a man who has not taken God for his helper, but has put his hope in the multitude of his riches. His cause is a weak and even a bad one, and, as I learn from persons worthy of belief, from the sole of its foot even to its head there is no soundness in it. What then? What does a man who is without a just cause expect to gain from him who watches over justice and protects equity? Does he suppose that he will be able to swallow up justice in the Curia, as he has done in England? He has swallowed up an ordinary stream and made nothing of it; and now flatters himself that he can take the river of Jordan also into his mouth. He has come accompanied by many, whom he has gained over by money or by entreaties. One alone has escaped to bring you word; one alone, at the peril of his life, stood fast as a wall for the house of Israel, nor did he worship the idol at the command of the King. He is alone, except that his righteousness bears him company; which escaped, as an

---

[1] Formerly No. 377; the former No. 346 is now No. 405.

honoured mother, with her son (Ecclus. xv. 2). What, then, will the Vicar of Peter do in this matter? Surely what Peter did with the man who thought that the gifts of God might be purchased with money (Acts viii. 20). If the Church has been founded upon a rock, the gates of hell shall not prevail against her (S. Matt. xvi. 18). I do not speak thus on my own account alone, but on the testimony of those who are moved by the Spirit of God.

LETTER CCCXLVII.[1] (*Circa* A.D. 1141.)

To the Same.

He recommends to the Pope the deputies of the Diocese of York, who are going to Rome on account of the matter of the Archbishop.

To his very dear lord and father, INNOCENT, supreme Pontiff, Brother BERNARD, called Abbot of Clairvaux, sends his humble duty.

These men whom you see before you are simple, honest, and God-fearing; it is the Spirit of God that sends them to the sight of your glory, and they have no other aim than to obtain justice. Cast your eyes, I pray you, upon these poor and wearied men,[2] who, not without cause, have come to you from far, not regarding the great distance by land, nor the peril of the sea; nor the snows of the Alps, nor the great cost of the journey, though they are poor. Let my lord then kindly see to it that neither the intrigue nor ambition of any one render such great fatigues useless; especially since they do not seek their own advantage, but those things which are of Jesus Christ. For not even an enemy, I suppose, can suspect them of being influenced in

[1] Formerly No. 378; the former No. 347 is now No. 391.

[2] Undoubtedly these were the Abbot and monks of Fountains, since they had shown themselves, like the monks of Rievaulx (of whom the two following Letters speak, also Nos. 353 and 360), extremely opposed to the intruded Bishop.

this matter by any private interest or by personal hatred, but only by the fear of God. Let, then, any one who is a servant of God, put himself on their side. If the barren tree shall encumber the ground any longer, to whom can I attach blame, except to him who holds the axe?

LETTER CCCXLVIII.[1] (A.D. 1141.)

To the Same.

On behalf of Arnulf, Bishop-elect of Lisieux.[2]

To his very dear father and lord, INNOCENT, by the grace of God supreme Pontiff, BERNARD, called Abbot of Clairvaux, sends his humble duty.

1. Blessed be God and the Father of our Lord Jesus Christ, Who has in our day preserved His Church, the spotless Spouse of His dear Son, free, and delivered her from grief and from the oppressions of the wicked. The schisms are extinct, the heresies have sunk into silence,[3] the necks of the proud and haughty are trodden under your feet. And, indeed, I have seen during the schism the head of the wicked lifted up, and lofty as the cedars of Libanus; yet, I passed by, and behold, he was not. During the heresy I saw a multitude of errors shooting up again, as it were, and flourishing, but the mouth of those speaking perverse things was stopped. The tyrant of Sicily[4] had lifted up his heart on high, and now is humbled under the mighty Hand of God; in short, there is none of any rank whatever over whom the Church of God by His mighty

---

[1] Formerly No. 388; the former No. 348 is now No. 407.

[2] Arnulph was Archdeacon of Séez, when he was elected in 1141 Bishop of Lisieux in Normandy; he was a learned man, and famous for the Letters which he wrote. Peter the Venerable also wrote to Innocent respecting his election (B. iv., Let. 7). This Letter of Bernard was first brought to light by John Picard, who placed it last, No. 367. Horst omitted it, but it has been recovered in *Spicil.* B. iii. Respecting Arnulph, see Let. 248.

[3] The reference is to the schisms of Anacletus and Victor, and the heresy of Peter Abaelard.

[4] Roger.

Hand and stretched-out Arm has not obtained the victory by your means.

2. Yet there remains still one adversary, the Count of Anjou, the Hammer of good men, and the enemy of peace, and of the liberty of the Church. He is persecuting the Church of Lisieux, in order that the Bishop of that Church shall not enter into the sheep-fold by the legitimate door, but in some other way. But what has been done cannot be undone. And furthermore, if the whole matter should be closely and carefully examined, it will be found that all has been done for the best, and that what has been done ought to be confirmed. All things concur to show this: the person chosen, the circumstances, he who has conducted it, and even the adversary who opposes it. For if you look to the person chosen, he is your dear son, in whom you are well pleased. If to the order of the proceedings, they have been carried out freely and canonically, and in proper order. If to the manager of them, he is a pious and God-fearing man. If to the adversary, behold he is a man who has not taken God for his help, but is hostile to the Church, and an enemy of the cross of Christ. Besides, in any affair in which it is doubtful which course to take, it is a most powerful reason for regarding a particular course as the better that it pleases the good and displeases the evil. But it is objected that the Count of Anjou has appealed to the Apostolic See. Wherefore, I pray you; what injury or loss has he to complain of? Far from being oppressed, it is he who is the oppressor; and it is not to relieve himself of an injustice that he has recourse to an appeal, but in order that by this means he may put an obstacle in the way of the consecration of the Bishop.

3. Since then in this matter not only the piety of him who has conducted it, but your affection for the person chosen, and the justice of his cause, combine to lead to the same conclusion, it seems superfluous and useless to make request on behalf of one whose humility has already had recourse to your authority. I will, however, who am but

dust and ashes, speak unto my Lord. Yes, I who am the humble servant of the Bride will speak unto the friends of the Bridegroom; let my discourse be welcome to Him. The Church, my lord, from the rising of the sun unto its setting, has been committed to your care. You ought, then, to be a wall and a rampart to her from the face of her enemy and persecutor. You ought to nourish her sons under the shadow of your wings. Sustain, therefore, the Bishop of Lisieux as a true son of the Roman Church, and send him back with the blessings of sweetness, so that his enemy may never say: I have prevailed against him. Gird on your sword, O Father, to raise up your son, to lay low the enemy, and to preserve the freedom of the Church. For we are not sons of the bond-woman, but of the free, and are sharers of the liberty wherewith Christ has made us free.

LETTER CCCXLIX.[1] (*Circa* A.D. 1141.)

To the Same.

He recommends a friend to the Pontiff.

To his very dear father and lord, INNOCENT, by the grace of God supreme Pontiff, Brother BERNARD, called Abbot of Clairvaux, sends his humble duty.

I am unwilling to enjoy alone the favour I have found in your eyes. I desire to share it with my friends. For I do not fear that there will not be enough both for me and for them. For it is so great that I am able to make a crowd of friends the sharers of it without fearing to find it empty when I shall come myself. What, therefore, I have freely received I will freely bestow, and your liberality makes me liberal with the gifts which you have given me. I recommend, then, to you the bearer of this letter, an estimable person. He is a friend, my lord, of the poor of Christ, and a servant of your servants. I entreat, my lord, that if

---

[1] Formerly No. 330; the former No. 349 is now No. 408.

he has any business with you, you will listen to him favourably, with your accustomed kindness, for my sake, or rather for his own, since he is so good a man as to deserve that he should obtain his petition because of his own merit.

LETTER CCCL.[1] (*Circa* A.D. 1141.)

TO THE SAME.

He asks for the Pope's blessing for one of his relatives.

The young man who will bring you this letter is reputed to be a brave and active soldier, and in order that he may perfect himself in actual warfare he is proceeding to Jerusalem. I, your son, entreat you at his request that in this good work which he is beginning he may have the benefit and the honour of your benediction and prayers. He is my relative, and, as the Prophet has said, I ought to take interest in those who are of my own flesh (Is. lviii. 7).

LETTER CCCLI.[2]

TO THE SAME.

He recommends certain poor persons.

I frequently write to you, and you receive letters and requests from me almost every day. I am placed under the dilemma of being either ungrateful to my friends or importunate towards you. My affection towards them incites me to write, but shamefacedness restrains me and modesty almost forbids me to discharge this duty of charity. But the Spouse of Christ has no asylum where she may lay her head or take refuge in the time of tribulation, except it be with the friend of her Bridegroom. These persons whom you see before you are poor, and sent as representatives of the poor. Through many dangers of land and sea

---

[1] Formerly No. 331; the former No. 350 is now No. 409.
[2] A new Letter; the former No. 351 is now No. 322.

they take refuge under the shadow of your wings, they resort to the rock of the Catholic faith and to the bosom of your apostolic piety since they are troubled in many things, and are free but in few from the tribulation and pain inflicted by the wicked. If you retain your ancient manner of acting and the office of your apostolate, you cannot bring yourself to desert the cause of the poor, nor to honour the countenance of the rich. I entreat you then, for these persons, for those by whom they are sent are my brethren and of our Order, so that you may incline the ear of your Piety to their prayers, in respect of their justice and for the love of Him who does not despise the prayers of the poor.

LETTER CCCLII.[1] (A.D. 1131.)

Privilege or Grant made by Pope Innocent II. to Saint Bernard.[2]

Innocent concedes very full privileges to Bernard and to the Cistercian Order on account of their great services to the Apostolic See.

Innocent, Bishop, and servant of the servants of God, to his beloved son Bernard, Abbot of Clairvaux, and to their successors regularly appointed for ever, etc.

To you, Abbot Bernard, my beloved son in the Lord, to your firm and indefatigable constancy, to the fervour of your piety, and the discretion which you displayed in defending the cause of S. Peter, and of the holy Roman Church your mother, when the schism of Peter Leonis was beginning; and to the zeal with which you opposed yourself as an impregnable bulwark before the house of God, and laboured to incline the minds of Kings and Princes, and of other persons both ecclesiastical and lay, by pressing arguments, made strong by reason, to the unity of the Catholic Church,

---

[1] A new Letter; the former No. 352 is now No. 389.

[2] It seems right that this *Privilegium* should find a place after the Letters of Bernard to Pope Innocent. It is to be found in *Spicilegium*, Vol. x. p. 383, in the History of the Abbey of Fontaines-Blanches, Diocese of Tours.

and the obedience of S. Peter, and of us; in great measure are due the happy condition in which the Church of God, and ourselves, are found.[1]

Wherefore, in order to give assent to your just wishes, we have fortified with the protection of the apostolical See the monastery of the Blessed Virgin Mary, Mother of God, over which, in the providence of God, you preside, with all the houses depending upon it. We ordain that all the possessions or goods whatsoever which it actually possesses justly and canonically at the present time, or in the future by the help of God shall possess, whether by the grant of Popes, or by the liberality of Kings or Princes, by the offerings of the faithful, or by any other just manner, shall remain firm and unimpaired to you and your successors. We forbid any Archbishop or Bishop to cite either you, or your successors, or any Abbot of the Cistercian Order, to any Council or Synod except for causes that concern the faith. And as the monastery of Cîteaux is the source and origin of this religious Order, let it deservedly enjoy this prerogative by our grant; that, whenever it shall be deprived of its own pastor, it may freely choose for itself any Abbot whatever, or monk, out of all the Abbeys of your Order, to preside over it, and may obtain the person chosen without any opposition. We grant to the other Abbeys of your Order which have one or more Abbeys dependent upon, or founded by them, the free power at the death of their own Abbot of choosing whomsoever they shall prefer from all the Abbeys under their obedience, or any monk whatever from all the Cistercian congregations. But those Abbeys which have no dependent houses may freely choose and have as their Abbot any monk out of all the congregations of the before-named Order. Further, let no Archbishop, Bishop, or Abbot presume to receive, or to retain, if received, any of your lay brothers (*conversos*) who are not monks, but who shall have made profession in any of your Houses, without your free consent. We ordain that no one presume to demand or receive of you tithes,

---
[1] These words are praised by Geoffrey. *Life*, B. iii. 22.

either on the lands which you and the brothers of your whole congregation cultivate with your own hands or at your own cost, or of the animals upon them. Let no one, therefore, etc.

The peace of our Lord Jesus Christ be upon those who preserve to the same place the things which belong to it; let them receive here below the recompense of that good action, and let them find before the tribunal of the Judge the rewards of eternal peace. Amen.

I, INNOCENT, Bishop of the Catholic Church.

I, MATTHEW, Bishop of Albano.

I, ROMANUS, Cardinal Deacon of S. Mary in Porticu.

I, JOHN, Cardinal Presbyter of S. Chrysogonus.

I, GREGORY, Cardinal Deacon of SS. Sergius and Bacchus.

Given at Lyons by the hand of HAIMERIC Cardinal Deacon and Chancellor of the holy Roman Church, the seventeenth February, indiction x., in the year of the Lord's Incarnation 1131, in the third year of the Pontificate of Pope Innocent II.

LETTER CCCLIII.[1] (*Circa* A.D. 1141.)

TO WILLIAM, ABBOT OF RIEVAULX.[2]

He warns William to bear with equanimity the unjust consecration of the Archbishop of York.

To his dear brother and co-Abbot, WILLIAM, Abbot of Rievaulx, Brother BERNARD of Clairvaux wishes the Spirit of counsel and strength.

I have heard what has been done about that Archbishop, and with the greatest regret. Knowing, therefore, your zeal, and fearing lest it might blaze up more than was proper, and not admit of wise moderation, which would be to the detriment of our Order, and to the harm of your

---

[1] Formerly No. 379; the former No. 353 is now No. 387.

[2] This was William, Abbot of Rievaulx, a Cistercian Abbey in the Diocese of York; it was he who was assisting S. Bernard, when the Letter to Robert (No. 1) was written to his dictation. About Rievaulx, see *Monast. Anglic.*, p. 727.

house, I have thought it proper to address to you some words of consolation; since when our own conscience does not accuse us of wrong, other evils may be borne with equanimity. I say it deliberately; neither the blame nor the sin belongs to you. You have resisted them as long as you were able; now, according to the judgment of S. Augustine, the wrong-doing of another cannot defile you, provided that you have not given assent to it in your heart, still less if you have protested against it with your mouth. For, he says; "Under two circumstances the wrong-doing of another does not defile you; if you do not consent, and if you protest."[1] Be therefore of good heart and do not be troubled. Respecting Ordination and other Sacraments, bear well in mind that He Who baptizes and He Who ordains is Christ the Lord, the Chief Bishop of our souls. But if any one is reluctant to receive Ordination from his hand, no one obliges you to [cause him to] be ordained. Yet I hold it to be quite certain that there is nothing to fear when the sacraments received are administered according to the rules of the Church. Otherwise, if we wished to avoid all evil men, though the Church bears with them, it would be needful to go out of the world. In conclusion, there will be no long delay in bringing the matter under the notice of the Pope, and what he orders or directs you will be able with a good conscience to hold and follow. In the meantime wait calmly and patiently.

LETTER CCCLIV.[2] (A.D. 1142.)

To Milisendis, Queen of Jerusalem, daughter of King Baldwin and wife of Fulk.

He advises the Queen how she ought to conduct herself now that her husband Fulk was dead.

To the most illustrious Queen of Jerusalem, M., BERNARD, Abbot of Clairvaux, wishes health, and that she may find grace in the sight of the Lord.

---

[1] Sermons on the Words of the Lord, No. lxxxviii., c. 18, n. 19.
[2] A new Letter; the former No. 354 is now No. 388.

If I looked only at your title of Queen, your power and your illustrious birth, it would seem to me that there was a certain unfitness in my writing to you, among the multiplied cares and business which trouble you in the midst of your Court. All these things are before the eyes of men, and those who are without them envy those who possess them, and think the man happy to whom they belong. But what blessedness is there in the possession of those things which are all destroyed, as it were, in a moment like the grass of the field, and fall in a moment like flowers? They are indeed pleasant, but their pleasantness alters; it is changeable, perishable, and temporary, because it is the pleasantness only of the flesh; and it is of the flesh and its good things that it is said, *All flesh is grass and the glory of it as the flower of grass* (Isaiah xl. 6). I ought not, therefore, to be withheld from writing to you by such things as those, since their favour is deceitful and their beauty vain. Receive, therefore, what I have in a few words to say: for although I might say much to you, yet I shall make my letter short, because of your many cares as well as mine. My counsels shall be short but salutary: deign to receive them from the distant land from whence they come, like a little seed which shall one day produce an abundant harvest. Receive, I say, advice from the hand of a friend, who seeks in offering it your honour only, and not any advantage of his own. You know that no one can be a more faithful counsellor than he who loves you alone, not the favours which he may receive from you. The King, your husband, is dead; the young King, your son, being still unable by his youth to bear the burden of the cares of State and to discharge the Royal office, the eyes of all are turned towards you, and upon you alone all the weight of government rests. You need, therefore, to put your hand to brave actions, and, though a woman, to show the spirit of a man; and to do those things which have to be done in the spirit of counsel and strength. It is of great consequence that you should take order for all things with such prudence and discretion that all who behold you may think you from your actions rather a King than a Queen. Let them not say among the nations: Where is the King of Jerusalem? But you will say: I am not sufficient for these things. For these are great matters, above my strength and my knowledge. These are the duties of a man, and I am but a woman, weak in body, changeable in heart, neither provident in counsel, nor accustomed to business. I know, my daughter, I know that these things are great, but I also know this, that although the waves of the sea are mighty, the Lord, who dwelleth on. High, is also mighty. These things are indeed great, but great is our Lord, and great is His power.

LETTER CCCLV.[1] (*Circa* A.D. 1142.)

TO THE SAME QUEEN.

He recommends to her some Religious of Prémontré, who were making pilgrimage to Jerusalem.

You see how greatly I presume on your goodness, since I venture to recommend others also to you. However, it would be as unnecessary as presumptuous perhaps for me to say much in commendation of these brethren of Prémontré, for they so commend themselves by their own merit that they have no need to be commended by another person. They will be found, if I mistake not, men of wisdom, fervent in spirit, patient in tribulation, powerful in word and work. They have put on the whole armour of God, and have girded themselves with the Sword of the Spirit, which is the Word of God, not against flesh and blood, but against Spiritual wickedness in high places. Receive them as warlike, and yet peaceful: gentle towards men, warlike only towards evil spirits. Rather, I should say, receive in them Christ Himself, who is the cause of their pilgrimage.

[1] Formerly No. 376; the former No. 355 is now No. 364.

LETTER CCCLVI.[1] (A.D. 1141.)
To Malachi, Archbishop of Ireland.[2]

He sends back to Malachi the Religious confided to him for training, and expresses regret that they are not as perfectly instructed and practised in the religious life as he could wish, on account of his many occupations.

To MALACHI, by the grace of God Bishop, and Legate of the apostolic See, Brother BERNARD, called Abbot of Clairvaux, wishes health and all the blessing that the prayer of a sinner (if it be of any avail) can venture to ask.

I have done what your Holiness directed, if not as well as I could have wished, yet as perfectly as was possible at this time. I am overwhelmed with affairs so numerous and difficult that I scarce know how I have been able to succeed in doing the little I have done. I send you only a few grains of seed, as you see, which may avail to sow a very small part of that field in which the true Isaac once went forth to meditate, when first Rebecca was led to him by the servant of Abraham his father, to be happily joined to him in an endless union (Gen. xxiv.), nor is that seed to be despised respecting which what was spoken in the time of our fathers is found to be fulfilled at this time in the midst of you. *If the Lord of Sabaoth had not left us a seed we should have been as Sodom and have been made like unto Gomorrah* (Isaiah i. 9). I then have sowed, let it be your duty to water, and God will give the increase. I salute through you all the saints which are among you, humbly commending myself to your prayers and to theirs. Farewell.

LETTER CCCLVII.[3] (A.D. 1142.)
To the Same.

He begs Malachi not only to continue his friendship for

---

[1] Formerly No. 216; the former No. 356 is now No. 369.

[2] Archbishop Usher, who gives this Letter as No. 43 in his Irish Letters, takes occasion to enter into many details about Mellifont and other Cistercian Monasteries of the same province.

[3] Formerly No. 317; the former No. 357 is now No. 370.

him, but to increase it; and he asks Malachi to give him proof of this by caring for and favouring the brethren he has sent.

To his very dear father and most reverend lord MALACHI, by the grace of God Bishop, Legate of the holy and apostolic See, the son of his Holiness Brother BERNARD, called Abbot of Clairvaux, wishes health, and sends the assurance of his humble prayers.

1. How sweet to me, lord and father, are your words! how pleasant the remembrance of your holiness! If I am capable of any feeling of affection, of devotedness, and of gratitude, it is due to the kindness of your feeling towards me. But there is no need of many words, where the feelings are strong; for I trust that the Spirit of God which is in you will bear witness with your spirit, that I am entirely devoted to you. You also, dear and longed for father, will not have forgotten the poor Religious, who is bound to you by bonds of charity, and whose soul bears you in everlasting remembrance. For I do not commend myself to you as if for the first time, since I now for a long time glory in the Lord, that my humble self has been favoured to find grace in the eyes of your Holiness; but I pray that your friendship, though not new, may increase daily. I commend to you my sons, or rather yours, the more earnestly as they are so far removed from me. You know how entire is my confidence in you, after God, since I sent them to you, as it seemed to me that it would be wrong not to yield to the request of your Holiness. Do that which seems good to you, only open to them the bowels of your kindness, and have a care of them. Let not your diligent solicitude grow cold on their behalf, nor the plantation perish which is the work of your right hand.

2. I have already learned both from your letter, and from the report of my brethren, that your house is in a prosperous state, and is multiplied both in temporal and spiritual things. I greatly congratulate you upon this, and render thanks with my whole heart both to God, and to your paternal solicitude. But as there is still need of much

vigilance, especially in a new country and among a population unaccustomed to a monastic form of religion, I entreat you in the Lord not to withdraw your hand, but to perfect happily what you have well begun. Concerning my brethren who have returned from that place, I should have been well pleased if they had remained; but it may be the case that those of your country whose characters are less disciplined, and who have shown a great repugnance for our observances, which were new to them, have been in great measure the reason for their return.

3. I have sent back to you Christian, my very dear son and yours, having instructed him as well as I could in all that concerns our Order, and I hope that he will be still more exact in observing them. Do not wonder that I have not sent any other brethren with him, since it is not easy to find fit persons who will willingly consent to go, nor was it my plan to oblige any to go against their will. My dear brother Robert[1] has acquiesced in my request for this time, like an obedient son. It will, therefore, be your part to render him all the assistance in your power, as well in buildings as in other things necessary, that the interests of your house may be promoted. I suggest to your Paternity, also, that you should persuade those religious, upon whom you are counting for the house you are about to found, to unite others with themselves by coming to their Order. That will be of the greatest advantage to the house, and you will be the better obeyed. May your Holiness continue in health, and be mindful of me before the Lord Christ.

[1] It is not quite clear who this Robert was. Perhaps he was the same as the holy man of that name, who is praised by Serlo in his "History of Fountains" (*Monast. Anglic.*, pp. 743 and 749). Formerly a monk at Whitby, he made common cause with the Religious, who left a monastery at York, and who are mentioned in Letter 95 and the following. Or it may have been Robert, the cousin of Bernard (Let. 1.)

LETTER CCCLVIII.[1] (A.D. 1142.)

To Pope Celestine.

He implores the assistance and influence of the Pope to obtain peace for Theobald, Count of Champagne.

That which Count Theobald asks of you I ask also; he is a son of peace, and we entreat you that it may be brought about by your assistance. Your Apostolate is one of peace; the position which you hold is a debtor to peace. All love peace, but few merit it. But it cannot be denied that your son is one of those who love peace; whether he merits it likewise it is for you to judge. And if neither he nor I merit it, the necessity of the Spouse of Christ, that is, the Church, requires it; and the friend of the Bridegroom will not distress her.[2] It belongs to the Apostolic See alone to extend its solicitude over all the Churches, that all may be united under it and in it; it is its duty, then, to be careful for all, to keep the unity of the Spirit in the bond of peace. Give us, then, this peace, send peace to us: if not to acquit yourself of an obligation towards us, at least because you ought to obey [the duty imposed upon you]. Enough for a command.

LETTER CCCLIX.[3] (A.D. 1143.)

The Community of Clairvaux to the Same Celestine.

They ask that the Abbot of Morimond may be forbidden to make a pilgrimage to Jerusalem.

To the sovereign Pontiff C., the little flock of Clairvaux offer the homage of a most devoted and humble obedience, and the assurance of their humble prayers.

---

[1] Formerly No. 374; the former No. 358 is now No. 376.

[2] After these words is added in the Vedastine Codex: *We have recommended and recommend Brother N., because he is to be commended.* The words of the same epistle which follow in that Codex begin a new line with this title, *To the Same*, as if it were another Letter. So says Edmund Martene (*Ampliss. Coll. Vet. Script. et Monum.*, p. 745).

[3] A new Letter; the former No. 359 is now No. 377.

Since we are happy to see you filling the place of Him who said that His daily charge was the care of all the Churches (2 Cor. xi. 28), notwithstanding that the ears of your piety are occupied with more important matters, our necessity obliges us to ask for a moment of your attention. Nor do we, though humble, fear that we shall be repulsed; He, too, will recompense you for listening to His poor, whom you will one day hear say respecting them, *That which ye have done unto one of the least of the brethren ye have done unto Me* (S. Matthew xxv. 40). For this is the cause, not of our community only, but of our entire Order. Certainly if your son, our superior and father, had been at home[1] at the time when this supplication is being addressed to you, he would either have come in person to your Majesty, or at least he would have written in his own name this deplorable complaint. But not to hold your charity longer in suspense, one of our brother Abbots, who is called of Morimond,[2] has had the levity to quit the monastery over which he presided under pretext of making the pilgrimage to Jerusalem, and it is said that it is his intention before he goes farther, to try to take your prudence by surprise, and to extort in some way from you the permission to do so. If you should give him any such license (which we trust will not happen) consider what disastrous consequences would follow to our Order; for by this example any Abbot who shall feel himself burdened by his pastoral charge will throw it off, since he will suppose that he may not unlawfully do so, especially among us, with whom the post of Superior is a great burden, but has not a great amount of honour. Furthermore, in order to complete the destruction of the house committed to his charge, he has taken with him the best and most exemplary of the brethren who were under him, among whom is one youth of good family, whom he had already (not without scandal) carried

---

[1] A gloss has crept into this passage to explain that "the Superior was then absent for some reason, and did not yet know what had happened."

[2] This was Raynauld, fourth Abbot after Abbot Arnold, who was the first Abbot, and who also abandoned his post (Let. 4). Raynauld had been Abbot fifteen years.

off from Cologne, as we believe you are aware, which scandal will be much increased by his carrying him off a second time. He will declare, perhaps, as we have heard, that he intends to observe in those countries all the rules of our Order, and that it is with this intention he has taken with him a certain number of Religious, but who does not perceive that in that land is more need of soldiers to fight than of monks to sing or pray? But our Order will receive the greatest detriment from this action of his: since it will be made easy for any Religious who takes it into his head to wander over the world, and he will have no scruple in pretending to undertake a pilgrimage to some country where he will be able to observe his Rule. We shall not be so presumptuous as to suggest what you will be pleased to do, or what order you will give in this matter, which we commit to your judgment.

LETTER CCCLX.[1] (A.D. 1143.)

To William, Abbot of Rievaulx.

He again exhorts William to resignation and patience.

To his very dear brother and co-Abbot, WILLIAM of Rievaulx, Brother BERNARD, called Abbot of Clairvaux, wishes health and the spirit of wisdom.

I have striven to the utmost of my power against the common evil, and if I have not succeeded in obtaining what I wished, yet the fruit of my labour remains with Him who suffers no good work to remain without recompense. This, then, is the true consolation of us and of all who strive for the truth, that there is laid up for us a crown of righteousness, which the righteous Judge shall bestow upon us in that day. Furthermore, I beg you now to bear in mind [what He has said], that if we suffer for righteousness sake happy are we, and that the wrong-doing of another person to which we have not consented, but have, on the contrary,

---

[1] Formerly No. 380; the former No. 360 is now No. 378.

protested against, cannot defile us. This, then, is our consolation, so that in our patience we must now possess our souls: and since we are unable to obtain help from men, let us hope for it from God, who will not despise those who hope in Him. For I trust in the mercy of our Heavenly Father, that every plant which He has not planted shall be plucked up, and that He will wither up with His malediction the barren fig tree, so that it shall not occupy the ground any longer. I beg and entreat, therefore, of you, my brother, to calm yourself, and not to trouble the flock which has been committed by God to your charge, but rather console yourself and strive bravely to serve the Lord in holiness, and He will deliver us from our enemies. I, however, have striven as far as I could to influence the Lord Bishop of Frascati,[1] who is charged with the functions of Legate in those parts, and he has faithfully promised me that if nothing better can be done for us, this, at least, he will observe, that under no circumstances will he deliver the pallium which he bears to the Archbishop if the Dean[2] (who is now become Bishop) shall not have made the statement on oath upon which the whole case depends; but that he will refer the cause to the Pope for decision.

LETTER CCCLXI.[3] (*Circa* A.D. 1144.)

To Archbishop Theobald,[4] on behalf of John of Salisbury.

Bernard, confiding in the friendship of Theobald, recommends John to him.

Nothing does me more honour or makes me more grateful to you than to see that my friends find favour in

---

[1] This was Ymar, who was Legate in England in the year 1143, in which this Letter was written. It was to him that Letters 219 and 230 were written.

[2] This was William of Sainte-Barbe, who from being Dean of York became Bishop of Durham (see Letter 235).

[3] Formerly No. 383; the former No. 361 is now No. 379.

[4] Theobald became Archbishop of Canterbury after having been a monk at Bec. Mention is made of him in Letter 238.

your eyes for my sake. Yet I seek not glory from man, but the Kingdom of God and His righteousness. Thus it is that I send to your Highness the bearer of this letter, John,[1] who is my friend and the friend of my friends, and I venture to ask for him the goodness and kindness which I feel assured you have for me, since I have always experienced it from you. For he has the testimony of all good men that he is very meritorious as well for his virtue as his knowledge. Nor have I learned this from those who use words rashly, but from my own sons, whose witness is for me as certain as if I had seen it with my own eyes. I had already recommended him to you in person, but now being absent from you, I recommend him so much the more earnestly and confidently, because I have learned from trustworthy witnesses how blameless are the life and character of the man. If, then, I have any interest with you, or rather because I believe that I have much, make for him some provision upon which he may sufficiently and honourably live, and deign to do this without delay, because he knows not whither to turn. In the meantime be so kind as to provide for his needs, and let me thus experience, my very dear father, the affection which you retain in your heart for me.

LETTER CCCLXII.[2] (A.D. 1145.)

To Robert Pullen,[3] Cardinal and Chancellor.

Bernard entreats him to show himself an efficient helper to Pope Eugenius, then recently elected, in the government of the Church.

[1] He was originally from Salisbury, and was an intimate friend of S. Thomas (Becket), Archbishop of Canterbury, to whom he attributed his obtaining the Bishopric of Chartres, as is shown by the commencement of most of his letters: " John, by the grace of God and the merits of the blessed martyr, Thomas, the humble minister of the Church of Chartres " (*Spicileg.* V. x. p. 391, where the word " merits " is omitted).

[2] Formerly No. 334; the former No. 362 is now No. 380.

[3] Otherwise *To the Chancellor Roland.* But the Cistercian MS. has *To Robert Pullen*, and I think more correctly: for, in the first place, Robert united with

LETTER CCCLXII.

To his lord and very dear friend ROBERT, by the grace of God Cardinal-Presbyter and Chancellor of the holy Roman Church, Brother BERNARD, called Abbot of Clairvaux, health and the assurance of his prayers.

1. I have received your letter with so much the greater pleasure that I hold you always in kindly remembrance. I can assure you that you have no need of letters of introduction to me, or of the praises of anyone, since it is a thing without doubt, in my mind, that the Spirit of truth testifies how sincerely I love you, and that I am loved by you; that Spirit, I say, by whom charity is spread abroad in our hearts. Blessed be God who according to His mercy has prevented our, or rather His, Eugenius with the blessings of sweetness, preparing a lantern for His Anointed; and has also sent before him a faithful man to be his helper, which is to me also a very great consolation. For when the vocation of my friend and his separation from his friend in whom he delighted in the Lord was a trouble to him, then the Lord, as I perceive plainly at this time, had thoughts of peace, and not of affliction, towards him, and was saying, *What I do thou knowest not now, but thou shalt know hereafter* (S. John xiii. 7). Wherefore be thou careful, my dear friend, for him to whom God has ordered that you should be a consoler and a counsellor; and watch carefully, according to the wisdom given to you, that he may not, through the multiplicity of affairs, fall into the snares of unworthy people, and be led into some decision unworthy of the apostolate of Eugenius.

2. Show yourself, therefore, my dear friend, what you ought to be in the post which you occupy, and in the high rank to which you have attained; employ bravely and prudently the zeal which is in you for God, to His glory,

S. Bernard in long and intimate friendship (Letter 205, to the Bishop of Rochester). Then he was a man remarkable for his learning, and this suits no one so well as Robert, who taught at Paris, and also with much success at Oxford. He is said to have been sent before as Chancellor, before the Pontificate of Eugenius, and to his help. All these particulars suit him much better than Roland, who was not made Chancellor until the eighth year of Eugenius (see notes to Letter 205). The doubt arises from the name being written only as R.

to your own salvation, and to the great good of the Church, so that you too may be able to say, *the grace of God which was in me was not in vain* (1 Cor. xv. 10). Up to this day you have lavished your learning faithfully and with great use upon a number of objects, as heaven and earth bear witness; but now the time is come to labour for God, and to employ all your powers to hinder the setting aside of His law by the wicked. Study, therefore, O Father, dearly-beloved and longed for, to be found a faithful and prudent servant of the Lord, even in this post which is committed to you; as far as regards yourself, show the simplicity of the dove, and for the Church, the spouse of the Lord, which is now entrusted to your care and faithfulness, show the wisdom of the serpent, so as to preserve her from the envenomed snares of the old malignant serpent, that thus in each of your virtues God may be glorified. I should have many things still to say to you; but there is no need of a long letter where the living voice is at hand. Wherefore, sparing your many occupations, as well as my own, I have put my words in the mouth of the brethren which are present before you; listen to them as to myself. Farewell.

LETTER CCCLXIII.[1] (A.D. 1146.)
To the Clergy and People of Eastern France.

Bernard exhorts them to take arms against the Infidels in defence of the Church in the East. In opposition to the incendiary appeals of a certain Religious, he tells them that the Jews are not to be persecuted, much less put to death.

To the lords and very dear fathers, the Archbishops and Bishops, with the whole Clergy and the faithful people of Eastern France and Bavaria, BERNARD, called Abbot of Clairvaux, desires that they may abound in the Spirit of strength.[2]

[1] Formerly No. 322; the former No. 363 is now No. 371.
[2] The inscription of this Letter in all editions which have hitherto appeared seems to me (it is Horst who speaks) far too narrow in respect of Bernard's

1. I write to you with respect to a matter which concerns the service of Christ, in whom is our salvation. This I say in order that the Lord's authority may excuse the unworthiness of the person who speaks; let the consideration of its usefulness to yourselves also excuse the faults of my address. I am, indeed, of small account; but I have no small love for you all in the bowels of Jesus Christ. This, now, is my reason for writing to you, that I may thus approach you as a whole. I would rather do so by word of mouth, if as well as the will the opportunity were afforded me. Behold, brethren, now is the acceptable time, now is the day of salvation. The earth also is moved and has trembled, because the God of heaven has begun to destroy the land which is His. His, I say, in which the Word of the Father evidently taught, and for more than thirty years dwelt a man among men. His, for He enlightened it with miracles, He consecrated it with His own blood; in it appeared the first fruits of His Resurrection. And now, for our sins, the enemies of the Cross have raised blaspheming heads; ravaging with the edge of the sword the land of promise. For they are almost on the point, if there be not One to withstand them, of bursting into the very city of the living God, of overturning the sanctuaries of our redemption, of polluting the holy places of the spotless Lamb with purple blood. Alas! they rage against the very shrine of the Christian Faith with blasphemous mouths, and would enter and trample down the very couch on which for us our Life lay down to sleep in death.

2. What are you doing then, O brave men? What are

purpose in writing it. Therefore I supply another and a fuller one, which is given by Otto of Frisingen (*de Gestis Frider.* i. 41). But I have since found the same Letter, not only on the same subject, but also in the same words, only with a different superscription, addressed to different nations, provinces, and cities. For I find in a MS. sent to me from England one inscribed *To the English People.* Edmund Martene (*Ampliss. Collect. Vet. Scriptor.* p. 745) says: "Ep. 363 in a MS. at S. James at Liège has this title: ' *Hanc Epistolam B. Bernardus abbas Claræ-Vallensis jam in extremis positus dictavit ad gentem Anglorum.*' " Baronius gives it, with only a few words changed, under the superscription: "To Manfred, Bishop of Brixen, and to the magistrates, knights, and all the people under his rule" (*Ad ann.* 1146, n. 15).

you doing, O servants of the Cross? Will you give what is holy to the dogs, and cast your pearls to swine? How many sinners there, confessing their sins with tears, have obtained pardon, after the defilement of the heathen has been purged by the swords of your fathers! The wicked man sees and is grieved, he gnashes with his teeth, and consumes away. He prepares the instruments of sin, and will leave no sign or trace of so great piety, if ever (which God forbid) he gain possession of this holiest of holy places. Verily that would be an irremediable grief to all time—because an irrecoverable loss, a vast disgrace to this most graceless generation, and an everlasting shame.

3. What are we then to think, brethren? Is the Lord's arm shortened so that it cannot save, because He calls His weak creatures to guard and restore His heritage? Can He not send more than twelve legions of angels, or just speak the word, and the land shall be set free? It is altogether in His power to effect, when he wishes; but I tell you, the Lord your God is trying you. He looks upon the sons of men, to see if there be any to understand, and seek, and bewail His error. For the Lord hath pity upon His people, and provides a sure remedy for those that are afflicted.

4. Think what care He uses for your salvation, and wonder; behold the abyss of His love, and trust Him, O ye sinners. He wills not your death, but that you may turn and live; for now he seeks occasion, not against you, but for your benefit. What opportunity of salvation has God not tried and sought out, when the Almighty deigns to summon to His service murderers, robbers, adulterers, perjurers, and those guilty of other crimes, as if they were a people that dealt righteously? Doubt Him not, O sinners; God is kind. If He willed to punish you, He not only would not seek your service, but would not accept it when offered. Again I say, weigh the riches of the goodness of the Highest God, hear his plan of mercy. He makes or feigns a need for Himself, while He desires to help your necessity. He wills to be held a debtor, that He may give

pay to those that fight for Him, pardon of sins, and everlasting glory. Therefore I may call it a highly-favoured generation, which has happened upon a time so full of indulgence, upon which has come that acceptable year of the Lord, a very jubilee. For this blessing is spread over the whole world, and all fly eagerly to the sign of life.[1]

5. Since, therefore, your land is fruitful in brave men, and is known to be full of robust youth, your praise is in the whole world, and the fame of your valour has filled the entire earth; gird up your loins, therefore, manfully, and take up arms prevailingly in zeal for the Christian name. Let not your former warlike skill cease, but that spirit of hatred, in which you are accustomed to strike down and kill one another, and in turn be overcome yourselves. How dire a madness goads those wretched men, when kinsmen strike each other's bodies with the sword, perchance causing the soul also to perish? But he does not escape who triumphs; the sword shall go through his own soul also, when he rejoices at having slain his enemy only. To enter such a combat is madness, not valour: not to be ascribed to bravery, but rather to foolishness. Now, O brave Knight, now, O warlike hero, you have a battle you may fight without danger: where it is glory to conquer, and gain to die. If you are a prudent merchant, if you are a desirer of this world: I show you some great bargains, see you lose them not. Take the sign of the Cross, and you shall gain pardon for every sin that you confess with contrite heart. The material itself being bought is worth little: if it be placed on a devout shoulder, it is without doubt worth no less than the kingdom of God. Therefore they have done well who have already taken the heavenly sign: well and wisely also will do the rest, if they hasten to lay upon their shoulders, like the first, the sign of salvation.

6. Besides, brethren, I warn you, and not only I, but

---

[1] That is, the sign of the Cross: as in n. 5, where an indulgence is granted to those who have taken the Cross, for all sins which they have confessed with a penitent heart. See Letter 423.

God's Apostle, *Believe not every spirit* (1 S. John iv. 1). We have heard and rejoice that the zeal of God abounds in you, but it behoves no mind to be wanting in wisdom. The Jews must not be persecuted, slaughtered, nor even driven out.[1] Inquire of the pages of Holy Writ. I know what is written in the Psalms as prophecy about the Jews, *God hath shown me,* says the Church, *thou shalt not slay my enemies, neither shall my people be ever forgotten.* They are living signs to us, representing the Lord's Passion. For this reason they are dispersed into all regions, that now they may pay the just penalty of so great a crime, that they may be witnesses of our redemption. Wherefore the Church, speaking in the same Psalm, says, *Scatter them in thy strength, and cast them down, O Lord my Protector* (Ps. lix. 11). So has it been. They have been dispersed, cast down. They undergo a hard captivity under Christian princes. Yet they shall be converted at evening-time, and remembrance of them shall be made in due season. Finally, when the multitude of the Gentiles shall have entered in, *then all Israel shall be saved* (Rom. xi. 25), saith the Apostle. Meanwhile, he who dies remains in death.

7. I do not enlarge on the lamentable fact that where there are no Jews, there Christian men judaize even worse than they in extorting usury, if, indeed, we may call them Christians, and not rather baptized Jews. If the Jews be utterly trampled down, how shall the promised salvation or conversion profit them in the end? Evidently if their salvation is to be waited for equally with that of the Gentiles the latter also should rather be preserved than attacked with the sword. But now when they begin to be violent against us, it behoves them to repel force with force who bear not the sword in vain. It is the part of Christian piety as much to overthrow the proud as to spare the conquered, those especially whose kingdom is yet promised, of whom came

---

[1] Bernard here speaks rightly and religiously, and that with far more reason than if they were Gentiles, because the Jews, living, are striking representatives of the Lord's Passion, and witnesses of Holy Writ; but not so the Gentiles. See Letter 364, Sermon 64, *in Cantica,* and *Liber ad Milites Templi,* c. 10.

the patriarchs, and of whom was Christ after the flesh, who is blessed for ever. Yet we must require of them according to the apostolic command, that they should set free from the bond of usury all who have taken the sign of the cross.

8. This also we must warn you, dearest brethren, that if any love to bear rule among you, and wish by hastening to anticipate the army of his country, that he by no means attempt to do it. If he pretend to have been sent by us, it is not true; or if he show letters as if given by us they are altogether false, I warn you, or obtained by fraud. It is the part of such to choose warlike and skilful leaders, and for the army of the Lord to set out together, that it may have strength everywhere, and not be able to sustain injury from any. There was in a former expedition, before Jerusalem was taken, a certain man, Peter by name,[1] of whom you (unless I mistake) have often heard mention. He went alone at the head of a mass of people who had entrusted themselves to his care, and led them into so great dangers that none, or at least very few, escaped dying by hunger or the sword. So there is fear lest, if you do likewise, the same fate should overtake you also, which may God, who is blessed for ever, avert from you. Amen.

LETTER CCCLXIV.[2] (A.D. 1146.)
To Peter, Abbot of Cluny.

He invites Peter to attend a meeting at Chartres in order to consult as to rendering help to the Church in the East.

To his very dear father PETER, by the grace of God the venerable Abbot of Cluny, Brother BERNARD, of Clairvaux, wishes health, and sends the assurance of his humble prayers.

---

[1] This celebrated Peter was known as the Hermit. We find a person of that name mentioned as Prior of Mont S. Quintin, near Peronne, in the *Necrology of Corbey*. There is much respecting Peter in William of Tyre, *History of the Crusade*, B. i., and James à Vitry, *Hist. Occidental.* c. 17.

[2] Formerly No. 355; the former No. 364 is now No. 381.

1. I imagine that the sad and lamentable groanings of the Church in the East have not failed to come to your ears, yes, even to the bottom of your heart. It becomes you, in the high post which you occupy, to show a sincere feeling of compassion for that Church, the common mother of all, in the sad state to which it is reduced, and in the great difficulties by which it is surrounded. The more elevated, I repeat, is the position which you hold, the more you ought to be consumed with an earnest zeal for the House of God. Otherwise, if we harden our hearts and affections at the sight of such misfortunes; where is our love towards God, or our charity towards our neighbours? If, then, we do not exert ourselves with all the earnestness in our power to find and supply a remedy to such great evils and dangers, how ungrateful should we not be shown to be to God, who shelters us in His tabernacle in the day of evil? and should we not merit to be punished the more severely, that we had shown ourselves neglectful both of God's glory, and of the salvation of our brethren? These considerations I have been led to suggest thus confidently and plainly, on account of the kindness with which your Excellence has deigned to honour my unworthiness.

2. Our fathers, then, the Bishops of France, with our lord the King and his nobles, have determined to meet on the third Sunday after Easter at the city of Chartres[1] in order to take counsel together about this great affair: and I trust that we may be favoured with your presence there also. For the advice of all the more eminent men is needed: and you will render a service not unacceptable to God, if you do not hold back from this business, but approve your zeal in a season so opportune, in a time of tribulation. For you know, dear father, that a friend is proved in time of adversity. I am convinced that your

[1] It was in this assembly that Bernard was chosen general in chief of the expedition, a title which he refused as being incompatible with his monastic profession and entirely foreign to his character (Let. 256 *ad Eugen.* n. 4). Letter 363, and the Letters of Suger, of which No. 133 is from Peter the Venerable, excusing himself from attending the meeting at Chartres on account of a General Chapter to be held at Cluny on the same day.

presence will be of great advantage to this expedition, as well because of the influence belonging to the holy Abbey of Cluny, over which, in God's Providence, you preside, as because of the wisdom and popularity which has been bestowed upon you for the honour of God and the good of your neighbours. May He deign to influence your mind, not to hesitate to come, and to give the advantage of your presence to His servants gathered in His name, and for zeal in His service.

LETTER CCCLXV.[1] (A.D. 1146.)

To Henry, Archbishop of Mayence.

He blames a monk named Ralph, who was instigating the faithful to the massacre of the Jews.

To the venerable lord and very dear father HENRY, Archbishop of Mayence, BERNARD, Abbot of Clairvaux, wishes health, and that he may find favour with God.

1. I have received your esteemed letter with the deep respect due to it; but my reply must be brief, on account of the multiplicity of business with which I am burdened. The confiding of your complaint to me is a sign and pledge of your affection, and a proof of your extreme humility. For who am I, and what is my father's house, that an Archbishop should refer to me a contempt of his authority and an injury to his metropolitan See? For am I not as a young child, not knowing how to come in and go out? But yet I am not ignorant of those words full of truth which proceed from the mouth of the Highest: *It is impossible but that offences come, but woe to him from whom they come* (S. Matt. xviii. 7). He[2] of whom you speak in your letter has received a

---

[1] Formerly No. 323; the former No. 365 is now No. 396.

[2] Ralph. Martene, *Ampliss. Collect. Vet. Scriptor.* p. 744. This Ralph or Rolf is described by Otto of Frisingen, *de Gestis Frider.* B. i. c. 37, as the author of a bloody persecution against the Jews. His seditious doctrines were resisted by Bernard, and he warned Ralph himself, who was then in extreme favour with the people of Mayence, not to violate all monastic rules by his wandering life, nor yet to assume the functions of a preacher by his own authority. Bernard brought him at length, by virtue of his vow of obedience, to retire to his

mission neither from men, nor through men, and certainly not from God. If he boasts that he is a monk and a hermit, and that therefore he has full power even to take the office of a preacher, let him learn what he ought to know, that the office of a Religious is that of penitence, not of preaching,[1] and that for a true Religious, towns are prisons and solitude a Paradise. It is not so with the man in question, for him it is solitude which is a prison and a town a Paradise. O man without feeling or modesty! whose foolishness has been placed, as it were, on a candlestick so that it may plainly appear to all in the house.

2. There are three things in him most worthy of blame: his usurpation of the right to preach, his contempt of the authority of the Bishop, and finally his inciting to murder. What new power is this? Do you suppose yourself greater than our father Abraham (Gen. xxii.), who laid down his sword at the bidding of him at whose command he had taken it up? Are you greater than the Prince of the Apostles who inquired of the Lord, *Lord, shall we strike with the sword?* (S. Luke xxii. 49). If you were instructed in all the wisdom of the Egyptians, that is the wisdom of this world which is foolishness towards God (1 Cor. iii. 19), and you reply to the question of Peter in a different manner than He did who said to Peter: Put up again thy sword into its sheath, for he who takes the sword shall perish by the sword (S. Matt. xxvi. 52). Does not the Church triumph a hundred times better over the Jews in convincing them every day of their error and in converting them to the faith, than if it were to exterminate them once for all by the edge of the sword? Does the Church universal from the rising of the sun even to its setting put up to God to no purpose that universal petition on behalf of the unbelieving Jews that our Lord God would take away the veil from their hearts and enable them to pass out of darkness into the light of truth? It would seem useless

monastery, much to the indignation of the people, who, if they had not been restrained by S. Bernard's reputation for sanctity, would have certainly risen in sedition against the loss of their favourite.—*Ibid.* c. 39.

[1] S. Jerome. *adv. Vigilant.* c. 6. See notes to Letter 89.

and vain to pray for them if she had not hope that though now without faith they will one day believe. But she understands with a pious insight that the Lord who renders good for evil and love for hatred has a purpose of grace towards them. Where is then that which is spoken, *See that thou slay them not* (Ps. lix. 11). Or this: *When the fulness of the Gentiles shall have come in then shall all Israel be saved* (Rom. xi. 25, 26). Or this: *The Lord doth build up Jerusalem and will gather together the outcasts of Israel?* (Ps. cxlvii. 2). Are you not the man who will make the Prophets liars and will render empty and useless all the treasures of the piety and mercy of Jesus Christ? Your doctrine is not yours, but that of your father who sent you. It is not surprising if you are as your master: *for he was a murderer from the beginning, a liar and the father of falsehood* (S. John viii. 44). O frightful knowledge; O infernal wisdom contrary to the Prophets, hostile to the Apostles, a subversion of piety and grace! O unclean heresy, sacrilegious deceiver, filled with the spirit of falsehood, which hath conceived sorrow and brought forth ungodliness (Ps. vii. 15). I would wish, but fear, to say more. In conclusion, to sum up briefly all that I think upon these matters: the man is great in his own eyes, full of the spirit of arrogance. His words and his actions reveal that he is striving to make a name for himself among the great of the earth, but he has not the means to succeed in his object. Farewell.

LETTER CCCLXVI.[1] (A.D. 1146.)

To the Abbess Hildegarde.[2]

He modestly rejects her praises: he warns her to recognise what she owes to the Grace of God: and begs her prayers for him and for his brethren.

[1] Formerly No. 386; the former No. 366 is now No. 410.

[2] She was the Abbess of the Monastery of Mont S. Rupert, near Bingen, in the Diocese of Mayence, and was celebrated for her prophetical utterances. Among the Letters of hers which are preserved in the *Bibliotheca Patrum*, there is one in

To his beloved daughter in Christ, HILDEGARDE, Brother BERNARD, called Abbot of Clairvaux, wishes health and all that the prayer of a sinner can obtain.

It seems to me that certain persons think very differently of so humble a person as myself, from that which my own conscience knows to be true: and that it is to be attributed not to my merits, but to the simplicity of mankind. Yet I hasten to reply to the sweet and charitable letter which you have had the goodness to write to me, although the number of my occupations obliges me to do so more briefly than I could wish. I congratulate you on the Grace of God which is in you, and kindly warn you to be careful to respond to it in a disposition of entire humility and devotion in order that you may retain this grace, knowing that *God resisteth the proud and giveth grace to the humble* (S. James iv. 6). That is the advice which I give to you, as far as in me lies, and the prayer that I make for you. But what am I to be able either to teach, or to give warning, to one in whom is the secret intuition and the anointing which teaches all things. For you are said to be so favoured as that the hidden things of Heaven are revealed to you, and that the Holy Spirit makes known to you those things which pass man's understanding. Wherefore I rather entreat and humbly pray that you would make remembrance of me before God, and of those who are joined with me in spiritual society. For I trust that when you are united to God in the Spirit, you will be able to help and profit us much. For *the fervent prayer of a righteous person availeth much* (S. James v. 16). As for me, I pray for you continually, that you may be strengthened in good, that your soul may be perfected, and you may be enabled to attain unto eternal joys: so that those who have put their hope in God may not be led to despair by seeing your failure: but may be, on the contrary, strengthened in good, and may

---

which she congratulates Bernard on the zeal which he had displayed in the preaching of the Crusade, and says that she "had seen him as it were a man in the sun two years before." John of Salisbury asks Magister Girard for some account of her visions, and says that she was very acceptable to Pope Eugenius.

progress from one degree of good to another, by beholding the blessings and graces which you have received from God.

LETTER CCCLXVII.[1] (*Circa* A.D. 1147.)
To the Chancellor G.

Bernard recommends to him the Bishop of Metz.

Your predecessor, the Chancellor Haimeric of good memory, held the Lord Bishop of Metz[2] in special affection; and as often as he sent messengers to Rome received them with great kindness and assisted them as much as he could. Wherefore I beg you to be so kind as to walk in his footsteps, and to assist with the arms of the Church that noble Bishop, who is placed in a position of great difficulty.

LETTER CCCLXVIII.[3] (*Circa* A.D. 1147.)
To the Cardinal-Deacon G.

Bernard gratefully thanks him for his affectionate letter, and the presents sent to him, and dissuades him from the love of riches and of earthly things.

To his lord and very dear friend G., by the grace of God Cardinal-Deacon in the holy Roman Church, Brother BERNARD, called Abbot of Clairvaux, health and the assurance of his devoted prayers.

1. I thank you in the Lord for having prevented me so liberally with the blessings of sweetness, and if there be any bowels of mercy, any affection or charity in me, the kindly humility and unaffected kindness of the mind of one so illustrious fully deserves it from me. For I knew already, and rejoiced over the earnest zeal in you, of which I had heard from my brethren; but now I feel myself so much

---

[1] Formerly No. 332; the former No. 367 is now No. 419.

[2] This was Guy Moricot de Vico, born at Pisa, who became Chancellor of the Roman Curia after Robert Pullen, in 1146. See Notes on Letter 334.

[3] Formerly No. 335; the former No. 368 is now No. 420.

more indebted to you for the affection so humble and
devoted with which you have commended yourself to so
humble a person as I. I would wish, indeed, to be sufficiently powerful with God to acquit myself of my obligation
to you. Wherefore I was anxious also to read to my
brethren the letter in which your heart is fully displayed—
a letter filled with devoted affection, with piety and grace ;
to show them also the blessing[1] which you had given to us,
and to direct as you had ordered, that the Holy Mysteries
of the Mass, should be celebrated in those very vessels, for
the memory of you and yours. May God make of you a
vessel to honour in His great house [which is His Church],
so that it may be our happiness to hear one day *He is for
me a vessel of election* (Acts ix. 15). This is our most
earnest prayer. For the Spirit of Truth is our witness, by
whom also *the love of God is spread abroad in our hearts*
(Romans v. 5), how greatly we long for you in the bowels
of Jesus Christ.

2. As it is in God alone that I feel for you the affection with
which my heart is full, not only is my intercession on your
behalf directed to this, but I wish you to pray for yourself
that you may perceive carefully how you ought to behave
yourself in the House of God, and to discharge the functions
of your ministry. For I say this, not of presumption, God
knows, but of charity, since *the judgment is severe upon
those who bear rule if they do not labour to rule profitably*
(Wisdom vi. 5) ; and, on the contrary, he who has ministered well shall *gain a good degree* (1 Tim. iii. 13). Do
you, then, my lord, dearly-beloved and longed for, study,
I beseech you, to avoid evil and to do good more and more ;
let no one see you seeking your own advantage in the
heritage of Christ, but be always mindful of the words of
the Apostle, *We have brought nothing into the world, and
it is certain that we can carry nothing out* (1 Tim. vi. 7).
Wherefore guard well your soul, since that is your im-

---

[1] *I.e.*, the gift of sacred vessels which Guy destined for the celebration of the
Holy Mysteries at Clairvaux. We shall see below that they were certainly of
gold or of silver.

mortal part. Let it not be able by any temptation to be torn away from, or uprooted from that disposition of which the Lord speaks in the Gospel: *What shall it profit a man if he shall gain the whole world and lose his own soul? or what shall a man give in exchange for his soul?* (S. Matt. xvi. 26). Unhappy, unspeakably unhappy, are they who spend all their lives in the enjoyment of their good things, so as to fall in an instant into the depths of hell! (Job xxi. 13). *They will carry away nothing of all that they possess when they perish, neither shall their glory descend with them* (Ps. xlix. 17); it is but a vapour, appearing for a moment (S. James iv. 15). Think of these things, my dear friend; meditate seriously upon them; grave them upon your heart, nor let them ever depart from your memory. Farewell.

LETTER CCCLXIX.[1] (*Circa* A.D. 1147.)

To Abbot Suger.

He congratulates Suger on the reformation of the Abbey of Ste. Geneviève, happily set on foot, and urges him to persevere in his undertaking.

To his very dear father and lord SUGER, by the grace of God the venerable Abbot of S. Denys, Brother BERNARD, of Clairvaux, health and the assurance of his prayers.

Blessed be God who by your hands has re-established the salutary reign of rule and discipline[2] in the Abbey of Ste. Geneviève. The Apostolic authority itself thanks you because you have set about a great work faithfully and effectually. I, too, with all those who love the Lord in truth, render to you such thanks as we can. I beg and earnestly entreat your Greatness that, according to the tenor of the Pope's letter, you would cause the work to proceed

---

[1] Formerly No. 356; the former No. 369 is now No. 338.
[2] Suger had established there Regular Canons of S. Augustine in place of the monks whom Pope Eugenius had sent thither to succeed the secular canons. The reference is to the same house in the following Letter, in which it is called Ste. Geneviève-du-Mont.

with all speed, that what has been grandly begun may go on from day to day and be happily accomplished. I regard it as unnecessary to ask your kind help for the Abbey of S. Victor,[1] because I am aware that the charge of all the religious houses has been committed to you. But it is needful to be particularly watchful over those in which the state of religion leaves much to be desired.

LETTER CCCLXX.[2] (*Circa* A.D. 1147.)

TO THE SAME.

He recommends to Suger the Abbey of Ste. Geneviève.

To his very dear father and lord SUGER, Abbot of S. Denys, Brother BERNARD, called Abbot of Clairvaux, health and the assurance of his friendship.

It behoves you to fulfil the duties of him who has left you in his stead,[3] or rather to do the work of the Lord your God, who has chosen you for the functions which you have to discharge. It is plainly the work of God to have restored religion and order in the Abbey of Ste. Geneviève-du-Mont; that new plantation finds in you its great guardian and helper. I entreat you that what you have well begun you will finish still better, and that you will oppose yourself as a wall for the defence of the house of Israel that man may not prevail against it. Be so kind, I entreat of you, as to raise up again the courage of the Abbot[4] of that place, who is easily cast down: that will be especially conducive to the honour of your person as well as to the saving of your soul, particularly at this time.

[1] See Letter 410.//
[2] Formerly No. 357; the former No. 370 is now No. 337.//
[3] Louis the Younger, before departing to the Crusade, had confided the Regency of the Kingdom to Abbot Suger. It is to this that Bernard refers when he says in the previous Letter that the care of Suger extended over all the religious houses of France, and in Letter 376, to the same, he calls him "the highest personage in the realm." In the same way he is addressed under the name of "Majesty" by Ulger, Bishop of Angers (*Letters of Suger*, No. 3).//
[4] Odo.

LETTER CCCLXXI.[1] (*Circa* A.D. 1147.)

To the Same.

Bernard opposes the marriage projected between the son of the Count of Anjou and the daughter of the King of France, on account of the impediment of consanguinity.

To the lord Abbot of S. Denys, Brother BERNARD, of Clairvaux, health and the assurance of his prayers.

I have written thus to the lord King:—

"You have undertaken an enterprise important and weighty, which no one is able to carry through except by the assistance of Divine strength. The business[2] in which you are engaged is above the powers of man, but that is easy to God which to men is impossible (S. Luke xviii. 27).

"Knowing this you ought to take the greatest care not in any way to repulse the help so necessary to you, nor by any project of yours to offend God and to deprive yourself of the furtherance of His grace. You ought, I repeat, now to take the greatest care never to provoke God so that He should be angry with you, should turn away His face, and withdraw His assistance from you. For this danger affects not the King alone, but the whole Church of God, since the cause which you have undertaken is also that of the whole world. Listen, and you will learn the cause which induces me to remind you of these facts. I am hastening indeed to your presence, as this letter shows, but I have formed the project of keeping the vigil of S. Mary Magdalene at Laon. Nevertheless, I have taken care to forewarn you by another letter of the danger which I am anxious that you should avoid. For I have heard that the Count of Anjou is pressing you to engage under oath your daughter to his

---

[1] Formerly No. 363; the former No. 371 is now No. 323.

[2] That is, the Crusade; wherefore this Letter was, no doubt, addressed to Louis the Younger, who wished to marry his eldest daughter, Mary, to the son of Fulk, Count of Anjou, who was also setting out to the East. But this marriage did not take place, and Mary espoused instead Henry, Count of Champagne.

son in marriage. Now this union is not only inexpedient, but it is not lawful; as well for other reasons as because of the impediment of consanguinity; since I know upon trustworthy information that the mother of the Queen, and of that young man, the son of the Count of Anjou, are related in the third degree. On this account permit me to urge you by no means to enter into this engagement, but to fear God and depart from evil. You have promised me that you would on no account do this without consulting me: and I should have done wrong if I had hidden from you my view. My advice then is by no means to go on with the affair. If you do, you will have acted both against my advice and that of many others who are your well-wishers; and also against the will of God. Do not think that after that God will accept your sacrifice, since it is made only in part: so that while you are combating on behalf of another kingdom, you do not leave your own in safety, while you order it against the will and the law of God, as also against what is honourable and advisable. I have now freed my own soul of responsibility: may God free yours also from lying lips and the deceitful tongue."

LETTER CCCLXXII.[1] (*Circa* A.D. 1147.)

To P.,[2] Bishop of Palencia, in Spain.

Bernard praises him for his humility, and particularly for his love of reading.

To his venerable lord and very dear father P., by the grace of God Bishop of Palencia, BERNARD, called Abbot of Clairvaux, wishes health, and prays that the Lord may prevent him with the blessings of sweetness.

Who will give me the wings of a dove that I may take my flight to repose within the odour of your sanctity? Your saintly life and the purity of your character have filled me with the odour of your sweetness, which seems to me,

---

[1] A new Letter; the former No. 372 is now No. 319.

[2] This was Peter: his name is found subscribed to the act of donation of the Abbey of Espina, made by Sanchia to S. Bernard (Manriquez under the year 1147, c. xviii. n. 3).

as it were, the odour of a fertile field which the Lord hath blessed. In it my soul is truly filled with marrow and fatness, and in such is the life of my spirit. For how can it be otherwise, when I hear of a man of lofty character and yet humble, full of cares and business, and yet peaceful, and trembling at the Word of the Lord. O rare bird upon the earth, humility conjoined with high station, and a tranquil mind in the midst of the hurry of business! You have made to rejoice, my lord, the soul of your servant; may the merciful Lord make yours also rejoice with the joy of His people. I have rejoiced with great joy on hearing such things as I had not expected reported of you. For my brethren, the bearers of your letter, reported to me your zeal in mortifying the flesh and reducing it to subjection, your habit of meditation, your love of reading, the gentleness of your manners, your kindness to all, and especially to those who are of the household of faith. But do not think, my dear father, that in speaking these words I intend to celebrate your praises. The word of blame spoken by the Prophet is before my mind: *Those who praise thee, my people, they deceive thee.*[1] I am unwilling, though a sinner, to pour upon your head the oil of sinful praise: but rather the oil of joy which proceeds from a pure heart and a good conscience, and faith unfeigned. Nor am I a trafficker in this oil; I have only too little with which to anoint myself for the arena of this world; but I cannot pass over in silence the virtues which are to the praise of Christ. Let not the creature, but the Creator be praised. Let Him who gives, not he who has received, be exalted: not he who plants nor he who waters are to be praised, for they are nothing, but He who gives the increase, that is God. I, then, will praise the hand which is stretched out to give, not that stretched out to receive: the praise of the Lord, and not of His servant shall come out of my mouth. Do thou, then, my dear father, recognize, if you are wise, or rather because you are wise, that the grace which is in you does not come

---

[1] Isaiah ix. 16, Vulg., but quoted probably from memory. The exact words are: *And there will be those who praise the people in order to seduce them, and those who are praised shall be given to destruction.*—[E.]

from yourself, but descends from the Father of Lights, since every good gift and every perfect gift is from above (S. James i. 17). I know that there are certain persons who have, as it were, a wise unwillingness to know the gifts which they have received from the Lord, so that they be not puffed up with pride nor fall into the snare of the devil. But it seems to me that I ought to know what I have received, in order that I may know what is wanting to me, and that I ought to know with the Apostle the things which have been bestowed upon me by God, in order that I may not be ignorant what I ought still to desire and pray for. For he who has received something and knows it not, is exposed to the double danger of being ungrateful for what he has received, and careless in preserving it. For how can any one render gratitude to a benefactor if he does not know that he has received anything from him? Or how will he be careful to guard that which he is not aware that he has received? Take away from me, O Lord, the blame of that ungrateful people of whom it is said: *They forgat what He had done and the wonderful works that He had showed for them* (Psalm lxxviii. 12). A benefit received, therefore, even according to the wise of this world, is to be graven deep in the tablets of the memory. It behoves us, then, that we should know how to take care of the gifts which we have received, and so that the grace of God in us may not be in vain: and that it may remain in us always, let us always render thanks to the Lord our God. I think it may be added, not unusefully, that you should proceed by three steps to the obtaining of grace and salvation: humility, faith, and fear. For humility is that quality to which grace is given, faith that in which it is received, fear that in which it is preserved. If we should wish to ascend to the throne of grace without the use of these three, I fear that it would be said to us, *Thou hast nothing to draw with, and the well is deep* (S. John iv. 11). Let us, then, in order to drink of the water of wisdom, have the rope of humility:[1] and let

---

[1] *Hæreditatis*: but surely we ought to read *humilitatis*, as in the next sentence.—[E.]

this humility be in mouth, in heart, and in action: which threefold cord is not easily broken. Let us have faith, as it were, for a water jar, and let it be great, so that much grace may be received in it: and let fear be, as it were, its cover, lest the water of wisdom be defiled with the impurities of vainglory: for it is written, *Every open vessel which hath no covering bound upon it shall be unclean* (Num. xix. 15). Your devotion to reading also, in which you embrace not only the writings of great men, but also, the trifles which I have penned, calls for some mention from me: so that you may perceive what joy your kindly feeling has given to my heart.

LETTER CCCLXXIII.[1] (*Circa* A.D. 1147).

From the Abbot of Sp.[2] to S. Bernard.

He complains of the weight of the charge laid upon him.

To his wished-for lord and very dear father BERNARD, Abbot of Clairvaux, his son, the unprofitable servant of the Abbey at Sp., wishes health and the blessing of all nations.

I have greatly desired that this letter should find you, if it were possible, free and disengaged from other business. For I have feared continually while writing, and think now with fear, of that man who desired to see Jesus, but was unable for the crowd because he was little of stature (S. Luke xix. 3). And it is not only your leisure that I desire, but also that I should find grace in your eyes. For what solace would your leisure alone be to me? May God pardon you, what have you done? Where have you placed me, being such an one as I am, whose powers are so little in proportion to the burden that I have to bear? It seems to me to be heavier than the sands of the sea. For what am

---

[1] A new Letter; the former No. 373 is now No. 411.

[2] No doubt of Espina, in the Diocese of Palencia, the founder of which was Sanchia, sister of the Emperor Alfonso, who gave the place to S. Bernard. Nivard, brother of Bernard, was sent thither with some companions. Manriquez does not mention the name of the first Abbot (*ad ann.* 1147, c. 18, n. 3).

I, and what is my father's house? Am I not a child who knows not how to come in or go out? What am I that I should be able with my own powers only to sustain, or rather raise up again the Abbey with which I am charged? It resembles an enclosure which is crumbling, or a wall in ruins. Such a business is above my powers, and I am consumed with useless labour. Still I strive even amidst my groans, but of what use are my labours and my groans? The diseases are of long standing, the plague an acute one, the mischief incurable except by a strong hand. Vices have been turned into habitudes, habitudes into custom, custom has become, as it were, a second nature, and is now a necessity. O how necessary it is that this necessity should be drawn out by the roots! But, I say it with tears, it has pushed such strong roots into the soil that they are too strong for me. So you see that I am absolutely wanting in the needful powers to give help. Even that brother who is the bearer of this letter, who was highly necessary to me, is leaving us. His charge was to teach the novices; they profited under his direction. I rejoiced in it, and hoped by the mercy of God a day might come when death might be swallowed up by life. I render this testimony in his favour, that as far as one man is permitted to judge of another, his conversation among us has been acceptable to God and pleasing to men. Therefore his departure cannot be without grief to me. You are able, my lord, to turn my sorrow into joy if I have found favour in your eyes. So far about these matters, other things the bearer will explain at greater length.

LETTER CCCLXXIV.[1] (A.D. 1148.)

TO THE BRETHREN IN IRELAND, ON THE OCCASION OF THE DEATH[2] OF THE BLESSED BISHOP MALACHI.

That the death of the Saints is a subject rather for joy

[1] Formerly No. 311; the former No. 374 is now No. 358.

[2] This took place on Nov. 2nd, 1148. See the *Life of S. Malachi*, by Bernard, and his two sermons on the same Saint.

than grief. That Clairvaux is honoured by the death and burial there of so great a man.

To the Religious in Ireland, and particularly to the congregations founded by Bishop Malachi of blessed memory, Brother BERNARD, called Abbot of Clairvaux, wishes health and the consolations of the Holy Spirit.

1. If we had here a continuing city, we should not have to shed abundant tears for the loss of so noble a fellow citizen. But if we are, as we ought, seeking one to come, it is a reason for no slight grief that we are deprived of so valuable a guide ; but yet, as we ought to temper zeal with knowledge, so grief ought to be moderated with the confidence of hope. No one ought to wonder that distress forces a groan from us, that the loss of a friend causes us to weep; yet we must set bounds to our affliction in presence of the great consolation we have, when we consider not the things which are seen, but the things which are not seen: for those which are seen are temporal, but those not seen are eternal. In the first place, that holy soul is to be congratulated on his safe attainment of Paradise, so that we may not be open to the charge of want of charity, and that be said to us which the Lord said to the Apostles : *If ye loved Me ye would rejoice because I go to the Father* (S. John xiv. 28). The spirit of our father has only preceded us into the presence of the Father of spirits. We should be wanting not only in charity, but be guilty of the highest ingratitude, if we did not rejoice that he through whom we have received so many benefits has passed from labour to rest, from danger to safety, from the world to the Father. If, then, it is a mark of pious affection to weep for Malachi dead, it is still more a mark of this to rejoice with Malachi living. Who doubts that he is living? Undoubtedly he lives, and that in a state of happiness. To the eyes of the ungodly he seemed to die, but he has entered into peace.

2. Furthermore, if we consider this death as it affects ourselves, it suggests to us another motive for joy and

gladness, because so faithful an advocate, so powerful a patron has preceded us to the court of Heaven, whose fervent charity cannot possibly forget his sons, and whose well-proved sanctity will find grace in the sight of God. For who is so bold as to suppose the holy Malachi either loves his sons less or is less able to be of service to them than before? For if he was loved by God before he quitted the earth, he receives now more certain proofs of that love; and since he had loved those that were his he loved them to the end. Far be it from us to suppose, O holy soul, that thy prayer is to be considered less efficacious when it is thine to offer it with increased ardour in the presence of the Divine Majesty; when thou no longer walkest in faith but reignest in the sight of God! Far be it from us to suppose that thy charity so unwearied is enfeebled when thou art at the very source of the Eternal charity, and art drinking long draughts of that Love for which thou didst thirst on earth whilst receiving only drops of it. Charity which is strong as death, yea, stronger than death itself, was not able to yield to death. Even when dying he was not unmindful of his sons, commending you most affectionately to God, and though I am so unworthy, entreating me also with his accustomed kindness and humility not to forget them even to the end. That is why I have thought myself bound to write to you, that you may know that I am entirely yours both in spiritual things, if there is anything in my poor powers that can ever through the merits of him our holy father be of service to you, and in temporal affairs, if opportunity should ever be given to me, I am ready to be of service to you with the greatest willingness.

3. And now, also, my dearly beloved, I deplore with my whole heart the heavy loss which the Church of Ireland has sustained; and I sympathize with you the more, as I am sensible that it imposes upon me greater duties on your behalf. God has indeed honoured us greatly in permitting that our house should be edified by the spectacle of his

blessed death, and enriched by the precious treasure of his body. Let it not be a source of regret to you that he should have his resting-place among us; for God has so ordered it according to the multitude of His mercy that as you possessed him while living, it should be given to us to possess him after his death. He was indeed, and is, a common father both to us and to you, for at the very time of his death his will in this respect was confirmed to us. Wherefore let us all be embraced as friends and brethren in the bonds of mutual charity, and as we were dear to so holy a father, let this spiritual relationship make us dear to each other.

4. I conclude by exhorting you, brethren, to follow diligently the steps of our blessed father, and that so much more earnestly as his holy life has become quite well known to you by the sight of it daily, for in this you will approve yourselves his true sons, if you follow bravely the directions which he gave; and as you saw in him and heard from him how you ought to walk, study thus to walk and to abound more and more, for *the wisdom of the sons is the glory of their father* (Prov. x. 1). As for me, the example before me of such great perfection had a great influence in dispersing my sloth and increasing my reverence. Would that he may draw us after him, and that the remembrance of his virtues may make us run the race that is set before us, more willingly and earnestly. Pray for us, and may Christ have us all in His holy keeping.

LETTER CCCLXXV.[1] (A.D. 1148.)

To Ida, Countess of Nevers.

He complains to the Countess that some of her vassals had done injury to the monks at Veselay.

To his beloved daughter in Christ, the Countess of NEVERS, Brother BERNARD, called Abbot of Clairvaux, wishes health, and assures her of his prayers.

[1] Formerly No. 390; the former No. 375 is now No. 316.

The venerable Abbot[1] of Vezelay complains that your vassals, and you yourself, prevent merchants and other persons from coming to Vezelay as they desire to do. Now since Count William[2] of happy memory freely acknowledged before the Bishop of Auxerre, and in my presence, that to act thus was unjust and wrong; let me advise and entreat that you should not act in this way any more. For I fear if you should continue such acts that you may do much injury both to yourself in this world, and to your husband where he is, which I should greatly regret. Follow, then, my advice, and cause all these acts of injustice to cease.

LETTER CCCLXXVI.[3] (A.D. 1149.)

To Abbot Suger.

He advises and requests that Suger should prevent certain noblemen from fighting a duel.

To his venerable father and lord SUGER, by the grace of God Abbot of St. Denys, Brother BERNARD, called Abbot of Clairvaux, wishes health and sends assurance of his prayers.

It is time, and there is urgent need, that you should now take up the sword of the Spirit, which is the Word of God, against a diabolical custom which is endeavouring to grow up a second time. Men who have just returned from the Crusade, Lord Henry, son of the Count, and Lord Robert, brother of the King, being enraged one against the other, have fixed one of those abominable meetings[4] to attack

---

[1] This was Pontius.

[2] This William had retired to the Chartreuse, as we have already mentioned; his son William had succeeded him in 1147.

[3] Formerly No. 358; the former No. 376 is now No. 355.

[4] *Nundinas*, i.e., the ninth day, and thence any settled appointment. What were these *nundinæ?* William of S. Thierry (*Life of S. Bernard*, B. 1. c. xi.) tells us in these terms :—" One day there arrived at Clairvaux an armed party of young nobles. . . . Lent was approaching, and all the young nobles who were engaged in the profession of arms traversed the country looking for those objectionable meetings which are called tourneys (*Turnetas*). Others call them tournaments (*Torneamentum*)." (Matthew of Paris, *Hist. Angl.*, p. 258.)

and slay each other, after the festival of Easter, being bent on violating all laws. Judge in what disposition of mind they have made the journey to Jerusalem, since they have returned in such a mood. How fitly can this be said of them:—*We would have healed Babylon, but she is not healed; they are stricken, but they have not grieved; they are consumed, but they have refused to receive correction* (Jer. li. 9, and v. 3). After so many hardships and perils; after the sufferings and the misfortunes which they have had to endure; when the realm is in peace, these two return to it only to disturb and throw it into confusion, and that in the absence of the King. I advise and entreat your Highness, since you are the chief person in the kingdom, to oppose this breach of the peace resolutely, and, either by persuasion or by force, prevent its taking place; your honour, the happiness of the kingdom, and the interest of the Church all require this of you. If I appeal to force, it is to that which belongs to ecclesiastical discipline. I am writing in this sense to the Archbishops of Rheims and of Sens, to the Bishops of Soissons and of Auxerre, to Count Theobald and Count Rodolph. Oppose yourself to these great evils both on account of the King and on account of the Pope, to whom the peace of the realm is a matter of concern.

LETTER CCCLXXVII.[1] (A.D. 1149.)

To the Same.

Bernard praises his zeal and care for the good of the kingdom, and approves of his having called together the Estates of the Realm to remedy certain dangers. He encourages him to continue his efforts for the benefit of all.

To his very dear father and lord SUGER, by the grace of God Abbot of S. Denys, Brother BERNARD, called Abbot of Clairvaux, wishes the spirit of wisdom and consolation.

[1] Formerly No. 359; the former No. 377 is now No. 346.

1. I have seen with extreme joy and pleasure the letter which your Highness has written to the Lord Archbishop of Tours. May the Most High bless you for the zeal and care with which you fulfil your charge of the realm of our most glorious King, so that he is freed in a measure from the troubles which threaten him at the present, and would speedily be upon him if they were not warded off with all your strength. It was, indeed, a counsel from God that you should call together the chief men, both of the State and of the Church, for deliberation; so that all who dwell on earth may see that he in whose hands the realm has been left is a devoted friend, a prudent counsellor, a strong and brave supporter to his Sovereign. And that Sovereign is one who is now in the service of the King whose kingdom is for ever and ever, who puts nations and kingdoms in movement so that the earthly land which belongs to the King of heaven, the land upon which His feet once stood, should not be lost. It was that King, I say, who when he was unrivalled in glory, abounding in riches, enjoying a secure peace, victorious in war, and in the prime of his youth, chose to exile himself from his own country, to serve in foreign lands, yet to serve Him whose service is royal. Who would dare to trouble his kingdom? who would venture upon such an impiety against the Lord and against His anointed? O, my lord King, I would that they were cut off who trouble thee! who seek harm to thee and thine whilst thou art remaining alone among foreign nations, so that the place might not be left desolate which the Lord hath chosen out of all lands to place His Name there.

2. Wherefore act bravely, and let your heart be strengthened, because the Lord God is with you, and protects the King who is in voluntary exile on His account. He who commands the winds and the sea will easily smooth the billows when they swell. The whole body of the Church of God will be with you, so that no one may rise up and make Israel to sin; and will thus support on the shoulders of all, the burden which is so heavy for yours. For now is the time when there is need for you to act as

becomes the place which you hold, the dignity with which you are invested, the power which you have received: so that your memory may be recalled, not only with blessing, but also with praise and admiration by every generation which shall succeed. You have to provide with care that so important a branch of the Church of God should not have the labour of assembling without good result, and that measures should be taken either to prevent or crush all blameable projects for breaking the peace. I have in mind, though myself humble and obscure, to address you all when you are assembled in the Name of the Lord, in a letter which, if it is of no service, will at least show the warmth of my feeling towards you. May He who has inspired you with this good purpose enable you also to carry it out with success; may He bruise Satan under your feet, so that in that assembly the Lord may be glorified, His Church honoured, the realm strengthened and steadied, and those who speak and do evil reduced to silence.

LETTER CCCLXXVIII.[1] (A.D. 1149.)
To the Same.

He asks assistance in grain for the Religious of the Diocese of Bourges.

To my very dear lord SUGER, by the grace of God the venerable Abbot of S. Denys, Brother BERNARD, Abbot of Clairvaux, wishes health and sends the assurance of his prayers.

We have in the Archdiocese of Bourges some brethren who are in want of bread; they are those from Maison Dieu, and I hear that the crops of corn of the lord King are very abundant, and, because abundant, they are not of great value. Therefore, I entreat you that out of those crops you would order such a supply to be bestowed upon those brethren as you shall see fit. For the King, whenever he was in that district, was accustomed to make some gift to them.

[1] Formerly No. 360; the former No. 378 is now No. 347.

LETTER CCCLXXIX.[1] (A.D. 1149.)

TO THE SAME.

He entreats Suger to come to the help of a certain Abbot who is in want.

To his lord and very dear father SUGER, by the grace of God the Reverend Abbot of S. Denys, Brother BERNARD, called Abbot of Clairvaux, health and his devoted prayers in Christ.

I send a poor Abbot to a rich one, that the need of the one may be relieved out of the abundance of the other. In so doing I yield to you the better part, according to that saying of the Truth that *it is better to give than to receive* (Acts xx. 35). Nor do I doubt that you would extend your bounty willingly and liberally to this one of the poor of Christ if you knew, as I do, his piety and probity, and the extreme necessity in which he is. He is burdened with debts, and he has not bread to eat, because his fields have produced only noxious herbs instead of grain. As your districts have not been stricken with the same sterility, I beg and entreat you of your charity to assist him, and you may be assured that whatever you shall be pleased to bestow upon him could not be devoted to a better object.

LETTER CCCLXXX.[2] (A.D. 1149.)

TO THE SAME.

On the unhappy state of the Church in the East.

To his very dear father and lord SUGER, by the grace of God Abbot of S. Denys, BERNARD, Abbot of Clairvaux, health and the assurance of his humble prayers.

The news which the Grand Master of the Temple and Brother John have brought I have received as joyfully as if

---

[1] Formerly No. 361; the former No. 379 is now No. 353. Among the Letters of Suger it is No. 93.

[2] Formerly No. 362; the former No. 380 is now No. 360.

I thought it came from God Himself. For the Church in the East utters such cries of distress now that whosoever does not sympathize with his whole heart is shown not to be a son of the Church. But though rejoiced at the news, I am distressed at the short notice you give me, which renders me unable to come to you at the time you named. I had promised the Bishop of Langres to meet him on that day for a conference on grave and important matters, which he had accepted in reliance upon me. I have, however, mentioned a time when, if convenient to you, I will gladly come to you with the same Bishop, who will be perhaps of great service in the conference which we are to hold.

END OF VOL. II.

INDEX.

A.

	PAGE
Abaelard, Note on	537
Abaelard, *Theologia* of	853
Abbot, Letter to a certain	866
Abbot of Sp. to S. Bernard	925
Absolution, what is meant by (Abaelard)	563
Alexander, Prior of Fountains, Letter to	842
Alfonso, King of Portugal, Letter to.	823
Anastasius, S., to the Brethren of	883
Andrew of Baudiment	650
Andrew, Uncle of Bernard, Letter to	794
Angoulême, Letter to Count of	807
Anselm, Bishop of Rochester	615
Archembald, Sub-dean of Orleans, murder of	476, 493
Arnold of Brescia	545, 598
Arnold of Chartres, Letter to	825
Atonement, Errors of Abaelard on the	558, 580, 860
Aubin, S., Letter to Abbot of	614
Augustine, S., on Charity	665

B.

Baldwin, Abbot of Riéti, Letter to	609
Bernard Desportes, Letters to	480, 482
Bernard, Prior of Portes, Letter to	729
Bernard, Abbot, of Italy, to Pope Innocent	879
Bernard, Abbot, of Italy, to Saint Bernard	881
Bernard on proposed marriage of Son of the Count of Anjou	921
Bertin, S., Abbey of	472
Beneventum, Loss of	521
Benedict, S., Rule of	665 *et seq.*
Bishops and Cardinals, The, of the Roman Court, Letters to	504, 541
Bishops at Sens, Letter to	537
Blois, Letter to Countess of	807
Bonami, Canon of Langres	499
Bourges, Archbishop of	631
Brethren in Ireland, Letter to the, on the death of Malachi	926
Bruno, Abbot of Chiarraville, Letter to	786
Burchard, Abbot of Balerne, Letter to	468

C.

	PAGE
Capua, Loss of	521
Cardinal G . . ., Letters to	862, 864, 917
Cardinal Presbyter, Letter to a	865
Celestine II., Letters to Pope	690, 900
Chancellor G . . ., Letter to	917
Charlieu, Abbey of	603
Church in the East, unhappy state of	934
Clairvaux, Position and Site of	460
Cluniacs and Cistercians, Causes of Strife between	654
Conception of B. V. M., Opinion of Bernard upon	512
Conrad, King of the Romans, Letters to	531, 717
Constance, Letter to Bishop of	598
Coronation of Louis the Younger	724
Crusade, Second, Failure of	794
Curia, Letter to Three Bishops of	630
Curia, Letters to the whole	693, 695

D.

Durham, William, Bishop of	691

E.

Eugenius, Letters to Pope, 698, 703, 705, 719, 721, 723, 727, 729, 732, 733, 750, 752, 754, 755, 757, 764, 765, 773, 776, 777, 779, 780, 782, 788, 790, 791, 793, 800, 803, 805, 814, 824

Eugenius, Letter of, to Cistercian Chapter	770
Eustace, Bishop of Valence, Letter to	532

F.

Faith, Abaelard on	574
Falco, Dean of Lyons	499
Falco, Dean of Lyons, Letter to	500
Falco, Archbishop-Elect of Lyons, Letter to	511
Fontevrault, Abbess of, her quarrel with Bishop of Angers	607
France, Eastern, Letter to Clergy and People of	906
Funerals, strange customs at	675

G.

Geoffrey, Abbot of S. Mary at York, Letter to	831
Gislebert, Archbishop of Tours	476
Godfrey, Prior, Letter to	839
Guido du Chatel, Letter to	593
Guido, the Legate, Letter to	601
Guy, Abbot of Pisa, Letter to	864

H.

	PAGE
Haimeric, Letters to	485, 493, 494, 529, 827, 871
Heloise, Abbess, her request	541, 781
Henry, Letter to Count	782
Henry, Archbishop of Sens, Letters to	530, 838
Henry, Archbishop of Mayence, Letter to	913
Henry, Letter to Cardinal	804
Henry Murdach, Abbot of Vauclair, Letter to	844
Herbert, Abbot of Dijon, Letters to	506, 689
Heresies of Abaelard, Heads of	556
Hildefonsus, Count of S. Eloy, Letter to	707
Hildegarde, Abbess, Letter to	915
Hugh, Archdeacon of Toul	520
Hugh, Bishop of Auxerre	625
Hugh, Abbot of Trois-Fontaines, Letter to	775
Hugo, a Novice, Letter to	845

I.

Ida, Countess of Nevers, Letter to	529
Incarnation, Errors of Abaelard on the	553, 576, 585
Ivo, Cardinal, Letter to	594

J.

Jerusalem, Letter to the Patriarch of	518
Jerusalem, Letters to the Queen of	616, 797
John of Crema, Letter to	495
John, Abbot of Buzay, Letter to	687
Joscelyn, Bishop of Soissons, Letters to	638, 641, 648, 877

K.

"Know Thyself," the, of Abaelard	543

L.

Laon, Letter to Bishop of	770
Legates of the Holy See, Letter to	811
Liege	475
Limoges, Letter to the Bishop of	858
Lothaire, the Emperor	475
Louis, King of France, Letters to	506, 634, 635, 648, 748, 787, 812, 813
Lyons, Letter to the Canons of	512

M.

	PAGE
Malachi, Bishop of Ireland, Letters to	875, 897
Martin, S., his choice of black robes	674
Matilda, Queen of England, Letter to	837
Mayence, Archbishop of	811 (*note*)
Memmius, S., first Bishop of Chalons	475
Milanese, Reconciliation of, by Bernard	835
Milisendis, Queen of Jerusalem, Letters to	894, 896
Montier Ramey, Letter to Abbot of	805

N.

Nicholas, Bishop of Cambray	624
Note to Letter 190 on Abaelard	549

O.

Obric, Canon of Langres	495
Odo, Abbot of S. Denys	791
Orleans	476, 484
Original Sin, Error of Abaelard on	561
Ostia, Tusculum and Præneste, Letters to Bishops of	682, 683, 686
Ostia, Letters to Bishop of	794, 799, 804, 815, 820

P.

Paulinus, Bishop of Nola, his Letter to Sulpicius Severus	674
Peter, Abbot of Cluny, Letters to	469, 472, 651, 760, 764, 911
Peter, Dean of Besancon, Letter to	603
Peter of Pisa, his deposition	623
Peter, Abbot of Cluny, Letter of, to S. Bernard	654, 759
Peter, Abbot of Moustier la Celle	802
Peter, Bishop of Palencia, Letter to	922
Philip, the intruded Archbishop of Tours, Letter to	478
Ponce, Archdeacon of Langres	499
Pope Innocent II., Letters to	473, 479, 483, 484, 486, 491, 493, 495, 501, 503, 505, 510, 520, 522, 523, 527, 528, 532, 543, 565, 591, 604, 606, 620, 621, 623, 624, 625, 626, 627, 629, 835, 840, 847, 859, 867, 873, 875, 885, 886, 887, 889, 890
Pope Innocent, Letter of, against Abaelard	595
Prémontré, Letter to Abbot of	735
Privilege given by Pope Innocent to S. Bernard	891

R.

Ralph, Abbot of Vaucelles	536
Ralph, Count of Vermandois, his divorce and remarriage	626
Ralph, a Monk, instigates a massacre of the Jews	913

	PAGE
Raynald, Archbishop of Rheims, Letter to	830
Reginald, Archbishop of Rheims	508
Revolt against Eugenius under Arnold of Brescia	712
Robert, Dean of Langres	495
Robert, Abbot of Dunes, Letters to	850, 851
Robert Pullen, Letter to	904
Rochester, Letter to Bishop of	614
Roger, King of Sicily, Letters to	617, 618, 619
Romans, Letter to the, on behalf of Pope Eugenius	712
Roman Pontiff, Letter to the	856
Rualene, Letter to Abbot	756

S.

	PAGE
Salamanca, Bishop of, S. Bernard's intercession for	621
Sanchia, sister of the Emperor of Spain	809
Seal of S. Bernard, the	457
Secular, Letter to a certain	801
Sens, Letter to the Clergy of	612
Sentences of Abaelard, S. Bernard on the	542
"Sic et Non" of	543
Simon of Cambray, Letter to	536
Soissons, Bishop of, Letters to	650, 758
Stephen, Bishop of Palestrina, Letter to	861
Stephen, Bishop of Præneste, Letter to	643
Suger, Abbot of S. Denys, Letters to	761, 919, 920, 921, 930, 931, 933, 934, 935
Suger, Letter of, to S. Bernard	762 (*note*)
S. Satyrus, Church of, the	475

T.

	PAGE
Theobald, Count of Champagne, Letter to	768
Theobald Notier, Archdeacon of Paris, his crime	492
Theobald, Archbishop of Canterbury, Letter on his behalf	621
Theobald, Abp., Letter to, on behalf of John of Salisbury	903
Theofred, S., Abbot of	686
Thomas, Prior of S. Victor, murder of	456
Thurstan, Archbishop of York, Letter to	840
Toulouse, Letter to people of	710
Trèves, Archbishop of	528
Trinity, Errors of Abaelard on the	552, 559, 565
Troyes, Letter to Bishop and Clergy of	613
,, ,, on behalf of Bishop of	479

U.

Ulger, Bishop of Angers, Letter to	607

V.

	PAGE
Vezelay, Abbey of, its reformation	474
Vezelay, Abbot of, election to See of Langres	496
Viterbo, Bernard's stay at	478, 479

W.

Warren, Abbot of S. Mary of the Alps, Letter to	743
William, Abbot, Letter of, to Geoffrey of Chartres	851
William, Abbot, Letter to	855
William, Abbot of Rievaulx, Letters to	893, 902

Y.

York, Disputed election to See of	690
York, Unjust consecration to the See of	893

www.ingramcontent.com/pod-product-compliance
Lightning Source LLC
Chambersburg PA
CBHW021426300426
44114CB00010B/669